The O'Leary Series

Microsoft® Office Word 2003

Introductory Edition

Timothy J. O'Leary

Arizona State University

Linda I. O'Leary

McGraw Hill **Technology Education**

Boston   Burr Ridge, IL   Dubuque, IA   Madison, WI   New York   San Francisco   St. Louis
Bangkok   Bogotá   Caracas   Kuala Lumpur   Lisbon   London   Madrid   Mexico City
Milan   Montreal   New Delhi   Santiago   Seoul   Singapore   Sydney   Taipei   Toronto

McGraw Hill Technology Education

MICROSOFT® OFFICE WORD 2003, INTRODUCTORY EDITION

Published by McGraw-Hill Technology Education, an imprint of the McGraw-Hill Companies, Inc. 1221 Avenue of the Americas, New York, NY, 10020. Copyright © 2004 by the McGraw-Hill Companies, Inc. All rights reserved. No part of this publication may be reproduced or distributed in any form or by any means, or stored in a database or retrieval system, without the prior written consent of The McGraw-Hill Companies, Inc., including, but not limited to, in any network or other electronic storage or transmission, or broadcast for distance learning.

Some ancillaries, including electronic and print components, may not be available to customers outside the United States.

This book is printed on acid-free paper.

3 4 5 6 7 8 9 0 QPD/QPD 0 9 8 7 6

ISBN-13: 978-0-07-283536-6
ISBN-10: 0-07-283536-2

Editor-in-Chief: *Bob Woodbury*
Sponsoring editor: *Don Hull*
Developmental editor: *Jennie Yates*
Marketing manager: *Andy Bernier*
Media producer: *Elizabeth Mavetz*
Project manager: *Jim Labeots*
Manager, new book production: *Heather D. Burbridge*
Coordinator freelance design: *Artemio Ortiz Jr.*
Photo research coordinator: *Ira C. Roberts*
Supplement producer: *Matthew Perry*
Senior digital content specialist: *Brian Nacik*
Cover design: *Asylum Studios*
Interior design: *Artemio Ortiz Jr.*
Typeface: *10.5/13 New Aster*
Compositor: *Rogondino & Associates/Cecelia G. Morales*
Printer: *Quebecor World Dubuque Inc.*

Library of Congress Control Number 2003111031

www.mhhe.com

McGraw-Hill Technology Education

At McGraw-Hill Technology Education, we publish instructional materials for the technology education market—in particular, for computer instruction in post secondary education that ranges from introductory courses in traditional four-year universities to continuing education and proprietary schools. McGraw-Hill Technology Education presents a broad range of innovative products—texts, lab manuals, study guides, testing materials, and technology-based training and assessment tools.

We realize that technology has created and will continue to create new mediums for professors and students to use in managing resources and communicating information to one another. McGraw-Hill Technology Education provides the most flexible and complete teaching and learning tools available and offers solutions to the changing needs of the classroom. McGraw-Hill Technology Education is dedicated to providing the tools for today's instructors and students, which will enable them to successfully navigate the world of Information Technology.

- McGraw-Hill/Osborne—This division of The McGraw-Hill Companies is known for its best-selling Internet titles, Harley Hahn's *Internet & Web Yellow Pages* and the *Internet Complete Reference*. For more information, visit Osborne at www.osborne.com.

- Digital Solutions—Whether you want to teach a class online or just post your "bricks-n-mortar" class syllabus, McGraw-Hill Technology Education is committed to publishing digital solutions. Taking your course online doesn't have to be a solitary adventure, nor does it have to be a difficult one. We offer several solutions that will allow you to enjoy all the benefits of having your course material online.

- Packaging Options—For more information about our discount options, contact your McGraw-Hill Sales representative at 1-800-338-3987 or visit our website at **www.mhhe.com/it**.

McGraw-Hill Technology Education is dedicated to providing
the tools for today's instructors and students.

What does this logo mean?

It means this courseware has been approved by the Microsoft® Office Specialist Program to be among the finest available for learning *Microsoft Office Word 2003, Microsoft Office Excel 2003, Microsoft Office Access 2003*, and *Microsoft Office PowerPoint 2003*. It also means that upon completion of this courseware, you may be prepared to take an exam for Microsoft Office Specialist qualification.

What is a Microsoft Office Specialist?

A Microsoft Office Specialist is an individual who has passed exams for certifying his or her skills in one or more of the Microsoft Office desktop applications such as Microsoft Word, Microsoft Excel, Microsoft PowerPoint, Microsoft Outlook, Microsoft Access, or Microsoft Project. The Microsoft Office Specialist Program typically offers certification exams at the "Specialist" and "Expert" skill levels.* The Microsoft Office Specialist Program is the only program in the world approved by Microsoft for testing proficiency in Microsoft Office desktop applications and Microsoft Project. This testing program can be a valuable asset in any job search or career advancement.

More Information:

To learn more about becoming a Microsoft Office Specialist, visit www.microsoft.com/officespecialist

To learn about other Microsoft Office Specialist approved courseware from McGraw-Hill Technology Education, visit http://www.mhhe.com/catalogs/irwin/it/mous/index.mhtml

---

* The availability of Microsoft Office Specialist certification exams varies by application, application version and language. Visit www.microsoft.com/officespecialist for exam availability.

Microsoft, the Microsoft Office Logo, PowerPoint, and Outlook are trademarks or registered trademarks of Microsoft Corporation in the United States and/or other countries, and the Microsoft Office Specialist logo is used under license from the owner.

Who benefits from Microsoft Office Specialist certification?

Employers

Microsoft Office Specialist certification helps satisfy employers' needs for qualitative assessments of employees' skills. Training, coupled with Microsoft Office Specialist certification, offers organizations of every size the ability to enhance productivity and efficiency by enabling their employees to unlock many advanced and laborsaving features in Microsoft Office applications. Microsoft Office Specialist certification can ultimately improve the bottom line.

Employees

Microsoft Office Specialist certification demonstrates employees' productivity and competence in Microsoft Office applications, the most popular business applications in the world. Achieving Microsoft Office Specialist certification verifies that employees have the confidence and ability to use Microsoft Office applications in meeting and exceeding their work challenges.

Instructors

Microsoft Office Specialist certification validates instructors' knowledge and skill in using Microsoft Office applications. It serves as a valuable credential, demonstrating their potential to teach students these essential applications. The Microsoft Office Specialist Authorized Instructor program is also available to those who wish to further demonstrate their instructional capabilities.

Students

Microsoft Office Specialist certification distinguishes students from their peers. It demonstrates their efficiency in completing assignments and projects, leaving more time for other studies. Improved confidence toward meeting new challenges and obstacles is yet another benefit. Achieving Microsoft Office Specialist certification gives students the marketable skills necessary to set them apart in the competitive job market.

To learn more about becoming a Microsoft Office Specialist, visit www.microsoft.com/officespecialist

To purchase a Microsoft Office Specialist certification exam, visit www.DesktopIQ.com

---

Brief Contents

Detailed Contents

Acknowledgments

The new edition of The O'Leary Series has been made possible only through the enthusiasm and dedication of a great team of people. Because the team spans the country, literally from coast to coast, we have utilized every means of working together including conference calls, FAX, e-mail, and document collaboration. We have truly tested the team approach and it works!

Leading the team from McGraw-Hill are Don Hull, Sponsoring Editor, and Jennie Yates, Developmental Editor. Their renewed commitment, direction, and support have infused the team with the excitement of a new project.

The production staff is headed by James Labeots, Project Manager, whose planning and attention to detail has made it possible for us to successfully meet a very challenging schedule. Members of the production team include: Artemio Ortiz, Designer; Pat Rogondino and Cecelia Morales, Compositors; Susan Defosset, Copy Editor; Heather Burbridge, Production Supervisor; Matthew Perry, Supplement Coordinator; and Elizabeth Mavetz, Media Producer. We would particularly like to thank Pat, Cecelia, and Susan—team members for many past editions whom we can always depend on to do a great job.

Finally, we are particularly grateful to a small but very dedicated group of people who helped us develop the manuscript. Colleen Hayes, Susan Demar, and Kathy Duggan have helped on the last several editions and continue to provide excellent developmental support. To Steve Willis, Carol Cooper, and Sarah Martin who provide technical expertise, youthful perspective, and enthusiasm, our thanks for helping get the manuscripts out the door and meeting the deadlines.

Preface

Introduction

The 20th century not only brought the dawn of the Information Age, but also rapid changes in information technology. There is no indication that this rapid rate of change will be slowing—it may even be increasing. As we begin the 21st century, computer literacy will undoubtedly become prerequisite for whatever career a student chooses. The goal of the O'Leary Series is to assist students in attaining the necessary skills to efficiently use these applications. Equally important is the goal to provide a foundation for students to readily and easily learn to use future versions of this software. This series does this by providing detailed step-by-step instructions combined with careful selection and presentation of essential concepts.

About the Authors

Tim and Linda O'Leary live in the American Southwest and spend much of their time engaging instructors and students in conversation about learning. In fact, they have been talking about learning for more than 25 years. Something in those early conversations convinced them to write a book, to bring their interest in the learning process to the printed page. Today, they are as concerned as ever about learning, about technology, and about the challenges of presenting material in new ways, both in terms of content and the method of delivery.

A powerful and creative team, Tim combines his years of classroom teaching experience with Linda's background as a consultant and corporate trainer. Tim has taught courses at Stark Technical College in Canton, Ohio, Rochester Institute of Technology in upper New York state, and is currently a professor at Arizona State University in Tempe, Arizona. Tim and Linda have talked to and taught students from ages 8 to 80, all of them with a desire to learn something about computers and the applications that make their lives easier, more interesting, and more productive.

About the Book

Times are changing, technology is changing, and this text is changing, too. Do you think the students of today are different from yesterday? There is no doubt about it—they are. On the positive side, it is amazing how much effort students will put toward things they are convinced are relevant to them. Their effort directed at learning application programs and exploring the Web seems at times limitless. On the other hand, students can often be shortsighted, thinking that learning the skills to use the application is the only objective. The mission of the series is to build upon and extend this interest by not only teaching the specific application skills but by introducing the concepts that are common to all applications, providing students with the confidence, knowledge, and ability to easily learn the next generation of applications.

Same Great Features as the Office XP Edition with some new additions!

- **Introduction to Computer Essentials**—A brief introduction to the basics of computer hardware and software (appears in Office Volume I only).

- **Introduction to Outlook**—A lab devoted to Microsoft Office Outlook 2003 basics (appears in Office Volume I only).

- **Introduction to Microsoft Office 2003**—Presents an overview to the Microsoft Office 2003 components: Office Word, Excel, Access, PowerPoint, and Outlook. Includes a hands-on section that introduces the features that are common to all Office 2003 applications, including using menus, task panes, and the Office Help system.

- **Lab Organization**—The lab text is organized to include main and subtopic heads by grouping related tasks. For example, tasks such as changing fonts and applying character effects appear under the "Formatting" topic head. This results in a slightly more reference-like approach, making it easier for students to refer back to the text to review. This has been done without losing the logical and realistic development of the case.

- **Relevant Cases**—Four separate running cases demonstrate the features in each application. Topics are of interest to students—At Arizona State University, over 600 students were surveyed to find out what topics are of interest to them.

- **Focus on Concepts**—Each lab focuses on the concepts behind the application. Students learn the concepts, so they can succeed regardless of the software package they might be using. The concepts are previewed at the beginning of each lab and summarized at the end of each lab.

- All **Numbered Steps** and bullets appear in left margin space making it easy not to miss a step.

- **Clarified Marginal Notes**—Marginal notes have been enhanced by more clearly identifying the note content with box heads and the use of different colors.

    Additional Information—Brief asides with expanded discussion of features.

    Having Trouble?—Procedural tips advising students of possible problems and how to overcome them.

    Another Method—Alternative methods of performing a procedure.

- **Focus on Careers**—A new feature, appearing at the end of each lab, which provides an example of how the material covered may be applied in the "real world."

- A **Microsoft Office Specialist Skills** table, appearing at the end of each lab, contains page references to Microsoft Office Specialist skills learned in the lab.

- **End-of-Chapter Material**

  - Screen Identification (appears in the first lab of each application)

  - Matching

  - Multiple Choice

  - Fill-In

  - True/False

  Hands-On Practice Exercises—Students apply the skills and concepts they learned to solve case-based exercises. Many cases in the practice exercises tie to a running case used in another application lab. This helps to demonstrate the use of the four applications across a common case setting. For example, the Adventure Travel Tours case used in the Word labs is continued in practice exercises in Excel, Access, and PowerPoint.

  - Step-by-Step

  - On Your Own

- **Rating System**—The 3-star rating system identifies the difficulty level of each practice exercise in the end-of-lab materials.

- **Continuing Exercises**—A continuing exercise icon identifies exercises that build off of exercises completed in earlier labs.

- **Working Together Labs**—At the completion of the brief and introductory texts, a final lab demonstrates the integration of the MS Office applications.

- **References**

  Command Summary—Provides a table of all commands used in the labs.

  Glossary of Key Terms—Includes definitions for all bolded terms used in the labs and included in the Key Terms list at the end of each lab.

  Data File List—Helps organize all data and solution files.

  Microsoft Office Specialist Certification Guide—Links all Microsoft Office Specialist objectives to text content and end-of-chapter exercises.

Instructor's Guide

We understand that, in today's teaching environment, offering a textbook alone is not sufficient to meet the needs of the many instructors who use our books. To teach effectively, instructors must have a full complement of supplemental resources to assist them in every facet of teaching from preparing for class, to conducting a lecture, to assessing students' comprehension. *The O'Leary Series* offers a fully-integrated supplements package and Web site, as described below.

Instructor's Resource Kit

The **Instructor's Resource Kit** contains a computerized Test Bank, an Instructor's Manual, and PowerPoint Presentation Slides. Features of the Instructor's Resource Kit are described below.

- **Instructor's Manual** The Instructor's Manual contains lab objectives, concepts, outlines, lecture notes, and command summaries. Also included are answers to all end-of chapter material, tips for covering difficult materials, additional exercises, and a schedule showing how much time is required to cover text material.

- **Computerized Test Bank** The test bank contains over 1,300 multiple choice, true/false, and discussion questions. Each question will be accompanied by the correct answer, the level of learning difficulty, and corresponding page references. Our flexible Diploma software allows you to easily generate custom exams.

- **PowerPoint Presentation Slides** The presentation slides will include lab objectives, concepts, outlines, text figures, and speaker's notes. Also included are bullets to illustrate key terms and FAQs.

Online Learning Center/Web Site

Found at **www.mhhe.com/oleary**, this site provides additional learning and instructional tools to enhance the comprehension of the text. The OLC/Web Site is divided into these three areas:

- **Information Center** Contains core information about the text, supplements, and the authors.

- **Instructor Center** Offers instructional materials, downloads, and other relevant links for professors.

- **Student Center** Contains data files, chapter competencies, chapter concepts, self-quizzes, flashcards, additional Web links, and more.

Skills Assessment

SimNet (Simulated Network Assessment Product) provides a way for you to test students' software skills in a simulated environment.

- Pre-testing options
- Post-testing options
- Course placement testing
- Diagnostic capabilities to reinforce skills
- Proficiency testing to measure skills
- Web or LAN delivery of tests.
- Computer-based training tutorials

For more information on skills assessment software, please contact your local sales representative, or visit us at **www.mhhe.com/it**.

Digital Solutions to Help You Manage Your Course

PageOut is our Course Web Site Development Center that offers a syllabus page, URL, McGraw-Hill Online Learning Center content, online exercises and quizzes, gradebook, discussion board, and an area for student Web pages.

Available free with any McGraw-Hill Technology Education product, PageOut requires no prior knowledge of HTML, no long hours of coding, and a way for course coordinators and professors to provide a full-course Web site. PageOut offers a series of templates—simply fill them with your course information and click on one of 16 designs. The process takes under an hour and leaves you with a professionally designed Web site. We'll even get you started with sample Web sites, or enter your syllabus for you! PageOut is so straightforward and intuitive, it's little wonder why over 12,000 college professors are using it. For more information, visit the PageOut Web site at www.pageout.net.

Online courses are also available. Online Learning Centers (OLCs) are your perfect solutions for Internet-based content. Simply put, these Centers are "digital cartridges" that contain a book's pedagogy and supplements. As students read the book, they can go online and take self-grading quizzes or work through interactive exercises. These also provide students appropriate access to lecture materials and other key supplements.

Online Learning Centers can be delivered through any of these platforms:

- Blackboard.com
- WebCT (a product of Universal Learning Technology)

McGraw-Hill has partnerships with WebCT and Blackboard to make it even easier to take your course online. Now you can have McGraw-Hill content delivered through the leading Internet-based learning tool for higher education.

Computing Concepts

Computing Essentials 2004 and *Computing Today* offer a unique, visual orientation that gives students a basic understanding of computing concepts. *Computing Essentials* and *Computing Today* are some of the few books on the market that are written by a professor who still teaches the courses every semester and loves it. The books encourage "active" learning with their exercises, explorations, visual illustrations, and inclusion of screen shots and numbered steps. While combining the "active" learning style with current topics and technology, these texts provide an accurate snapshot of computing trends. When bundled with software application lab manuals, students are given a complete representation of the fundamental issues surrounding the personal computing environment.

Select features of these texts include:

- **Using Technology**—Engaging coverage of hot, high-interest topics, such as phone calls via the Internet, using the Internet remotely with a Personal Digital Assistant (PDA), and Client and Server operating systems. These Web-related projects direct the student to explore current popular uses of technology.

- **Expanding Your Knowledge**—Geared for those who want to go into greater depth on a specific topic introduced within the chapter. These projects meet the needs of instructors wanting more technical depth of coverage.

- **Building Your Portfolio**—Develops critical thinking and writing skills while students examine security, privacy, and ethical issues in technology. By completing these exercises, students will be able to walk away from the class with something to show prospective employers.

- **Making IT Work for You**—Based on student surveys, *Computing Essentials* identified several special interest topics and devoted a two-page section on each in the corresponding chapter. Making IT Work for You sections engage students by presenting high interest topics that directly relate to the concepts presented in the chapter. Topics include downloading music from the Internet, creating personal Web sites, and using the Internet to make long-distance phone calls. Many of these are supported by short video presentations that will be available via CD and the Web.

- **On the Web Explorations**—Appear throughout the margins of the text and encourage students to go to the Web to visit several informative and established sites in order to learn more about the chapter's featured topic.

- **A Look to the Future Sections**—Provide insightful information about the future impact of technology and forecasts of how upcoming enhancements in the world of computing will play an important and powerful role in society.

- **End-of-Chapter Material**—A variety of material including objective questions (key terms, matching, multiple choice, and short answer completion) and critical thinking activities. This will help to reinforce the information just learned.

STUDENT'S GUIDE

As you begin each lab, take a few moments to read the **Case Study** and the Concept Preview. The case study introduces a real-life setting that is interwoven throughout the entire lab, providing the basis for understanding the use of the application. Also, notice the Additional Information, Having Trouble?, and Another Method boxes scattered throughout the book. These tips provide more information about related topics, help get you out of trouble if you are having problems, and offer suggestions on other ways to perform the same task. Finally, read the text between the steps. You will find the few minutes more it takes you is well worth the time when you are completing the practice exercises.

Many learning aids are built into the text to ensure your success with the material and to make the process of learning rewarding. The pages that follow call your attention to the key features in the text.

Objectives
Appear at the beginning of the lab and identify the main features you will be learning.

Case Study
Introduces a real-life setting that is interwoven throughout the lab, providing the basis for understanding the use of the application.

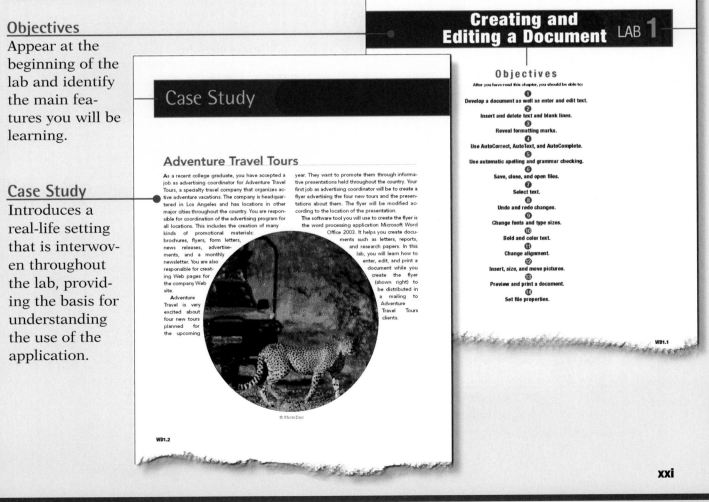

Creating and Editing a Document   LAB 1

Objectives
After you have read this chapter, you should be able to:

1. Develop a document as well as enter and edit text.
2. Insert and delete text and blank lines.
3. Reveal formatting marks.
4. Use AutoCorrect, AutoText, and AutoComplete.
5. Use automatic spelling and grammar checking.
6. Save, close, and open files.
7. Select text.
8. Undo and redo changes.
9. Change fonts and type sizes.
10. Bold and color text.
11. Change alignment.
12. Insert, size, and move pictures.
13. Preview and print a document.
14. Set file properties.

WD1.1

Case Study

Adventure Travel Tours

As a recent college graduate, you have accepted a job as advertising coordinator for Adventure Travel Tours, a specialty travel company that organizes active adventure vacations. The company is headquartered in Los Angeles and has locations in other major cities throughout the country. You are responsible for coordination of the advertising program for all locations. This includes the creation of many kinds of promotional materials: brochures, flyers, form letters, news releases, advertisements, and a monthly newsletter. You are also responsible for creating Web pages for the company Web site.

Adventure Travel is very excited about four new tours planned for the upcoming year. They want to promote them through informative presentations held throughout the country. Your first job as advertising coordinator will be to create a flyer advertising the four new tours and the presentations about them. The flyer will be modified according to the location of the presentation.

The software tool you will use to create the flyer is the word processing application Microsoft Word Office 2003. It helps you create documents such as letters, reports, and research papers. In this lab, you will learn how to enter, edit, and print a document while you create the flyer (shown right) to be distributed in a mailing to Adventure Travel Tours clients.

© PhotoDisc

WD1.2

xxi

• Objectives, Case Study
• Concept Preview, Another Method, Having Trouble?

Concept Preview
Provides an overview to the concepts that will be presented throughout the lab.

Another Method
Offers additional ways to perform a procedure.

Having Trouble?
Helps resolve potential problems as you work through each lab.

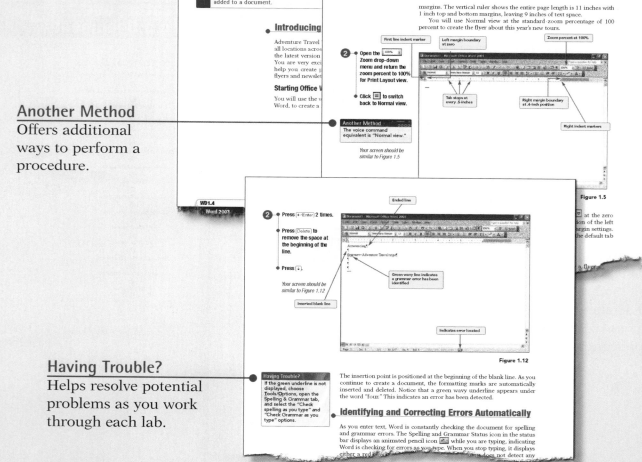

Numbered and Bulleted Steps, Additional Information

Numbered and Bulleted Steps

Provide clear Step-by-Step Instructions on how to complete a task, or series of tasks.

Additional Information

Offers brief asides with expanded coverage of content.

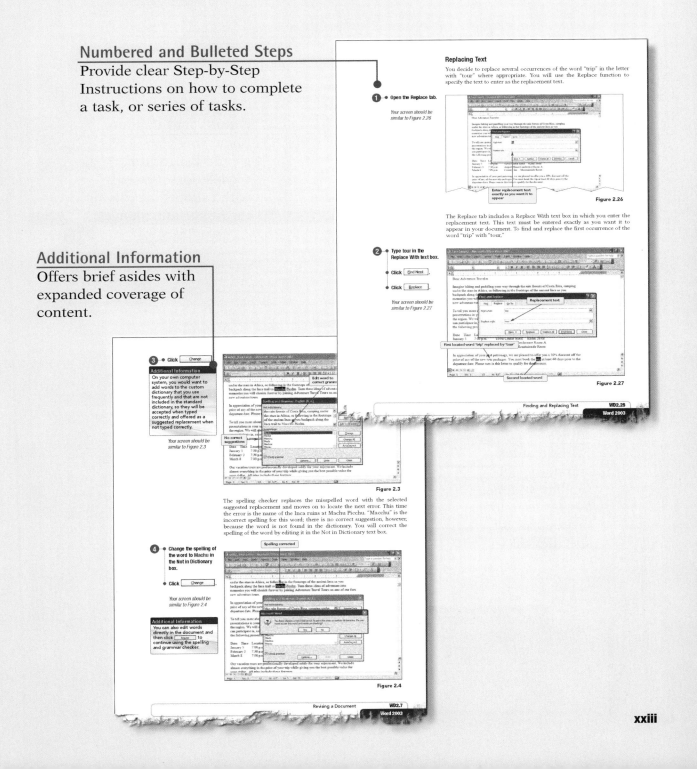

Figures and Callouts, Tables

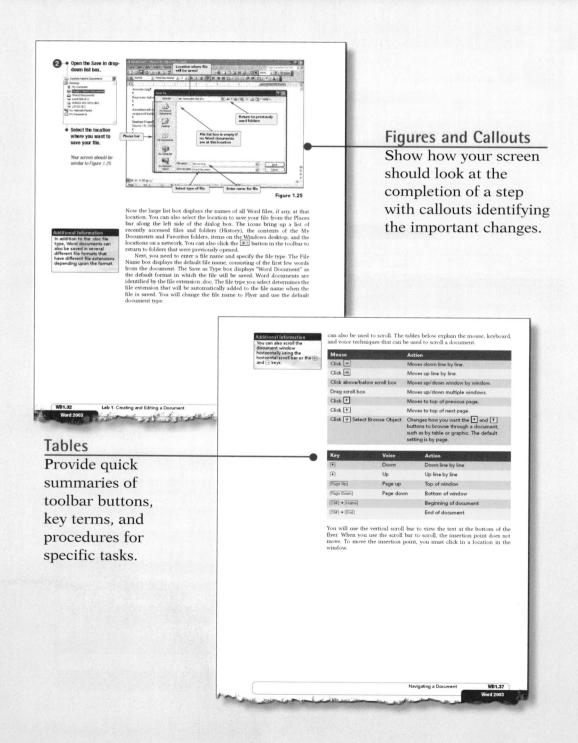

Figures and Callouts
Show how your screen should look at the completion of a step with callouts identifying the important changes.

Tables
Provide quick summaries of toolbar buttons, key terms, and procedures for specific tasks.

• Focus on Careers, Concept Summary

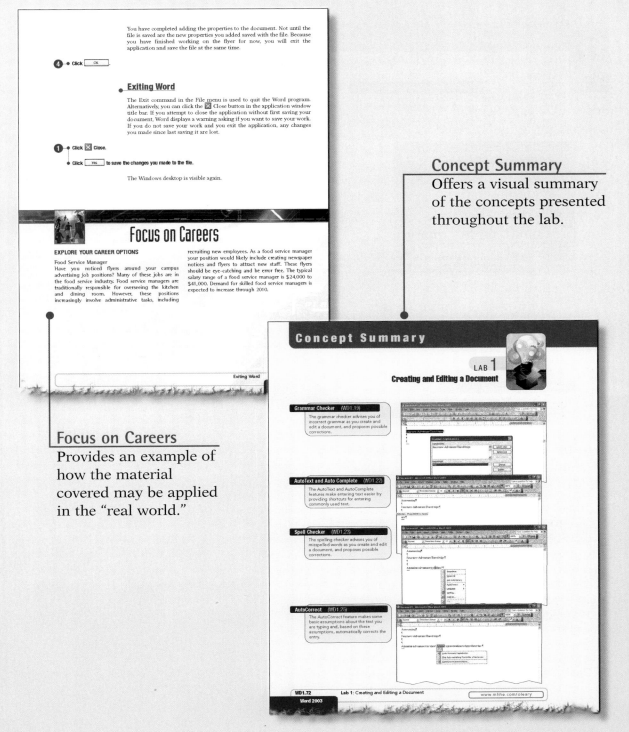

Concept Summary
Offers a visual summary of the concepts presented throughout the lab.

Focus on Careers
Provides an example of how the material covered may be applied in the "real world."

Key Terms and Microsoft Office Specialist Skills, Command Summary

Key Terms and Microsoft Office Specialist Skills

Includes a list of all bolded terms with page references and a table showing the Microsoft Office Specialist certification skills that were covered in the lab.

Command Summary

Provides a table of commands and keyboard and toolbar shortcuts for all commands used in the lab.

---

lab review

LAB 3
Creating Reports and Tables

key terms

alignment WD1.58	font size WD1.51	sans serif font WD1.51
AutoComplete WD1.22	format WD1.11	select WD1.6
AutoCorrect WD1.25	formatting mark WD1.14	selection rectangle WD1.65
AutoText WD1.22	Formatting toolbar WD1.5	serif font WD1.51
character formatting WD1.50	grammar checker WD1.16	sizing handles WD1.65
cursor WD1.5	graphic WD1.60	Smart Tag WD1.29
custom dictionary WD1.23	Insert mode WD1.40	soft space WD1.58
default WD1.68	insertion point WD1.5	source program WD1.60
document window WD1.5	main dictionary WD1.23	spelling checker WD1.23
drawing object WD1.60	object WD1.60	Standard toolbar WD1.5
edit WD1.11	Overtype mode WD1.41	thumbnail WD1.62
embedded object WD1.60	pane WD1.6	TrueType WD1.52
end-of-file marker WD1.5	paragraph formatting WD1.50	typeface WD1.51
file property WD1.69	picture WD1.60	word wrap WD1.28
font WD1.51	ruler WD1.5	

microsoft office specialist skills

The Microsoft Office Specialist (MOS) certification program is designed to measure your proficiency in performing basic tasks using the Office 2003 applications. Getting certified demonstrates that you have the skills and provides a valuable industry credential for employment. After completing this lab, you have learned the following Microsoft Office Specialist skills:

Skill	Description	Page
Creating Content	Insert and edit text, symbols, and special characters	WD1.XX
	Insert frequently used and predefined text	WD1.XX,
	Insert, position, and size graphics	WD1.XX
Formatting Content	Format text	WD1.XX
	Format paragraphs	WD1.XX
Formatting and Managing Documents	Preview and print documents	WD1.XX
	Review and modify document properties	WD1.XX
	Save documents in appropriate formats for different uses	WD1.XX
	Print documents, envelopes, and labels	WD1.XX
	Preview documents and Web pages	WD1.XX
	Change and organize document views and windows	WD1.XX

---

command summary

Command	Shortrtcut Key	Button	Voice	Action
File/Page Setup				Changes layout of page including margins, paper size, and paper source
File/Versions				Saves, opens, and deletes document versions
Edit/Cut	Ctrl + X		Cut	Cuts selection to Clipboard
Edit/Copy	Ctrl + C		Copy	Copies selection to Clipboard
Edit/Paste	Ctrl + V		Paste	Pastes item from Clipboard
Edit/Find	Ctrl + F			Locates specified text
Edit/Replace	Ctrl + H			Locates and replaces specified text
Insert/Break/Page break	Ctrl + ⏎Enter			Inserts hard page break
Insert/Date and Time				Inserts current date or time, maintained by computer system, in selected format
Insert/AutoText				Enters predefined text
Insert/AutoText/AutoText				Create new AutoText entries
Insert/Picture/AutoShapes		AutoShapes ▾		Inserts selected AutoShape
Format/Font/Font/ Underline style/Single	Ctrl + U	U		Underlines selected text with a single line
Format/Paragraph/Indents and Spacing/Special/First Line				Indents first line of paragraph from left margin
Format/Paragraph/Indents and Spacing/Line Spacing	Ctrl + #			Changes amount of white space between lines
Format/Bullets and Numbering				Creates a bulleted or numbered list
Format /Tabs				Specifies types and position of tab stops
Format/Styles and Formatting				Displays the Styles and Formatting Task pane

Lab Exercises

Reinforce the terminology and concepts presented in the lab through Screen Identification, Matching, Multiple Choice, True/False, and Fill-in questions.

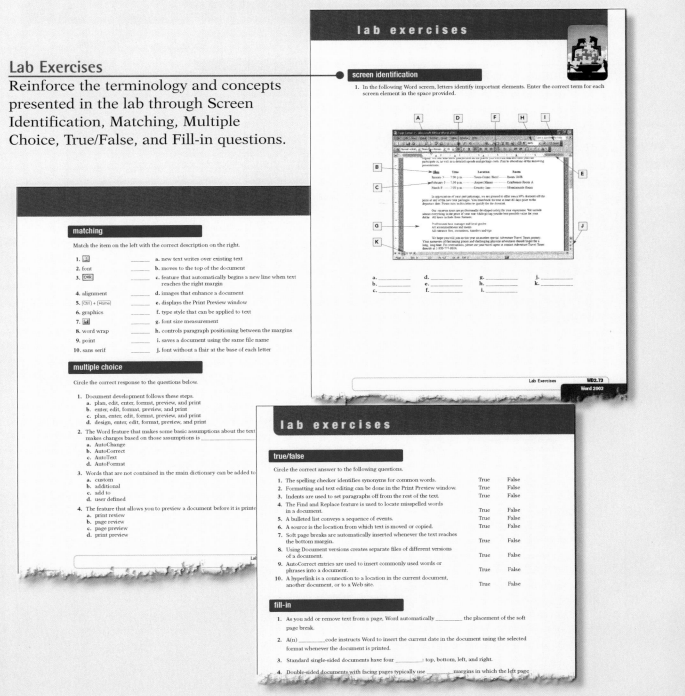

lab exercises

screen identification

1. In the following Word screen, letters identify important elements. Enter the correct term for each screen element in the space provided.

a. _____   d. _____   g. _____   j. _____
b. _____   e. _____   h. _____   k. _____
c. _____   f. _____   i. _____

Lab Exercises WD2.73
Word 2003

matching

Match the item on the left with the correct description on the right.

1. ☐ _____ a. new text writes over existing text
2. font _____ b. moves to the top of the document
3. OVR _____ c. feature that automatically begins a new line when text reaches the right margin
4. alignment _____ d. images that enhance a document
5. Ctrl + Home _____ e. displays the Print Preview window
6. graphics _____ f. type style that can be applied to text
7. ☐ _____ g. font size measurement
8. word wrap _____ h. controls paragraph positioning between the margins
9. point _____ i. saves a document using the same file name
10. sans serif _____ j. font without a flair at the base of each letter

multiple choice

Circle the correct response to the questions below.

1. Document development follows these steps.
   a. plan, edit, enter, format, preview, and print
   b. enter, edit, format, preview, and print
   c. plan, enter, edit, format, preview, and print
   d. design, enter, edit, format, preview, and print

2. The Word feature that makes some basic assumptions about the text makes changes based on those assumptions is _____
   a. AutoChange
   b. AutoCorrect
   c. AutoText
   d. AutoFormat

3. Words that are not contained in the main dictionary can be added to _____
   a. custom
   b. additional
   c. add to
   d. user defined

4. The feature that allows you to preview a document before it is printed _____
   a. print review
   b. page review
   c. page preview
   d. print preview

lab exercises

true/false

Circle the correct answer to the following questions.

1. The spelling checker identifies synonyms for common words. True False
2. Formatting and text editing can be done in the Print Preview window. True False
3. Indents are used to set paragraphs off from the rest of the text. True False
4. The Find and Replace feature is used to locate misspelled words in a document. True False
5. A bulleted list conveys a sequence of events. True False
6. A source is the location from which text is moved or copied. True False
7. Soft page breaks are automatically inserted whenever the text reaches the bottom margin. True False
8. Using Document versions creates separate files of different versions of a document. True False
9. AutoCorrect entries are used to insert commonly used words or phrases into a document. True False
10. A hyperlink is a connection to a location in the current document, another document, or to a Web site. True False

fill-in

1. As you add or remove text from a page, Word automatically _____ the placement of the soft page break.

2. A(n) _____ code instructs Word to insert the current date in the document using the selected format whenever the document is printed.

3. Standard single-sided documents have four _____: top, bottom, left, and right.

4. Double-sided documents with facing pages typically use _____ margins in which the left page

• Lab Exercises: Step-by-Step, On Your Own

Lab Exercises

Provide hands-on practice and develop critical thinking skills through step-by-step and on-your-own practice exercises. These exercises have a rating system from easy to difficult and test your ability to apply the knowledge you have gained in each lab. Exercises that build off of previous exercises are noted with a 🔄 Continuing Exercise icon.

On Your Own

lab exercises

step-by-step

Writing a Memo ★

1. Adventure Travel Tours is planning to update its World Wide Web site in the near future. You have been asked to solicit suggestions from the travel agents about changes they would like to see made to the current Web site. You decide to send all the travel agents a memo asking them for their input. Your completed memo is shown here.

   a. Open a blank Word document and create the following memo in Normal view. Press [Tab] twice after you type colons (:) in the To, From, and Date lines. This will make the information following the colons line up evenly. Enter a blank line between paragraphs.

   To: **Travel Agents**
   From: **Student Name**
   Date: **[Current date]**

   Next month we plan to begin work on updating the current Adventure Travel Tours Web site. In preparation for this project, I would like your input about the current Web site. In the next few days as you use the Web site, pay attention to such things as the layout, colors, and content. Then send your comments back to me about both the positive and negative features of the current Web site and suggestions for changes you would like to see made in the new Web site.

   Thank you in advance for your input.

   b. Turn on the display of formatting marks.

   c. Correct any spelling and grammar errors that are identified.

   d. Delete the word "current" from the first and second sentences. Delete the phrase "such things ... third sentence. Insert the text "ease of use," after the word "colors," in the third ... paragraph beginning with the third sentence. Include a blank line between ... size for the entire memo to 14 pt and the alignment of the body of the memo to ... line insert the AutoText reference line "RE:".

Lab 1: Creating and Editing a Document   www.mhhe.com/oleary

---

p. Increase the font size of the line above "Roast Coffee" to 18 pt. Reset its line spacing to single. Insert a blank line below it.

q. Copy the remaining paragraph from the wd02_Coffee Flyer document, and insert it at the bottom of the new document. Include two blank lines between the table and the paragraph.

r. Bold and center the final paragraph. Remove the hyperlink format from the URL. Format the URL as italic, bold, and red.

s. Increase the top, left, and right margins to 1.5 inches.

t. Create the Explosion 1 AutoShape from Stars and Banners. Enter and center the word **Sale!** in red within it, and choose the gold fill color. Size the shape appropriately. Move the shape to the top left corner of the document. Delete the drawing canvas.

u. Add your name and a field with the current date several lines below the final paragraph.

v. Save the document as Coffee Flyer2. Preview and print it.

on your own

Requesting a Reference ★

1. Your first year as a biology major is going well and you are looking for a summer internship with a local research lab. You have an upcoming interview and want to come prepared with a letter of reference from your last position. Write a business letter directed to your old supervisor, Rachel McVey, at your former lab, AMT Research. Use the modified block letter style shown in the lab. Be sure to include the date, a salutation, two paragraphs, a closing, and your name as a signature. Spell-check the document, save the document as Reference Letter, and print it.

Long Distance Rates Survey ★

2. American Consumer Advocates conducted a survey in October, 2002 comparing the costs of long distance rates. Create a tabbed table using the information shown below. Bold and underline the column heads. Add style 2 tab leaders to the table entries. Above the table, write a paragraph explaining the table contents.

Company	Per Minute	Monthly Fee	Customer Service Wait
Zone LD	3.5¢	$2.00	Less than 1 minute
Pioneer Telephone	3.9¢	none	1 minute
Capsule	3.9¢	none	17 minutes
ECG	4.5¢	$1.99	5 minutes
IsTerra	4.9¢	none	10 minutes

Include your name and the date below the table. Save the document as Phone Rates and print the document.

Introduction to Microsoft Office 2003

Objectives

After completing the Introduction to Microsoft Office 2003, you should be able to:

1
Describe Office System 2003.

2
Describe the Office 2003 applications.

3
Start an Office 2003 application.

4
Recognize the basic application window features.

5
Use menus, shortcut menus, and shortcut keys.

6
Use toolbars and task panes.

7
Use Office Help.

8
Exit an Office 2003 application.

What Is Microsoft Office System 2003?

Microsoft Office System 2003 is a comprehensive, integrated system of programs, servers and services designed to solve a wide array of business needs. Although the programs can be used individually, they are designed to work together seamlessly making it easy to connect people and organizations to information, business processes and each other. The applications include tools used to create, discuss, communicate, and manage projects. If you share a lot of documents with other people, these features facilitate access to common documents. This version has expanded and refined the communication and collaboration features and integration with the World Wide Web. In addition, several new interface features are designed to make it easier to perform tasks and help users take advantage of all the features in the applications.

The Microsoft Office System 2003 is packaged in different combinations of components. The major components and a brief description are provided in the following table.

Component	Description
Microsoft Office 2003	
Office Word 2003	Word Processor
Office Excel 2003	Spreadsheet
Office Access 2003	Database manager
Office PowerPoint 2003	Presentation graphics
Office Outlook 2003	Desktop information manager
Office FrontPage 2003	Web site creation and management
Office InfoPath 2003	Creates XML forms and documents
Office OneNote 2003	Note-taking
Office Publisher 2003	Desktop publishing
Office Visio 2003	Drawing and diagramming
Office SharePoint Portal Server v2.0 and Services	

The five components of Microsoft Office 2003—Word, Excel, Access, PowerPoint, and Outlook—are the applications you will learn about in this series of labs. They are described in more detail in the following sections.

Office Word 2003

Office Word 2003 is a word processing software application whose purpose is to help you create text-based documents. Word processors are one of the most flexible and widely used application software programs. A word processor can be used to manipulate text data to produce a letter, a report, a memo, an e-mail message, or any other type of correspondence.

Two documents you will produce in the first two Word labs, a letter and flyer, are shown here.

A letter containing a tabbed table, indented paragraphs, and text enhancements is quickly created using basic Word features.

March 25, 2005

Dear Adventure Traveler:

Imagine hiking and paddling your way through the rain forests of Costa Rica, camping under the stars in Africa, or following in the footsteps of the ancient Inca as you backpack along the Inca trail to Machu Picchu. Turn these dreams of adventure into memories you will cherish forever by joining Adventure Travel Tours on one of our four new adventure tours.

To tell you more about these exciting new adventures, we are offering several presentations in your area. These presentations will focus on the features and cultures of the region. We will also show you pictures of the places you will visit and activities you can participate in, as well as a detailed agenda and package costs. Plan to attend one of the following presentations:

Date	Time
January 5 ----- 7:00 p.m. --------
February 3 ---- 7:30 p.m. --------
March 8 ------- 7:00 p.m. --------

In appreciation of your past patro[...] price of any of the new tour packages. Y[...] departure date. Please turn in this letter t[...]

Our vacation tours are professior[...] almost everything in the price of your to[...] dollar. All tours include these features:

- **Professional tour manager and**
- **All accommodations and meals**
- **All entrance fees, excursions, t**

We hope you will join us this ye[...] Your memories of fascinating places an[...] long, long time. For reservations, please[...] directly at 1-800-777-0004.

Announcing

New Adventure Travel Tours

Attention adventure travelers! Attend an Adventure Travel presentation to learn about some of the earth's greatest unspoiled habitats and find out how you can experience the adventure of a lifetime. This year we are introducing four new tours and offering you a unique opportunity to combine many different outdoor activities while exploring the world.

India Wildlife Adventure
Inca Trail to Machu Picchu
Safari in Tanzania
Costa Rica Rivers and Rain Forests

Presentation dates and times are January 5 at 7:00 p.m., February 3 at 7:30 p.m., and March 8 at 7:00 p.m. All presentations are held at convenient hotel locations. The hotels are located in downtown Los Angeles, in Santa Clara, and at the airport.

Call 1-800-777-0004 for presentation locations, a full color brochure, and itinerary information, costs, and trip dates.

Visit our
Web site at
www.AdventureTravelTours.com

A flyer incorporating many visual enhancements such as colored text, varied text styles, and graphic elements is both eye-catching and informative.

The beauty of a word processor is that you can make changes or corrections as you are typing. Want to change a report from single spacing to double spacing? Alter the width of the margins? Delete some paragraphs and add others from yet another document? A word processor allows you to do all these things with ease.

Word 2003 includes many group collaboration features to help streamline how documents are developed and changed by group members. You can also create and send e-mail messages directly from within Word using all its features to create and edit the message. In addition, you can send an entire document as your e-mail message, allowing the recipient to edit the document directly without having to open or save an attachment.

Word 2003 is closely integrated with the World Wide Web, detecting when you type a Web address and automatically converting it to a hyperlink. You can also create your own hyperlinks to locations within documents, or to other documents, including those at external locations such as a Web site or file server. Its many Web-editing features, including a Web Page Wizard that guides you step by step, help you quickly create a Web page.

Office Excel 2003

Office Excel 2003 is an electronic worksheet that is used to organize, manipulate, and graph numeric data. Once used almost exclusively by accountants, worksheets are now widely used by nearly every profession. Marketing professionals record and evaluate sales trends. Teachers record grades and calculate final grades. Personal trainers record the progress of their clients.

Excel includes many features that not only help you create a well-designed worksheet, but one that produces accurate results. Formatting features include visual enhancements such as varied text styles, colors, and graphics. Other features help you enter complex formulas and identify and correct formula errors. You can also produce a visual display of data in the form of graphs or charts. As the values in the worksheet change, charts referencing those values automatically adjust to reflect the changes.

Excel also includes many advanced features and tools that help you perform what-if analysis and create different scenarios. And like all Office 2003 applications, it is easy to incorporate data created in one application into another. Two worksheets you will produce in Labs 2 and 3 of Excel are shown on the next page.

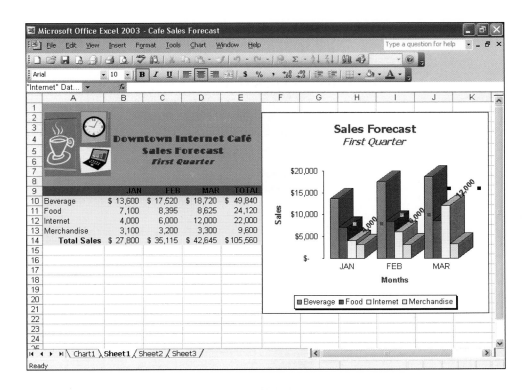

A worksheet showing the quarterly sales forecast containing a graphic, text enhancements, and a chart of the data is quickly created using basic Excel features.

A large worksheet incorporating more complex formulas, visual enhancements such as colored text, varied text styles, and graphic elements is both informative and attractive.

You will see how easy it is to analyze data and make projections using what-if analysis and what-if graphing in Lab 3 and to incorporate Excel data in a Word document as shown in the following figures.

Changes you make in worksheet data while performing what-if analysis are automatically reflected in charts that reference that data.

Worksheet data and charts can be copied and linked to other Office documents such as a Word document.

www.mhhe.com/oleary

Office Access 2003

Office Access 2003 is a relational database management application that is used to create and analyze a database. A database is a collection of related data. In a relational database, the most widely used database structure, data is organized in linked tables. Tables consist of columns (called fields) and rows (called records). The tables are related or linked to one another by a common field. Relational databases allow you to create smaller and more manageable database tables, since you can combine and extract data between tables.

The program provides tools to enter, edit, and retrieve data from the database as well as to analyze the database and produce reports of the output. One of the main advantages of a computerized database is the ability to quickly add, delete, and locate specific records. Records can also be easily rearranged or sorted according to different fields of data, resulting in multiple table arrangements that provide more meaningful information for different purposes. Creation of forms makes it easier to enter and edit data as well. In the Access labs you will create and organize the database table shown below.

A relational database can be created and modified easily using basic Access features.

Organizing records into sorted order in a database makes the information more meaningful and easier to use.

Forms make entering and editing data easy.

Another feature is the ability to analyze the data in a table and perform calculations on different fields of data. Additionally, you can ask questions or query the table to find only certain records that meet specific conditions to be used in the analysis. Information that was once costly and time-consuming to get is now quickly and readily available. This information can then be quickly printed out in the form of reports ranging from simple listings to complex, professional-looking reports in different layout styles, or with titles, headings, subtotals, or totals.

A database can be queried to locate and display only specified information.

A professional-looking report can be quickly generated from information contained in a database.

Office PowerPoint 2003

Office PowerPoint 2003 is a graphics presentation program designed to help you produce a high-quality presentation that is both interesting to the audience and effective in its ability to convey your message. A presentation can be as simple as overhead transparencies or as sophisticated as an on-screen electronic display. In the first two PowerPoint labs you will create and organize the presentation shown on the next page.

A presentation consists of a series of pages or "slides" presenting the information you want to convey in an organized and attractive manner.

When running an onscreen presentation, each slide of the presentation is displayed full-screen on your computer monitor or projected onto a screen.

Office Outlook 2003

Office Outlook 2003 is a personal information manager (PIM) program that is designed to get you organized and keep you organized. PIMs, also known as desktop managers, are designed to maximize your personal productivity by making it efficient and easy to perform everyday tasks such as scheduling meetings, recording contact information, and communicating with others, to name a few. Outlook 2003 includes an integrated e-mail program, a calendar, and contact and task management features.

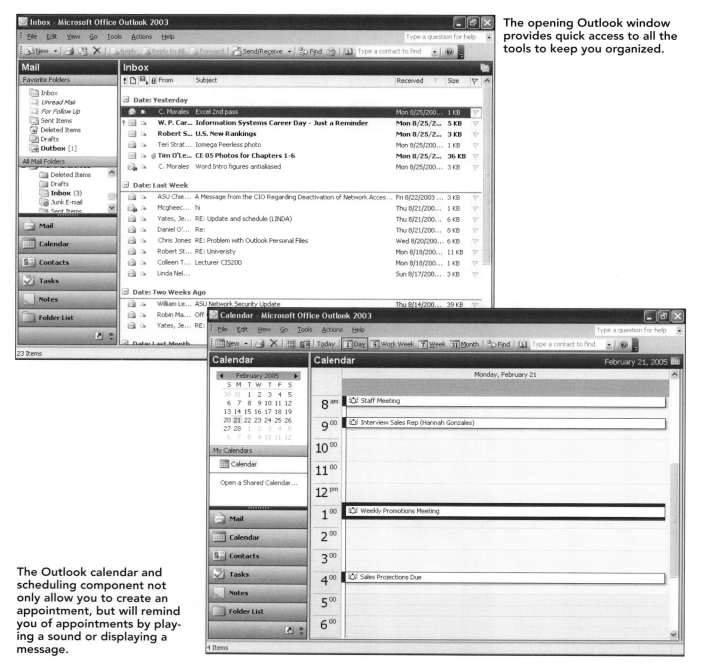

The opening Outlook window provides quick access to all the tools to keep you organized.

The Outlook calendar and scheduling component not only allow you to create an appointment, but will remind you of appointments by playing a sound or displaying a message.

Common Office 2003 Features

Now that you know a little about each of the applications in Microsoft Office 2003, we will take a look at some of the features that are common to all Office 2003 applications. This is a hands-on section that will introduce you to the features and allow you to get a feel for how Office 2003 works. Although Word 2003 will be used to demonstrate how the features work, only common features will be addressed. These features include using menus, Office Help, task panes, toolbars, and starting and exiting an application. The features that are specific to each application will be introduced individually in each application text.

Starting an Office 2003 Application

There are several ways to start an Office 2003 application. The two most common methods are by using the Start menu or by clicking a desktop shortcut for the program if it is available. If you use the Start menu, the steps will vary slightly depending on the version of Windows you are using.

1 • Click **start** to display the Start menu.

• Select All Programs.

• Select
  Microsoft Office .

• Choose
  Microsoft Office Word 2003 .

OR

1 • Double-click the shortcut on the desktop.

2 • If necessary, click Maximize in the title bar to maximize the window.

Your screen should be similar to Figure 1

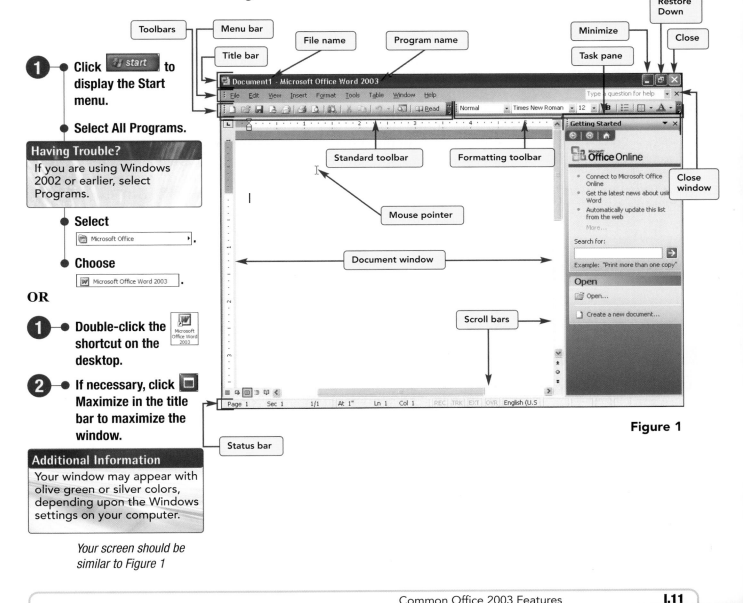

Toolbars · Menu bar · Title bar · File name · Program name · Minimize · Restore Down · Close · Task pane · Standard toolbar · Formatting toolbar · Office Online · Close window · Mouse pointer · Document window · Scroll bars · Status bar

Figure 1

The Word program is started and displayed in a window on the desktop. The left end of the application window title bar displays the file name followed by the program name, Microsoft Office Word 2003. The right end of the title bar displays the ▬ Minimize, ⬜ Restore Down, and ✕ Close buttons. They perform the same functions and operate in the same way as all Windows versions.

The **menu bar** below the title bar displays the application's program menu. The right end displays the document window's ✕ Close Window button. As you use the Office applications, you will see that the menu bar contains many of the same menus, such as File, Edit, and Help. You will also see several menus that are specific to each application.

The **toolbars** located below the menu bar contain buttons that are mouse shortcuts for many of the menu items. Commonly, the Office applications will display two toolbars when the application is first opened: Standard and Formatting. They may appear together on one row (as in Figure 1), or on separate rows.

The large center area of the program window is the **document window** where open application files are displayed. Currently, there is a blank Word document open. In Word, the mouse pointer appears as I when positioned in the document window and as a $\natural$ when it can be used to select items. The **task pane** is displayed on the right side of the document window. Task panes provide quick access to features as you are using the application. As you perform certain actions, different task panes automatically open. In this case, since you just started an application, the Getting Started task pane is automatically displayed, providing different ways to create a new document or open an existing document.

The **status bar** at the bottom of the window displays location information and the status of different settings as they are used. Different information is displayed in the status bar for different applications.

On the right and bottom of the document window, are vertical and horizontal scroll bars. A **scroll bar** is used with a mouse to bring additional lines of information into view in a window. The vertical scroll bar is used to move up or down, and the horizontal scroll bar moves side to side in the window.

As you can see, many of the features in the Word window are the same as in other Windows applications. The common user interface makes learning and using new applications much easier.

Using Menus

A menu is one of many methods you can use to accomplish a task in a program. When opened, a menu displays a list of commands. When an Office program menu is first opened, it may display a short version of commands. The short menu is a personalized version of the menu that displays basic and frequently used commands and hides those used less often. An expanded version will display automatically after the menu is open for a few seconds.

1 ● Click **F**ile to open the File menu.

● Point to each menu in the menu bar to see the full menu for each.

● Point to the **V**iew menu.

Your screen should be similar to Figure 2

Figure 2

Many commands have images next to them so you can quickly associate the command with the image. The same image appears on the toolbar button for that feature. Menus may include the following features (not all menus include all features):

Feature	Meaning
Ellipsis (...)	Indicates a dialog box will be displayed.
▶	Indicates a submenu will be displayed.
Dimmed	Indicates the command is not available for selection until certain other conditions are met.
Shortcut key	A key or key combination that can be used to execute a command without using the menu.
Checkmark	Indicates a toggle type of command. Selecting it turns the feature on or off. A checkmark indicates the feature is on.
Underlined letter	Indicates the letter you can type to choose the command.

On the View menu, two options, Task Pane and Ruler, are checked, indicating these features are on. The Task Pane option also displays the shortcut key combination, Ctrl + F1, after the option. This indicates the command can be chosen by pressing the keys instead of using the menu. The Footnotes option is dimmed because it is not currently available. The Toolbars option will display a submenu when selected, and the Zoom command a dialog box of additional options.

Once a menu is open, you can select a command from the menu by pointing to it. A colored highlight bar, called the **selection cursor**, appears over the selected command.

2 ● **Point to the Toolbars command to select it and display the submenu.**

Your screen should be similar to Figure 3

Figure 3

Currently there are three selected (checked) Toolbar options: Standard, Formatting, and although not technically a toolbar, the Task Pane. If other toolbars are selected in your menu, this is because once a toolbar has been turned on, it remains on until turned off.

To choose a command, you click on it. When the command is chosen, the associated action is performed. You will close the task pane and any other open toolbars and display the Drawing toolbar.

3 ● Click on Task Pane to turn off this feature.

● Open the View menu again, select Toolbars, and if it is not already selected, click on the Drawing toolbar option to turn it on.

● If necessary, choose View/Toolbars again and deselect any other toolbar options (there should be 3 selected toolbar options).

Your screen should be similar to Figure 4

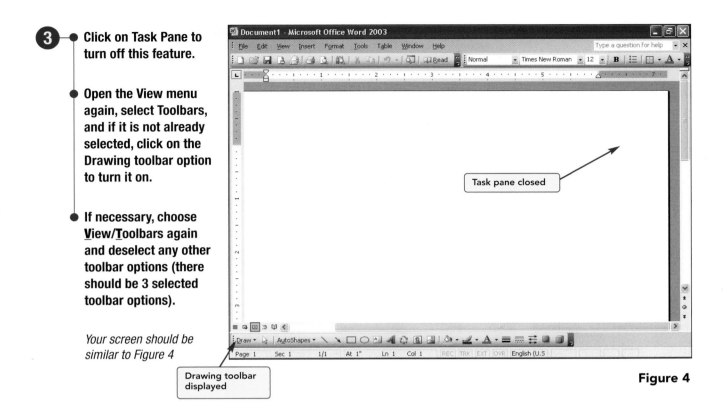

Drawing toolbar displayed

Figure 4

The task pane is closed and the Drawing toolbar is displayed above the status bar. Any other toolbars that were open which you deselected are closed.

Using Shortcut Menus

Another way to access menu options is to use the **shortcut menu**. The shortcut menu is opened by right-clicking on an item on the screen. This menu displays only those options associated with the item. For example, right-clicking on any toolbar will display the toolbar menu options only. You will use this method to hide the Drawing toolbar again.

1 ● **Point to the Drawing toolbar and right-click.**

Your screen should be similar to Figure 5

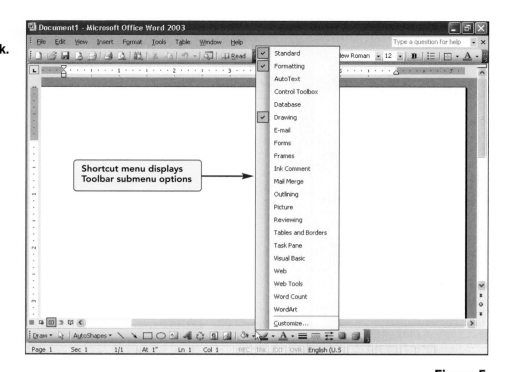

Shortcut menu displays Toolbar submenu options

Figure 5

Additional Information

The Customize option can be used to change features of toolbars and menus.

The shortcut menu displays only the Toolbar submenu options on the View menu. Using a shortcut menu saves time over selecting the main menu command sequence.

2 ● **Choose Drawing to turn off this feature.**

Your screen should be similar to Figure 6

Drawing toolbar closed

Figure 6

The Drawing toolbar is no longer displayed.

Using Shortcut Keys

A third way to perform a command is to use the shortcut key or key combination associated with a particular command. If you will recall, the shortcut key associated with the **V**iew/Tas**k** Pane command is Ctrl + F1. To use the key combination, you hold down the first key while pressing the second.

1 ➤ Hold down Ctrl and press the F1 function key.

Having Trouble?

Function keys are located above the numeric keys on the keyboard.

Your screen should be similar to Figure 7

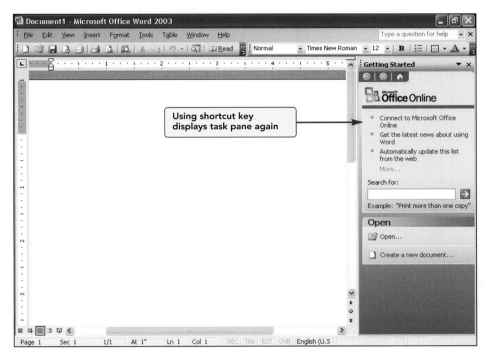

Using shortcut key displays task pane again

Figure 7

The task pane is displayed again. Using shortcut keys is the quickest way to perform many actions; however, you need to remember the key combination in order to use it.

Using Toolbars

Initially, Word displays two toolbars, Standard and Formatting, below the menu bar (see Figure 3). The **Standard toolbar** contains buttons that are used to complete the most frequently used menu commands. The **Formatting toolbar** contains buttons that are used to change the appearance or format of the document. There are many features that can be used to make working with toolbars easier.

Displaying Toolbars on Separate Rows

The default toolbar arrangement is to display both toolbars on one row. Because there is not enough space to display all the buttons on both toolbars on a single row, many buttons are hidden. The Toolbar Options button located at the end of a toolbar displays a drop-down button list of those buttons that are not displayed. Toolbars initially display the basic buttons. Like menus, they are personalized automatically, displaying those buttons you use frequently and hiding others. When you use a button from this list, it then is moved to the toolbar, and a button that has not been used recently is moved to the Toolbar Options list. It also contains an option to display the toolbars on separate rows. You will use this option to quickly see all the toolbar buttons.

1 ● **Click** 🔳 **Toolbar Options.**

● **Choose S̲how Buttons on Two Rows.**

Toolbars displayed on two rows

Toolbar options button

Figure 8

Another Method

You can also use **T̲**ools/**C̲**ustomize/**O̲**ptions, or choose **C̲**ustomize/**O̲**ptions from the toolbar shortcut menu and select "Show Standard and Formatting toolbars on two rows."

Your screen should be similar to Figure 8

Additional Information

The Add or Remove Buttons option allows you to customize existing toolbars by selecting those buttons you want to display and by creating your own customized toolbars.

The two toolbars now occupy separate rows, providing enough space for all the buttons to be displayed. Now using 🔳 Toolbar Options is no longer necessary, and when selected only displays the options to return the toolbars display to one row and the Add or Remove Buttons option.

When a toolbar is open, it may appear docked or floating. A **docked toolbar** is fixed to an edge of the window and displays a vertical bar 🔳, called the move handle, on the left edge of the toolbar. Dragging this bar up or down allows you to move the toolbar. If multiple toolbars share the same row, dragging the bar left or right adjusts the size of the toolbar. If docked, a toolbar can occupy a row by itself, or several can be on a row together. A **floating toolbar** appears in a separate window and can be moved anywhere on the desktop.

2 ● Point to the move handle of the Standard toolbar and, when the mouse pointer appears as ✛, drag the toolbar into the document window.

Your screen should be similar to Figure 9

Docked toolbar

Floating toolbar

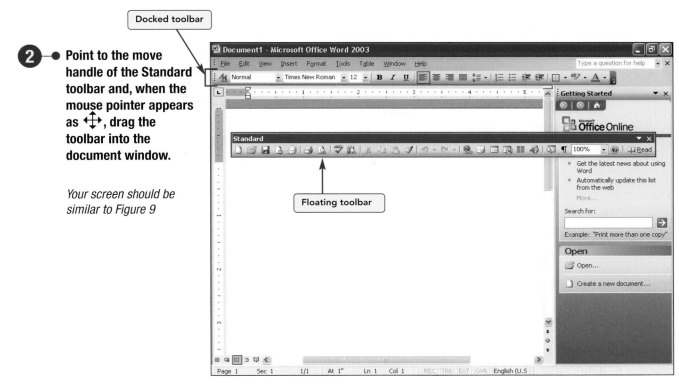

Figure 9

The Standard toolbar is now a floating toolbar and can be moved to any location in the window by dragging the title bar. If you move a floating toolbar to the edge of the window, it will attach to that location and become a docked toolbar. A floating toolbar can also be sized by dragging the edge of the toolbar.

Toolbars docked and displayed on two rows again

3 ● Drag the title bar of the floating toolbar (the mouse pointer appears as ✛) to move the toolbar to the row below the Formatting toolbar.

● Move the Formatting toolbar below the Standard toolbar.

● Align both toolbars with the left edge of the window by dragging the move handle horizontally.

Your screen should be similar to Figure 10

Figure 10

The two toolbars again occupy two rows. To quickly identify the toolbar buttons, you can display the button name by pointing to the button.

4 ● **Point to any button on the Standard toolbar.**

Your screen should be similar to Figure 11

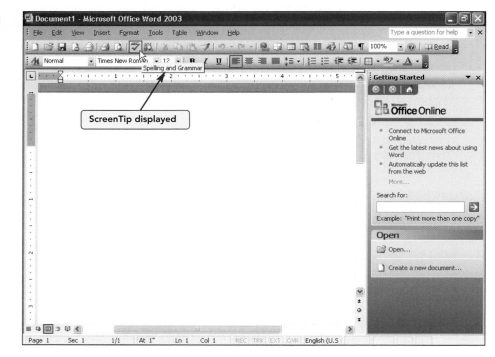

Figure 11

A ScreenTip containing the button name appears next to the mouse pointer. Clicking on a button will perform the associated action. You will use the Help button to access Microsoft Word Help.

5 ● **Click** **Microsoft Office Word Help.**

Another Method
You can also choose **H**elp/ Microsoft Office Word **H**elp, or press F1 to access Help.

Your screen should be similar to Figure 12

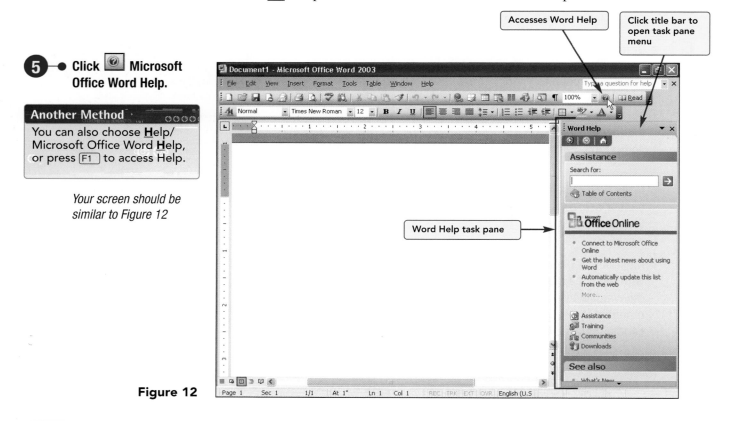

Figure 12

The Getting Started task pane is replaced by the Microsoft Word Help task pane. The name of the task pane appears in the task pane title bar.

Using Task Panes

Task panes appear automatically when certain features are used. They can also be opened manually from the task pane menu. Clicking the task pane title bar displays a drop-down menu of other task panes you can select. In Word there are 14 different task panes. You will redisplay the Getting Started task pane. Then you will quickly return to the previously displayed task pane using the Back toolbar button in the task pane.

Additional Information

You can drag the pane divider line to adjust the width of the pane. When there is more information in the pane than can be displayed, [▲] and [▼] appear to scroll the information into view.

1 ● **Click on the task pane title bar.**

| Word Help | ▼ |
| Getting Started |
| ✓ Help |
| Search Results |
| Clip Art |
| Research |
| Clipboard |
| New Document |
| Shared Workspace |
| Document Updates |
| Protect Document |
| Styles and Formatting |
| Reveal Formatting |
| Mail Merge |
| XML Structure |

● **Choose Getting Started.**

Another Method

You can also click the [🏠] Home button to quickly display the Getting Started task pane.

● **Click [◀] Back.**

Your screen should be similar to Figure 13

Displays Next task pane after ⊕ is used

Displays Getting Started task pane

Displays previous task panes

Enter topic to search on

Starts search

Scrolls task pane

Figure 13

The Help task pane is displayed again. Likewise, clicking the [▶] Forward button will display the task pane that was viewed before using [◀] Back.

Using Office Help

There are several ways you can get help. One method is to conduct a search of the available help information by entering a sentence or question you want help on in the Search text box of the Help task pane. Notice the insertion point is positioned in the Search text box. This indicates it is ready for you to type an entry. You will use this method to learn about getting Help while you work.

Additional Information

Although you can also simply enter a word or phrase in the Search box, the best results occur when you type a complete sentence or question.

Type How do I get help? **in the Search box.**

If the insertion point is not displayed in the Search box, simply click in the box to activate it.

● **Click** **Start Searching.**

Your screen should be similar to Figure 14

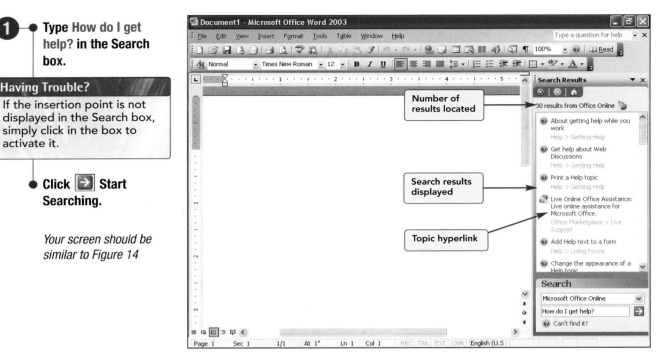

Figure 14

In addition to being connected to the Internet, the Online Content settings must be selected. Click Online Content Settings in the Help task pane and select all the options to turn on these features.

The number of results located and where they were found is displayed at the top of the list.

If you are connected to the Internet, the Microsoft Office Online Web site is searched and the results are displayed in the Search Results task pane. If you are not connected, the offline help information that is provided with the application and stored on your computer is searched. Generally the search results are similar, but fewer in number.

The Search Results pane displays a list of located results. The results are shown in order of relevance, with the most likely matches at the top of the list. Each result is a **hyperlink** or connection to the information located on the Online site or in Help on your computer. Clicking the hyperlink accesses and displays the information associated with the hyperlink.

You want to read the information in the topic "About getting help while you work."

2 • **From the Search Results list click the "About getting help while you work" hyperlink.**

Additional Information

When you point to the hyperlink, it appears underlined and the mouse pointer appears as 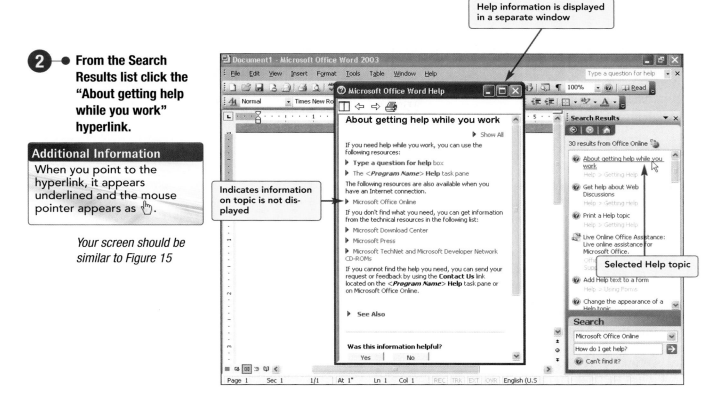.

Your screen should be similar to Figure 15

Figure 15

The information on the selected topic is displayed in a separate Help window. The Help window on your screen will probably be a different size and arrangement than in Figure 15. Depending on the size of your Help window, you may need to scroll the window to see all the Help information provided. As you are reading the help topic, you will see many subtopics preceded with ▶. This indicates the information in the subtopic is not displayed. Clicking on the subtopic heading displays the information about the topic.

3 If necessary, use the scroll bar to scroll the Help window to see the information on this topic.

● Scroll back up to the top of the window.

Additional Information

Clicking the scroll arrows scrolls the text in the window line by line, and dragging the scroll bar up or down moves to a general location within the window area.

● Click the "Type a question for help box" subtopic.

● Click the "The <Program name> Help task pane" subtopic.

● Read the information on both subtopics.

Your screen should be similar to Figure 16

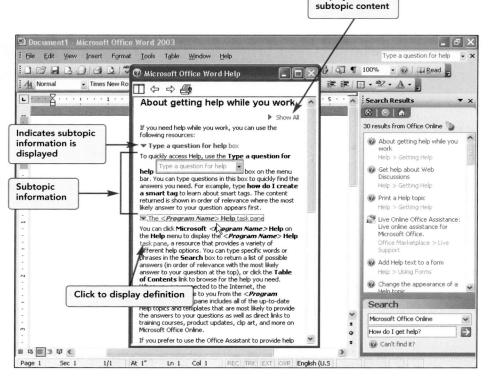

Figure 16

The ▶ preceding the subtopic has changed to ▼ indicating the subtopic content is displayed. The selected subtopics provide information about accessing Help using the "Type a question for help" box and the Help task pane. Notice the blue words "task pane" within the subtopic content. This indicates that clicking on the text will display a definition of the term. You can continue to click on the subtopic headings to display the information about each topic individually, or you can click Show All to display all the available topic information.

4 • Click "task pane" to see the definition.

• Click Show All at the top of the Help window.

• Scroll the window to see the Microsoft Office Online subtopic.

• Read the information on this subtopic.

Your screen should be similar to Figure 17

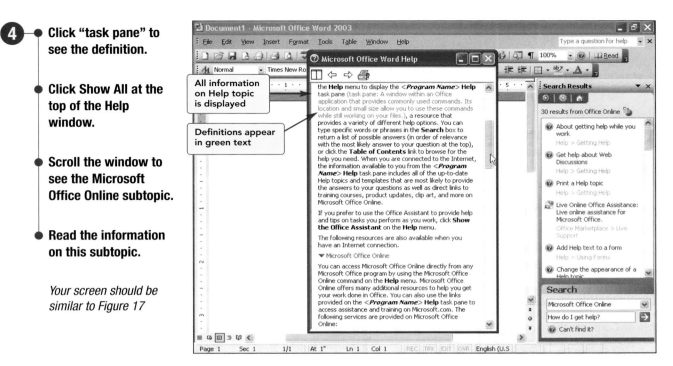

Figure 17

The information under all the subtopics is fully displayed, including definitions.

Using the Help Table of Contents

Another source of help is to use the Help table of contents. Using this method allows you to browse the Help topics to locate topics of interest to you.

1 • Click ☒ Close in the Help window title bar to close the Help window.

• Click ⊕ Back in the task pane.

• Click Table of Contents (below the Search box).

Your screen should be similar to Figure 18

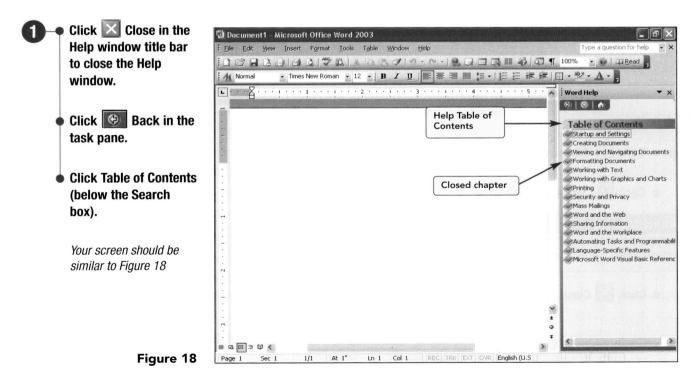

Figure 18

lab exercises

step-by-step

Using an Office Application ★

1. All Office 2003 applications have a common user interface. You will explore the Excel 2003 application and use many of the same features you learned about while using Word 2003 in this lab.

   a. Use the Start menu or a shortcut icon on your desktop to start Office Excel 2003. Close the Getting Started Task Pane.

   b. What shape is the mouse pointer when positioned in the document window area? _____

   c. Excel also has nine menus. Which menu is not the same as in Word? _____ Open the Tools Menu. How many commands in the Tools menu will display a submenu when selected? _____ How many commands are listed in the Formula Auditing submenu? _____

   d. Click on a blank space near the Formatting toolbar to open the toolbar shortcut menu. How many toolbars are available in Excel? _____

   e. Display the Chart toolbar. Dock the Chart toolbar above the Status bar. Change it to a floating toolbar. Close the Chart toolbar.

   f. Use the shortcut key combination to display the Task Pane. How many Task Panes are available? _____

   g. Display the Help Task Pane and search for help information on "worksheet." How many search results were returned? _____ Read the "About viewing workbooks and worksheets" topic. What is the definition of a worksheet? _____
   _____

   h. Close the Help window. Close the Excel window to exit the program.

on your own

Exploring Microsoft Help ★

1. In addition to the Help information you used in this lab, Office 2003 Online Help also includes many interactive tutorials. Selecting a Help topic that starts a tutorial will open the browser program on your computer. Both audio and written instructions are provided. You will use one of these tutorials to learn more about using Office 2003. Start Word 2003 and search for Help on "shortcut keys." Then select the "Work with the Keyboard in Office" topic. Follow the directions in the tutorial to learn about this feature. When you are done, close the browser window and the Word window.

Overview of Microsoft Office Word 2003

What Is Word Processing?

Office Word 2003 is a word processing software application whose purpose is to help you create any type of written communication. A word processor can be used to manipulate text data to produce a letter, a report, a memo, an e-mail message, or any other type of correspondence. Text data is any letter, number, or symbol that you can type on a keyboard. The grouping of the text data to form words, sentences, paragraphs, and pages of text results in the creation of a document. Through a word processor you can create, modify, store, retrieve, and print part or all of a document.

Word processors are one of the most widely used applications software programs. Putting your thoughts in writing, from the simplest note to the most complex book, is a time-consuming process. Even more time-consuming is the task of editing and retyping the document to make it better. Word processors make errors nearly nonexistent—not because they are not made, but because they are easy to correct. Word processors let you throw away the correction fluid, scissors, paste, and erasers. Now, with a few keystrokes, you can easily correct errors, move paragraphs, and reprint your document.

Word 2003 Features

Word 2003 excels in its ability to change or edit a document. Editing involves correcting spelling, grammar, and sentence-structure errors. In addition, you can easily revise or update existing text by inserting or deleting text. For example, a document that lists prices can easily be updated to reflect new prices. A document that details procedures can be revised by deleting old procedures and inserting new ones. This is especially helpful when a document is used repeatedly. Rather than recreating the whole document, you change only the parts that need to be revised.

Revision also includes the rearrangement of selected areas of text. For example, while writing a report, you may decide to change the location of a single word or several paragraphs or pages of text. You can do it easily by cutting or removing selected text from one location, then pasting or placing the selected text in another location. The selection can also be copied from one document to another.

Another time saver is word wrap. As you enter text you do not need to decide where to end each line, as you do on a typewriter. When a line is full, the program automatically wraps the text down to the next line.

To help you produce a perfect document, Word 2003 includes many additional support features. The AutoCorrect feature checks the spelling and grammar in a document as text is entered. Many common errors are corrected automatically for you. Others are identified and a correction suggested. While you enter text, the AutoComplete feature may suggest entire phrases that can be quickly inserted based on the first few characters you type. The words and phrases are included in a list of AutoText entries provided with Word 2003, or they may be ones you have included yourself. A thesaurus can be used to display alternative words that have a meaning similar or opposite to a word you entered. A Find and Replace feature can be used to quickly locate specified text and replace it with other text throughout a document.

A variety of Wizards are included in Word 2003 that provide step-by-step assistance while you produce many common types of documents, such as business letters, faxes, resumes, or reports. Templates also can be used to produce many of these documents without the step-by-step guidance provided by the Wizard.

You can also easily control the appearance or format of the document. Formatting includes such operations as changing the line spacing and margin widths, adding page numbers, and displaying page headers and footers. You can also quickly change how your text is aligned with the left or right margin. For example, text can be centered between the margins, or justified—evenly aligned on both the left and right margins. Perhaps the most noticeable formatting feature is the ability to apply different fonts (type styles and sizes) and text appearance changes such as bold, italics, and color to all or selected portions of the document. Additionally, you can add color shading behind individual pieces of text or entire paragraphs and pages to add emphasis. Automatic formatting can be turned on to automatically format text as you type by detecting when to apply selected formats to text as it is entered. In addition, Word 2003 includes a variety of tools that automate the process of many common tasks, such as creating tables, form letters, and columns.

Group collaboration on projects is common in industry today. Word 2003 includes many features to help streamline how documents are developed and changed by group members. A discussion feature allows multiple people to insert remarks in the same document without having to route the document to each person or reconcile multiple reviewers' comments. A feature called versioning allows you to save multiple versions of the same document so that you can see exactly who did what on a document and when. You can easily consolidate all changes and comments from different reviewers in one simple step and accept or reject changes as needed.

To further enhance your documents, you can insert many different types of graphic elements. You can select from over 150 border styles that can be applied to areas of text such as headings, or around graphics or entire pages. The drawing tools supplied with Word 2003 can be used to create your own drawings, or you can select from over 100 adjustable AutoShapes and modify them to your needs. All drawings can be further enhanced with 3-D effects, shadows, colors, and textures. Additionally, you can produce fancy text effects using the WordArt tool. More complex pictures can be inserted in documents by scanning your own, using supplied or purchased clip art, or downloading images from the World Wide Web.

Word 2003 is closely integrated with the World Wide Web. It detects when you are typing a Web address and converts it to a hyperlink automatically for you. You can also create your own hyperlinks to locations within documents, or to other documents, including those at external locations such as a Web site or file server. Word's many Web-editing features help you quickly create a Web page. Among these is a Web Page Wizard that guides you step by step through the process of creating a Web page. Themes can be used to quickly apply unified design elements and color schemes to your Web pages. Frames can be created to make your Web site easier for users to navigate. Pictures, graphic elements, animated graphics, sound, and movies can all be used to increase the impact of your Web pages.

You can also create and send e-mail messages directly from within Word 2003, using all its features to create and edit the message. You can also send an entire document directly by e-mail. The document becomes the message. This makes collaboration easy because you can edit the document directly without having to open or save an attachment.

Case Study for Office Word 2003 Labs

As a recent college graduate, you have accepted a job as advertising coordinator for Adventure Travel Tours, a specialty travel company that organizes active adventure vacations. The company is headquartered in Los Angeles and has locations in other major cities throughout the country. Your duties include the creation of brochures, flyers, form letters, news releases, advertisements, and a monthly newsletter, all of which promote Adventure Travel's programs. You are also responsible for working on the company Web site.

Brief Version

Lab 1: Adventure Travel has developed four new tours for the upcoming year and needs to promote them, partly through informative presentations held throughout the country. Your first job as advertising coordinator is to create a flyer advertising the four new tours and the presentations about them.

Lab 2: Your next project is to create a letter to be sent to past clients along with your flyer. The letter briefly describes Adventure Travel's four new tours and invites clients to attend an informational presentation.

Lab 3: Part of your responsibility as advertising coordinator is to gather background information about the various tour locations. You will write a report providing information about Tanzania and Peru for two of the new tours.

Working Together: Adventure Travel has a company Web site. You will convert the flyer you developed to promote the new tours and presentations to be used on the Web site.

Before You Begin

To the Student

The following assumptions have been made:

- Microsoft Office Word 2003 has been properly installed on your computer system.

- You have the data files needed to complete the series of Word 2003 labs and practice exercises. These may be supplied by your instructor and are also available at the online learning center Web site found at www.mhhe.com/oleary.

- You are already familiar with how to use Microsoft Windows and a mouse.

To the Instructor

A complete installation of Microsoft Office 2003 is required in which all components are available to students while completing the labs.

Please be aware that the following settings are assumed to be in effect for the Office Word 2003 program. These assumptions are necessary so that the screens and directions in the labs are accurate.

- The Getting Started task pane is displayed when Word is started. (Use Tools/Options/View/Startup Task Pane.)

- The ScreenTips feature is active. (Use Tools/Options/View/ScreenTips.)

- The status bar is displayed. (Use Tools/Options/View/Status bar.)

- The horizontal and vertical scroll bars are displayed. (Use Tools/Options/View/Horizontal scroll bar/Vertical scroll bar.)

- The Wrap to Window setting is off. (Use Tools/Options/View/Wrap to Window.)

- The Smart Tags feature is active. (Use Tools/Options/View/Smart tags.)

- The Mark Formatting Inconsistencies option is off. (Use Tools/Options/Edit/Mark formatting inconsistencies.)

- The Paste Options buttons are displayed. (Use Tools/Options/Edit/Show Paste Options buttons.)

- Background repagination is on. (Use Tools/Options/General/Background repagination.)

- The feature to check spelling and grammar as you type is on. (Use Tools/Options/Spelling & Grammar/Check spelling as you type/Check grammar as you type.)

- All AutoCorrect features are on. (Use Tools/AutoCorrect Options/AutoCorrect and select all options.)

- In the Introduction to Microsoft Office 2003 lab, the Standard and Formatting toolbars are displayed on one row. In all other labs they are displayed on two rows. (Use Tools/Customize/Options/Show Standard and Formatting toolbars on two rows.)
- Full menus are displayed after a short delay. (Use Tools/Customize/Options/Show full menus after a short delay.)
- Language is set to English (US). (Use Tools/Language/Set Language.)
- AutoComplete Suggestions are displayed. (Use Insert/AutoText/Auto-Text/ Show AutoComplete Suggestions.)
- The feature to access Online Help is on. (Choose Online Content Settings from the Help task pane and select the Show content and links from Microsoft Office Online option.)
- The Research tools include the Encarta World Dictionary, Thesaurus, MSN Search and Encyclopedia.
- The Office Assistant feature is off. (Right-click on the Assistant character, choose Options, and clear the Use the Office Assistant option.)
- All default settings for the Normal document template are in effect.

In addition, all figures in the manual reflect the use of a standard VGA display monitor set at 800 by 600. If another monitor setting is used, there may be more or fewer lines of text displayed in the windows than in the figures. This setting can be changed using Windows setup.

Microsoft Office Language Bar

The Microsoft Office Language Bar may also be displayed when you start the application. Commonly, it will appear on the title bar, however, it may appear in other locations depending upon your setup. The Language bar provides buttons to access and use the Speech Recognition and Handwriting recognition features.

Instructional Conventions

Hands-on instructions you are to perform appear as a sequence of numbered steps. Within each step, a series of bullets identifies the specific actions that must be performed. Step numbering begins over within each topic heading throughout the lab.

Command sequences you are to issue appear following the word "Choose." Each menu command selection is separated by a /. If the menu command can be selected by typing a letter of the command, the letter will appear underlined and bold. Items that need to be selected will follow the word "Select" and will appear in black text. You can select items with the mouse or directional keys. (See Example A.)

Example A

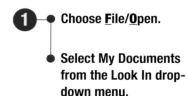

1 ● Choose **F**ile/**O**pen.

● Select My Documents from the Look In drop-down menu.

Commands that can be initiated using a button and the mouse appear following the word "Click." The icon (and the icon name if the icon does not include text) is displayed following "Click." The menu equivalent, keyboard shortcut, and/or voice command appear in an Another Method margin note when the action is first introduced. (See Example B.)

Example B

1 ● Click 🖿 **Open.**

Another Method
The menu equivalent is **File/Open**, the keyboard shortcut is Ctrl + O, and the voice command is "Open file."

Plain blue text identifies file names you need to select or enter. Information you are asked to type appears in blue and bold. (See Example C.)

Example C

1 ● **Open the document** wd01_Flyer.

● **Type Adventure Travel presents four new trips.**

Creating and Editing a Document

Objectives

After completing this lab, you will know how to:

1 Develop a document as well as enter and edit text.

2 Insert and delete text and blank lines.

3 Reveal formatting marks.

4 Use AutoCorrect, AutoText, and AutoComplete.

5 Use automatic spelling and grammar checking.

6 Save, close, and open files.

7 Select text.

8 Undo and redo changes.

9 Change fonts and type sizes.

10 Bold and color text.

11 Change alignment.

12 Insert, size, and move pictures.

13 Preview and print a document.

14 Set file properties.

Adventure Travel Tours

As a recent college graduate, you have accepted a job as advertising coordinator for Adventure Travel Tours, a specialty travel company that organizes active adventure vacations. The company is headquartered in Los Angeles and has locations in other major cities throughout the country. You are responsible for coordination of the advertising program for all locations. This includes the creation of many kinds of promotional materials: brochures, flyers, form letters, news releases, advertisements, and a monthly newsletter. You are also responsible for creating Web pages for the company Web site.

Adventure Travel is very excited about four new tours planned for the upcoming year.

They want to promote them through informative presentations held throughout the country. Your first job as advertising coordinator will be to create a flyer advertising the four new tours and the presentations about them. The flyer will be modified according to the location of the presentation.

The software tool you will use to create the flyer is the word processing application Microsoft Office Word 2003. It helps you create documents such as letters, reports, and research papers. In this lab, you will learn how to enter, edit, and print a document while you create the flyer (shown right) to be distributed in a mailing to Adventure Travel Tours clients.

© PhotoDisc

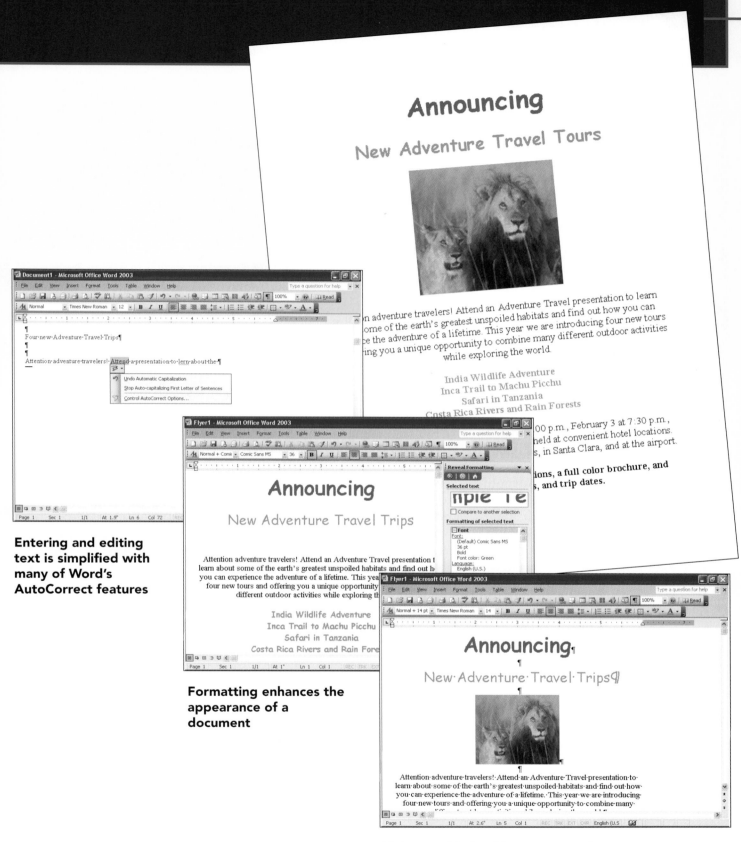

Entering and editing text is simplified with many of Word's AutoCorrect features

Formatting enhances the appearance of a document

Pictures add visual interest to a document

① Grammar Checker The grammar checker advises you of incorrect grammar as you create and edit a document, and proposes possible corrections.

② AutoText and AutoComplete The AutoText and AutoComplete features make entering text easier by providing shortcuts for entering commonly used text.

③ Spelling Checker The spelling checker advises you of misspelled words as you create and edit a document, and proposes possible corrections.

④ AutoCorrect The AutoCorrect feature makes some basic assumptions about the text you are typing and, based on these assumptions, automatically corrects the entry.

⑤ Word Wrap The word wrap feature automatically decides where to end a line and wrap text to the next line based on the margin settings.

⑥ Font and Font Size A font, also commonly referred to as a typeface, is a set of characters with a specific design that has one or more font sizes.

⑦ Alignment Alignment is the positioning of text on a line between the margins or indents. There are four types of paragraph alignment: left, centered, right, and justified.

⑧ Graphics A graphic is a non-text element or object, such as a drawing or picture that can be added to a document.

Introducing Office Word 2003

Adventure Travel Tours has recently upgraded their computer systems at all locations across the country. As part of the upgrade, they have installed the latest version of the Microsoft Office suite of applications, Office System 2003. You are very excited to see how this new and powerful application can help you create professional letters and reports as well as eye-catching flyers and newsletters.

Starting Office Word 2003

You will use the word processing application included in Office System 2003, Word 2003, to create a flyer promoting the new tours and presentations.

Formatting toolbar

Standard toolbar

Document window

Menu bar

Ruler

Task pane

1 ● **Start Office Word 2003.**

Having Trouble?

See "Common Office 2003 Features," page I.11, for information on how to start the application and use menus, toolbars, task panes, and other features that are common to all Office 2003 applications.

● **If necessary, maximize the Word 2003 application window.**

● **To display the standard window view, choose View/Normal.**

Additional Information

You will learn about the different document views shortly.

● **If necessary, display the Standard and Formatting toolbars on 2 rows.**

Having Trouble?

Choose **T**ools/**C**ustomize/ **O**ptions/**S**how Standard and Formatting toolbars on two rows, to make this change.

Your screen should be similar to Figure 1.1

Insertion point

End-of-file marker

Mouse pointer

Figure 1.1

Exploring the Word 2003 Window

The menu bar below the title bar displays the Word program menu. It consists of nine menus that provide access to the commands and features you will use to create and modify a document.

The toolbars, normally located below the menu bar, contain buttons that are mouse shortcuts for many of the menu items. The **Standard toolbar** contains buttons for the most frequently used menu commands. The **Formatting toolbar** contains buttons that are used to change the appearance or format of the document. Word includes 21 toolbars, many of which appear automatically as you use different features. Your screen may display other toolbars if they were on when the program was last exited.

The large area below the toolbars is the **document window**. It currently displays a blank Word document. The **ruler**, displayed at the top of the document window, shows the line length in inches and is used to set margins, tab stops, and indents. The **insertion point**, also called the **cursor**, is the blinking vertical bar that marks your location in the document. The solid horizontal line is the **end-of-file marker**. Because this document contains no text, the insertion point appears at the first character space on the first line.

The task pane is displayed on the right side of the document window. A **pane** is a separate area in a window that you can view and scroll independently. Word includes 14 task panes, which are displayed depending on the task being performed. Since you just started Word, the Getting Started task pane is automatically displayed. This task pane provides different ways to create a new document or open an existing document.

The mouse pointer may appear as an I-beam (see Figure 1.1) or a left- or right-facing arrow, depending on its location in the window. When it appears as an I-beam, it is used to move the insertion point, and when it appears as an arrow, it is used to select items.

1 ● Move the mouse pointer into the left edge of the document window to see it appear as ⇗.

● Move the mouse pointer to the menu bar to see it appear as ⇗.

Your screen should be similar to Figure 1.2

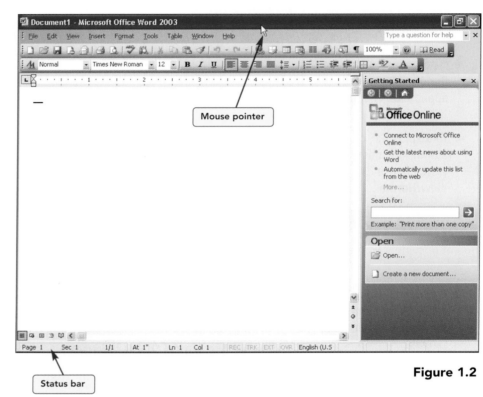

Figure 1.2

The indicators on the **status bar** show both the location of the text that is displayed in the document window as well as the location of the insertion point in a document. The numbers following the indicators specify the exact location in the document. The indicators are described in the following table.

Indicator	Meaning
Page	Indicates the page of text displayed onscreen.
Sec	Indicates the section of text displayed onscreen. A large document can be broken into sections.
1/1	Indicates the number of the page displayed onscreen, and the total number of pages in the document.
At	Indicates the vertical position in inches of the insertion point from the top of the page.
Ln	Indicates the line of text where the insertion point is located.
Col	Indicates the horizontal position of the insertion point in number of characters from the left margin.

Creating New Documents

When you first start Word, a new blank document is opened. It is like a blank piece of paper that already has many predefined settings. These settings, called default settings, are generally the most commonly used settings. You will use the blank document to create the flyer for Adventure Travel Tours. You do not need to use the task pane, so you will close it to see the entire document window.

1 ● Click ⊠ Close in the task pane title bar to close the task pane.

Another Method
The menu equivalent is **V**iew/Tas**k** Pane and the keyboard shortcut is Ctrl + F1 . The voice command is "Task pane" to show it and "Hide task pane" to hide it.

Your screen should be similar to Figure 1.3

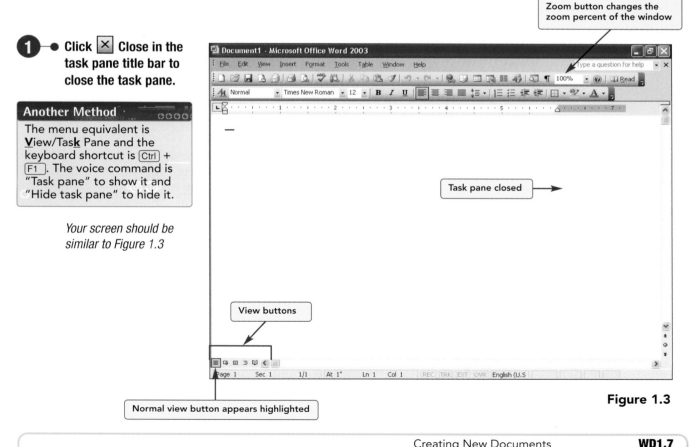

Zoom button changes the zoom percent of the window

Task pane closed →

View buttons

Normal view button appears highlighted

Figure 1.3

Viewing and Zooming a Document

To verify several of the default document settings more easily, you can switch to another document view. Word includes several views that are used for different purposes. You can change views using the View menu commands or the view buttons located to the left of the horizontal scroll bar. The different document views are described in the table below.

Document View	Command	Button	Effect on Text
Normal	**V**iew/**N**ormal		Shows text formatting and simple layout of the page. This is the best view to use when typing, editing, and formatting text.
Web Layout	**V**iew/**W**eb Layout		Shows the document as it will appear when viewed in a Web browser. Use this view when creating Web pages or documents that will be displayed on the screen only.
Print Layout	**V**iew/**P**rint Layout		Shows how the text and objects will appear on the printed page. This is the view to use when adjusting margins, working in columns, drawing objects, and placing graphics.
Reading Layout	**V**iew/**R**eading Layout		Automatically scales the content of the document to fit the screen so that pages are easy to read and browse. Use to review a document and add comments and highlighting.
Outline	**V**iew/**O**utline		Shows the structure of the document. This is the view to use to plan and reorganize text in a document.
Full Screen	**V**iew/**F**ull Screen		Shows the document only, without menu bar, toolbars, status bar, or any other features. Useful for viewing and reading large documents.

The view you see when first starting Word is the view that was in use when the program was last exited. Currently, your view is Normal view, as shown in Figure 1.3. You can tell which view is in use by looking at the view buttons. The button for the view that is in use appears highlighted.

In addition, you can change the amount of information displayed in the document window by "zooming in" to get a close-up view or "zooming out" to see more of the document at a reduced view. The default display, 100 percent, shows the characters the same size they will be when printed. You can increase the onscreen character size up to five times the normal display (500 percent) or reduce the character size to 10 percent. The zoom setting for each view is set independently and remains in effect until changed to another zoom setting.

You will switch to Print Layout view and "zoom out" on the document to see the entire page so you can better see the default document settings.

1 • Click ▣ **Print Layout View** (located to the left of the horizontal scroll bar).

Additional Information

The view buttons display the button name in a ScreenTip when you point to them.

• **Choose View/Zoom/Whole Page/** [OK] .

Your screen should be similar to Figure 1.4

Having Trouble?

If your zoom percentage is different, this is a function of the monitor you are using.

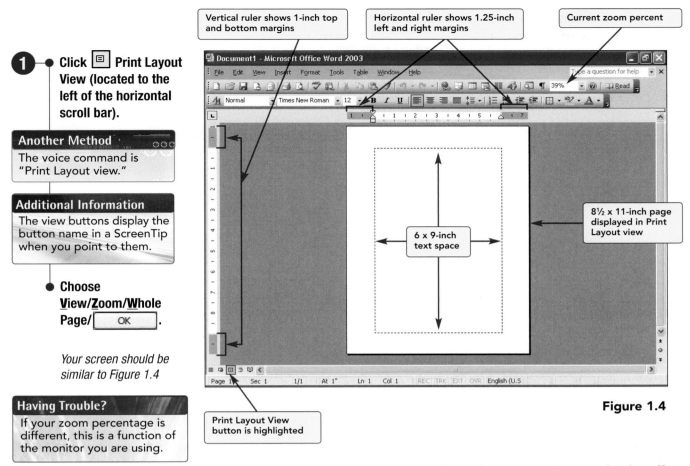

Vertical ruler shows 1-inch top and bottom margins

Horizontal ruler shows 1.25-inch left and right margins

Current zoom percent

8½ x 11-inch page displayed in Print Layout view

6 x 9-inch text space

Print Layout View button is highlighted

Figure 1.4

The zoom percentage shown in the Zoom button on the Standard toolbar has decreased to 39 percent in order to display the entire page. Print Layout view displays the current page of your document as it will appear when printed. All four edges of the paper are visible. This view also displays a vertical ruler that shows the vertical position of text.

The default document settings include a standard paper-size setting of 8.5 by 11 inches, 1-inch top and bottom margins, and 1.25-inch left and right margins. Other default settings include tab stops at every half inch and single line spacing. You can verify many of the default document settings by looking at the information displayed in the rulers. The margin boundaries on both ends of the horizontal ruler show the location of the left margin at zero and the right margin at 6-inches. The ruler shows that the distance between the left and right margins is 6 inches. Knowing that the default page size is 8.5 inches wide, this leaves 2.5 inches for margins: 1.25 inches for equal-sized left and right margins. The vertical ruler shows the entire page length is 11 inches with 1 inch top and bottom margins, leaving 9 inches of text space.

You will use Normal view at the standard zoom percentage of 100 percent to create the flyer about this year's new tours. This time you will use the [31% ▼] Zoom button on the Standard toolbar to change the Zoom percentage. The buttons on this toolbar are identified below.

Figure 1.5

The ruler also displays other default settings. The symbol ▽ at the zero position is the first line indent marker and marks the location of the left paragraph indent. The symbol △ on the right end of the ruler line at the 6-inch position marks the right paragraph indent. The indent locations are the same as the left and right margin settings. The dimmed tab marks below each half-inch position show the default tab stop setting of every half inch.

Developing a Document

Your first project with Adventure Travel Tours is to create a flyer about four new tours. The development of a document follows several steps: plan, enter, edit, format, and preview and print.

Step	Description
Plan	The first step in the development of a document is to understand the purpose of the document and to plan what your document should say.
Enter	After planning the document, you enter the content of the document by typing the text using the keyboard. Text can also be entered using the handwriting and speech recognition features.
Edit	Making changes to your document is called **editing**. While typing, you probably will make typing and spelling errors that need to be corrected. This is one type of editing. Another is to revise the content that you have entered to make it clearer, or to add or delete information.
Format	Enhancing the appearance of the document to make it more readable or attractive is called **formatting**. This step is usually performed when the document is near completion, after all editing and revising have been done. It includes many features such as boldfaced text, italics, and bulleted lists.
Preview and Print	The last step is to preview and print the document. Previewing displays the document onscreen as it will appear when printed, allowing you to check the document's overall appearance and make any final changes before printing.

You will find that you will generally follow these steps in the order listed above for your first draft of a document. However, you will probably retrace steps such as editing and formatting as the final document is developed.

During the planning phase, you spoke with your manager regarding the purpose of the flyer and the content in general. The primary purpose of the flyer is to promote the new tours. A secondary purpose is to advertise the company in general.

You plan to include specific information about the new tours in the flyer as well as general information about Adventure Travel Tours. The content also needs to include information about the upcoming new tour presentations. Finally, you want to include information about the Adventure Travel Web site.

Entering Text

Now that you understand the purpose of the flyer and have a general idea of the content, you are ready to enter the text.

Text is entered using the keyboard. As you type, you will probably make simple typing errors that you want to correct. Word includes many features that make entering text and correcting errors much easier. These features include checking for spelling and grammar errors, auto correction, and word wrap. You will see how these features work while entering the title and first paragraph of the flyer.

Additional Information

You can also enter and edit text in Dictation mode using the Speech Recognition feature.

Typing Text

To enter text in a new document, simply begin typing the text. The first line of the flyer will contain the text 'Announcing four new Adventure Travel trips.' As you begin to enter this line of text, include the intentional error identified in italic.

1 ━ ● Type Announcing four new*w*.

Your screen should be similar to Figure 1.6

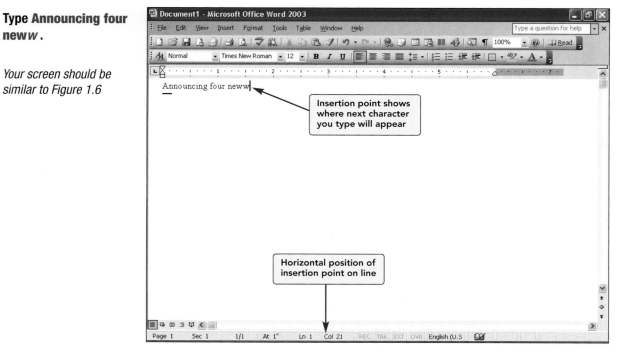

Figure 1.6

Notice that as you type, the insertion point moves to the right and the character appears to the left of the insertion point. The location of the insertion point shows where the next character will appear as you type. Also, the status bar reflects the new horizontal position of the insertion point on the line. As you can see from the first three indicators, page 1 of section 1 of a document consisting of only 1 page (1/1) is displayed on your screen. The next three indicators show the position of the insertion point. Currently, the insertion point is positioned at the 1-inch location from the top of the page, on line 1 from the top margin and column 21 from the left margin.

Using Backspace and Delete

You have made a typing error by typing an extra w in the word new. Removing typing entries to change or correct them is one of the basic editing tasks. Corrections may be made in many ways. Two of the most important editing keys are the ⌈Backspace⌋ key and the ⌈Delete⌋ key. The ⌈Backspace⌋ key removes a character or space to the left of the insertion point. It is particularly useful when you are moving from right to left (backward) along a line of text. The ⌈Delete⌋ key removes the character or space to the right of the insertion point and is most useful when moving from left to right along a line.

You will correct the error and continue typing the first line.

1 • Press Backspace to remove the extra w.

• Press Spacebar.

• Type **Adventure Travel trips** and correct any typing errors as you make them using Backspace or Delete.

Another Method

Using voice dictation you would say "Backspace" and "Delete."

Your screen should be similar to Figure 1.7

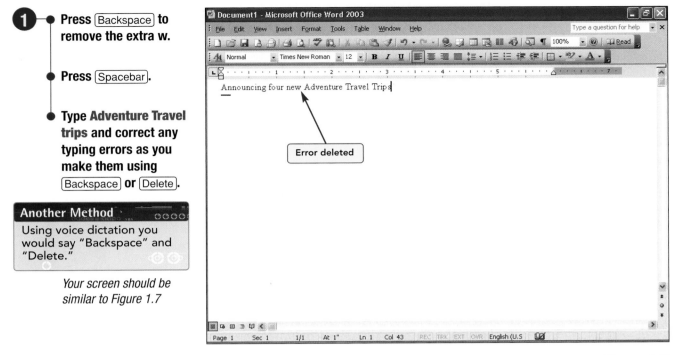

Announcing four new Adventure Travel Trips

Error deleted

Figure 1.7

Ending a Line and Inserting Blank Lines

Now you are ready to complete the first line of the announcement. To end a line and begin another line, you simply press ←Enter. The insertion point moves to the beginning of the next line. If you press ←Enter at the beginning of a line, a blank line is inserted into the document. If the insertion point is in the middle of a line of text and you press ←Enter, all the text to the right of the insertion point moves to the beginning of the next line.

1 ● **Press** ⏎Enter **3 times.**

Your screen should be similar to Figure 1.8

Blank lines inserted →

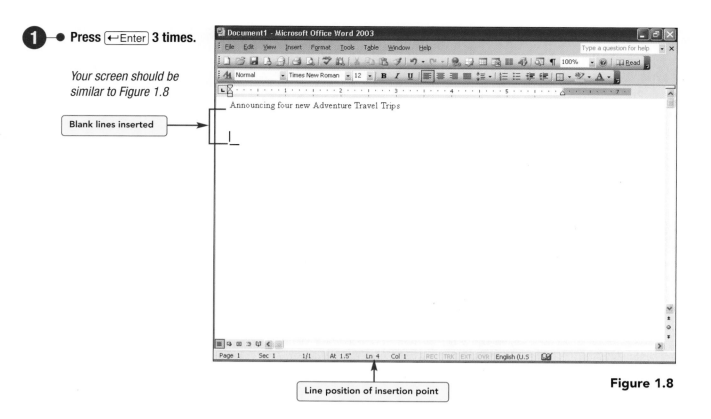

Line position of insertion point

Figure 1.8

Pressing the first ⏎Enter ended the first line of text and inserted a blank line. The next two inserted blank lines. The status bar now shows that the insertion point is positioned at the left margin (1.5 inches), on line 4, column 1 of the page.

Revealing Formatting Marks

While you are creating your document, Word automatically inserts **formatting marks** that control the appearance of your document. Word's default screen display does not show this level of detail. Sometimes, however, it is helpful to view the underlying formatting marks. Displaying these marks makes it easy to see, for example, if you have added an extra space between words or at the end of a sentence. Because you may use this feature frequently, you can access it quickly using the ¶ Show/Hide ¶ button on the Standard toolbar.

1 Click ¶ Show/Hide ¶ (on the Standard toolbar).

Another Method

The menu equivalent is **T**ools/**O**ptions/View/All, and the keyboard shortcut is Ctrl + ⇧Shift + *. The voice command is "Show formatting marks."

Your screen should be similar to Figure 1.9

Inserted blank lines by pressing ←Enter

Entered space by pressing Spacebar

Ended line by pressing ←Enter

Figure 1.9

The document now displays the formatting marks. The ¶ character on the line above the insertion point represents the pressing of ←Enter that created the blank line. The ¶ character at the end of the text represents the pressing of ←Enter that ended the line and moved the insertion point to the beginning of the next line. Between each word, a dot shows where the Spacebar was pressed. Formatting marks do not appear when the document is printed. You can continue to work on the document while the formatting marks are displayed, just as you did when they were hidden.

Additional Information

You can display selected formatting marks using **T**ools/**O**ptions/View and selecting the formatting marks you want to see.

Moving Through Text

After text is entered into a document, you need to know how to move around within the text to correct errors or make changes. The keyboard, mouse, or voice commands can be used to move through the text in the document window. Depending on what you are doing, one method may be more efficient than another. For example, if your hands are already on the keyboard as you are entering text, it may be quicker to use the keyboard rather than take your hands off to use the mouse.

Moving Using the Keyboard

Additional Information

Voice commands are also shown in the following table.

You use the arrow keys located on the numeric keypad or the directional keypad to move the insertion point in a document. The keyboard directional keys are described in the following table.

Key	Voice	Movement
→	Right	One character to right
←	Left	One character to left
↑	Up	One line up
↓	Down	One line down
Ctrl + →	Next word	One word to right
Ctrl + ←	Back word	One word to left
Home	Home	Left end of line
End	Go end	Right end of line

Additional Information

You can use the directional keys on the numeric keypad or the dedicated directional keypad area. If using the numeric keypad, make sure the Num Lock feature is off, otherwise numbers will be entered in the document. The Num Lock indicator light above the keypad is lit when on. Press Num Lock to turn it off.

Holding down a directional key or key combination moves quickly in the direction indicated, saving multiple presses of the key. Many of the Word insertion point movement keys can be held down to execute multiple moves. You will use many of these keys to quickly move through the text.

1 ● Press ↑ 3 times.

● Press → 5 times.

● Press Ctrl + → 4 times.

● Press End.

● Hold down ← until the insertion point is positioned to the left of the "A" in "Adventure." If you move too far to the left along the line, use → to move back to the correct position.

● Press Home.

Your screen should be similar to Figure 1.10

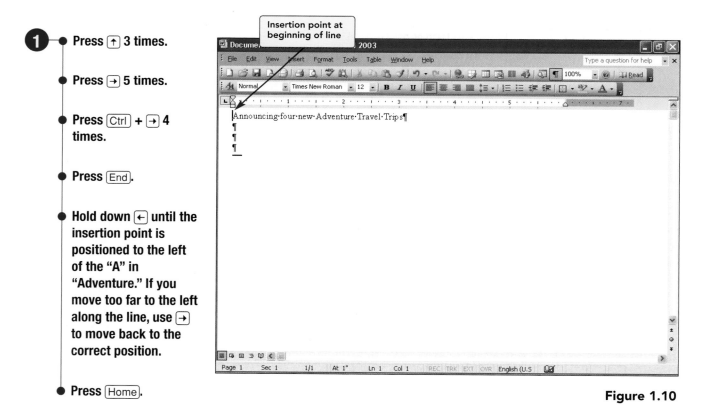

Figure 1.10

The insertion point first moved up three lines, then five character spaces to the right, four words to the right, then quickly to the end of the line. You then held down the direction key to quickly move character by character to the left, and finally to the beginning of the line.

Moving Using the Mouse

You use the mouse to move the insertion point to a specific location in a document. When you can use the mouse to move the insertion point, it is shaped as an I-beam. However, when the mouse pointer is positioned in the unmarked area to the left of a line (the left margin), it changes to an arrow 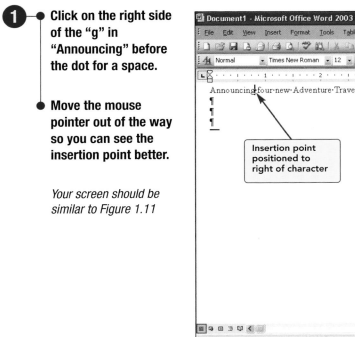. When the mouse is in this area, it can be used to highlight (select) text.

You have decided you want the flyer heading to be on two lines, with the word "Announcing" on the first line. To do this, you will insert a blank line after this word. You will move the insertion point to the location in the text where you want to insert the blank line.

1 ● Click on the right side of the "g" in "Announcing" before the dot for a space.

● Move the mouse pointer out of the way so you can see the insertion point better.

Your screen should be similar to Figure 1.11

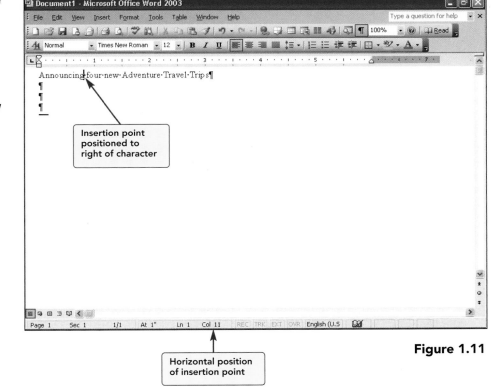

Insertion point positioned to right of character

Horizontal position of insertion point

Figure 1.11

The insertion point should now be positioned to the right of the g, and the status bar shows the column location of the insertion point as column 11. Next, you will start a new line and enter a blank line.

2 • Press ←Enter 2 times.

• Press Delete to remove the space at the beginning of the line.

• Press ↓.

Your screen should be similar to Figure 1.12

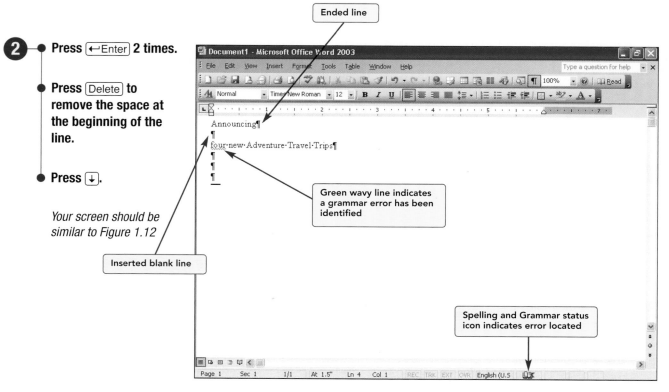

Ended line

Green wavy line indicates a grammar error has been identified

Inserted blank line

Spelling and Grammar status icon indicates error located

Figure 1.12

The insertion point is positioned at the beginning of the blank line. As you continue to create a document, the formatting marks are automatically inserted and deleted. Notice that a green wavy underline appears under the word "four." This indicates an error has been detected.

Identifying and Correcting Errors Automatically

As you enter text, Word is constantly checking the document for spelling and grammar errors. The Spelling and Grammar Status icon in the status bar displays an animated pencil icon [icon] while you are typing, indicating Word is checking for errors as you type. When you stop typing, it displays either a red checkmark [icon], indicating the program does not detect any errors, or a red X [icon], indicating the document contains an error. In many cases, Word will automatically correct errors for you. In other cases, it identifies the error by underlining it. The different colors and designs of underlines indicate the type of error that has been identified. In addition to identifying the error, Word provides suggestions as to the possible correction needed.

Checking Grammar

In addition to the green wavy line under "four," the Spelling and Grammar Status icon appears as [icon]. This indicates that a spelling or grammar error has been located. The green wavy underline indicates it is a grammar error.

Concept 1

Grammar Checker

1 The **grammar checker** advises you of incorrect grammar as you create and edit a document, and proposes possible corrections. Grammar checking occurs after you enter punctuation or end a line. If grammatical errors in subject-verb agreements, verb forms, capitalization, or commonly confused words, to name a few, are detected, they are identified with a wavy green line. You can correct the grammatical error by editing it or you can open the shortcut menu for the identified error and display a suggested correction. Because not all identified grammatical errors are actual errors, you need to use discretion when correcting the errors.

1 ● **Right-click the word "four" to open the shortcut menu.**

Having Trouble?

Review shortcut menus in the "Common Office 2003 Features" section (page I.11). If the wrong shortcut menu appears, you probably did not have the I-beam positioned on the error with the green wavy line. Press [Esc] or click outside the menu to cancel it and try again.

Your screen should be similar to Figure 1.13

Figure 1.13

Additional Information

A dimmed menu option means it is currently unavailable.

The first item on the Grammar shortcut menu is the suggested correction, "Four." The grammar checker indicates you should capitalize the first letter of the word because it appears to be the beginning of a sentence. It also includes three available commands that are relevant to the item, described below.

Command	Effect
Ignore Once	Instructs Word to ignore the grammatical error in this sentence.
Grammar	Opens the grammar checker and displays an explanation of the error.
Look Up	Provides help about the grammatical error.

To make this correction, you could simply choose the correction from the shortcut menu and the correction would be inserted into the document. Although in this case you can readily identify the reason for the error, sometimes the reason is not so obvious. In those cases, you can open the grammar checker to find out more information.

2 ● **Choose Grammar.**

Your screen should be similar to Figure 1.14

Figure 1.14

The Grammar dialog box identifies the possible grammatical error in the upper text box and the suggested correction in the Suggestions box. The line in the document containing the error is also highlighted (selected) to make it easy for you to see the location of the error. You will make the suggested change.

3 • Click [Change].

• **Move to the blank line at the end of the document.**

Your screen should be similar to Figure 1.15

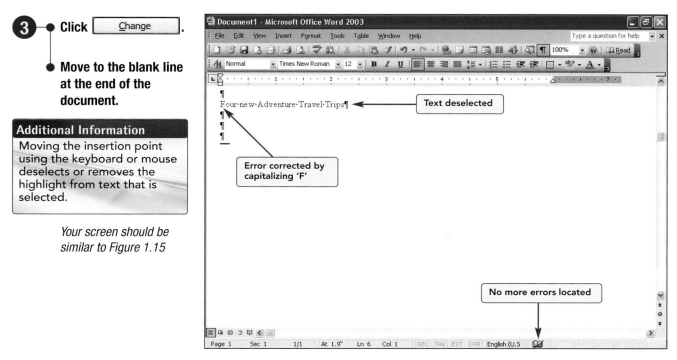

Figure 1.15

The error is corrected, the wavy green line is removed, and the Spelling and Grammar Status icon returns to .

Using AutoText and AutoComplete

Now you are ready to type the text for the first paragraph of the flyer.

1 • Type **atte**.

Your screen should be similar to Figure 1.16

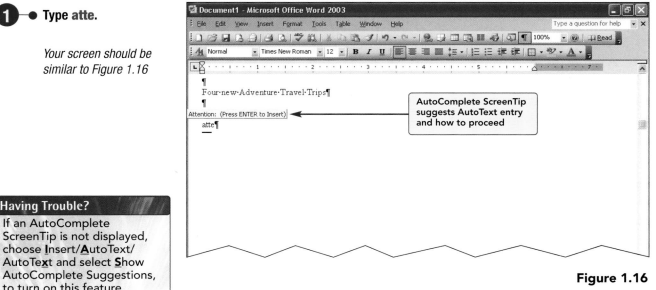

Figure 1.16

A ScreenTip appears displaying "Attention: (Press ENTER to Insert)." This is Word's AutoText and AutoComplete feature.

2 The AutoText and AutoComplete features make entering text easier by providing shortcuts for entering commonly used text. The **AutoText** feature includes entries, such as commonly used phrases, that can be quickly inserted into a document. The AutoText entries can be selected and inserted into the document using the Insert/AutoText command. Word's standard AutoText entries include salutations and closing phrases. You can also add your own entries to the AutoText list, which can consist of text or graphics you may want to use again. Common uses are for a company name, mailing address, and a distribution list for memos.

Additionally, if the **AutoComplete** feature is on, a ScreenTip appears as you type the first few characters of an AutoText entry, suggesting the remainder of the AutoText entry you may want to use. You can choose to accept the suggestion to insert it into the document or to ignore it.

The AutoComplete ScreenTip suggests that you may be typing "Attention:." Because this is the word you are typing, you will accept the suggestion. However, you do not need the colon and will delete it. Then you will continue typing the line, including the intentional spelling error.

2 • **Press** ←Enter.

• **Press** Backspace **to delete the colon.**

• **Press** Spacebar.

• **Type adventure travellars!.**

• **Press** Spacebar.

Your screen should be similar to Figure 1.17

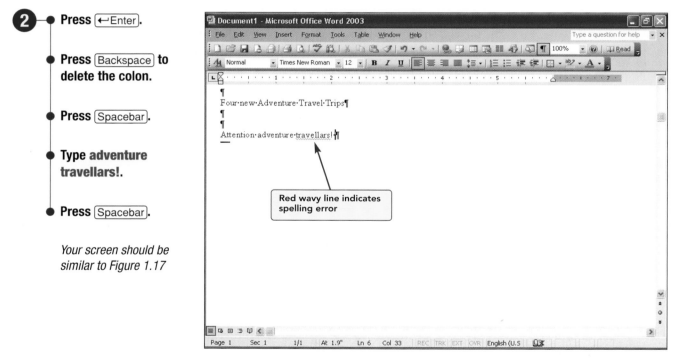

Figure 1.17

Checking Spelling

As soon as you complete a word by entering a space or punctuation, the program checks the word for spelling accuracy.

Concept 3

Spelling Checker

3 The **spelling checker** advises you of misspelled words as you create and edit a document, and proposes possible corrections. The spelling checker compares each word you type to a **main dictionary** of words supplied with the program. Although this dictionary includes most common words, it may not include proper names, technical terms, and so on. If the word does not appear in the main dictionary, it checks the **custom dictionary**, a dictionary that you can create to hold words you commonly use but that are not included in the main dictionary. If the word does not appear in either dictionary, the program identifies it as misspelled by displaying a red wavy line below the word. You can then correct the misspelled word by editing it. Alternatively, you can display a list of suggested spelling corrections for that word and select the correct spelling from the list to replace the misspelled word in the document.

Word automatically identified the word "travellars" as misspelled by underlining it with a wavy red line. The quickest way to correct a misspelled word is to select the correct spelling from a list of suggested spelling corrections displayed on the shortcut menu.

1 ● Right-click on "travellars" to display the shortcut menu.

Another Method
You can also position the insertion point on the item you want to display a shortcut menu for and press ⬆Shift + F10 to open the shortcut menu.

Your screen should be similar to Figure 1.18

Figure 1.18

A shortcut menu of suggested correct spellings is displayed. In this case, there is only one suggested correction, which happens to be correct. The shortcut menu also includes several related menu options, described in the following table.

Option	Effect
Ignore All	Instructs Word to ignore the misspelling of this word throughout the rest of this session.
Add to Dictionary	Adds the word to the custom dictionary list. When a word is added to the custom dictionary, Word will always accept that spelling as correct.
AutoCorrect	Adds the word to the AutoCorrect list so Word can correct misspellings of it automatically as you type.
Language	Sets the language format, such as French, English, or German, to apply to the word.
Spelling	Starts the spell-checking program to check the entire document. You will learn about this feature in Lab 2.
Look Up	Searches the reference tools to locate similar words and definitions.

Sometimes there are no suggested replacements because Word cannot locate any words in its dictionary that are similar in spelling; or the suggestions are not correct. If this occurs, you need to edit the word manually. In this case the suggestion is correct.

2 ● Choose "travelers."

Your screen should be similar to Figure 1.19

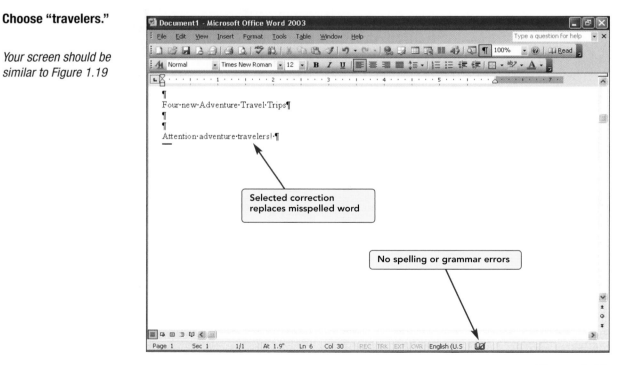

Figure 1.19

The spelling correction you selected replaces the misspelled word in the document. The Spelling and Grammar status icon returns to 📖, indicating that as far as Word is able to detect, the document is free from errors.

Using AutoCorrect

As soon as you complete a word by entering a space or punctuation, the program checks the word for accuracy. When you complete a sentence and start another, additional checks are made. This is part of the AutoCorrect feature of Word.

Concept 4
AutoCorrect

4 The **AutoCorrect** feature makes some basic assumptions about the text you are typing and, based on these assumptions, automatically corrects the entry. The AutoCorrect feature automatically inserts proper capitalization at the beginning of sentences and in the names of days of the week. It will also change to lowercase letters any words that were incorrectly capitalized because of the accidental use of the Caps Lock key. In addition, it also corrects many common typing and spelling errors automatically.

One way the program automatically makes corrections is by looking for certain types of errors. For example, if two capital letters appear at the beginning of a word, Word changes the second capital letter to a lowercase letter. If a lowercase letter appears at the beginning of a sentence, Word capitalizes the first letter of the first word. If the name of a day begins with a lowercase letter, Word capitalizes the first letter. When Spelling Checker provides a single suggested spelling correction for the word, the program will automatically replace the incorrect spelling with the suggested replacement.

Another way the program makes corrections is by checking all entries against a built-in list of AutoCorrect entries. If it finds the entry on the list, the program automatically replaces the error with the correction. For example, the typing error "withthe" is automatically changed to "with the" because the error is on the AutoCorrect list. You can also add words to the AutoCorrect list that you want to be automatically corrected.

Enter the following text, including the errors (identified in italics).

● Press → twice to move to the end of the line.

● Type **attend a** **present*aa*tion to *lern* abou*tt*he.**

● Press Spacebar.

Your screen should be similar to Figure 1.20

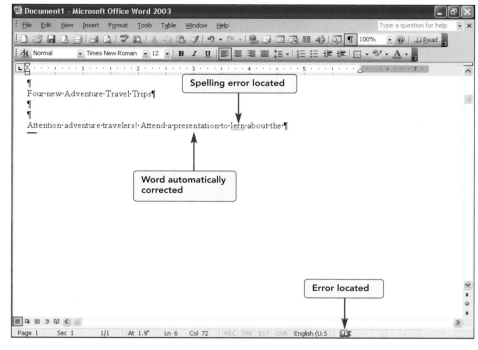

Spelling error located

Word automatically corrected

Error located

Figure 1.20

Having Trouble?

The "Capitalize first letter of sentences" and "Replace text as you type" AutoCorrect features must be on. Use **T**ools/**A**uto Correct Options and select these options if necessary.

Having Trouble?

If your screen does not display the blue box, choose **T**ools/**A**utoCorrect Options and select the Show AutoCorrect Options button check box.

The first letter of the word "attend" was automatically capitalized because as you were typing, the program determined that it is the first word in a sentence. In a similar manner it corrected the spelling of "presentation" and separated the words "about the" with a space. The AutoCorrect feature corrected the spelling of "presentation" because it was the only suggested correction for the word supplied by the Spelling Checker. The word "lern" was not corrected because there are several suggested corrections on the Spelling shortcut menu.

When you rest the mouse pointer near text that has been corrected automatically or move the insertion point onto the word, a small blue box appears under the first character of the word. The blue box changes to the 🗗• AutoCorrect Options button when you point directly to it.

2 • Point to the word "Attend" to display the blue box.

• Point to the blue box.

• Click 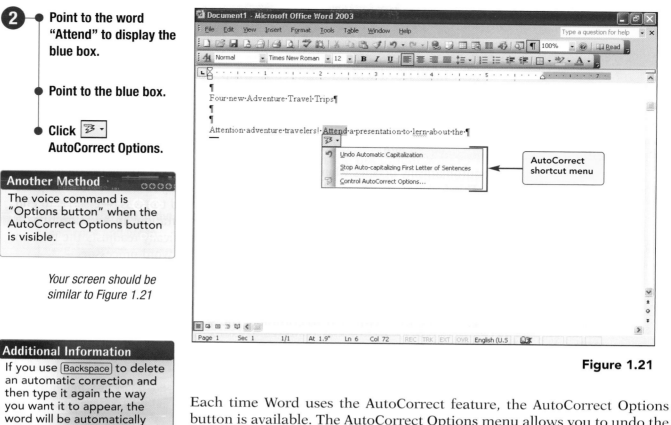 AutoCorrect Options.

Another Method

The voice command is "Options button" when the AutoCorrect Options button is visible.

Your screen should be similar to Figure 1.21

Additional Information

If you use [Backspace] to delete an automatic correction and then type it again the way you want it to appear, the word will be automatically added to the exceptions list.

Document1 - Microsoft Office Word 2003

File Edit View Insert Format Tools Table Window Help

Normal   Times New Roman   12

¶
Four·new·Adventure·Travel·Trips¶
¶
¶
Attention·adventure·travelers!··Attend·a·presentation·to·lern·about·the·¶

Undo Automatic Capitalization
Stop Auto-capitalizing First Letter of Sentences
Control AutoCorrect Options...

→ AutoCorrect shortcut menu

Page 1   Sec 1   1/1   At 1.9"   Ln 6   Col 72   REC TRK EXT OVR English (U.S

Figure 1.21

Each time Word uses the AutoCorrect feature, the AutoCorrect Options button is available. The AutoCorrect Options menu allows you to undo the AutoCorrection or to permanently disable the AutoCorrection for the remainder of your document. The Control AutoCorrect Options command can also be used to change the settings for this feature. In some cases, you may want to exclude a word from automatic correction. You can do this by manually adding the word to an exception list using **T**ools/**A**utoCorrect Options/**E**xceptions. You want to keep this AutoCorrection.

3 • Click outside the menu to close it.

• Open the spelling shortcut menu for "lern" and select "learn."

The spelling is corrected, and the spelling indicator in the status bar indicates that the document is free of errors.

Using Word Wrap

Now you will continue entering more of the paragraph. As you type, when the text gets close to the right margin, do not press ⏎Enter to move to the

2 ● **Open the Save In drop-down list box.**

● **Select the location where you want to save your file.**

Your screen should be similar to Figure 1.25

Figure 1.25

Now the large list box displays the names of all Word files, if any, at that location. You can also select the location to save your file from the Places bar along the left side of the dialog box. The icons bring up a list of recently accessed files and folders (My Recent Documents), the contents of the My Documents folder, items on the Windows desktop, and the locations on your computer or on a network. You can also click the ⊚ button in the toolbar to return to folders that were previously opened.

Next, you need to enter a file name and specify the file type. The File Name box displays the default file name, consisting of the first few words from the document. The Save as Type box displays "Word Document" as the default format in which the file will be saved. Word documents are identified by the file extension .doc. The file type you select determines the file extension that will be automatically added to the file name when the file is saved. You will change the file name to Flyer and use the default document type.

3 • Double-click in the File Name text box.

• Type **Flyer**.

Additional Information

The file name can be entered in either uppercase or lowercase letters and will appear exactly as you type it.

• Click [Save].

Your screen should be similar to Figure 1.26

New file name

Closes document

Four·new·Adventure·Travel·Trips¶

Attention·adventure·travelers!·Attend·a·presentation·to·learn·about·the·earth's·greatest·unspoiled·habitats·and·find·out·how·you·can·experience·an·adventure·of·a·lifetime.¶

Student·Name¶
March·7,·2005¶

Figure 1.26

The document is saved as Flyer.doc at the location you selected, and the new file name is displayed in the Word title bar.

Closing a File

Finally, you want to close the document while you attend your meeting.

1 • Click ☒ Close Window in the menu bar.

Another Method

The menu equivalent is **F**ile/**C**lose and the keyboard shortcut is Ctrl + F4. The voice command is "Close document."

Your screen should be similar to Figure 1.27

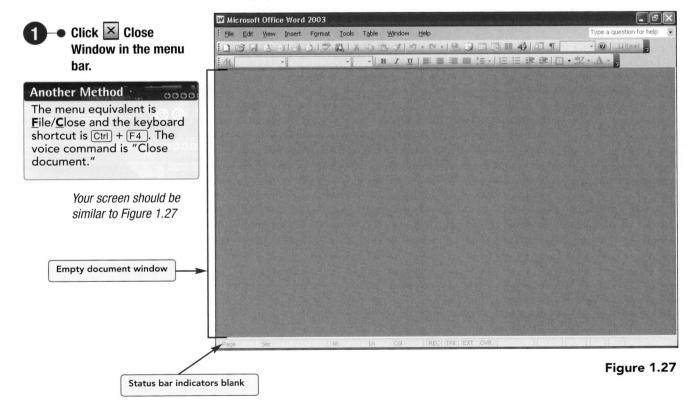

Empty document window

Status bar indicators blank

Figure 1.27

Because you did not make any changes to the document since saving it, the document window is closed immediately. If you had made additional changes, the program would ask whether you wanted to save the file before closing it. This prevents the accidental closing of a file that has not been saved first. Now the Word window displays an empty document window, and the status bar indicators are dimmed because no documents are open.

Opening a File

You asked your assistant to enter the remaining information in the flyer for you while you attended the meeting. Upon your return, you find a note from your assistant on your desk. The note explains that he had a little trouble entering the information and tells you that he saved the revised file as Flyer1. You want to open the file and continue working on the flyer.

Because opening a file is a very common task, there are many ways to do it. You can use the **F**ile/**O**pen command; the keyboard shortcut is Ctrl + O or Open in the Standard toolbar. Additionally, a recently used file can be opened quickly by selecting it from the list of file names displayed at the bottom of the File menu. You can also use the Getting Started task pane to open files and create new files. Like the File menu, the Getting Started task pane displays the names of recently used files.

Additional Information

The default setting is to display the last four recently used files in the File menu.

1 • Choose **V**iew/Tas**k** Pane.

• If necessary, display the Getting Started task pane.

• Click More in the Open section of the task pane.

Another Method

The voice command is "Open file."

Your screen should be similar to Figure 1.28

Figure 1.28

In the Open dialog box, you specify the location and name of the file you want to open. The Look In drop-down list box displays the last specified location, in this case the location where you saved the Flyer document. The large list box displays the names of all Word documents. As in the Save As dialog box, the Places bar can be used to quickly locate files.

When selecting a file to open, it is often helpful to see a preview of the file first. To do this you can change the dialog box view.

2 • **If the Look In location is not correct, select the location containing your data files from the Look In drop-down list box.**

• **Select** wd01_Flyer1.doc.

• **Open the** 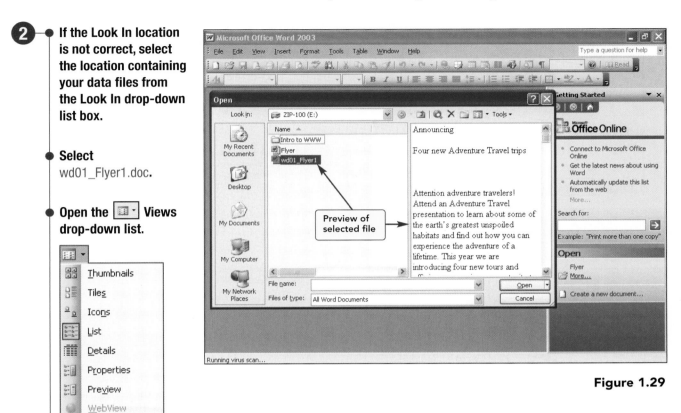 **Views drop-down list.**

• **Choose** ▤ **Preview.**

Your screen should be similar to Figure 1.29

Figure 1.29

A preview of the selected file consisting of the first few lines of text in the document is displayed in the right pane of the dialog box. You will return the view to the list of file names and open this file.

3 ● **Open the** 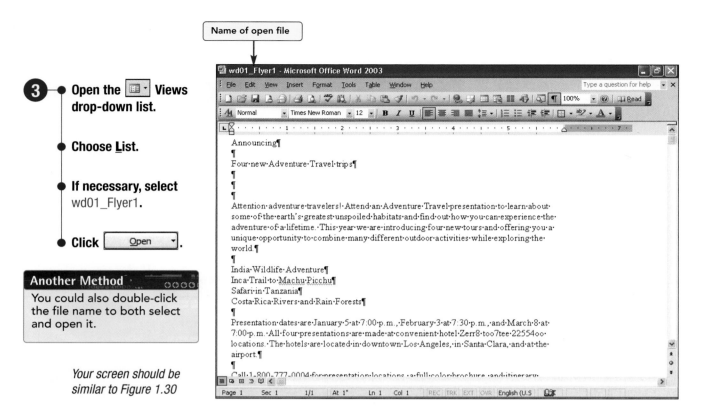 **Views drop-down list.**

● **Choose List.**

● **If necessary, select wd01_Flyer1.**

● **Click** Open ▾ .

Another Method

You could also double-click the file name to both select and open it.

Your screen should be similar to Figure 1.30

Figure 1.30

The file is opened and displayed in the document window. This file contains the text of the rest of the first draft of the flyer. The formatting marks are displayed because this feature is still on.

Navigating a Document

As documents increase in size, they cannot be easily viewed in their entirety in the document window and much time can be spent moving to different locations in the document. Word includes many features that make it easy to move around in a large document. The basic method is to scroll through a document using the scroll bar or keyboard. Another method is to move directly to a page or other identifiable item in the document, such as a table. You can also quickly return to a previous location, or browse through a document to a previous page or item.

Other features that help move through a large document include searching the document to locate specific items, and using the Document Map or a table of contents. You will learn about many of these features in later labs.

Scrolling a Document

Now that more information has been added to the document, the document window is no longer large enough to display the entire document. To bring additional text into view in the window, you can scroll the document using either the scroll bars or the keyboard. Again, both methods are useful, depending on what you are doing. Voice commands can also be used to scroll. The tables below explain the mouse, keyboard, and voice techniques that can be used to scroll a document.

Mouse	Action
Click ⌄	Moves down line by line.
Click ⌃	Moves up line by line.
Click above/below scroll box	Moves up/down window by window.
Drag scroll box	Moves up/down multiple windows.
Click ⬆	Moves to top of previous page.
Click ⬇	Moves to top of next page.
Click ⊙ Select Browse Object	Changes how you want the ⬇ and ⬇ buttons to browse through a document, such as by table or graphic. The default setting is by page.

Key	Voice	Action
↓	Down	Down line by line
↑	Up	Up line by line
Page Up	Page up	Top of window
Page Down	Page down	Bottom of window
Ctrl + Home		Beginning of document
Ctrl + End		End of document

You will use the vertical scroll bar to view the text at the bottom of the flyer. When you use the scroll bar to scroll, the insertion point does not move. To move the insertion point, you must click in a location in the window.

1 ● Click ☑ in the vertical scroll bar 10 times.

● Click anywhere in the last line to move the insertion point.

Your screen should be similar to 1.31

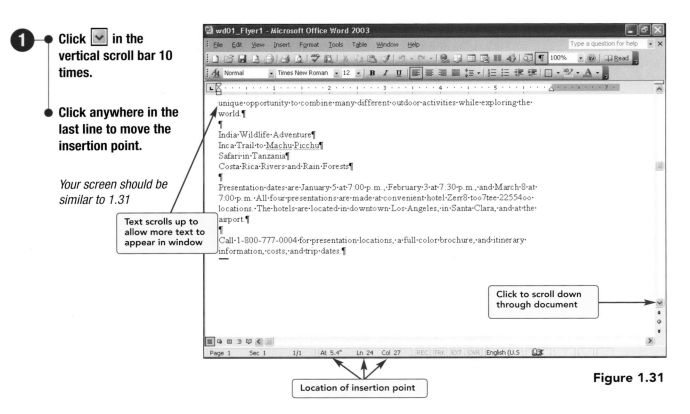

Text scrolls up to allow more text to appear in window

Click to scroll down through document

Location of insertion point

Figure 1.31

The text at the beginning of the flyer has scrolled off the top of the document window, and the text at the bottom of the flyer is now displayed.

You can also scroll the document using the keyboard. While scrolling using the keyboard, the insertion point also moves. The insertion point attempts to maintain its position in a line as you scroll up and down through the document. In a large document, scrolling line by line can take a while. You will now try out several of the mouse and keyboard scrolling features that move by larger jumps.

Having Trouble?

If your screen scrolls differently, this is a function of the type of monitor you are using.

2 ● Hold down ⬆ for several seconds until the insertion point is on the first line of the flyer.

● Click below the scroll box in the scroll bar.

● Drag the scroll box to the middle of the scroll bar.

● Press Ctrl + End.

Your screen should be similar to Figure 1.32

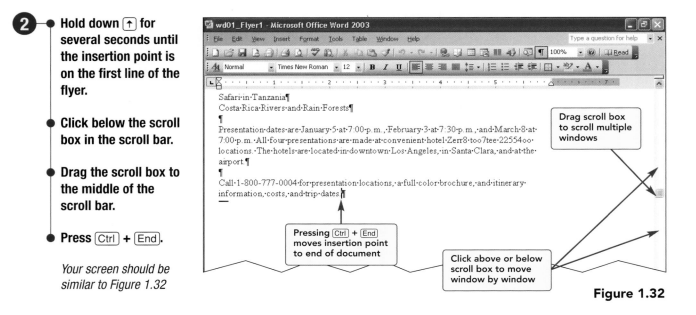

Drag scroll box to scroll multiple windows

Pressing Ctrl + End moves insertion point to end of document

Click above or below scroll box to move window by window

Figure 1.32

The insertion point is now at the end of the document. Using these features makes scrolling a large document much more efficient. Remember that when scrolling using the mouse, if you want to start working at that location, you must click at the new location to move the insertion point.

Editing Documents

While entering text and creating a document, you will find that you will want to edit or make changes and corrections to the document. Although many of the errors are identified and corrections are made automatically for you, others must be made manually. You learned how to use the Backspace and Delete keys earlier to correct errors. But deleting characters one at a time can be time consuming. Now you will learn about several additional editing features that make editing your work more efficient.

After entering the text of a document, you should proofread it for accuracy and completeness and edit the document as needed. After looking over the flyer, you have identified several errors that need to be corrected and changes you want to make to the content. The changes you want to make are shown below.

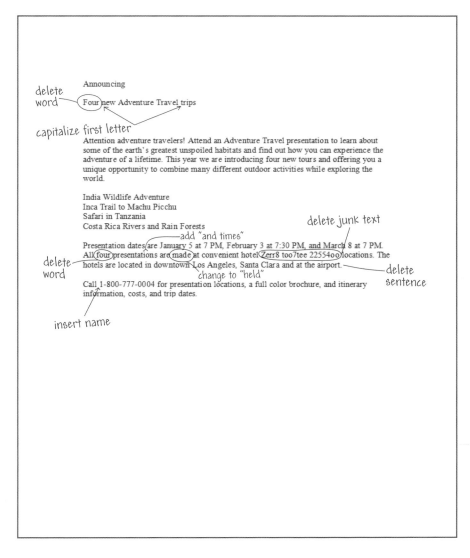

Ignoring Spelling Errors

You first notice that the spelling checker has identified the names of one of the tour locations as misspelled, though in fact it is spelled correctly. This is because it is not in the dictionary. You will instruct Word to accept the spelling of this name and all other words it encounters having the same spelling until you exit the Word application.

1 ● **Scroll to the top of the document.**

● **Right-click on "Machu" to open the Spelling shortcut menu.**

● **Choose Ignore All.**

● **In the same manner, tell Word to ignore the spelling of Picchu.**

Your screen should be similar to Figure 1.33

Figure 1.33

The red underlines are removed from each word. If you type any of these words again, they will not be identified as misspelled.

Inserting Text

As you continue to check the document, you see that the first sentence of the paragraph below the list of trips is incorrect. It should read: "Presentation dates and times are . . ." The sentence is missing the words "and times." In addition, you want to change the word "made" to "held" in the following sentence. These words can easily be entered into the sentence without retyping by using either Insert or Overtype mode.

In **Insert mode** new characters are inserted into the existing text by moving the existing text to the right to make space for the new characters. You will insert the words "and times" after the word "dates" in the first sentence.

1

Move to "a" in "are" (in the first sentence paragraph below the list of tours).

Additional Information

Throughout these labs, when instructed to move to a specific letter in the text, this means to move the insertion point to the left side of the character.

Type and times.

Press Spacebar.

Your screen should be similar to Figure 1.34

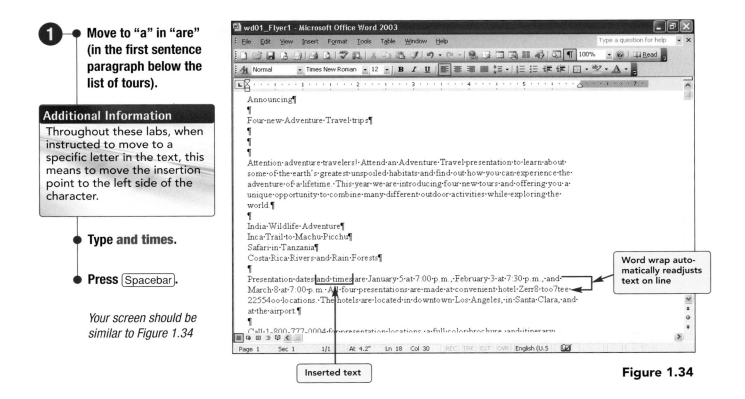

Figure 1.34

The inserted text pushes the existing text on the line to the right, and the word wrap feature automatically readjusts the text on the line to fit within the margin settings.

In the second sentence, you want to change the word "made" to "held." You could delete this word and type in the new word, or you can use the Overtype mode to enter text in a document. When you use **Overtype mode**, new text replaces existing text as you type. You will switch to this mode to change the word.

② ● Move to the "m" of "made."

● Double-click in the status bar.

● Type **held**.

Your screen should be similar to Figure 1.35

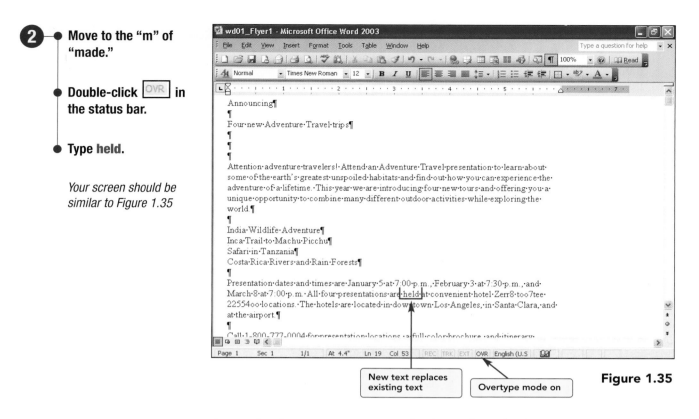

New text replaces existing text

Overtype mode on

Figure 1.35

As each character was typed, the selected character (or space) was replaced with the character being typed. Also notice that the OVR status indicator button letters are now bold, indicating the Overtype mode is on.

③ ● Double-click OVR.

Another Method
You can also turn Overtype mode on and off by pressing [Insert] or by choosing **T**ools/**O**ptions/Edit/Overtype mode.

Overtype mode is off and Insert mode is restored.

Deleting a Word

You next want to delete the word "four" from the same sentence. The [Ctrl] + [Delete] key combination deletes text to the right of the insertion point to the beginning of the next group of characters. In order to delete an entire word, you must position the insertion point at the beginning of the word.

Additional Information
The [Ctrl] + [Backspace] key combination deletes text to the left of the insertion point to the beginning of the next group of characters.

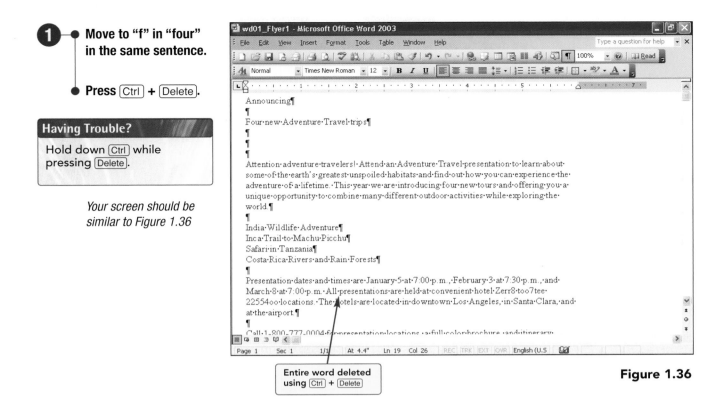

1 Move to "f" in "four" in the same sentence.

● Press Ctrl + Delete.

Having Trouble?

Hold down Ctrl while pressing Delete.

Your screen should be similar to Figure 1.36

Entire word deleted using Ctrl + Delete

Figure 1.36

Selecting and Deleting Text

As you continue proofreading the flyer, you see that the end of this sentence contains a section of junk characters. To remove these characters, you could use Delete and Backspace to delete each character individually, or Ctrl + Delete or Ctrl + Backspace to delete each word or group of characters. This is very slow, however. Several characters, words, or lines of text can be deleted at once by first selecting the text and then pressing Delete. Text that is selected is highlighted.

To select text using the mouse, first move the insertion point to the beginning or end of the text to be selected, and then drag to highlight the text you want selected. You can select as little as a single letter or as much as the entire document. You can quickly select a standard block of text. Standard blocks include a sentence, paragraph, page, tabular column, rectangular portion of text, or the entire document. The following table summarizes the mouse techniques used to select standard blocks.

To Select	Procedure
Word	Double-click in the word.
Sentence	Press Ctrl and click within the sentence.
Line	Click to the left of a line when the mouse pointer is ᐟᐟ.
Multiple lines	Drag up or down to the left of a line when the mouse pointer is ᐟᐟ.
Paragraph	Triple-click on the paragraph or double-click to the left of the paragraph when the mouse pointer is a ᐟᐟ.
Multiple paragraphs	Drag to the left of the paragraphs when the mouse pointer is ᐟᐟ.
Document	Triple-click or press Ctrl and click to the left of the text when the mouse pointer is ᐟᐟ.

You can also select text with the keyboard or voice commands as shown in the following table.

To Select	Keyboard	Voice
Next space or character.	⇧Shift + →	
Previous space or character.	⇧Shift + ←	
Next word.	Ctrl + ⇧Shift + →	Select next word
Previous word.	Ctrl + ⇧Shift + ←	Select last word
Text going backward to beginning of paragraph.	Ctrl + ⇧Shift + ↑	Select last line
Text going forward to end of paragraph.	Ctrl + ⇧Shift + ↓	Select next line
Entire current paragraph.		Select paragraph
Entire document.	Ctrl + A	Select all

To remove highlighting to deselect text, simply click anywhere in the document or press any directional key.

The section of characters you want to remove follow the word "hotel" in the second line of the paragraph below the list of trips.

1 ● **Move to "Z" (following the word "hotel").**

● **Drag to the right until all the text including the space before the word "locations" is highlighted.**

Your screen should be similar to Figure 1.37

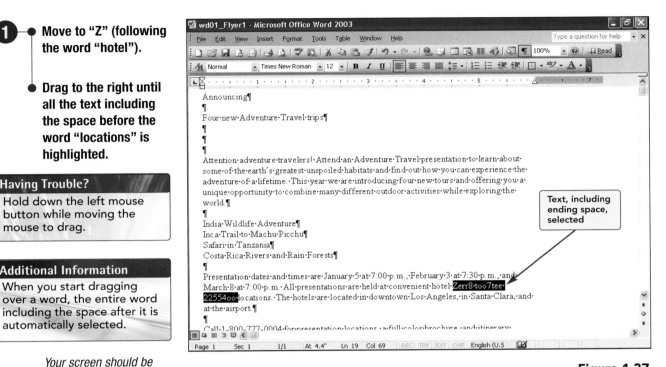

Figure 1.37

The characters you do not want are selected. Text that is selected can then be modified using many different Word features. In this case, you want to remove the selected text.

2 ● **Press Delete.**

Your screen should be similar to Figure 1.38

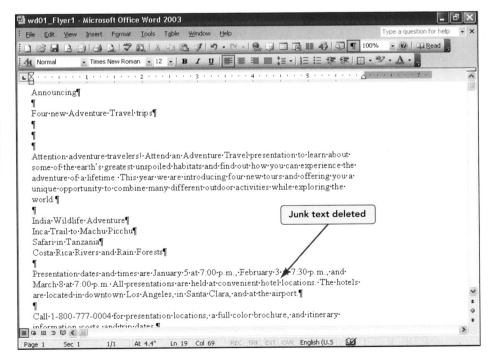

Figure 1.38

You also decide to delete the entire last sentence of the paragraph.

3 • Hold down Ctrl and click anywhere in the third sentence of the paragraph below the list of trips.

• Press Delete.

Your screen should be similar to Figure 1.39

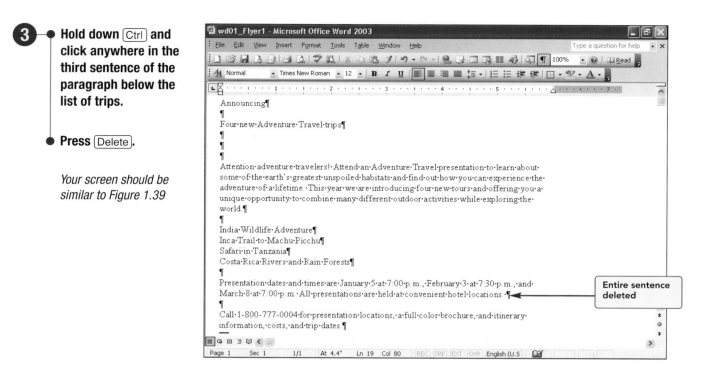

Figure 1.39

Undoing Editing Changes

After removing the sentence, you decide it may be necessary after all. To quickly restore this sentence, you can use [↺] Undo to reverse your last action or command.

1 • Click [↺] Undo.

Another Method

The menu equivalent is Edit/Undo (The action to be undone follows the command.) The keyboard shortcut is Ctrl + Z and the voice command is "Undo."

Your screen should be similar to Figure 1.40

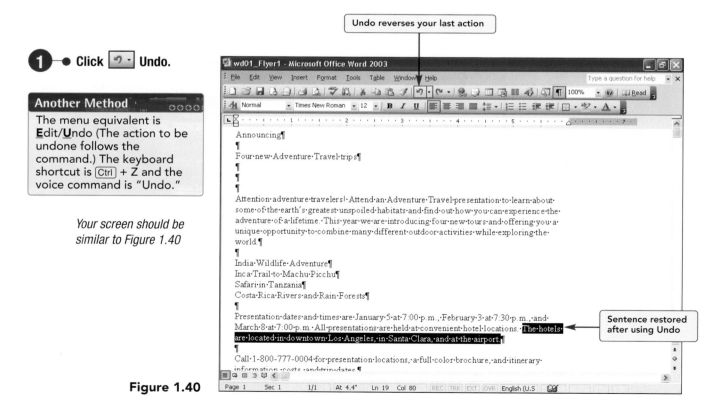

Figure 1.40

Undo returns your last deletion and restores it to its original location in the text, regardless of the current insertion point location. Notice that the Undo button includes a drop-down list button. Clicking this button displays a list of the most recent actions that can be reversed, with the most recent action at the top of the list. When you select an action from the drop-down list, you also undo all actions above it in the list.

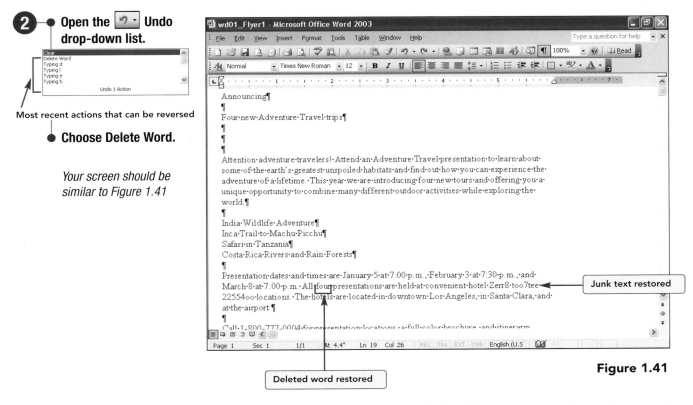

2 ● **Open the** [↻ ▾] **Undo drop-down list.**

Most recent actions that can be reversed

● **Choose Delete Word.**

Your screen should be similar to Figure 1.41

Deleted word restored

Junk text restored

Figure 1.41

The junk characters and the word "four" are restored. Immediately after you undo an action, the [↺ ▾] Redo button is available so you can restore the action you just undid. You will restore your corrections and then save the changes you have made to the document to a new file.

3 • Click 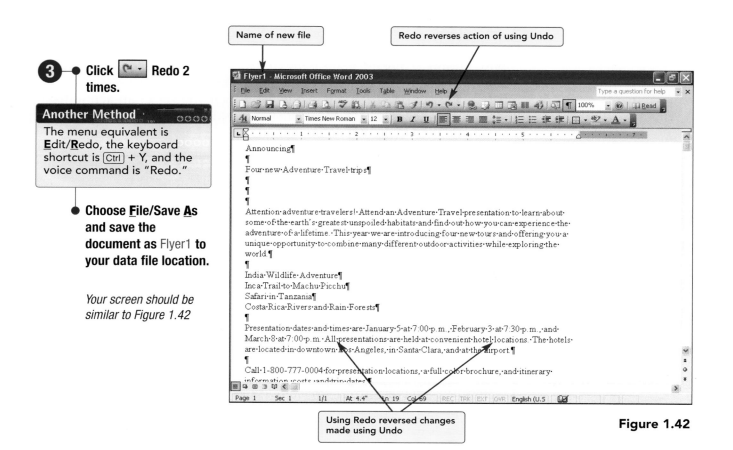 Redo 2
times.

Another Method

The menu equivalent is
Edit/**R**edo, the keyboard
shortcut is Ctrl + Y, and the
voice command is "Redo."

• Choose **F**ile/Save **A**s
and save the
document as Flyer1 to
your data file location.

*Your screen should be
similar to Figure 1.42*

Name of new file

Redo reverses action of using Undo

Flyer1 - Microsoft Office Word 2003

File   Edit   View   Insert   Format   Tools   Table   Window   Help   Type a question for help

Normal   Times New Roman   12

Announcing¶
¶
Four·new·Adventure·Travel·trips¶
¶
¶
¶
Attention·adventure·travelers!·Attend·an·Adventure·Travel·presentation·to·learn·about·
some·of·the·earth's·greatest·unspoiled·habitats·and·find·out·how·you·can·experience·the·
adventure·of·a·lifetime.·This·year·we·are·introducing·four·new·tours·and·offering·you·a·
unique·opportunity·to·combine·many·different·outdoor·activities·while·exploring·the·
world.¶
¶
India·Wildlife·Adventure¶
Inca·Trail·to·Machu·Picchu¶
Safari·in·Tanzania¶
Costa·Rica·Rivers·and·Rain·Forests¶
¶
Presentation·dates·and·times·are·January·5·at·7:00·p.m.,·February·3·at·7:30·p.m.,·and·
March·8·at·7:00·p.m.·All·presentations·are·held·at·convenient·hotel·locations.·The·hotels·
are·located·in·downtown·Los·Angeles,·in·Santa·Clara,·and·at·the·airport.¶
¶
Call·1-800-777-0004·for·presentation·locations,·a·full·color·brochure,·and·itinerary·
information ·costs ·and·trip·dates ¶

Page 1   Sec 1   1/1   At 4.4"   Ln 19   Col 69   REC TRK EXT OVR   English (U.S

Using Redo reversed changes
made using Undo

Figure 1.42

The new file name, Flyer1, is displayed in the window title bar. The
original document file, wd01_Flyer1, is unchanged.

Repeatedly using the ⟲ Undo or ⟳ Redo buttons performs the
actions in the list one by one. So that you can see what action will be
performed, these button's ScreenTips identify the action.

Changing Case

You also want to delete the word "Four" from the second line of the flyer
title and capitalize the first letter of each word. Although you could
change the case individually for the words, you can quickly change both
using the Change Case command on the Format menu.

1
- **Press** [Ctrl] + [Home] **to move to the beginning of the document.**

- **Move to "F" in "Four."**

- **Press** [Ctrl] + [Delete].

- **Click in the left margin to select the entire title line.**

- **Choose Format/Change Case.**

Your screen should be similar to Figure 1.43

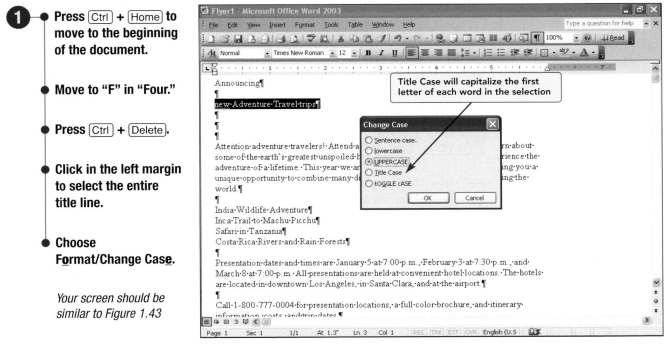

Figure 1.43

The Change Case dialog box allows you to change the case of selected words and sentences to the desired case without having to make the change manually. You want the title to appear in Title Case. In addition, since you have finished editing the flyer for now, you will also turn off the display of formatting marks.

2
- **Select Title Case.**

- **Click** OK .

- **Click anywhere to deselect the title line.**

- **Click** ¶ **Show/Hide ¶.**

Your screen should be similar to Figure 1.44

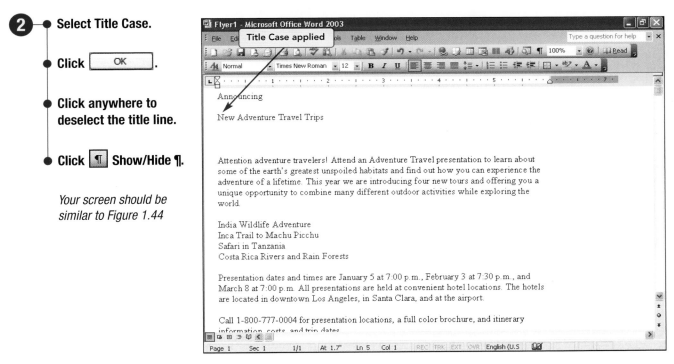

Figure 1.44

The first letter of each word in the title is now capitalized and the highlight is removed from the text. The document returns to normal display. As you have seen, in many editing situations it is helpful to display the formatting marks. However, for normal entry of text, you will probably not need the marks displayed. Now that you know how to turn this feature on and off, you can use it whenever you want when entering and editing text.

Formatting a Document

Because this document is a flyer, you want it to be easy to read and interesting to look at. Applying different formatting to characters and paragraphs can greatly enhance the appearance of the document. **Character formatting** consists of formatting features that affect the selected characters only. This includes changing the character style and size, applying effects such as bold and italics to characters, changing the character spacing and adding animated text effects. **Paragraph formatting** features affect an entire paragraph. A paragraph consists of all text up to and including the paragraph mark. Paragraph formatting features include how the paragraph is positioned or aligned between the margins, paragraph indentation, spacing above and below a paragraph, and line spacing within a paragraph.

Revealing Document Formatting

Word allows you to quickly check the formatting in a document using the Reveal Formatting task pane.

1 ● Choose F**o**rmat/Re**v**eal Formatting.

● Move to the top of the document.

Your screen should be similar to Figure 1.45

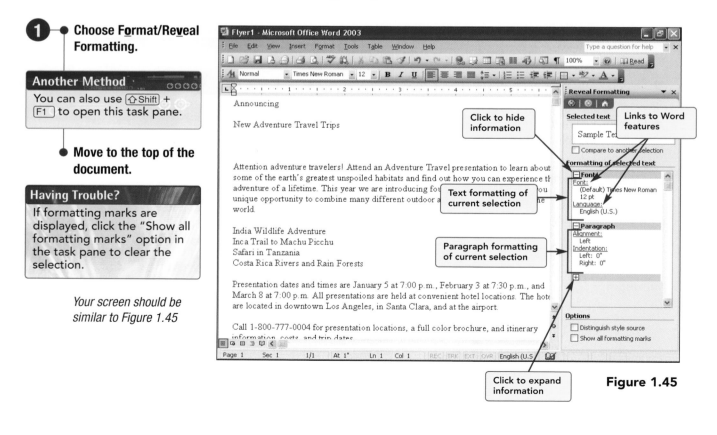

Figure 1.45

The Reveal Formatting task pane displays information about the formatting for the currently selected text and paragraph. Because you have not changed any of these settings, it displays the default document settings. It can also be used to modify these settings. The blue underlined text in the task pane indicates items that are links to Word features, providing faster access to the feature when this pane is displayed than using the menu.

Changing Fonts and Font Sizes

The first formatting change you want to make is to use different fonts and font sizes in the flyer.

Concept 6

Font and Font Size

6   A **font**, also commonly referred to as a **typeface,** is a set of characters with a specific design. The designs have names such as Times New Roman and Courier. Using fonts as a design element can add interest to your document and give readers visual cues to help them find information quickly.

Two basic types of fonts are serif and sans serif. **Serif fonts** have a flair at the base of each letter that visually leads the reader to the next letter. Two common serif fonts are Roman and Times New Roman. Serif fonts generally are used for text in paragraphs. **Sans serif fonts** do not have a flair at the base of each letter. Arial and Helvetica are two common sans serif fonts. Because sans serif fonts have a clean look, they are often used for headings in documents. A good practice is to use only two types of fonts in a document, one for text and one for headings. Too many styles can make your document look cluttered and unprofessional.

Each font has one or more sizes. **Font size** is the height and width of the character and is commonly measured in points, abbreviated "pt." One point equals about 1/72 inch, and text in most documents is 10 pt or 12 pt.

Several common fonts in different sizes are shown in the table below.

Font Name	Font Type	Font Size
Arial	Sans serif	This is 10 pt This is 16 pt.
Courier New	Serif	This is 10 pt. This is 16 pt.
Times New Roman	Serif	This is 10 pt. This is 16 pt.

To change the font before typing the text, use the command and then type. All text will appear in the specified setting until another font setting is selected. To change a font setting for existing text, select the text you want to change and then use the command. If you want to apply font formatting to a word, simply move the insertion point to the word and the formatting is automatically applied to the entire word.

First you want to increase the font size of all the text in the flyer to make it easier to read.

Your screen should be similar to Figure 1.46

Figure 1.46

The current font settings are displayed, reflecting the default document setting of Times New Roman with a font size of 12 points. The Preview box displays an example of the currently selected font setting.

Notice the description of the font below the Preview box. It states that the selected font is a TrueType font. **TrueType** fonts are fonts that are automatically installed when you install Windows. They appear onscreen exactly as they will appear when printed. Some fonts are printer fonts, which are available only on your printer and may look different onscreen than when printed. Courier is an example of a printer font.

You will increase the font size to 14 points. As you select the option, the Preview box displays how it will appear.

② ● **Scroll the Size list box and select 14.**

● **Click** [OK].

Your screen should be similar to Figure 1.47

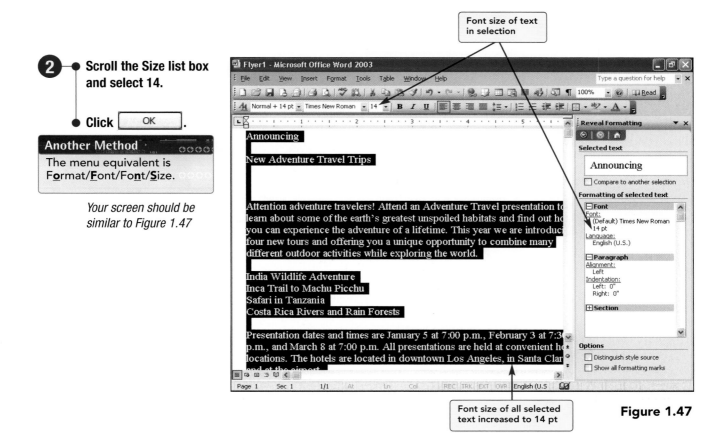

Figure 1.47

Font size of text in selection

Font size of all selected text increased to 14 pt

The font size of all text in the document has increased to 14 points, making the text much easier to read. The Font Size button in the Formatting toolbar and in the task pane displays the new point size setting for the text at the location of the insertion point.

Next you will change the font and size of the two title lines. Another way to change the font and size is to use the buttons on the Formatting toolbar. The Formatting toolbar buttons are identified below.

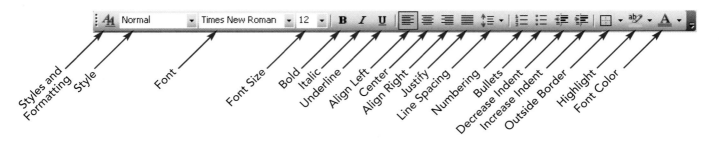

3 • Click anywhere on the word "Announcing."

• Open the [Times New Roman ▾] Font drop-down list.

Additional Information
Font names are listed in alphabetical order and appear in their actual font.

Times New Roman ▾
- 𝕋 Abadi MT Condensed
- 𝕋 **Abadi MT Condensed Extra Bold**
- 𝕋 Abadi MT Condensed Light
- 𝕋 ALGERIAN
- 𝕋 Andy
- 𝕋 Arial
- 𝕋 **Arial Black**
- 𝕋 Arial Narrow
- 𝕋 **Arial Rounded MT Bold**
- 𝕋 Arial Unicode MS
- 𝕋 Baskerville Old Face
- 𝕋 Comic Sans MS

• Scroll the list and choose Comic Sans MS.

Having Trouble?
If this font is not available on your computer, choose a similar font.

• Open the [14 ▾] Font Size drop-down list.

14 ▾
8
9
10
11
12
14
16
18
20
22
24
26

• Scroll the list and choose 36.

Your screen should be similar to Figure 1.48

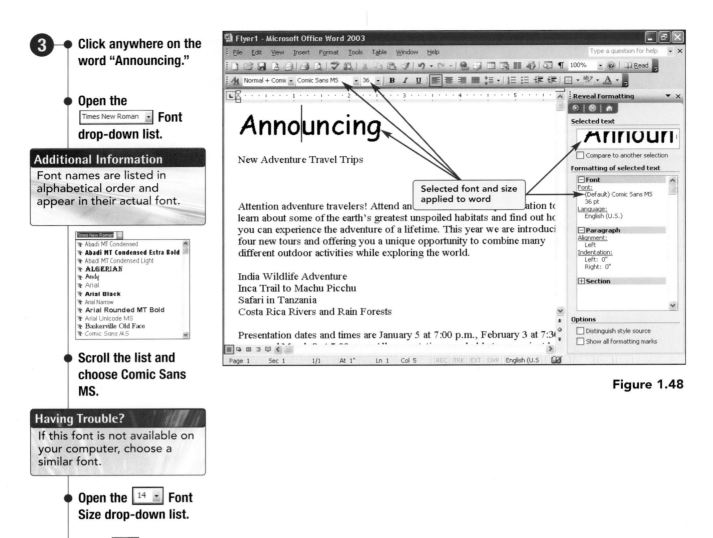

Figure 1.48

The selected font and size have been applied to the word, making the title line much more interesting and eye-catching. The Font and Font Size buttons as well as the information displayed in the Reveal Formatting task pane reflect the settings in use at the location of the insertion point.

4 ● Select the second title line.

● Change the font to Comic Sans MS with a font size of 24.

● Select the list of four tours.

● Change the font to Comic Sans MS.

● Click anywhere on the highlighted text to deselect it.

Your screen should be similar to Figure 1.49

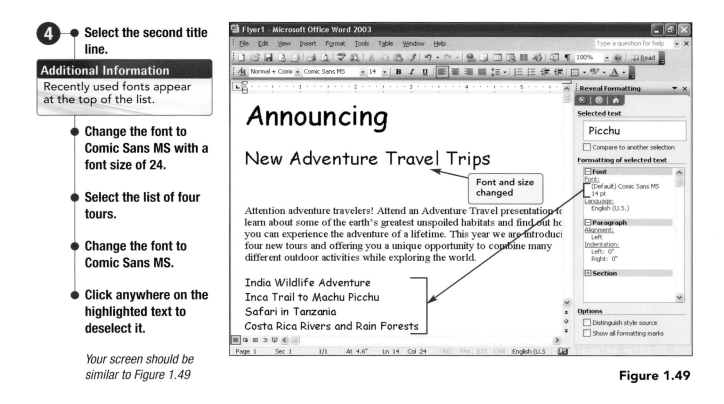

Figure 1.49

Applying Character Effects

Next you want to liven up the flyer by adding character effects such as color and bold to selected areas. The table below describes some of the effects and their uses.

Format	Example	Use
Bold, italic	**Bold** *Italic*	Adds emphasis.
Underline	Underline	Adds emphasis.
Strikethrough	~~Strikethrough~~	Indicates words to be deleted.
Double strikethrough	~~Double Strikethrough~~	Indicates words to be deleted.
Superscript	"To be or not to be."[1]	Used in footnotes and formulas.
Subscript	H_2O	Used in formulas.
Shadow	Shadow	Adds distinction to titles and headings.
Outline	Outline	Adds distinction to titles and headings.
Small caps	SMALL CAPS	Adds emphasis when case is not important.
All caps	ALL CAPS	Adds emphasis when case is not important.
Hidden		Prevents selected text from displaying or printing. Hidden text can be viewed by displaying formatting marks.
Color	**Color** Color **Color**	Adds interest

First you will add color and bold to the top title line. The default font color setting is Automatic. This setting automatically determines when to use black or white text. Black text is used on a light background and white text on a dark background.

1 • **Click anywhere on the word "Announcing."**

• **Open the** 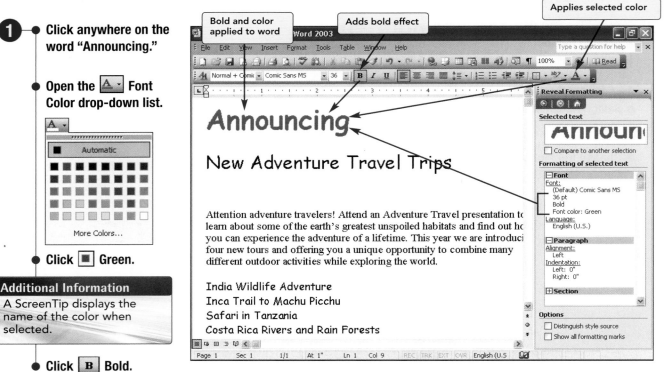 **Font Color drop-down list.**

• **Click** ■ **Green.**

• **Click** **B** **Bold.**

Your screen should be similar to Figure 1.50

Figure 1.50

The selected color and bold effect have been applied to the entire word. The buttons and task pane information reflect the settings associated with the text at the insertion point. The Font Color button appears in the last selected color. This color can be quickly applied to other selections now simply by clicking the button.

Next you will add color and bold to several other areas of the flyer.

2
- Select the entire second title line.

- Change the font color to orange and add bold.

- Select the list of four trips.

- Click 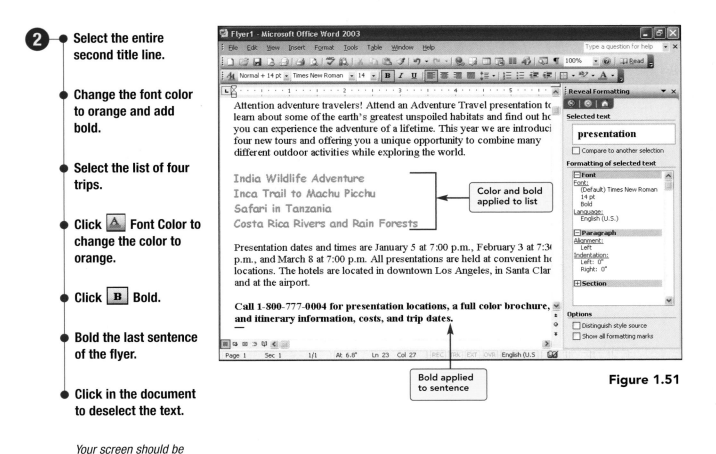 Font Color to change the color to orange.

- Click **B** Bold.

- Bold the last sentence of the flyer.

- Click in the document to deselect the text.

Your screen should be similar to Figure 1.51

Figure 1.51

Setting Paragraph Alignment

The final formatting change you want to make is to change the paragraph alignment.

Concept 7

Alignment

7 **Alignment** is the positioning of text on a line between the margins or indents. There are four types of paragraph alignment: left, centered, right, and justified. The alignment settings affect entire paragraphs and are described in the table below.

Alignment		Effect on Text Alignment
	Left	Aligns text against the left margin of the page, leaving the right margin ragged or uneven. This is the most commonly used paragraph alignment type and therefore the default setting in all word processing software packages.
	Centered	Centers each line of text between the left and right margins. Center alignment is used mostly for headings or centering graphics on a page.
	Right	Aligns text against the right margin, leaving the left margin ragged. Use right alignment when you want text to line up on the outside of a page, such as a chapter title or a header.
	Justified	Aligns text against the right and left margins and evenly spaces out the words by inserting extra spaces, called **soft spaces**, that adjust automatically whenever additions or deletions are made to the text. Newspapers commonly use justified alignment so the columns of text are even.

The commands to change paragraph alignment are under the **F**ormat/ **P**aragraph/**I**ndents and Spacing/Ali**g**nment menu. However, it is much faster to use the keyboard shortcuts, toolbar buttons, or voice commands shown below.

Alignment	Keyboard Shortcut	Button	Voice
Left	[Ctrl] + L		Left justify
Centered	[Ctrl] + E		Centered
Right	[Ctrl] + R		Right justify
Justified	[Ctrl] + J		

You want to change the alignment of all paragraphs in the flyer from the default of left-aligned to centered.

1
- Press [Ctrl] + **A** to select the entire document.

- Click ≡ Center (on the Formatting toolbar).

- Press [Ctrl] + [Home].

Your screen should be similar to Figure 1.52

Text on each line is centered be-tween right and left margins

Buttons indicate feature is in use at selection

Current paragraph alignment

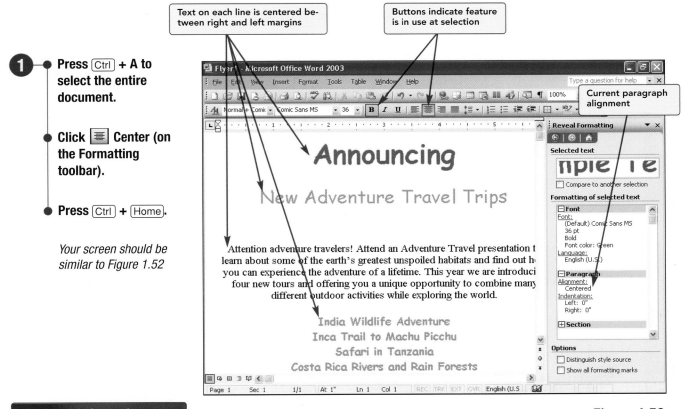

Figure 1.52

Each line of text is centered evenly between the left and right page margins. The Reveal Formatting task pane paragraph alignment setting shows the new alignment is centered. Now that you have finished formatting the document, you will close the task pane and save the flyer again using the same file name.

2
- Click ✕ Close in the task pane title bar.

- Click 💾 Save to save the file using the same file name.

Working with Graphics

Finally, you want to add a graphic to the flyer to add interest.

Concept 8
Graphics

8   A **graphic** is a non-text element or object, such as a drawing or picture, that can be added to a document. An **object** is an item that can be sized, moved, and manipulated.

A graphic can be a simple **drawing object** consisting of shapes such as lines and boxes. A drawing object is part of your Word document. A **picture** is an illustration such as a graphic illustration or a scanned photograph. Pictures are graphics that were created using another program and are inserted in your Word document as embedded objects. An **embedded object** becomes part of the Word document and can be opened and edited from within the Word document using the **source program**, the program in which it was created. Any changes made to the embedded object are not made to the original picture file because they are independent. Several examples of drawing objects and pictures are shown below.

| drawing object | graphic illustration | photograph |

Add graphics to your documents to help the reader understand concepts, to add interest, and to make your document stand out from others.

Inserting a Picture

Picture files can be obtained from a variety of sources. Many simple drawings called clip art are available in the Clip Organizer that comes with Microsoft Office 2003. You can also create picture files using a scanner to convert any printed document, including photographs, to an electronic format. Most images that are scanned and inserted into documents are stored as Windows bitmap files (.bmp). All types of pictures, including clip art, photographs, and other types of images, can be found on the Internet. These files are commonly stored as .jpg or .pcx files. Keep in mind that any images you locate on the Internet may be copyrighted and should only be used with permission. You can also purchase CDs containing graphics for your use.

You want to add a picture to the flyer below the two title lines. You will move to the location in the document where you want to insert the graphic and then open the Clip Art task pane to locate a graphic.

1
Click ¶ Show/Hide to display formatting marks.

Move to the middle blank line below the second title line.

Choose **Insert/Picture/Clip Art**.

Your screen should be similar to Figure 1.53

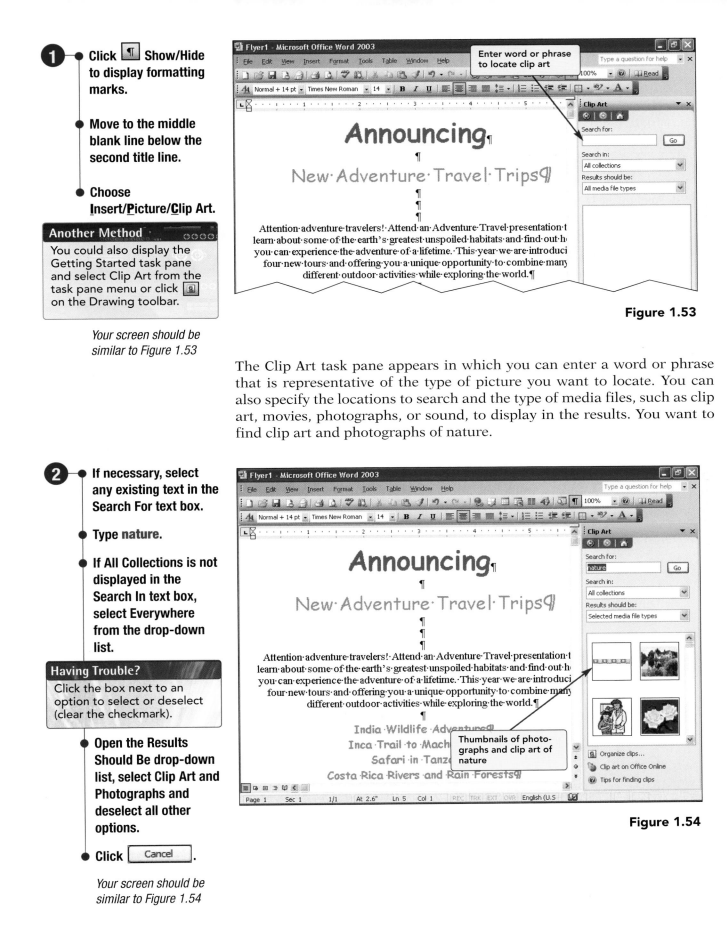

Figure 1.53

The Clip Art task pane appears in which you can enter a word or phrase that is representative of the type of picture you want to locate. You can also specify the locations to search and the type of media files, such as clip art, movies, photographs, or sound, to display in the results. You want to find clip art and photographs of nature.

2
If necessary, select any existing text in the Search For text box.

Type **nature**.

If All Collections is not displayed in the Search In text box, select Everywhere from the drop-down list.

Open the Results Should Be drop-down list, select Clip Art and Photographs and deselect all other options.

Click [Cancel].

Your screen should be similar to Figure 1.54

Figure 1.54

The program searches all locations on your computer and, if you have an Internet connection established, Microsoft's Clip Art and Media Web site for clip art and graphics that match your search term. The Results area displays **thumbnails**, miniature representations of pictures, of all located graphics. Pointing to a thumbnail displays a ScreenTip containing the keywords associated with the picture and information about the picture properties. It also displays a drop-down list bar that accesses the item's shortcut menu.

3 ● **Point to any thumbnail to see a ScreenTip.**

● **Scroll the list to view additional images.**

Your screen should be similar to Figure 1.55

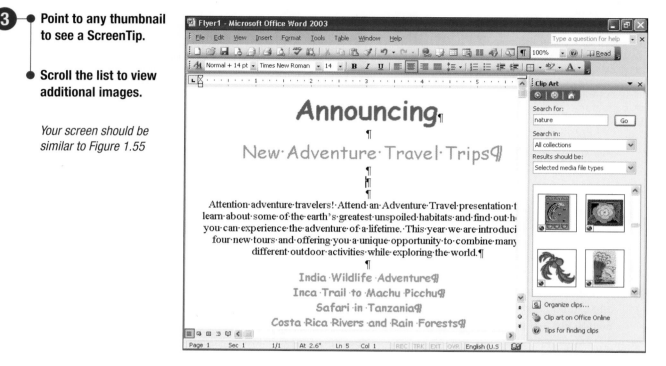

Figure 1.55

Because so many pictures were located, you decide to narrow your search to display pictures of animals only. Additionally, because it is sometimes difficult to see the graphic, you can preview it in a larger size.

4

- Select the word "nature" in the Search For text box and type **animal**.
- Click Cancel.
- If necessary, expand and scroll the results area to see the graphic of a tiger.
- Point to the tiger graphic and click next to the graphic to open the shortcut menu.

  Insert
  Copy
  Delete from Clip Organizer
  Copy to Collection...
  Move to Collection...
  Edit Keywords...
  Find Similar Style
  Preview/Properties

- Choose **Preview/Properties**.

  Your screen should be similar to Figure 1.56

Preview Properties dialog box provides more information about the selected graphic

Figure 1.56

Because the search term is more specific, fewer results are displayed. The Preview/Properties dialog box displays the selected graphic larger so it is easier to see. It also displays more information about the properties associated with the graphic. You think this looks like a good choice and will insert it into the document.

5

- Click Close to close the dialog box.
- Click on the graphic to insert it in the document.

Another Method

You could also choose **Insert** from the thumbnail's shortcut menu.

- Click ☒ in the task pane title bar to close it.

  Your screen should be similar to Figure 1.57

Selected picture inserted and centered in document

Figure 1.57

The picture is inserted in the document at the insertion point. It is centered because the paragraph in which it was placed is centered. Although you think this graphic looks good, you want to see how a photograph of a lion you recently received from a client would look instead. The photograph has been saved as a picture image.

6 Choose
Insert/**P**icture/**F**rom
File.

Another Method

You could also click 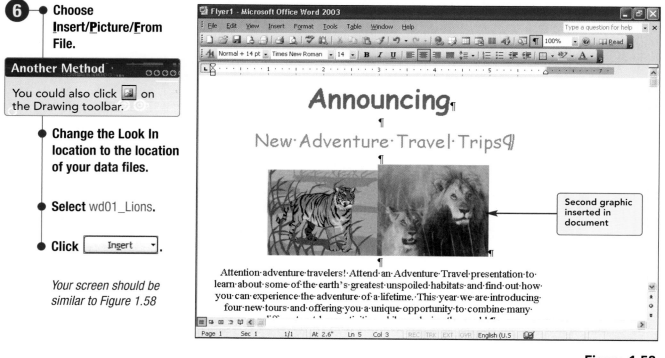 on the Drawing toolbar.

Change the Look In location to the location of your data files.

Select wd01_Lions.

Click [Insert].

Your screen should be similar to Figure 1.58

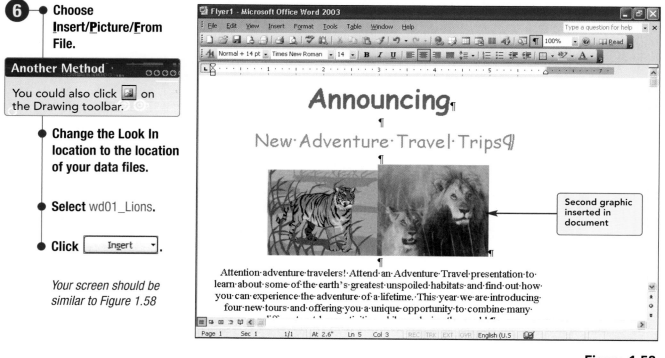

Second graphic inserted in document

Figure 1.58

The lion picture is inserted next to the clip art.

Deleting a Graphic

There are now two graphics in the flyer. You decide to use the lion picture and need to remove the graphic of the tiger. To do this, you select the graphic and delete it.

1 • **Click on the tiger clip art graphic.**

Your screen should be similar to Figure 1.59

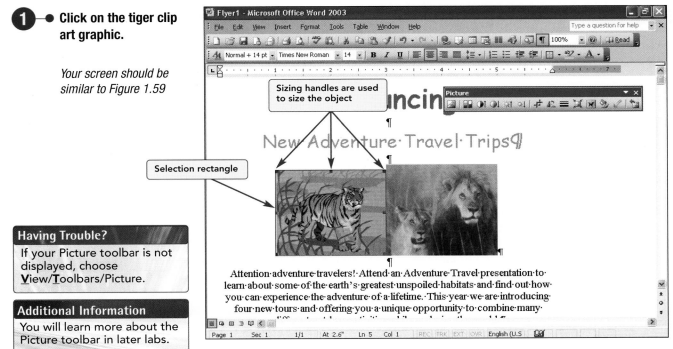

Figure 1.59

The picture is surrounded by a **selection rectangle** and eight boxes, called **sizing handles**, indicating it is a selected object and can now be deleted, sized, moved, or modified. The Picture toolbar automatically appears and is used to modify the selected picture object.

2 • **Press** Delete.

Your screen should be similar to Figure 1.60

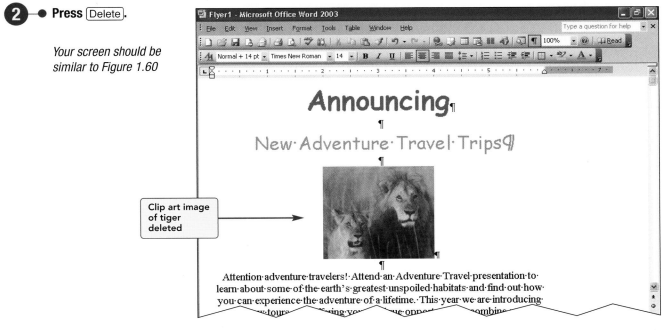

Figure 1.60

The tiger graphic is removed.

Sizing a Graphic

Usually, when a graphic is inserted, its size will need to be adjusted. A graphic object can be manipulated in many ways. You can change its size, add captions, borders, or shading, or move it to another location. A graphic object can be moved anywhere on the page, including in the margins or on top of or below other objects, including text. The only places you cannot place a graphic object are into a footnote, endnote, or caption. In this case, you want to increase the picture's size. To size a graphic, you select it and drag the sizing handles to increase or decrease the size of the object. The mouse pointer changes to ↔ when pointing to a handle. The direction of the arrow indicates the direction in which you can drag to size the graphic. You want to increase the image to approximately 3 inches wide by 2.5 inches high.

1 ● **Click on the Lions graphic to select it.**

● **Point to the lower right corner handle.**

● **With the pointer as a ↖, drag outward from the picture to increase the size to approximately 3 by 2.5 inches (use the ruler as a guide and refer to Figure 1.61).**

● **Click anywhere in the document to deselect the graphic.**

● **Turn off the display of formatting marks.**

● **Click 🖫 Save.**

Your screen should be similar to Figure 1.61

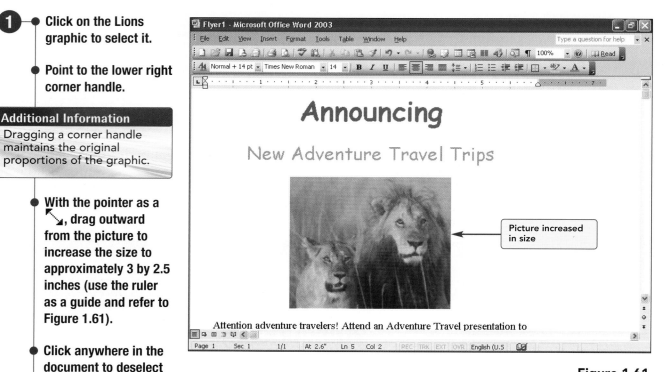

Figure 1.61

Previewing and Printing a Document

Although you still plan to make several formatting changes to the document, you want to give a copy of the flyer to the manager to get feedback regarding the content and layout. To save time and unnecessary printing and paper waste, it is always a good idea to first preview your document onscreen to see how it will appear when printed.

Previewing the Document

Previewing your document before printing it allows you to look over each page and make necessary adjustments before printing it.

1 ● Click 🔲 **Print Preview (on the Standard toolbar).**

Another Method
The menu equivalent is **F**ile/Print Pre**v**iew and the voice command is "Print preview."

● **If necessary, change the zoom to Whole Page.**

Your screen should be similar to Figure 1.62

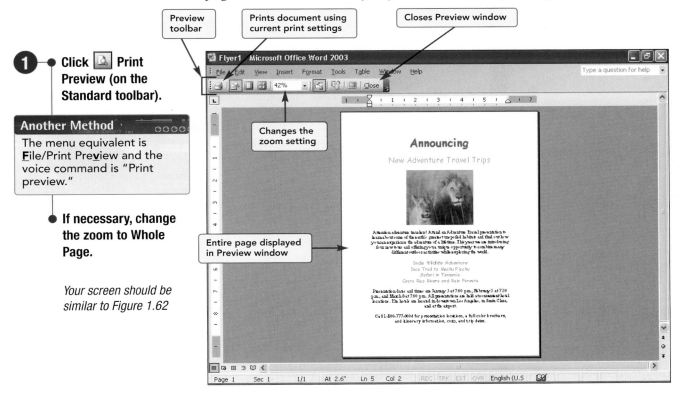

Figure 1.62

The Print Preview window displays a reduced view of how the current page will appear when printed. This view allows you to check your page layout before printing. The flyer looks good and does not appear to need any further modifications immediately.

The Preview window also includes its own toolbar. You can print the flyer directly from the Preview window using the 🖨 Print button; however, you do not want to send the document directly to the printer just yet.

Printing the Document

First you need to add your name to the flyer and check the print settings.

1 ● Click [Close].

● Add **your name at** before the phone number in the last sentence of the flyer.

● **If necessary, make sure your printer is on and ready to print.**

● Choose **File/Print**.

Another Method ○○○○

The keyboard shortcut for the Print command is [Ctrl] + P. Clicking [🖨] Print on the Standard toolbar will print the active document immediately using the current print settings.

Your screen should be similar to Figure 1.63

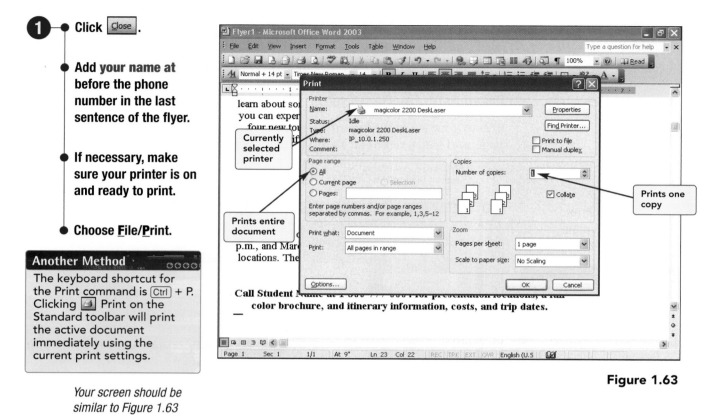

Figure 1.63

Note: Please consult your instructor for printing procedures that may differ from the following directions.

From the Print dialog box, you need to specify the printer you will be using and the document settings. The printer that is currently selected is displayed in the Name drop-down list box in the Printer section of the dialog box.

The Page Range area of the Print dialog box lets you specify how much of the document you want printed. The range options are described in the following table:

Option	Action
All	Prints entire document.
Current page	Prints selected page or page the insertion point is on.
Pages	Prints pages you specify by typing page numbers in the dialog box.
Selection	Prints selected text only.

The **default** range setting, All, is the correct setting. In the Copies section, the default setting of one copy of the document is acceptable. You will print using the default print settings.

2 ● If you need to change the selected printer to another printer, open the **N**ame drop-down list box and select the appropriate printer (your instructor will tell you which printer to select).

● Click [OK].

Your printer should be printing the document. The printed copy of the flyer should be similar to the document shown in the Case Study at the beginning of the lab.

Setting File Properties

You have finished working on the flyer for now and want to save the changes you have made to the file. Along with the content of the file, each file can include additional **file properties** or settings that are associated with the file. Some of these properties are automatically generated. These include statistics, such as the number of words in the file, and general information, such as the date the document was created and last modified. Others, such as the author of the file, are properties that you can add to the file.

Documenting a File

You will look at the file properties and add documentation to identify you as the author and a title for the document.

1 ● Choose **F**ile/Properties

● Open the General tab.

Your screen should be similar to Figure 1.64

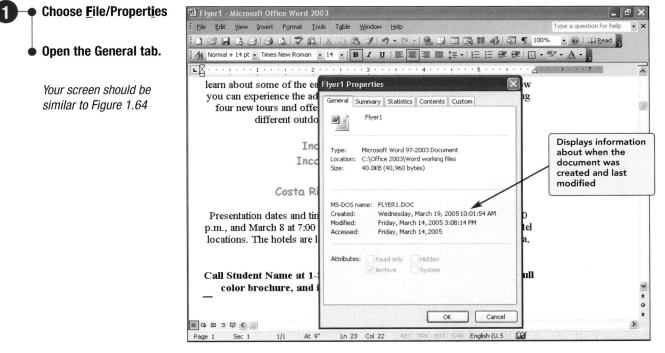

Figure 1.64

The General tab displays information about the type, location, and size of the document as well as information about when the document was created and modified. Next you will look at the document statistics.

2 ● **Open the Statistics tab.**

Your screen should be similar to Figure 1.65

Number of pages, words, lines, and paragraphs in the document

Figure 1.65

Another Method

You can also use **T**ools/**W**ord Count or display the Word Count toolbar to review the document statistics.

Additional Information

Saving a preview picture increases the file size.

This tab identifies who last saved the document, the revision number, and the total editing time in minutes. The table identifies the number of pages, words, lines, paragraphs, and so forth that are included in the document.

Now you want to add your own documentation to the file. Along with the documentation, you can save a picture of the first page of the file for previewing in the Open dialog box. Unlike the preview you saw when you opened the file earlier, which displayed the text of the first few lines of the document, saving a preview picture displays a graphic representation of the entire first page of the document.

3 ● **Open the Summary tab.**

Additional Information

The first few words in the first line of a document are used as the default title.

● **Enter New Tour Flyer as the title and your name as the author.**

● **Select the "Save preview picture" option.**

Your screen should be similar to Figure 1.66

Saves a preview picture of the document

Figure 1.66

You have completed adding the properties to the document. Not until the file is saved are the new properties you added saved with the file. Because you have finished working on the flyer for now, you will exit the application and save the file at the same time.

4 ● Click OK .

Exiting Word

The Exit command in the File menu is used to quit the Word program. Alternatively, you can click the ⊠ Close button in the application window title bar. If you attempt to close the application without first saving your document, Word displays a warning asking if you want to save your work. If you do not save your work and you exit the application, any changes you made since last saving it are lost.

1 ● Click ⊠ Close.

● Click Yes to save the changes you made to the file.

> **Another Method**
> The keyboard shortcut for the Exit command is
> Alt + F4.

The Windows desktop is visible again.

Focus on Careers

EXPLORE YOUR CAREER OPTIONS

Food Service Manager
Have you noticed flyers around your campus advertising job positions? Many of these jobs are in the food service industry. Food service managers are traditionally responsible for overseeing the kitchen and dining room. However, these positions increasingly involve administrative tasks, including recruiting new employees. As a food service manager your position would likely include creating newspaper notices and flyers to attract new staff. These flyers should be eye-catching and error-free. The typical salary range of a food service manager is $24,000 to $41,000. Demand for skilled food service managers is expected to increase through 2010.

concept summary

LAB 1
Creating and Editing a Document

Grammar Checker (WD1.19)

The grammar checker advises you of incorrect grammar as you create and edit a document, and proposes possible corrections.

AutoText and AutoComplete (WD1.22)

The AutoText and AutoComplete features make entering text easier by providing shortcuts for entering commonly used text.

Spelling Checker (WD1.23)

The spelling checker advises you of misspelled words as you create and edit a document, and proposes possible corrections.

AutoCorrect (WD1.25)

The AutoCorrect feature makes some basic assumptions about the text you are typing and, based on these assumptions, automatically corrects the entry.

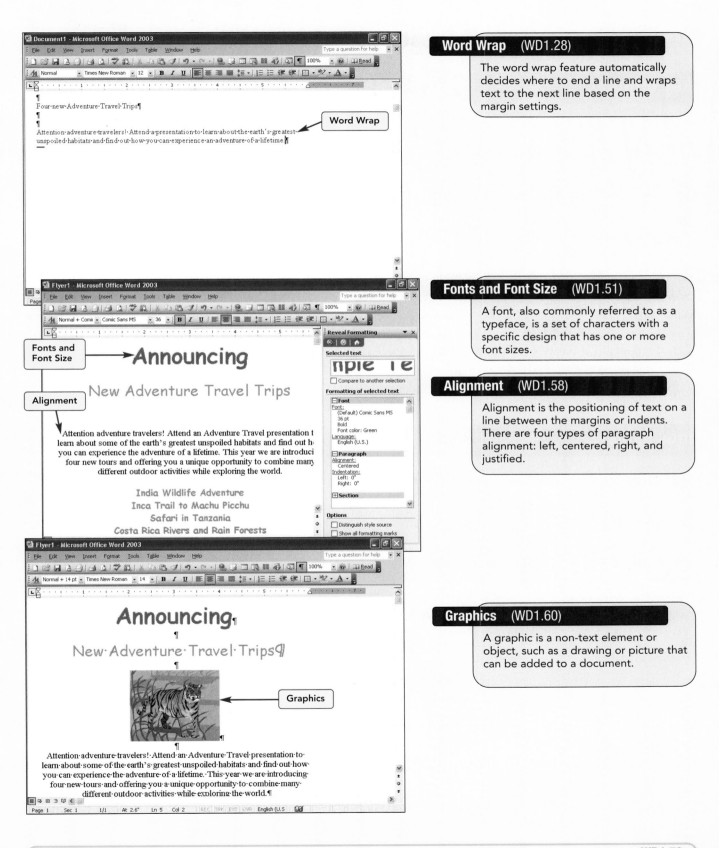

Word Wrap (WD1.28)

The word wrap feature automatically decides where to end a line and wraps text to the next line based on the margin settings.

Fonts and Font Size (WD1.51)

A font, also commonly referred to as a typeface, is a set of characters with a specific design that has one or more font sizes.

Alignment (WD1.58)

Alignment is the positioning of text on a line between the margins or indents. There are four types of paragraph alignment: left, centered, right, and justified.

Graphics (WD1.60)

A graphic is a non-text element or object, such as a drawing or picture that can be added to a document.

key terms

alignment WD1.58	font size WD1.51	sans serif font WD1.51
AutoComplete WD1.22	format WD1.11	select WD1.6
AutoCorrect WD1.25	formatting mark WD1.14	selection rectangle WD1.65
AutoText WD1.22	Formatting toolbar WD1.5	serif font WD1.51
character formatting WD1.50	grammar checker WD1.19	sizing handles WD1.65
cursor WD1.5	graphic WD1.60	Smart Tag WD1.29
custom dictionary WD1.23	Insert mode WD1.40	soft space WD1.58
default WD1.68	insertion point WD1.5	source program WD1.60
document window WD1.5	main dictionary WD1.23	spelling checker WD1.23
drawing object WD1.60	object WD1.60	Standard toolbar WD1.5
edit WD1.11	Overtype mode WD1.41	thumbnail WD1.62
embedded object WD1.60	pane WD1.6	TrueType WD1.52
end-of-file marker WD1.5	paragraph formatting WD1.50	typeface WD1.51
file property WD1.69	picture WD1.60	word wrap WD1.28
font WD1.51	ruler WD1.5	

mos skills

The Microsoft Office Specialist (MOS) certification program is designed to measure your proficiency in performing basic tasks using the Office 2003 applications. Getting certified demonstrates that you have the skills and provides a valuable industry credential for employment. After completing this lab, you have learned the following Microsoft Office Word Specialist skills:

Skill	Description	Page
Creating Content	Insert and edit text, symbols, and special characters	WD1.11
	Insert frequently used and predefined text	WD1.21
	Insert, position, and size graphics	WD1.60
Formatting Content	Format text	WD1.50
	Format paragraphs	WD1.57
Formatting and Managing Documents	Preview and print documents	WD1.67
	Review and modify document properties	WD1.69
	Print documents, envelopes, and labels	WD1.67
	Preview documents and Web pages	WD1.67
	Change and organize document views and windows	WD1.8

command summary

Command	Shortcut Key	Button	Voice	Action
File/**N**ew	Ctrl + N	📄	New file	Opens new document
File/**O**pen	Ctrl + O	📂	Open	Opens existing document file
File/**C**lose	Ctrl + F4	✕	Close Document	Closes document
File/**S**ave	Ctrl + S	💾	Save	Saves document using same file name
File/Save **A**s				Saves document using a new file name, type, and/or location
File/Print Pre**v**iew		🔍	Print Preview	Displays document as it will appear when printed
File/**P**rint	Ctrl + P	🖨	Print	Prints document using selected print settings
File/Proper**t**ies				Displays file statistics, summary, and property settings
File/E**x**it	Alt + F4	✕		Exits Word program
Edit/**U**ndo	Ctrl + Z	↩	Undo	Restores last editing change
Edit/**R**edo	Ctrl + Y	↪	Redo	Restores last Undo or repeats last command or action
Edit/Cle**a**r/**C**ontents	Delete			Deletes characters you do not want
Edit/Select A**l**l	Ctrl + A			Selects all text in document
View/**N**ormal		☰	Normal View	Shows text formatting and simple layout of page
View/**W**eb Layout		▣	Web Layout View	Shows document as it will appear when viewed in a Web browser
View/**P**rint Layout		▤	Print Layout View	Shows how text and objects will appear on printed page
View/**R**eading Layout		📖		Scales document to fit screen as pages in a book
View/**O**utline		▤		Shows structure of document

command summary (continued)

Command	Shortcut Key	Button	Voice	Action
View/**Fu**ll Screen			View full screen	Displays document only, without application features such as menu bars or toolbars
View/**R**uler				Displays/hides horizontal ruler bar
View/**Z**oom/**W**hole Page				Fits entire page on screen
Insert/**A**utoText/AutoText/**S**how/AutoComplete suggestions				Turns on AutoComplete feature
Insert/**P**icture/**C**lip Art		[button]		Accesses Clip Organizer and inserts selected clip
Insert/**P**icture/**F**rom File		[button]		Inserts selected picture
Format/**F**ont/Font/**F**ont		Times New Roman		Changes typeface
F**o**rmat/**F**ont/Fo**n**t/**F**ont Style/Bold	Ctrl + B	**B**	On bold	Makes selected text bold
F**o**rmat/**F**ont/Fo**n**t/**S**ize		12		Changes font size
F**o**rmat/**F**ont/Fo**n**t/**C**olor		A		Changes text to selected color
Format/**P**aragraph/**I**ndents and Spacing/Ali**g**nment/Center	Ctrl + E	[button]	Centered	Centers text between left and right margins
Format/**P**aragraph/**I**ndents and Spacing/Ali**g**nment/Justified	Ctrl + J	[button]		Aligns text equally between left and right margins
Format/**P**aragraph/**I**ndents and Spacing/Ali**g**nment/Left	Ctrl + L	[button]	Left justify	Aligns text to left margin
Format/**P**aragraph/**I**ndents and Spacing/Ali**g**nment/Right	Ctrl + R	[button]	Right justify	Aligns text to right margin
Format/Change Cas**e**				Changes case of selected text
Format/Re**v**eal Formatting	⇧Shift + F1			Opens Reveal Formatting task pane

command summary (continued)

Command	Shortcut Key	Button	Voice	Action
F**o**rmat/P**i**cture				Changes format settings associated with selected picture
Tools/**W**ord Count				Reviews document statistics
Tools/**A**utoCorrect Options/**E**xceptions			Options button	Displays or hides AutoCorrect option buttons
Tools/**A**utoCorrect Options/S**h**ow AutoCorrect Options buttons			Options button	Displays or hides AutoCorrect option buttons
Tools/**C**ustomize/**O**ptions/**S**howStandard and Formatting toolbars				Displays Standard and Formatting toolbars on two rows
Tools/**O**ptions/Edit/O**v**ertype Mode	Insert	OVR		Switches between Insert and Overtype modes
Tools/**O**ptions/Spelling and Grammar				Changes settings associated with Spelling and Grammar checking
Tools/**O**ptions/View/A**l**l	Ctrl + ⇧Shift + *	¶		Displays or hides formatting marks
Tools/**O**ptions/Save				Changes settings associated with saving files

lab exercises

screen identification

1. In the following Word screen, letters identify important elements. Enter the correct term for each screen element in the space provided.

Possible answers for the screen identification are:

Scrolls down	Show/Hide	A. _____
Normal view	Zoom	B. _____
tab mark	Center	C. _____
Formatting toolbar	Spelling and grammar	D. _____
Save	status icon	E. _____
Print layout view	Redo	F. _____
Overtype	Bold	G. _____
Font color	Status bar	H. _____
Print Preview	Scroll bar	I. _____
Standard toolbar	Graphic	J. _____
Font	Paragraph mark	K. _____
Undo	tab stop	

L. _____
M. _____
N. _____
O. _____
P. _____
Q. _____
R. _____
S. _____
T. _____
U. _____
V. _____

matching

Match the item on the left with the correct description on the right.

1. 🔍   _____   **a.** new text writes over existing text

2. font   _____   **b.** moves to the top of the document

3. OVR   _____   **c.** feature that automatically begins a new line when text reaches the right margin

4. alignment   _____   **d.** images that enhance a document

5. Ctrl + Home   _____   **e.** displays the Print Preview window

6. graphics   _____   **f.** type style that can be applied to text

7. 💾   _____   **g.** font size measurement

8. word wrap   _____   **h.** controls paragraph positioning between the margins

9. point   _____   **i.** saves a document using the same file name

10. sans serif   _____   **j.** font without a flair at the base of each letter

11. A ▾

multiple choice

Circle the correct response to the questions below.

1. Document development follows these steps.
   a. plan, edit, enter, format, preview, and print
   b. enter, edit, format, preview, and print
   c. plan, enter, edit, format, preview, and print
   d. design, enter, edit, format, preview, and print

2. The Word feature that makes some basic assumptions about the text entered and automatically makes changes based on those assumptions is _____.
   a. AutoChange
   b. AutoCorrect
   c. AutoText
   d. AutoFormat

3. Words that are not contained in the main dictionary can be added to the _____ dictionary.
   a. custom
   b. additional
   c. add to
   d. user defined

4. The feature that allows you to preview a document before it is printed is _____.
   a. print review
   b. page review
   c. page preview
   d. print preview

5. When text is evenly aligned on both margins it is _____.
   a. center aligned
   b. justified
   c. left aligned
   d. right aligned

6. Words that may be spelled incorrectly in a document are indicated by a _____.
   a. green wavy line
   b. red wavy line
   c. blue wavy line
   d. purple dotted underline

7. Font sizes are measured in _____.
   a. inches
   b. points
   c. bits
   d. pieces

8. The _____ feature automatically decides where to end a line and where the next line of text begins based on the margin settings.
   a. line wrap
   b. word wrap
   c. wrap around
   d. end wrap

9. A set of characters with a specific design is called a(n) _____.
   a. style
   b. font
   c. AutoFormat
   d. design

true/false

Circle the correct answer to the following questions.

1.	A wavy red line indicates a potential grammar error.	True	False
2.	The first three steps in developing a document are: plan, enter, and edit.	True	False
3.	Text can be entered in a document in either the Insert or Overtype mode.	True	False
4.	The Delete key erases the character to the right of the insertion point.	True	False
5.	The automatic word wrap feature checks for typing errors.	True	False
6.	The Word document file name extension is .wrd.	True	False
7.	Font sizes are measured in inches.	True	False
8.	Word inserts hidden marks into a document to control the display of text.	True	False
9.	The AutoCorrect feature automatically identifies and corrects certain types of errors.	True	False

fill-in

1. A small blue box appearing under a word or character indicates that the
_____ feature was applied.

2. If a word is underlined with purple dots, this indicates a(n) _____.

3. The _____ feature displays each page of your document in a reduced size so you
can see the page layout.

4. To size a graphic evenly, click and drag the _____ in one corner of the graphic.

5. It is good practice to use only _____ types of fonts in a document.

6. When you use _____, new text replaces existing text as you type.

7. The _____ sits on the right side of the window and contains buttons and icons to
help you perform common tasks, such as opening a blank document.

8. Use _____ when you want to keep your existing document with the original name and
make a copy with a new name.

9. The _____ window displays a reduced view of how the current page will
appear when printed.

10. The _____ feature includes entries, such as commonly used phrases, that
can be quickly inserted into a document.

Hands-On Exercises

step-by-step

Writing a Memo ★

1. Adventure Travel Tours is planning to update its World Wide Web site in the near future. You have been asked to solicit suggestions from the travel agents about changes they would like to see made to the current Web site. You decide to send all the travel agents a memo asking them for their input. Your completed memo is shown here.

   a. Open a blank Word document and create the following memo in Normal view. Press [Tab⇆] twice after you type colons (:) in the To, From, and Date lines. This will make the information following the colons line up evenly. Enter a blank line between paragraphs.

      To: Travel Agents
      From: Student Name
      Date: [Current date]

      Next month we plan to begin work on updating the current Adventure Travel Tours Web site. In preparation for this project, I would like your input about the current Web site. In the next few days as you use the Web site, pay attention to such things as the layout, colors, and content. Then send your comments back to me about both the positive and negative features of the current Web site and suggestions for changes you would like to see made in the new Web site.

      Thank you in advance for your input.

   To: Travel Agents
   From: Student Name
   Date: [Current date]
   RE: Web Site Revision

   Next month we plan to begin work on updating the Adventure Travel Tours Web site. In preparation for this project, I would like your input about the Web site.

   In the next few days as you use the Web site, pay attention to the layout, colors, ease of use, and content. Then send your comments back to me about both the positive and negative features of the current Web site and suggestions for changes you would like to see made in the new Web site.

   Thank you in advance for your input.

   b. Turn on the display of formatting marks.

   c. Correct any spelling and grammar errors that are identified.

   d. Delete the word "current" from the first and second sentences. Delete the phrase "such things as" from the third sentence. Insert the text "ease of use," after the word "colors," in the third sentence.

   e. Start a new paragraph beginning with the third sentence. Include a blank line between paragraphs.

   f. Change the font size for the entire memo to 14 pt and the alignment of the body of the memo to justified.

   g. Under the Date line insert the AutoText reference line "RE:".

h. Press `Tab ⇆` twice and type **Web Site Revision**. Insert a blank line below the reference line.

i. Save the document as Web Site Memo in your data file location.

j. Include your name in the file properties as author and the file name as the title.

k. Preview and print the document.

Writing a Newspaper Article ★ ★

2. You work for the Animal Rescue Foundation, a nonprofit organization that rescues and finds homes for unwanted animals. In next week's newspaper, you plan to run an article to try to encourage people from the community to support the Foundation by joining the Animal Angels volunteer group. Your completed article is shown here.

a. Enter the following information in a new Word document in Normal view, pressing `←Enter` where indicated.

Volunteers Needed! `←Enter` (4 times)

The Animal Rescue Foundation is in need of your help. Over the past 6 months, we have seen a 20 percent increase in the number of rescued animals. With the increase in animals, we need more people to join Animal Angels, our volunteer group. `←Enter` (2 times)

Our volunteer program is both diverse and flexible; no matter how hectic your schedule, we can find a place for you. Quite simply, it is our goal to have volunteers actively involved in many areas of our organization—from providing direct care for the animals to contributing to the every day functioning of our shelter and programs to furthering animal welfare and our mission of finding a loving home for each animal. Here are just some of the opportunities that await you. `←Enter` (2 times)

Foster parent `←Enter`
Work at adoption fairs `←Enter`
Provide obedience training `←Enter`
Pet grooming specialists `←Enter`
Repair, organize, and distribute donations `←Enter`
Greeters and matchmakers `←Enter`
Adoption counselor `←Enter`
Follow-up on adoptions `←Enter`
Kennel and animal care assistants `←Enter`
Special event volunteers `←Enter`
Grounds maintenance keepers `←Enter`

Volunteers Needed!

The Animal Rescue Foundation is in need of your help. Over the past six months, we have seen a *20 percent* increase in the number of rescued animals. With the increase in animals, we need more people to join Animal Angels, our volunteer group.

Our volunteer program is both diverse and flexible, no matter how hectic your schedule, we can find a place for you. It is our goal to have volunteers actively involved in many areas of our organization--from providing direct care for the animals to contributing to the every day functioning of our shelter and programs to furthering animal welfare and our mission of finding a loving home for each animal. Here are just some of the opportunities that await you.

Foster parent
Work at adoption fairs
Socialize the cats
Provide obedience training
Pet grooming specialists
Repair, organize, and distribute donations
Greeters and matchmakers
Adoption counselor
Kennel and animal care assistants
Special event volunteers
Grounds maintenance keepers
Humane educators

Thank you for your interest in giving your time and energy to the abused, homeless, and neglected animals that come to us each year. It is our desire that the time you spend here will be as rewarding for you as it is for the animals. We are proud of our organization and would like for you to become a part of the team.

Please call us at 603-555-1313 to join us!

Student Name
[Current Date]

Communication specialists [←Enter]
Humane educators [←Enter] (2 times)

Thank you for your interest in giving your time and energy to the abused, homeless, and neglected animals that come to us each year. It is our desire that the time you spend here will be as rewarding for you as it is for the animals. We are proud of our organization and would like for you to become a part of the team.
[←Enter] (2 times)

Please call us at 603-555-1313 to join us! [←Enter]

b. Correct any spelling or grammar errors. Save the document as Volunteers Needed.

c. Turn on the display of formatting marks. Check the document and remove any extra blank spaces between words or at the end of lines.

d. Switch to Print Layout view and center the title. Change the title font to Broadway (or a font of your choice), 16 pt.

e. In the first paragraph, change the number 6 to the word "six." Add italics and bold to the text "20 percent." Delete the phrase "Quite simply," from the second paragraph. Capitalize the following word, "It."

f. Justify the three main paragraphs. Center and bold the list of ways they can help.

g. Delete the "Communication specialists" and "Follow-up on adoptions" items from the list. Add "Socialize the cats" as the third item in the list.

h. Center, bold, and increase the font size to 14 pt of the last sentence.

i. Below the title insert the clip art graphic of the veterinarian and child holding a cat by searching on the keyword "animal." Center it and reduce the size of the graphic.

j. Add your name and the current date on separate lines several lines below the last line. Left-align both lines. Turn off the display of formatting marks.

k. Preview the document and if necessary reduce the graphic some more to fit the document on a single page.

l. Include your name in the file properties as author and the file name as the title.

m. Save the document again. Print the document.

WD1.84
Lab 1: Creating and Editing a Document
www.mhhe.com/oleary
Word 2003

Creating a Grand Opening Flyer ★ ★

3. The Downtown Internet Cafe is planning a grand opening celebration. The cafe combines the relaxed atmosphere of a coffee house with the fun of using the Internet. You want to create a flyer about the celebration that you can give to customers and also post in the window of other local businesses about the celebration. Your completed flyer is shown here.

a. Open a new Word document and enter the following text in Normal view, pressing ⏎Enter where indicated.

Grand Opening Celebration ⏎Enter (2 times)

Downtown Internet Cafe ⏎Enter (2 times)

Your neighborhood coffee shop ⏎Enter (4 times)

Stop on by and enjoy an excellent dark Italian Roast coffee, premium loose teas, blended drinks and quality light fare of sandwiches, pitas and salads. ⏎Enter (2 times)

Starting Monday, July 1st and continuing all week through Sunday, July 7th we will take 20% off all espresso, cappuccino and latte drinks. Plus take $1.00 off any sandwich order. With any specialty coffee drink order, you will also receive 15 FREE minutes of high-speed Internet access. ⏎Enter (2 times)

So enjoy a drink and then get online with the fastest connection in the neighborhood! ⏎Enter (6 times)

2314 Telegraph Avenue ⏎Enter

Cafe Hours: Sunday - Thursday 8:00 A.M. to 9:00 P.M. Friday and Saturday 8:00 A.M. to 12:00 A.M. ⏎Enter

Grand Opening Celebration

Downtown Internet Cafe

Your neighborhood coffee shop

Stop on by and enjoy an excellent dark Italian Roast coffee, premium loose teas, blended drinks and quality light fare of sandwiches, pitas and salads.

Starting Monday, July 1st and continuing all week through Sunday, July 7th we will take 20% off all espresso, cappuccino and latte drinks. Plus take $1.00 off any sandwich order. With any specialty coffee drink order, you will also receive 15 FREE minutes of high-speed Internet access.

So enjoy a drink and then get online with the fastest connection in the neighborhood!

2314 Telegraph Avenue
Cafe Hours: Sunday - Thursday 8:00 A.M. – 9:00 P.M. Friday - Saturday 8:00 A.M. - 12:00 P.M.

Student Name
[Current Date]

b. Correct any spelling and grammar errors that are identified.

c. Save the document as Grand Opening.

d. Type **Join Us for Live Entertainment!** after the location and hours. Use the Undo Typing feature to remove this sentence.

e. Turn on the display of formatting marks. Center the entire document.

f. Switch to Print Layout view. Change the first line to a font color of red, font type of Arial Rounded MT Bold or a font of your choice, and size of 24 pt.

g. Change the second line to a font color of blue, font type of Arial Rounded MT Bold or a font of your choice, and size of 36 pt.

h. Change the third line to a font color of red and a font size of 16 pt.

i. Increase the font size of the three paragraphs to 14 points.

j. Insert the graphic file wd01_coffee (from your data files) on the middle blank line below the third title line.

k. Size the graphic to be approximately 2 by 3 inches using the ruler as a guide.

l. Add your name and the current date, left-aligned, on separate lines two lines below the last line. Turn off the display of formatting marks.

m. Preview the document. If necessary, reduce the size of the pictures so the entire flyer fits on one page.

n. Include your name in the file properties as author and the file name as the title. Save and print the flyer.

Preparing a Lecture on Note-Taking Skills ★ ★ ★

4. You teach a college survival skills class and have recently read about the results of a survey conducted by the Pilot Pen Company of America about note-taking skills. The survey of 500 teenagers found that students typically begin taking classroom notes by sixth grade and that only half had been taught how to take classroom notes. It also found that those students trained in note-taking earned better grades. Note taking becomes increasingly important in high school and is essential in college. Lecture notes are a key component for mastering material. In response to the survey, the pen manufacturer came up with 10 tips for better note-taking. You started a document of these tips that you plan to use to supplement your lecture on this topic. You will continue to revise and format the document. The revised document is shown here.

a. Open the Word document wd01_Note Taking Skills.

b. Turn on the display of formatting marks.

c. Correct any spelling and grammar errors that are identified. Save the document as **Note Taking Skills**.

d. Switch to Print Layout view. Change the font of the title line to a font of your choice, 18 pt. Center and add color of your choice to the title line.

e. In the Write Legibly tip, delete the word "cursive" and add the word "an erasable" before the word "pen." Change the tip heading "Use Margins" to "Use Wide Margins."

Tips for Taking Better Classroom Notes

Be Ready
Review your assigned reading and previous notes you've taken before class. Bring plenty lots of paper and a sharpened pencil, an erasable pen or a pen that won't skip or smudge. Write the class name, date and that day's topic at the top the page.

Write Legibly
Print if your handwriting is poor. Use a pencil or an erasable pen if you cross out material a lot so that your notes are easier to read. Take notes in one-liners rather than paragraph form. Skip a line between ideas to make it easier to find information when you're studying for a test.

Use Wide Margins
Leave a wide margin on one side of your paper so you'll have space to write your own thoughts and call attention to key material. Draw arrows or stars beside important information like dates, names and events. If you miss getting a date, name, number or other fact, make a mark in the margin so you'll remember to come back to it.

Fill in Gaps
Check with a classmate or your teacher after class to get any missing names, dates, facts or other information you couldn't write down.

Mark Questionable Material
Jot down a "?" in the margin beside something you disagree with or do not think you recorded correctly. When appropriate, ask your teacher, classmate, or refer to your textbook, for clarification.

Student Name
[Current Date]

f. Above the Mark Questionable Material tip, insert the following tip:

Fill in Gaps

Check with a classmate or your teacher after class to get any missing names, dates, facts or other information you couldn't write down.

g. Increase the font size of the tip heading lines to 14 pt, bold, and a color of your choice.

h. Change the alignment of the paragraphs to justified. Use Undo Changes to return the alignment to left. Use Redo Changes to return the paragraphs to justified again.

i. Insert a clip art graphic of your choice (search on "pen") below the title. Size it appropriately and center it.

j. Add your name and the current date, centered, on separate lines two lines below the last line.

k. Include your name in the file properties as author and the file name as the title. Save the document. Preview and print the document.

Writing an Article on Water Conservation ★★★

5. Each month the town newsletter is included with the utility bill. This month the main article is about conserving water. You started the column a few days ago and just need to continue the article by adding a few more suggestions. Then you need to edit and format the text and include a graphic to enhance the appearance of the article. Your completed article is shown here.

a. Open the file named wd01_Conserve Water and enter the following suggestions in the category indicated. Be sure to leave a blank line above each category heading.

Personal Use Tips

Turn the water off when brushing your teeth or shaving

Keep a jug of cold water in the refrigerator instead of letting the tap run until cool

Repair Tips

Repair dripping faucets by replacing washers

Outdoor Tips

When washing the car, use soap and water from a bucket. Use a hose with a shut-off nozzle for the final rinse

b. Use Undo Changes to remove the last sentence. Use Redo Changes to return the last sentence to the document.

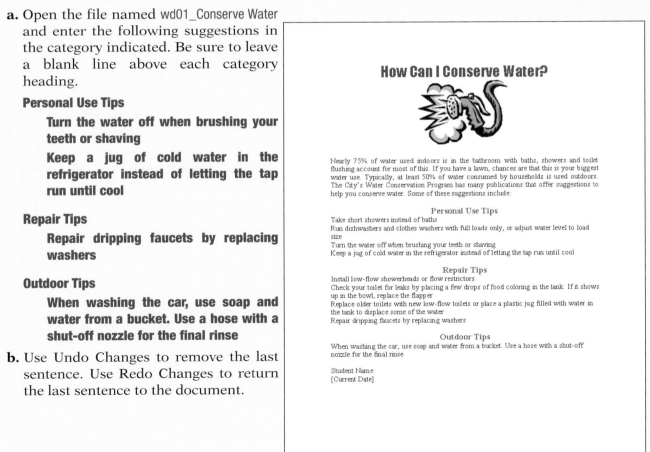

c. Turn on the display of formatting marks.

d. Correct any spelling and grammar errors. Save the document as Water Conservation.

e. Switch to Print Layout view. Center the title. Change the font to Impact with a point size of 24. Add a color of your choice to the title.

f. Change the three category heads to bold with a type size of 14 pt. Center the heads. Use the same color as in the title for the heads.

g. Change the alignment of the introductory paragraph to justified.

h. Insert the picture wd01_water hose (from your data files) below the main title of the article.

i. Size the picture to be 2 inches wide (use the ruler as a guide). Center it below the title.

j. Add your name and the current date two lines below the last line.

k. Include your name in the file properties as author and the file name as the title. Save the document again. Preview and print the document.

on your own

Creating a Cruise Flyer ★

1. Adventure Travel Tours is offering a great deal on a cruise to Hawaii. Using the features of Word you have learned so far, create a flyer that will advertise this tour. Be sure to use at least two colors of text, two sizes of text, and two kinds of paragraph alignment. Include a graphic from the Clip Organizer. Include your name at the bottom of the flyer. Include your name in the file properties as author and the file name as the title. Save the document as Hawaii Cruise Flyer.

Creating a Computer Lab Rules Flyer ★

2. You work in the computer lab of your school and have been asked to create a flyer to post that identifies the rules students should follow when using the computer workstations. Create a flyer that explains the five most important rules to follow while working in the computer lab. Use a piece of clip art to liven up your flyer. Include different font sizes, paragraph alignments, and other formatting features to make the flyer attractive. Apply different font colors for each rule. Include your name at the bottom of the flyer. Include your name in the file properties as author and the file name as the title. Save the document as Lab Rules.

CPR Training Memo ★ ★

3. Lifestyle Fitness Club has decided to require that all employees know how to perform CPR and has organized two classes to teach the procedure. You want to notify all employees about the classes by including a memo with their pay check. Using Hands-On Exercise 1 as a model, provide information about when and where the classes will be held. Include information about how people sign up for the class. Also, advise them that they will be paid for their time while attending the class. Include your name in the file properties as author and the file name as the title. Save the memo as CPR Classes.

Keeping Your Computer Clean ★★★

4. Wherever you work, in a bakery, repair shop, retail store, or your own home office, all types of environmental factors from dust to cat hair can cause havoc with your computer. It is important to keep your personal computers clean to prevent such problems as an overheated monitor, malfunctioning keyboard, or even a crashed hard drive. Using the Web as a resource, research how to clean your computer. Then write a one-page report on your findings that includes information on cleaning three areas: monitor, keyboard, and CPU. Include a title at the top of the document and your name and the current date below the title. Center the title lines. Use at least two colors of text, two sizes of text, and two kinds of paragraph alignment. Include a graphic from the Clip Organizer. At the end of the document, include references to the sources you used. Include your name in the file properties as author and the file name as the title. Save the document as Computer Cleaning.

Writing a Career Report ★★★

5. Using the library or the Web, research information about your chosen career. Write a one-page report about your findings that includes information on three areas: Career Description; Educational Requirements; Salary and Employment projections. Include a title at the top of the document and your name and the current date below the title. Center the title lines. Justify the paragraphs. At the end of the document, include references to the sources you used. Include your name in the file properties as author and the file name as the title. Save the document as Career Report.

Revising and
Refining a Document

Objectives

After completing this lab, you will know how to:

1 Use the Spelling and Grammar tool and the Thesaurus.

2 Move, cut, and copy text and formats.

3 Control document paging.

4 Find and replace text.

5 Insert the current date.

6 Change margins, line spacing, and indents.

7 Create a tabbed table.

8 Add color highlighting and underlines to text.

9 Create numbered and bulleted lists.

10 Use an AutoText entry.

11 Insert and Modify an AutoShape.

12 Edit in Print Preview.

13 Create document versions.

Case Study

Adventure Travel Tours

After creating the rough draft of the new tours flyer, you showed the printed copy to your manager at Adventure Travel Tours. Your manager then made several suggestions for improving the flyer's style and appearance. In addition, you created a letter to be sent to clients along with your flyer. The letter briefly describes Adventure Travel's four new tours and invites clients to attend an informational presentation. Your manager likes the idea, but also wants the letter to include information about the new Adventure Travel Tours Web site and a 10 percent discount for early booking.

In this lab, you will learn more about editing documents so you can reorganize and refine both your flyer and a rough draft of the letter to clients. You will also learn to use many more of the formatting features included in Office Word 2003 so you can add style and interest to your documents. Formatting features can greatly improve the appearance and design of any document you produce, so that it communicates its message more clearly. The completed letter and revised flyer are shown here.

© Corbis

Features such as the Spelling Checker, Thesaurus, Move and Copy, and Find and Replace make it easy to revise and refine your document.

Formatting and page layout changes such as margin adjustments, indented paragraphs, and tabbed tables help improve the readability and style of the document.

Graphic enhancements such as AutoShapes add interest to a document.

WD2.3

Word displays a question dialog box advising you that the correction to the word is not found in its dictionaries and asking you to confirm that you want to continue.

5 ● Click [Yes].

● Click [Ignore All] for the next located word, Picchu.

Your screen should be similar to Figure 2.5

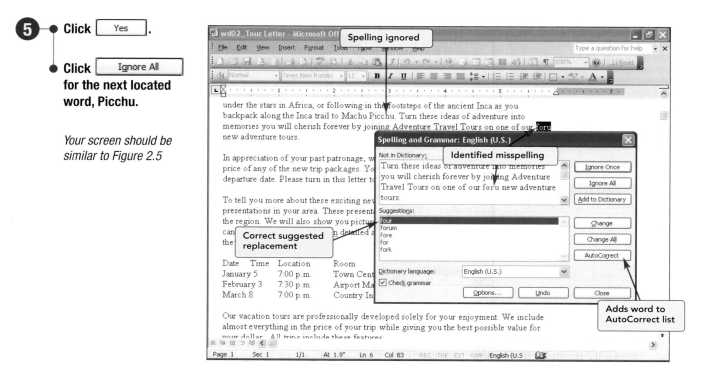

Figure 2.5

The spelling of the word "Picchu" is ignored, and the word is no longer identified as misspelled. If this word is used in other locations in this document, the spelling will be accepted.

The next located error, "foru," is a typing error that you make frequently when typing the word four. The correct spelling is selected in the Suggestions list box. You want to change it to the suggested word and add it to the list of words that are automatically corrected.

Additional Information

The [Ignore Once] option accepts the word as correct for this occurrence only.

6 ● Click [AutoCorrect].

Having Trouble?

If a dialog box appears telling you an AutoCorrect entry already exists for this word, simply click [Yes] to continue.

Your screen should be similar to Figure 2.6

Figure 2.6

The word is corrected in the document. Because you also added it to the AutoCorrect list, in the future whenever you type this word incorrectly as "foru," it will automatically be changed to "four." The next five errors that will be identified and their causes are shown in the following table

Identified Error	Cause	Action	Result
new	Repeated word	Delete	Duplicate word "new" is deleted
we is	Subject-verb disagreement	Change	we are
cOsts	Inconsistent capitalization	Change	costs
an detailed	Grammatical error	Change	a

7 • **Click** [Delete] **to delete the repeated word "new."**

• **Continue to respond to the spelling and grammar checker by clicking** [Change] **for the next three identified errors.**

• **Click** [OK] **in response to the message telling you that the spelling and grammar check is complete.**

• **Move to the top of the document and save the revised document as** Tour Letter2 **to the appropriate data file location.**

Your screen should be similar to Figure 2.7

Figure 2.7

Document is free of spelling and grammar errors

Using the Thesaurus

The next text change you want to make is to find a better word for "ideas" in the first paragraph and "happy" in the second paragraph. To help find a similar word, you will use the thesaurus tool.

Concept 1

Thesaurus

1 Word's **thesaurus** is a reference tool that provides synonyms, antonyms, and related words for a selected word or phrase. **Synonyms** are words with a similar meaning, such as "cheerful" and "happy." **Antonyms** are words with an opposite meaning, such as "cheerful" and "sad." Related words are words that are variations of the same word, such as "cheerful" and "cheer." The Thesaurus can help to liven up your documents by adding interest and variety to your text.

First you need to identify the word you want looked up by moving the insertion point onto the word. Then you use the thesaurus to suggest alternative words. The quickest way to get synonyms is to use the shortcut menu for the word you want to replace.

1 ● Right-click on the word "ideas" (first paragraph, third sentence).

● Select Synonyms.

Your screen should be similar to Figure 2.8

Figure 2.8

The Synonyms shortcut menu lists two words with similar meanings. You decide to replace "ideas" with "dreams." Then you will look for a synonym for "happy." You will use the Research pane to locate synonyms this time.

2 • Choose "dreams" from the Shortcut menu.

• With the insertion point in the word "happy" (first sentence, second paragraph), hold down ⬆Shift and press F7.

Another Method

The menu equivalent is **T**ools/**L**anguage/**T**hesaurus. You can also use **T**ools/**R**esearch or use 🔲 Research to open the Research task pane and enter the word in the Search For box.

• If necessary, select Thesaurus: English from the search scope list box.

Your screen should be similar to Figure 2.9

Figure 2.9

The Research task pane opens and the word the insertion point is on is displayed in the Search For text box. The list box displays words that have similar meanings for the word "happy" with a meaning of "content (adj)." The best choice from this list is "pleased." To see whether any other words are closer in meaning, you will look up synonyms for the word "pleased."

3 • Choose "pleased."

Additional Information

You can also choose Look Up from the word's drop-down menu to look up synonyms for the word.

Your screen should be similar to Figure 2.10

Figure 2.10

The word "pleased" is the new search term, and the list displays synonyms, as well as an antonym, for this word. You decide to use "pleased" and will return to the previous list and insert the word into the document.

4 ● Click 🔄 to display the list for the word "happy."

● Open the "pleased" synonym drop-down menu.

● Choose **I**nsert.

● Close the Research task pane.

Your screen should be similar to Figure 2.11

Figure 2.11

The word "happy" is replaced with the selected word from the thesaurus.

Moving and Copying Selections

After looking over the letter, you decide to add the company name in several other locations and to change the order of paragraphs. To make these changes quickly, you can move and copy selections.

Concept 2

Move and Copy

2   Text and graphic selections can be moved or copied to new locations in a document or between documents, saving you time by not having to recreate the same information. A selection that is moved is cut from its original location, called the **source**, and inserted at a new location, called the **destination**. A selection that is copied leaves the original in the source and inserts a duplicate at the destination.

When a selection is cut or copied, the selection is stored in the **system Clipboard**, a temporary Windows storage area in memory. It is also stored in the **Office Clipboard**. The system Clipboard holds only the last cut or copied item, whereas the Office Clipboard can store up to 24 items that have been cut or copied. This feature allows you to insert multiple items from various Office documents and paste all or part of the collection of items into another document.

Using Copy and Paste

You want to include the company name in the last paragraph of the letter in two places. Because the name has already been entered in the first paragraph, you will copy it instead of typing the name again.

- Select "Adventure Travel Tours" (first paragraph, last sentence).

- Click 📋 Copy.

- Move to the beginning of the word "journey" (last paragraph, first sentence).

- Click 📋 Paste.

Your screen should be similar to Figure 2.12

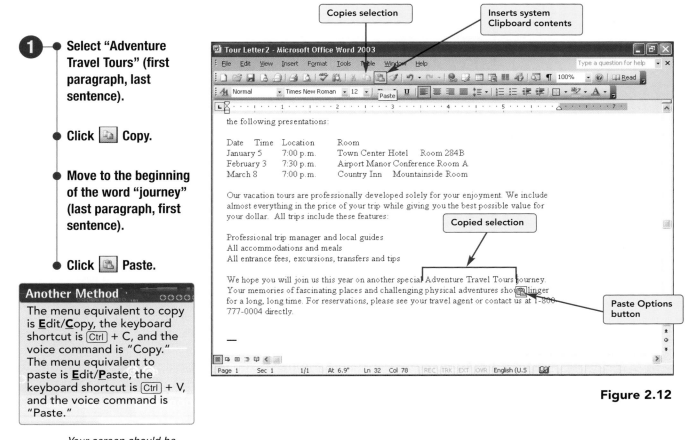

Figure 2.12

The copied selection is inserted at the location you specified. The 📋 Paste Options button appears automatically whenever a selection is pasted. It is used to control the format of the pasted item.

2 ● **Click the** 🔳 **Paste Options button.**

Your screen should be similar to Figure 2.13

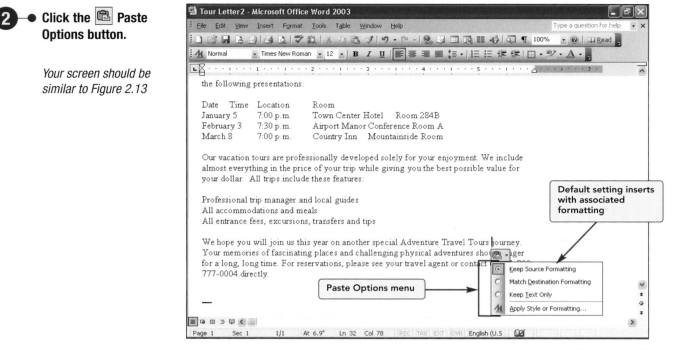

Figure 2.13

The options are used to specify whether to insert the item with the same formatting that it had in the source, to change it to the formatting of the surrounding destination text, or to insert text only (from a selection that is a combination of text and graphics). You can also apply new formatting to the selection. The default, to keep the formatting from the source, is appropriate. Next, you want to insert the company name in place of the word "us" in the last sentence of the letter.

3 ● **Click outside the menu to close it.**

● **Select "us" (last sentence).**

● **Right-click on the selection and choose Paste from the shortcut menu.**

Your screen should be similar to Figure 2.14

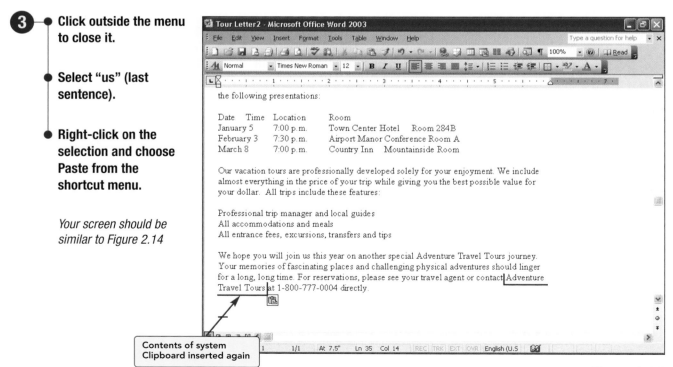

Figure 2.14

The selected text was deleted and replaced with the contents of the system Clipboard. The system Clipboard contents remain in the Clipboard until another item is copied or cut, allowing you to paste the same item multiple times.

Using Cut and Paste

You want the paragraph about the 10 percent discount (second paragraph) to follow the list of presentation dates. To do this, you will move the paragraph from its current location to the new location. The Cut and Paste commands on the Edit menu are used to move selections. You will use the shortcut menu to select the Cut command.

1 ● **Select the second paragraph including the blank line below the paragraph.**

Having Trouble?

Drag in the space to the left of the paragraph to select it.

● **Right-click on the selection to display the shortcut menu.**

Another Method

The Cut shortcuts are or Ctrl + X and the voice command is "Cut."

● **Choose Cut.**

Your screen should be similar to Figure 2.15

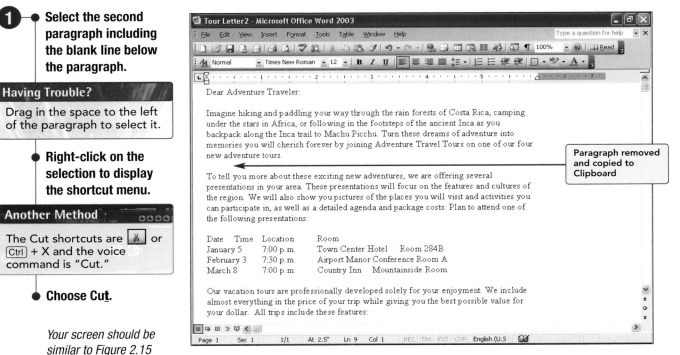

Paragraph removed and copied to Clipboard

Figure 2.15

The selected paragraph is removed from the source and copied to the Clipboard. Next, you need to move the insertion point to the location where the text will be inserted and paste the text into the document from the Clipboard.

2 ● Move to the beginning of the paragraph below the list of presentation dates.

● Click 🔲 Paste.

Another Method

You can also choose **P**aste from the shortcut menu.

● If necessary, scroll down to view the pasted paragraph.

Your screen should be similar to Figure 2.16

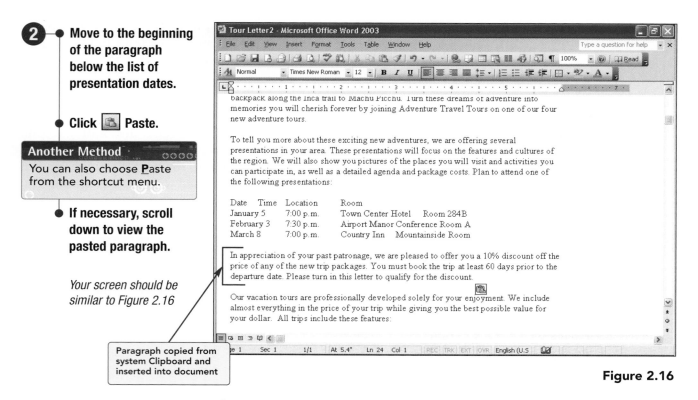

Paragraph copied from system Clipboard and inserted into document

Figure 2.16

The cut paragraph is reentered into the document at the insertion point location. That was much quicker than retyping the whole paragraph!

Using Drag and Drop

Finally, you also decide to move the word "directly" in the last paragraph so that the sentence reads ". . . contact Adventure Travel Tours directly at 1-888-777-0004." Rather than use Cut and Paste to move this text, you will use the **drag and drop** editing feature. This feature is most useful for copying or moving short distances in a document.

To use drag and drop to move a selection, point to the selection and drag it to the location where you want the selection inserted. The mouse pointer appears as ▷ as you drag, and a temporary insertion point shows you where the text will be placed when you release the mouse button.

Additional Information

You can also use drag and drop to copy a selection by holding down Ctrl while dragging. The mouse pointer shape is ▷.

1 ● Select "directly" (last word in last paragraph).

● Drag the selection to before "at" in the same sentence.

Additional Information

You can also move or copy a selection by holding down the right mouse button while dragging. When you release the mouse button, a shortcut menu appears with the available move and copy options.

Your screen should be similar to Figure 2.17

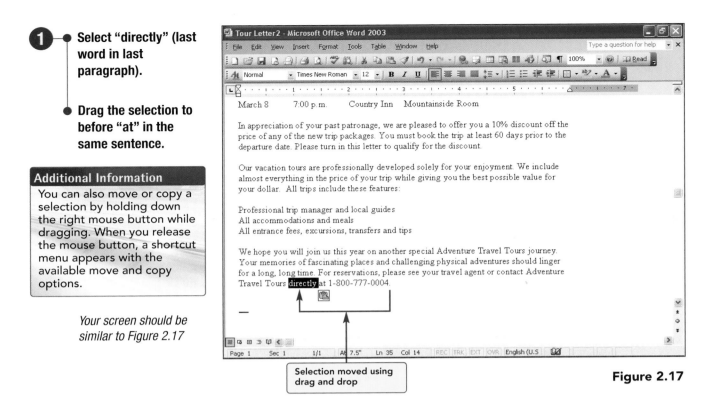

Figure 2.17

The selection is moved to the new location.

Copying Between Documents

You plan to include the flyer with the letter to be mailed to clients. To do this, you will open the flyer document and copy it into the letter document file. Because all Office 2003 applications allow you to open and use multiple files at the same time, this is a very simple procedure.

1 ● Move to the top of the document.

● Click ☐ Save.

● Open the wd02_Flyer2 document.

Additional Information

Sometimes you may want to open several files at once. To do this you can select multiple files from the Open dialog box by holding down (Ctrl) while clicking on each file name. If the files are adjacent, you can click the first file name, hold down (⇧Shift) and click on the name of the last file.

Your screen should be similar to Figure 2.18

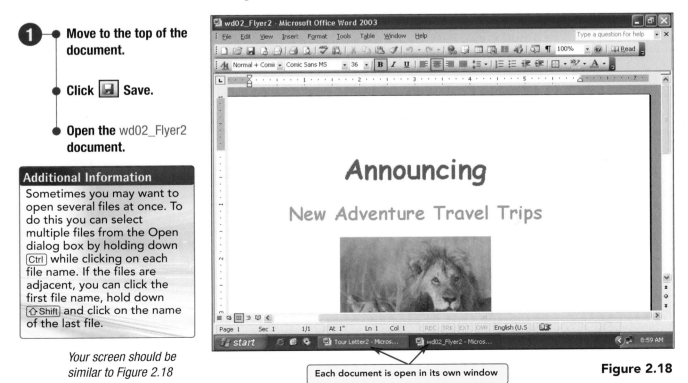

Figure 2.18

The flyer document is opened and displayed in a separate window. It contains the insertion point, which indicates that it is the **active window**, or the window in which you can work. The taskbar displays a button for each open document window; it can be used to switch quickly from one window to the other.

You can also display both open documents on the screen at once to make it easy to compare documents or to move information between documents.

2 • Choose **W**indow/Compare Side **b**y Side with Tour Letter2.

Your screen should be similar to Figure 2.19

Additional Information
The Arrange All command divides the screen horizontally.

Figure 2.19

The two document windows are arranged side-by-side on the screen. The active window displays the insertion point and is the document you can work in. Simply clicking on the other document makes it active. When you use this feature, the documents in both windows will scroll together so you can compare text easily. If you are not comparing text, this feature can be turned off so that they scroll independently. The Compare Side by Side toolbar automatically appears and is used to control the window arrangement and action.

You will copy the entire flyer to the bottom of the letter document using drag and drop. To copy between documents using drag and drop, hold down the right mouse button while dragging. When you release the button, a shortcut menu appears where you specify the action you want to perform. If you drag using the left mouse button, the selection is moved by default.

Synchronous scrolling   Reset window position

3 • Click ▾ 3 times in the wd02_Flyer2 window scrollbar to see both windows scroll.

• Click 🗐 **Synchronous Scrolling** in the Compare Side by Side toolbar to turn off this feature.

• Click ▾ 3 times in the wd02_Flyer2 window scrollbar to scroll the active window only.

• Select the entire flyer.

Having Trouble?
Triple-click in the left margin to quickly select the entire document.

• Right-drag the selection to the blank line immediately below the last paragraph of the letter.

• Release the mouse button and choose **C**opy Here from the shortcut menu.

• Click | Close Side by Side | to return the display to a single document window.

Your screen should be similar to Figure 2.20

Another Method
If you did not want to arrange windows, you could just copy the selection in the active window, click on the taskbar button of the other open window to make it active, and then paste the selection in the document.

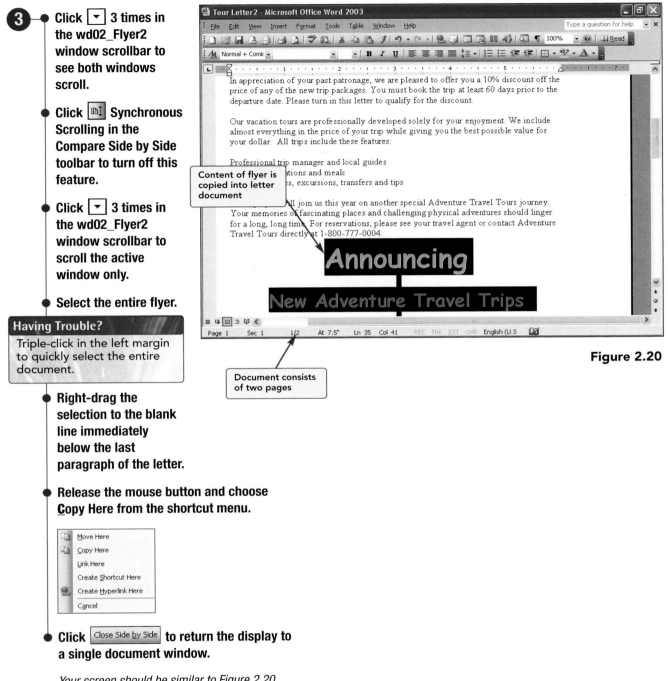

Figure 2.20

The letter now consists of two pages. Notice the status bar shows the insertion point location is on page 1/2.

Controlling Document Paging

As text and graphics are added to a document, Word automatically starts a new page when text extends beyond the bottom margin setting. The beginning of a new page is identified by a page break.

Concept 3

Page Break

3 A **page break** marks the point at which one page ends and another begins. Two types of page breaks can be used in a document: soft page breaks and hard page breaks. As you fill a page with text or graphics, Word inserts a **soft page break** automatically when the bottom margin is reached and starts a new page. As you add or remove text from a page, Word automatically readjusts the placement of the soft page break.

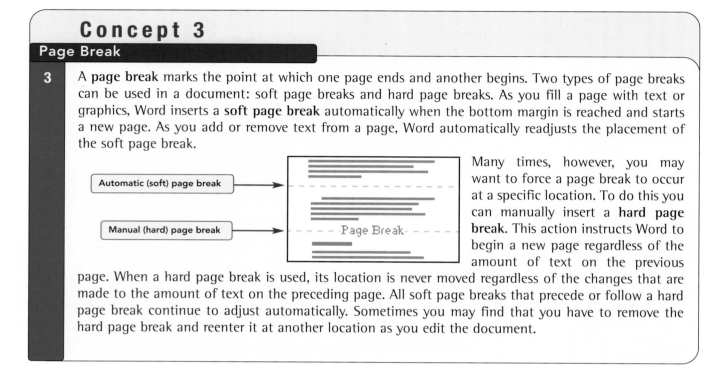

Many times, however, you may want to force a page break to occur at a specific location. To do this you can manually insert a **hard page break**. This action instructs Word to begin a new page regardless of the amount of text on the previous page. When a hard page break is used, its location is never moved regardless of the changes that are made to the amount of text on the preceding page. All soft page breaks that precede or follow a hard page break continue to adjust automatically. Sometimes you may find that you have to remove the hard page break and reenter it at another location as you edit the document.

You will switch back to Normal view to see the soft page break that was entered in the document.

1 ● Click in the document to deselect the flyer text.

● Switch to Normal view.

● If necessary, scroll the document to see the dotted page break line.

Additional Information

As you drag the scroll box, a ScreenTip displays the number of the page that is displayed in the window.

Your screen should be similar to Figure 2.21

Figure 2.21

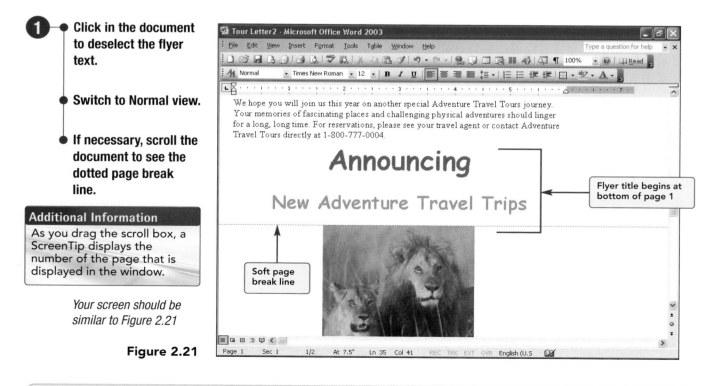

To show where one page ends and another begins, Word displays a dotted line across the page to mark the soft page break.

Inserting a Hard Page Break

Many times the location of the soft page break is not appropriate. In this case, the location of the soft page break displays the flyer title on the bottom of page 1 and the remaining portion of the flyer on page 2. Because you want the entire flyer to print on a page by itself, you will manually insert a hard page break above the flyer title.

1 ● **Move to the end of the last line at the end of the letter.**

● **Press** Ctrl + ←Enter.

Another Method

The menu equivalent is **I**nsert/**B**reak/**P**age break.

● **Save the document again.**

Your screen should be similar to Figure 2.22

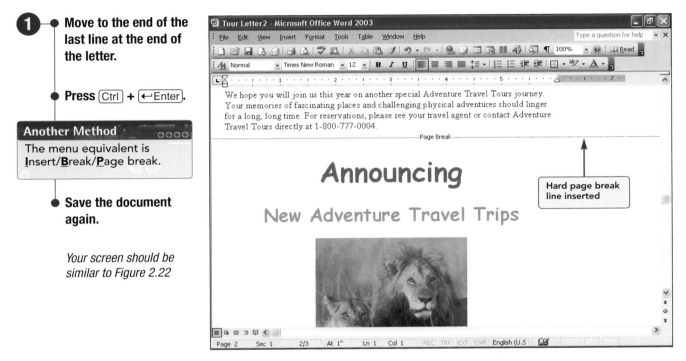

Figure 2.22

Additional Information

To remove a hard page break, simply select the hard page break line and press Delete.

A dotted line and the words "Page Break" appear across the page above the flyer title, indicating that a hard page break was entered at that position.

Finding and Replacing Text

As you continue proofing the letter, you notice that the word "trip" is used frequently. You think that the letter would read better if the word "tour" was used in place of "trip" in some instances. To do this, you will use the Find and Replace feature.

Concept 4

Find and Replace

4 To make editing easier, you can use the Find and Replace feature to find text in a document and replace it with other text as directed. For example, suppose you created a lengthy document describing the type of clothing and equipment needed to set up a world-class home gym, and then you decided to change "sneakers" to "athletic shoes." Instead of deleting every occurrence of "sneakers" and typing "athletic shoes," you can use the Find and Replace feature to perform the task automatically.

You can also find and replace occurrences of special formatting, such as replacing bold text with italicized text, as well as find and replace formatting marks. Additionally, special characters and symbols, such as an arrow or copyright symbol, can be easily located or replaced. This feature is fast and accurate; however, use care when replacing so that you do not replace unintended matches.

Finding Text

First, you will use the Find command to locate all occurrences of the word "trip" in the document.

1 ● **Move the insertion point to the top of the document.**

Another Method

Reminder: Use Ctrl + Home to quickly move to the top of the document.

● **Choose Edit/Find.**

Another Method

The keyboard shortcut is Ctrl + F. You can also open the Find and Replace dialog box by clicking the ● Select Browse Object button in the vertical scroll bar and selecting 🔍 Find from the menu.

Your screen should be similar to Figure 2.23

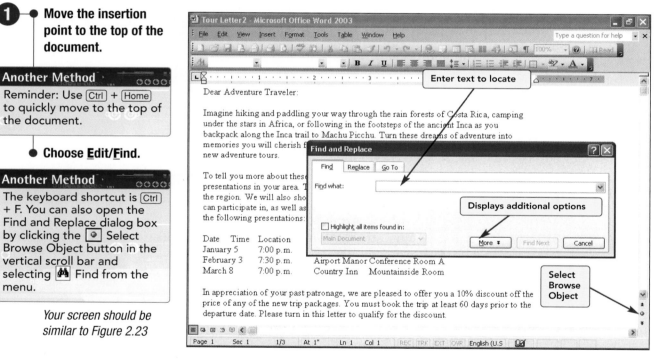

Figure 2.23

The Find and Replace dialog box is used to define the information you want to locate and replace. In the Find What text box, you enter the text you want to locate. In addition, you can use the search options to refine the search.

② → • Click [More ▼].

Your screen should be similar to Figure 2.24

Searches entire document

Hides search options

Use these options to refine your search

Figure 2.24

The additional options can be combined in many ways to help you find and replace text in documents. They are described in the table below.

Option	Effect on Text
Match case	Finds only those words in which the capitalization matches the text you typed.
Find whole words only	Finds matches that are whole words and not part of a larger word. For example, finds "cat" only and not "catastrophe" too.
Use wildcards	Fine-tunes a search; for example, c?t finds "cat" and "cot" (one-character matches), while c*t finds "cat" and "court" (searches for one or more characters).
Sounds like (English)	Finds words that sound like the word you type; very helpful if you do not know the correct spelling of the word you want to find.
Find all word forms (English)	Finds and replaces all forms of a word; for example, "buy" will replace "purchase," and "bought" will replace "purchased."
Format ▼	Finds text with formatting characteristics specified and/or replaces text with specified formatting. If no Find text is specified, locates all occurrences of specified formatting.
Special ▼	Finds/replaces all occurrences of special characters.

When you enter the text to find, you can type everything lowercase, because the Match Case option is not selected. If Match Case is not selected, the search will not be **case sensitive**. This means that lowercase letters will match both upper- and lowercase letters in the text.

Also notice that the Search option default setting is All, which means Word will search the entire document, including headers and footers. You can also choose to search Up or Down the document. These options search in the direction specified but exclude the headers, footers, footnotes, and comments from the area to search. Because you want to search the entire document, All is the appropriate setting. You will hide the search options again and begin the search.

Additional Information

You will learn about headers, footers, footnotes, and comments in later labs.

3 ● Click [Less ▲] to close the advanced search options.

● Type **trip** in the Find What text box.

● Click [Find Next].

Your screen should be similar to Figure 2.25

Additional Information

If the search does not begin at the top of the document, when Word reaches the end of the document it asks if you want to continue searching from the beginning of the document. You can also highlight text to restrict the search to a selection.

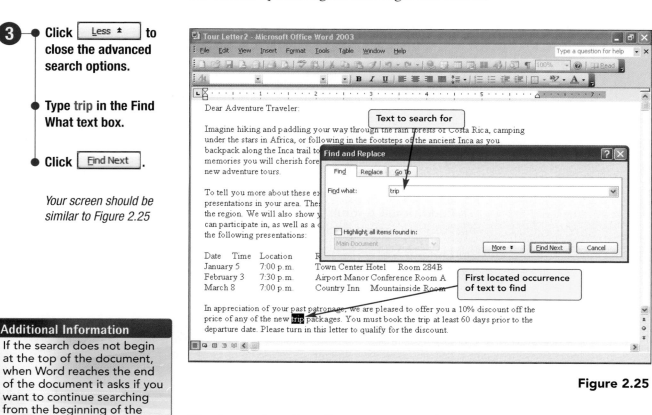

Figure 2.25

Word searches for all occurrences of the text to find beginning at the insertion point, locates the first occurrence of the word "trip," and highlights it in the document.

4 ● Continue to click [Find Next] to locate all occurrences of the word.

● Click [OK] when Word indicates the entire document has been searched.

The word "trip" is used seven times in the document.

Replacing Text

You decide to replace several occurrences of the word "trip" in the letter with "tour" where appropriate. You will use the Replace feature to specify the text to enter as the replacement text.

1 ● **Open the Replace tab.**

Your screen should be similar to Figure 2.26

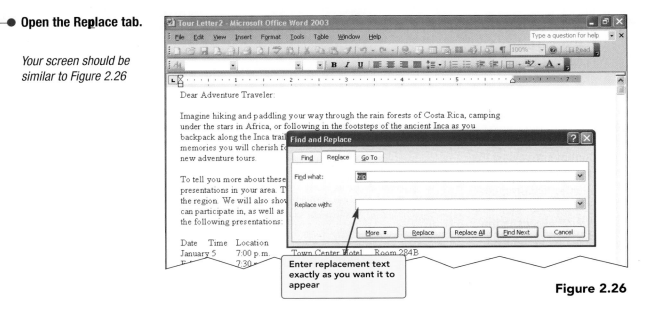

Enter replacement text exactly as you want it to appear

Figure 2.26

The Replace tab includes a Replace With text box in which you enter the replacement text. This text must be entered exactly as you want it to appear in your document. To find and replace the first occurrence of the word "trip" with "tour,"

2 ● **Type tour in the Replace With text box.**

● **Click** Find Next .

● **Click** Replace .

Your screen should be similar to Figure 2.27

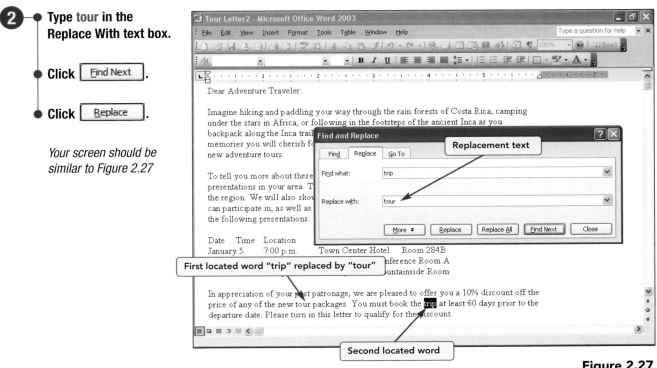

Replacement text

First located word "trip" replaced by "tour"

Second located word

Figure 2.27

Word replaced the first located word with "tour" and has highlighted the second occurrence of the word "trip." You do not want to replace this occurrence of the word. You will continue the search without replacing the highlighted text.

3 ● **Click** `Find Next` **to skip this occurrence and locate the next occurrence.**

● **Replace the next located occurrence.**

● **Continue to review the document, replacing all other occurrences of the word "trip" with "tour,"** *except* **on the final line of the flyer.**

● **Click** `Find Next`.

● **Click** `OK` **to close the information dialog box.**

● **Click** `Close` **to close the Find and Replace dialog box.**

Your screen should be similar to Figure 2.28

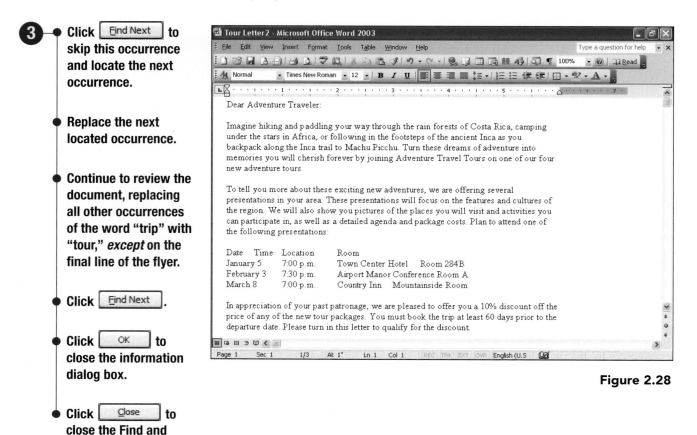

Figure 2.28

When using the Find and Replace feature, if you wanted to change all the occurrences of the located text, it is much faster to use `Replace All`. Exercise care when using this option, however, because the search text you specify might be part of another word and you may accidentally replace text you want to keep. If this happens, you could use Undo to reverse the action.

Inserting the Current Date

The last text change you need to make is to add the date to the letter. The Date and Time command on the Insert menu inserts the current date as maintained by your computer system into your document at the location of the insertion point. You want to enter the date on the first line of the letter, five lines above the salutation.

1 ● If necessary, move to the "D" in "Dear" at the top of the letter.

● Press ⏎Enter 4 times to insert four blank lines.

● Move to the first blank line.

● Choose Insert/Date and Time.

Your screen should be similar to Figure 2.29

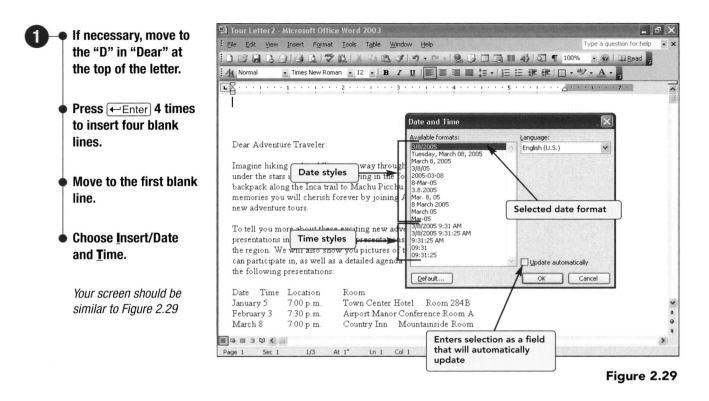

Figure 2.29

Additional Information

The current time can also be inserted into a document using the same procedure.

From the Date and Time dialog box, you select the style in which you want the date displayed in your document. The Available Formats list box displays the format styles for the current date and time. You want to display the date in the format Month XX, 2XXX, the third format setting in the list.

You also want the date to be updated automatically whenever the letter is sent to new Adventure Tours travelers. You use the Update Automatically option to do this, which enters the date as a field.

Concept 5

Field

5 A **field** is a placeholder that instructs Word to insert information into a document. The **field code** contains the directions as to the type of information to insert or action to perform. Field codes appear between curly brackets {}, also called braces. The information that is displayed as a result of the field code is called the **field result**. Many field codes are automatically inserted when you use certain commands; others you can create and insert yourself. Many fields update automatically when the document changes. Using fields makes it easier and faster to perform many common or repetitive tasks.

2
- Select the third format setting.

- If necessary, select <u>U</u>pdate Automatically to display the checkmark.

- Click [OK].

Your screen should be similar to Figure 2.30

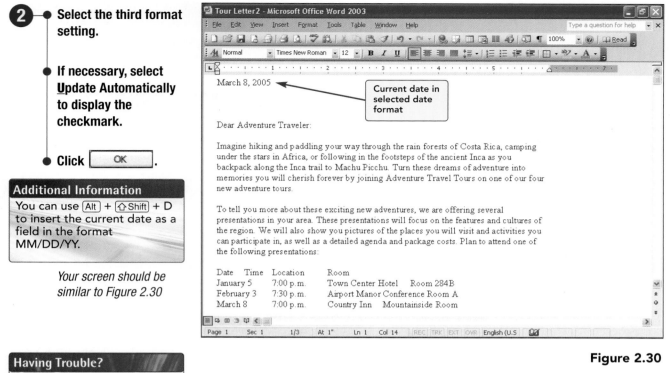

Figure 2.30

The current date is entered in the document in the format you selected. The date is the field result. You will display the field code to see the underlying instructions.

3
- Right-click on the date and choose <u>T</u>oggle Field Codes from the shortcut menu.

Your screen should be similar to Figure 2.31

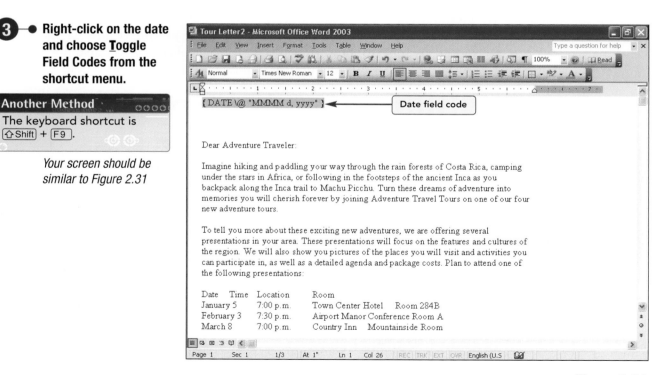

Figure 2.31

The field code includes the field name (DATE) followed by the field properties, in this case the date format instructions. Whenever this document is printed, Word will print the current system date using this format. The field result and code may appear with a shaded background depending upon the setting selected in your program. To show or remove field shading choose Tools/Options/View and then select Never, Always, or When Selected from the field shading box. The shading does not print.

4 ● Press [⇧ Shift] + [F9] to display the field result again.

● Save the document.

Modifying Page Layout

Next the manager has suggested that you make several formatting changes to improve the appearance of the letter and flyer. Many formatting features that can be used in a document affect the layout of an entire page. These formatting features include page margin settings, vertical alignment of text on a page, headers and footers, and orientation of text on a page.

Changing Margin Settings

One of the first changes you will make is to change the page margin settings.

Concept 6
Page Margin

6 The **page margin** is the blank space around the edge of a page. Generally, the text you enter appears in the printable area inside the margins. However, some items can be positioned in the margin space. You can set different page margin widths to alter the appearance of the document.

Standard single-sided documents have four margins: top, bottom, left, and right. Double-sided documents with facing pages, such as books and magazines, also have four margins: top, bottom, inside, and outside. These documents typically use mirror margins in which the left page is a mirror image of the right page. This means that the inside margins are the same width and the outside margins are the same width. (See the illustrations below.)

You can also set a "gutter" margin that reserves space on the left side of single-sided documents, or on the inside margin of double-sided documents, to accommodate binding. There are also special margin settings for headers and footers. (You will learn about these features in Lab 3.)

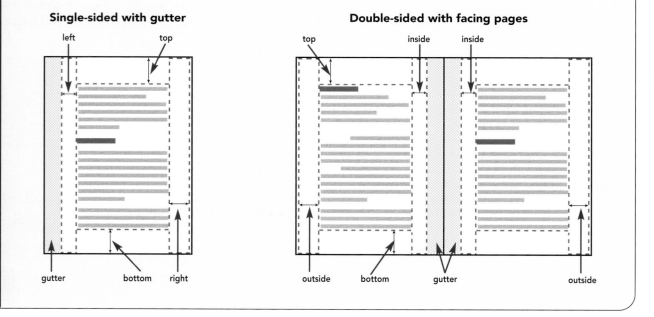

Single-sided with gutter

left   top

gutter   bottom   right

Double-sided with facing pages

top   inside   inside

outside   bottom   gutter   outside

To see how the changes you make to margin settings will look on the page, you will first change the document view to Print Layout view and Page Width zoom.

1 ● Click ▣ **Print Layout View.**

● **Open the** `100%` **Zoom drop-down menu and choose Page Width.**

● **If the ruler is not displayed, choose View/Ruler to turn it on.**

Your screen should be similar to Figure 2.32

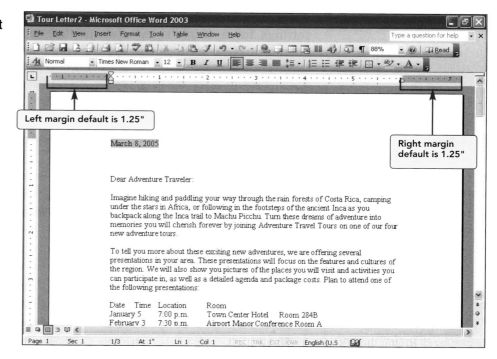

Left margin default is 1.25"

Right margin default is 1.25"

Figure 2.32

The default left and right margin settings of 1.25 inches are now easy to see. As you make changes to the margin settings next, you will be able to easily see the change in the layout of the document on the page.

You would like to see how the letter would look if you changed the right and left margin widths to 1 inch. The Page Setup command on the File menu is used to change settings associated with the layout of the entire document.

2 ● **Choose File/Page Setup.**

● **If necessary, open the Margins tab.**

Another Method

You can also double-click on the ruler to display the Page Setup dialog box.

Your screen should be similar to Figure 2.33

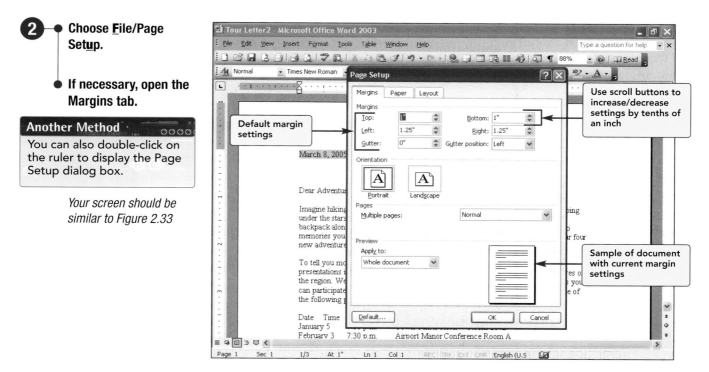

Default margin settings

Use scroll buttons to increase/decrease settings by tenths of an inch

Sample of document with current margin settings

Figure 2.33

Concept 7
Indents

7   To help your reader find information quickly, you can **indent** paragraphs from the margins. Indenting paragraphs sets them off from the rest of the document. There are four types of indents, and their effects are described below.

Indent	Effect on Text	Indent	Effect on Text
Left Left→	Indents the entire paragraph from the left margin. To "outdent" or extend the paragraph into the left margin, use a negative value for the left indent.	**First Line** First line	Indents the first line of the paragraph. All following lines are aligned with the left margin.
Right ←Right	Indents the entire paragraph from the right margin. To outdent or extend the paragraph into the right margin, use a negative value for the right indent.	**Hanging** Hanging	Indents all lines after the first line of the paragraph. The first line is aligned with the left margin. A hanging indent is typically used for bulleted and numbered lists.

You want to change the letter style from the block paragraph style to the modified block style. You will begin by indenting the first line of the first paragraph.

1 • Return the zoom to Page Width.

• Right-click anywhere in the first paragraph.

• Choose Paragraph from the shortcut menu.

• If necessary, open the Indents and Spacing tab.

Another Method
The menu equivalent is **F**ormat/**P**aragraph.

Your screen should be similar to Figure 2.36

Figure 2.36

The Indents and Spacing tab shows that the left and right indentation settings for the current paragraph are 0. This setting aligns each line of the paragraph with the margin setting. Specifying an indent value would indent each line of the selected paragraph the specified amount from the margin. However, you only want to indent the first line of the paragraph.

2 • From the Special drop-down list box, select First line.

Your screen should be similar to Figure 2.37

Figure 2.37

The default first line indent setting of 0.5 inch displayed in the By text box is acceptable. The Preview area shows how this setting will affect a paragraph.

3 ● Click [OK].

Your screen should be similar to Figure 2.38

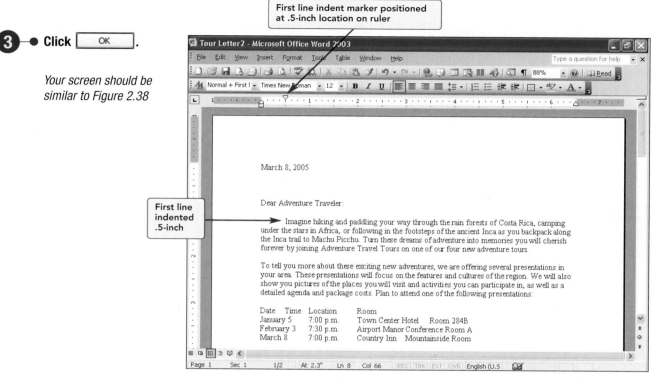

Figure 2.38

The first line of the paragraph indents a half inch from the left margin. The text in the paragraph wraps as needed, and the text on the following line begins at the left margin. Notice that the First Line Indent marker on the ruler moved to the 0.5-inch position. This marker controls the location of the first line of text in the paragraph.

A much quicker way to indent the first line of a paragraph is to press [Tab↹] at the beginning of the paragraph. When the insertion point is positioned at the beginning of a line, pressing [Tab↹] indents the first line of the paragraph to the first tab stop from the left margin. A **tab stop** is a marked location on the horizontal ruler that indicates how far to indent text when the [Tab↹] key is pressed. The default tab stops are every .5 inch.

4 ● Move to the beginning of the second paragraph.

● Press Tab.

Your screen should be similar to Figure 2.39

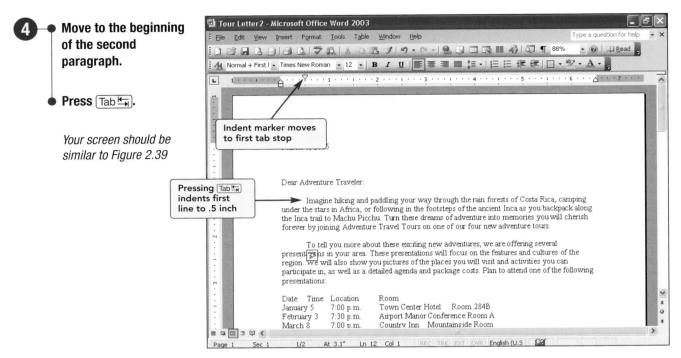

Indent marker moves to first tab stop

Pressing Tab indents first line to .5 inch

Dear Adventure Traveler:

Imagine hiking and paddling your way through the rain forests of Costa Rica, camping under the stars in Africa, or following in the footsteps of the ancient Inca as you backpack along the Inca trail to Machu Picchu. Turn these dreams of adventure into memories you will cherish forever by joining Adventure Travel Tours on one of our four new adventure tours.

To tell you more about these exciting new adventures, we are offering several presentations in your area. These presentations will focus on the features and cultures of the region. We will also show you pictures of the places you will visit and activities you can participate in, as well as a detailed agenda and package costs. Plan to attend one of the following presentations:

Date	Time	Location	Room
January 5	7:00 p.m.	Town Center Hotel	Room 284B
February 3	7:30 p.m.	Airport Manor Conference Room A
March 8	7:00 p.m.	Country Inn	Mountainside Room

Figure 2.39

Indenting the line using Tab moves the first line to the first tab stop and also moves the indent marker to that position on the ruler. If the insertion point was positioned anywhere else within the line of text, pressing Tab would move the text to the right of the insertion point to the next tab stop and the indent marker would not move.

You can indent the remaining paragraphs individually, or you can select the paragraphs and indent them simultaneously by either using the Format menu or dragging the upper indent marker on the ruler.

Additional Information

To indent an entire paragraph, click in front of any line except the first line and press Tab.

5 ● Select the remaining text on page 1.

● Drag the First Line Indent marker on the ruler to the 0.5-inch position.

Additional Information

A ScreenTip identifies the First Line Indent marker when you point to it.

● If necessary, scroll the window to display the entire selection.

Your screen should be similar to Figure 2.40

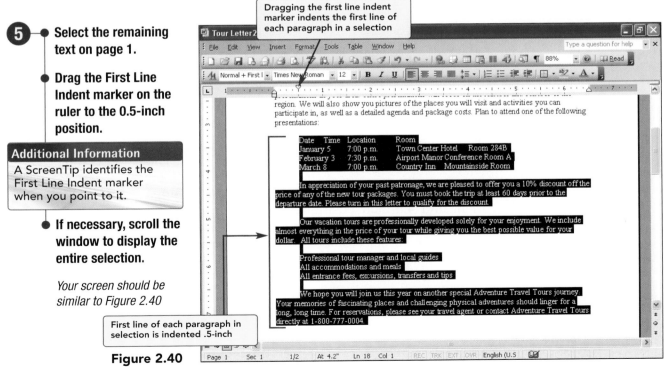

Dragging the first line indent marker indents the first line of each paragraph in a selection

region. We will also show you pictures of the places you will visit and activities you can participate in, as well as a detailed agenda and package costs. Plan to attend one of the following presentations:

Date	Time	Location	Room
January 5	7:00 p.m.	Town Center Hotel	Room 284B
February 3	7:30 p.m.	Airport Manor Conference Room A
March 8	7:00 p.m.	Country Inn	Mountainside Room

In appreciation of your past patronage, we are pleased to offer you a 10% discount off the price of any of the new tour packages. You must book the trip at least 60 days prior to the departure date. Please turn in this letter to qualify for the discount.

Our vacation tours are professionally developed solely for your enjoyment. We include almost everything in the price of your tour while giving you the best possible value for your dollar. All tours include these features:

Professional tour manager and local guides
All accommodations and meals
All entrance fees, excursions, transfers and tips

We hope you will join us this year on another special Adventure Travel Tours journey. Your memories of fascinating places and challenging physical adventures should linger for a long, long time. For reservations, please see your travel agent or contact Adventure Travel Tours directly at 1-800-777-0004.

First line of each paragraph in selection is indented .5-inch

Figure 2.40

The first line of each paragraph in the selection is indented. Notice that each line of the date and time information is also indented. This is because each line ends with a paragraph mark. Word considers each line a separate paragraph.

Setting Tab Stops

Next you want to improve the appearance of the list of presentation times and dates. The date and time information was entered using tabs to separate the different columns of information. However, because the default tab stops are set at every 0.5 inch, the columns are not evenly spaced. You want to reformat this information to appear as a tabbed table of information so that it is easier to read as shown below.

Date	Time	Location	Room
January 5 ----- 7:00 pm -----------Town Center Hotel -------Room 284B			
February 3 ---- 7:30 pm -----------Airport Manor -------------Conference Room A			
March 8 ------- 7:00 pm -----------Country Inn----------------Mountainside Room			

To improve the appearance of the data, you will create custom tab stops that will align the data in evenly spaced columns. The default tab stops of every 0.5 inch are visible on the ruler as light vertical lines below the numbers. As with other default settings, you can change the location of tab stops in the document.

You can also select from five different types of tab stops that control how characters are positioned or aligned with the tab stop. The following table explains the five tab types, the tab marks that appear in the tab alignment selector box (on the left end of the horizontal ruler), and the effects on the text.

Tab Type	Tab Mark	Effects on Text	Example
Left	∟	Extends text to right from tab stop	left
Center	⊥	Aligns text centered on tab stop	center
Right	⌐	Extends text to left from tab stop	right
Decimal	⊥·	Aligns text with decimal point	35.78
Bar	I	Draws a vertical line through text at tab stop		

To align the data, you will place three left tab stops at the 1.5-inch, 2.75-inch, and 4.5-inch positions. You can quickly specify custom tab stop locations and types using the ruler. To select a type of tab stop, click the tab alignment selector box to cycle through the types. Then, to specify where to place the selected tab stop type, click on the location in the ruler. As you specify the new tab stop settings, the table data will align to the new settings.

1 Select the line of table headings and the three lines of data.

- If necessary, click the tab alignment selector box until the left tab icon 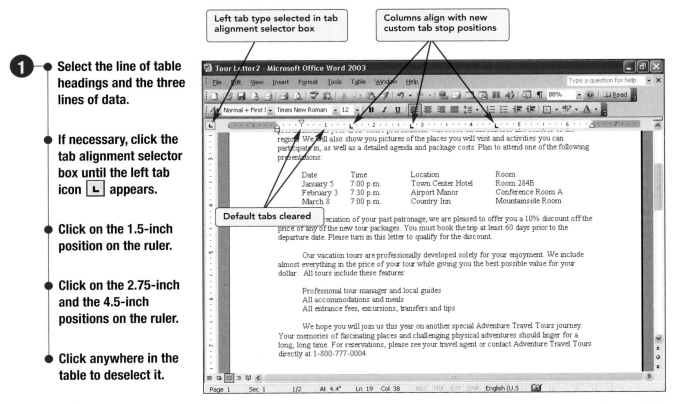 appears.

- Click on the 1.5-inch position on the ruler.

- Click on the 2.75-inch and the 4.5-inch positions on the ruler.

- Click anywhere in the table to deselect it.

Your screen should be similar to Figure 2.41

Figure 2.41

The three tabbed columns appropriately align with the new tab stops. All default tabs to the left of the custom tab stops are cleared. After looking at the columns, you decide the column headings would look better centered over the columns of data. To make this change, you will remove the three custom tabs for the heading line by dragging them off the ruler and then add three center tab stops.

2 Move to anywhere in the heading line.

• Drag the three left tab stop marks off the ruler.

• Click the tab alignment selector box until the center tab icon ⊥ appears.

• Set a center tab stop at the .75-inch, 1.75-inch, 3.25-inch, and 5-inch positions.

Your screen should be similar to Figure 2.42

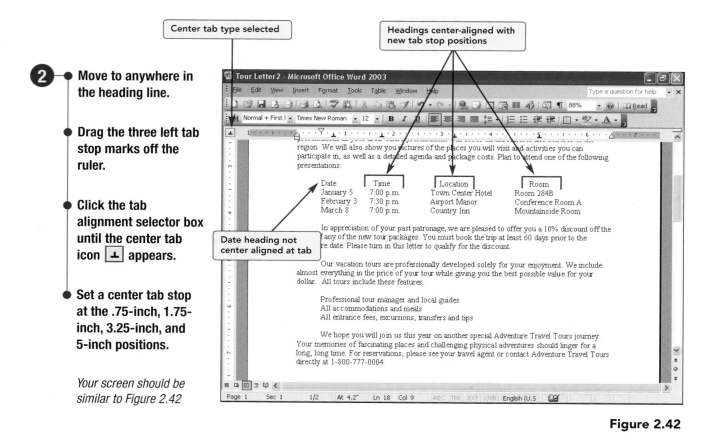

Center tab type selected

Headings center-aligned with new tab stop positions

Date heading not center aligned at tab

Figure 2.42

The Time, Location, and Room headings are appropriately centered on the tab stops. However, the Date heading still needs to be indented to the .75 tab stop position by pressing Tab ⇆.

3 If necessary, move to the "D" in "Date."

• Press Tab ⇆.

Your screen should be similar to Figure 2.43

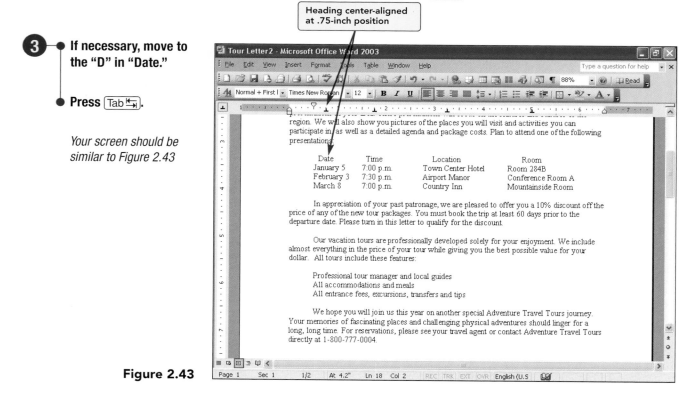

Heading center-aligned at .75-inch position

Figure 2.43

The Date heading is now centered at the .75-inch tab stop. As you can see, setting different types of tab stops is helpful for aligning text or numeric data vertically in columns. Using tab stops ensures that the text will indent to the same set location. Setting custom tab stops instead of pressing [Tab ⇥] or [Spacebar] repeatedly is a more professional way to format a document, as well as faster and more accurate. It also makes editing easier because you can change the tab stop settings for several paragraphs at once.

Adding Tab Leaders

To make the presentation times and location data even easier to read, you will add tab leaders to the table. **Leader characters** are solid, dotted, or dashed lines that fill the blank space between tab stops. They help the reader's eye move across the blank space between the information aligned at the tab stops.

1 ● Select the three lines of presentation information, excluding the heading line.

● Choose **F**ormat/**T**abs.

Your screen should be similar to Figure 2.44

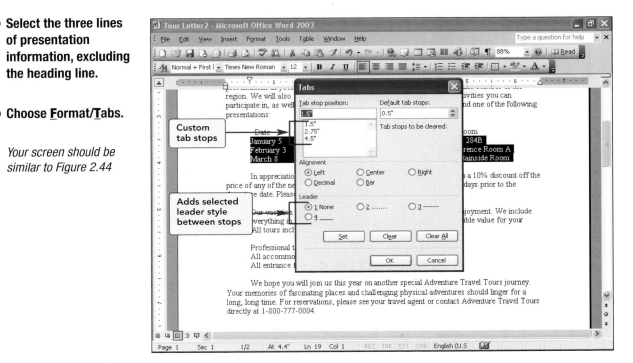

Figure 2.44

Notice that the Tabs dialog box displays the custom tabs you set on the ruler. You can set tab positions in the dialog box by entering the tab positions in the text box. The current tab leader setting is set to None for the 1.5-inch tab stop. You can select from three styles of tab leaders. You will use the third tab leader style, a series of dashed lines. The tab leader fills the empty space to the left of the tab stop. Each tab stop must have the leader individually set.

2

- Select **3** --------.

- Click [Set].

- Select the 2.75-inch tab stop setting from the Tab Stop Position list box.

- Select **3** --------.

- Click [Set].

- In a similar manner, set the tab leader for the 4.5-inch tab.

- Click [OK].

- Click in the table to deselect the text.

Your screen should be similar to Figure 2.45

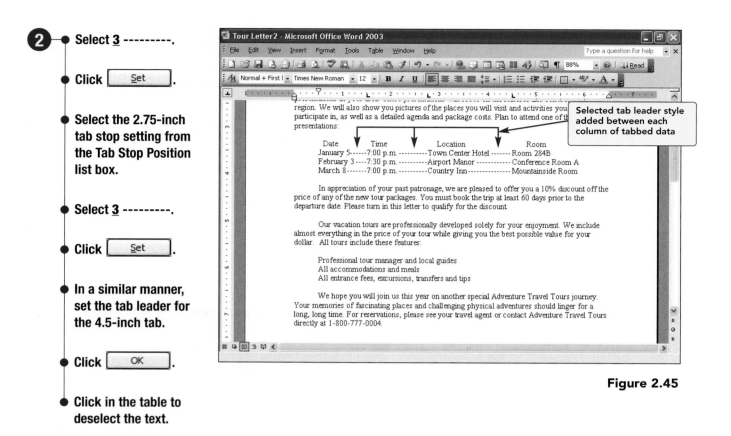

Figure 2.45

The selected leader style has been added to the blank space between each column of tabbed text.

Changing Line Spacing

You also want to increase the spacing between the lines in the table to make the presentation data even easier to read.

8 Adjusting the **line spacing**, or the vertical space between lines of text, helps set off areas of text from others and when increased makes it easier to read and edit text. The default setting of single line spacing accommodates the largest font in that line, plus a small amount of extra space. If a line contains a character or object, such as a graphic, that is larger than the surrounding text, the spacing for that line is automatically adjusted. Additional line spacing settings are described in the table below.

Spacing	Effect
1.5 lines	Spacing is one and a half times that of single line spacing.
Double (2.0)	Spacing is twice that of single line spacing.
At least	Uses a value specified in points as the minimum line spacing that is needed to fit the largest font or graphic on the line.
Exactly	Uses a value specified in points as a fixed line spacing amount that is not adjusted, making all lines evenly spaced. Graphics or text that is too large will appear clipped.
Multiple	Uses a percentage value to increase or decrease the spacing. For example, 1.3 will increase the spacing by 33 percent.

In addition to changing line spacing within paragraphs, you can also change the spacing before or after paragraphs. For example, the line spacing of text within paragraphs could be set to single and the spacing between paragraphs to double.

1 ● Select the table including the heading line.

● Open the 🔀 Line Spacing drop down menu.

Another Method

The menu equivalent is **Fo**rmat/**P**aragraph/**I**ndents and Spacing/**Li**ne Spacing

● Choose 1.5 lines from the Line Spacing drop-down list.

Another Method

You can also use Ctrl + # to change the line spacing to the number specified.

● Click in the table to deselect the text.

Your screen should be similar to Figure 2.46

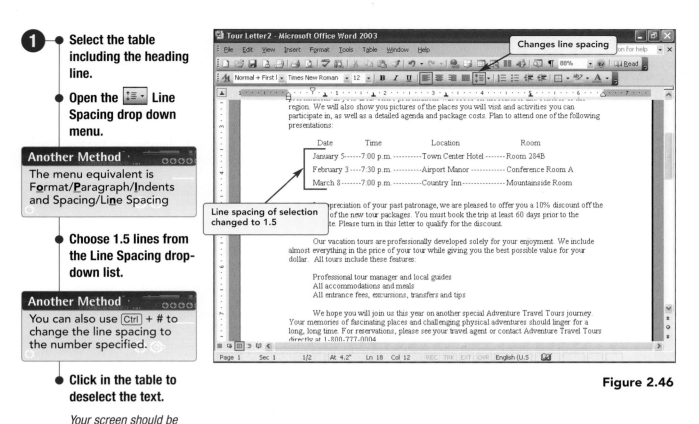

Figure 2.46

The line spacing within the selection has increased to 1.5 lines.

More Character Formatting

As you look at the letter, you still feel that the table of presentation dates and times does not stand out enough. You can add emphasis to information in your documents by formatting specific characters or words. Applying color shading behind text is commonly used to identify areas of text that you want to stand out. It is frequently used to mark text that you want to locate easily as you are revising a document. Italics, underlines, and bold are other character formats that add emphasis and draw the reader's attention to important items. Word applies character formatting to the entire selection or to the entire word at the insertion point. You can apply formatting to a portion of a word by selecting the area to be formatted first.

Adding Color Highlighting

First, you want to see how a color highlight behind the tabbed table of presentation times and locations would look.

1 • Open the Highlight drop-down list.

• Select the turquoise color from the color palette.

Additional Information
The mouse pointer appears as ✍ when positioned on text, indicating the highlighting feature is on.

• Select the entire table.

Another Method
You can also select the area you want to highlight first and then click 🖉 to apply the current color selection.

• Click 🖉 to turn off the highlighting feature.

Your screen should be similar to Figure 2.47

Another Method
You can also press Esc to turn off highlighting.

Additional Information
When you use highlights in a document you plan to print in black and white, select a light color so the text is visible.

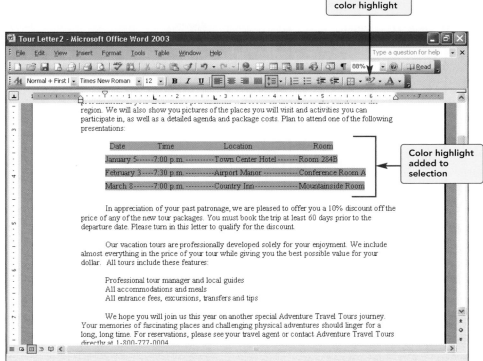

Figure 2.47

Although the highlight makes the table stand out, it does not look good.

Underlining Text

Instead, you decide to bold and underline the headings. The default underline style is a single black line. In addition, Word includes 15 other types of underlines.

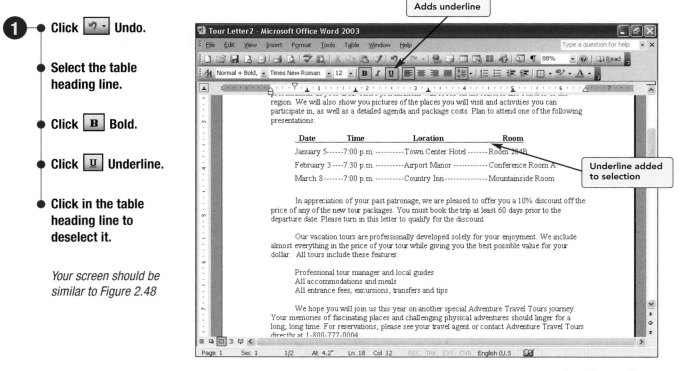

1
- Click ↺ Undo.

- Select the table heading line.

- Click **B** Bold.

- Click U Underline.

- Click in the table heading line to deselect it.

Your screen should be similar to Figure 2.48

Figure 2.48

All the words are bold, and a single black underline has been added below the entire selection. You decide you want the underline to appear under each word only and to stand out more. To do this, you will select another underline style and apply the underline to the word individually. When the insertion point is positioned on a word, the selected underline style is applied to the entire word.

2
- Click 🔄 Undo to remove the underline.
- Deselect the heading line.
- Right-click on the "Date" heading in the table.
- Choose **F**ont from the shortcut menu.
- If necessary, open the Font tab.
- Open the **U**nderline style drop-down list box.

Your screen should be similar to Figure 2.49

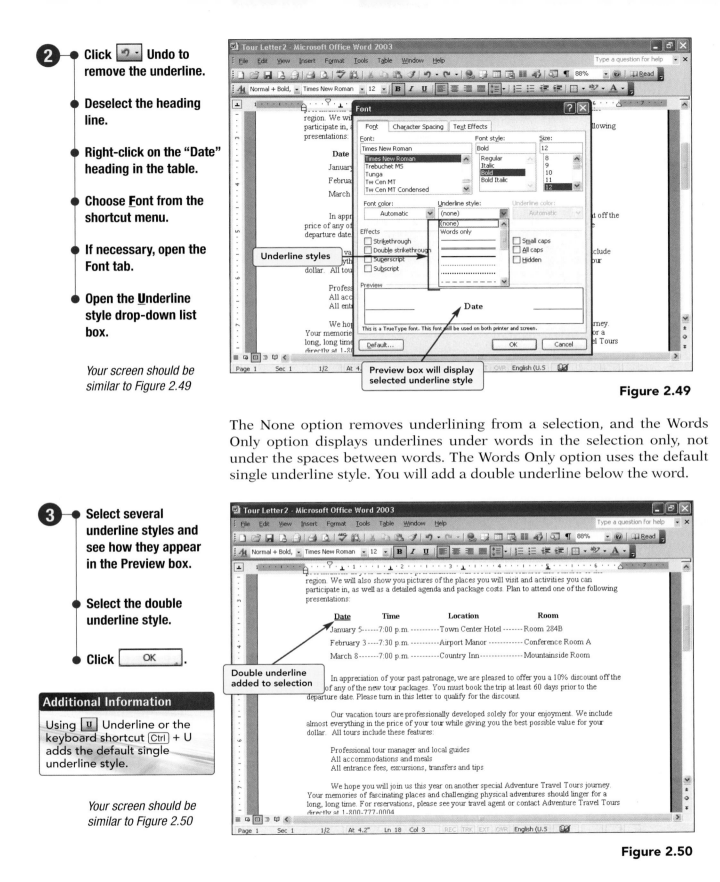

Figure 2.49

The None option removes underlining from a selection, and the Words Only option displays underlines under words in the selection only, not under the spaces between words. The Words Only option uses the default single underline style. You will add a double underline below the word.

3
- Select several underline styles and see how they appear in the Preview box.
- Select the double underline style.
- Click [OK].

Additional Information

Using 🅄 Underline or the keyboard shortcut [Ctrl] + U adds the default single underline style.

Your screen should be similar to Figure 2.50

Figure 2.50

The selected word is underlined using the double underline style.

Copying Formats with Format Painter

You want to quickly apply the same formats to the other headings. To do this you can use the **Format Painter**. This feature applies the formats associated with the current selection to new selections. If the selection is a paragraph (including the paragraph mark), the formatting is applied to the entire paragraph. If the selection is a character, the format is applied to a character, word, or selection you specify. To turn on the feature, move the insertion point to the text whose formats you want to copy and click the Format Painter button. Then select the text to which you want the formats applied. The format is automatically applied to an entire word simply by clicking on the word. To apply the format to more or less text, you must select the area. If you double-click the Format Painter button, you can apply the format multiple times.

1
- If necessary, click on the "Date" heading.
- Double-click Format Painter.
- Click on the "Time" and "Location" headings.
- Click to turn off Format Painter.

Another Method

You can press Esc to turn off Format Painter.

Your screen should be similar to Figure 2.51

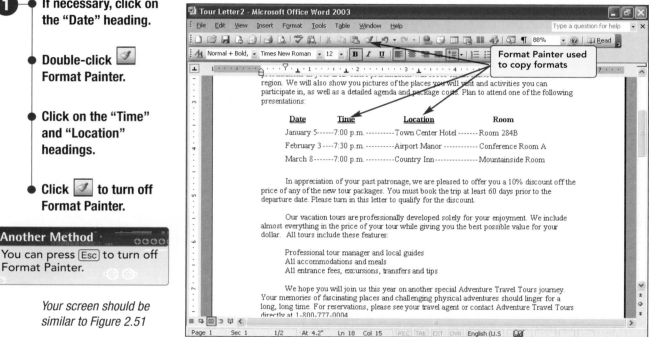

Figure 2.51

Applying Formats Using the Styles and Formatting Task Pane

The last heading to format is Room. Another way to apply existing formatting is to use the Styles and Formatting task pane.

Task pane

1 ● Click **44** **Styles and Formatting on the Formatting toolbar.**

Another Method

The menu equivalent is **Format/Styles and Formatting.**

Your screen should be similar to Figure 2.52

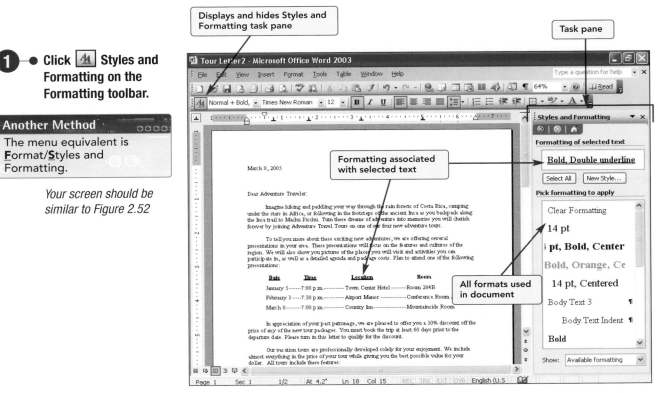

Formatting associated with selected text

All formats used in document

Figure 2.52

Using the Styles and Formatting task pane, you can apply styles, create new styles, and modify existing styles. The formatting associated with the selected text appears in the Formatting of Selected text box at the top of the pane. The names of all other formats available are listed in the Pick Formatting to Apply list box. The names are in alphabetical order and are displayed using the associated formatting. To apply an existing format to a selection, you can pick the format from this list.

2 ● Click on the "Room" table heading.

● Scroll the list box and click Bold, Double underline .

Your screen should be similar to Figure 2.53

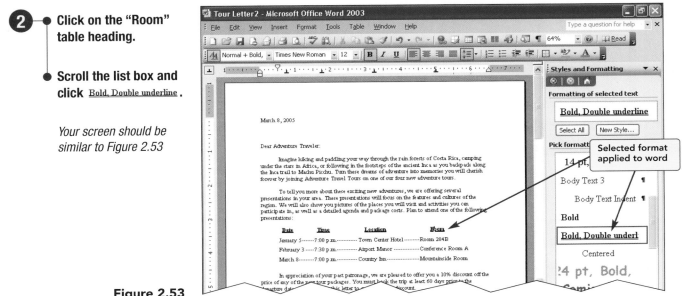

Selected format applied to word

Figure 2.53

The selected formatting is applied to the word.

3 ● Click 🔤 **Styles and Formatting** to hide the task pane.

● **Save the document again.**

Creating Lists

The next change you want to make is to display the three lines of information about tour features as an itemized list so that they stand out better from the surrounding text.

Concept 9
Bulleted and Numbered Lists

9 Whenever possible, add bullets or numbers before items in a list to organize information and to make your writing clear and easy to read. Word includes many basic bullet, a dot or other symbol, and number formats from which you can select. Additionally, there are many picture bullets available. If none of the predesigned bullet or number formats suits your needs, you can also create your own customized designs.

Use a **bulleted list** when you have several items in a paragraph that logically make a list. A bulleted list displays one of several styles of bullets before each item in the list. You can select from several types of symbols to use as bullets and you can change the color, size, and position of the bullet.

Use a **numbered list** when you want to convey a sequence of events, such as a procedure that has steps to follow in a certain order. A numbered list displays numbers or letters before the text. Word automatically increments the number or letter as you start a new paragraph. You can select from several different numbering schemes to create your numbered lists.

Use an **outline numbered list** to display multiple outline levels that show a hierarchical structure of the items in the list. There can be up to nine levels.

Numbering a List

Because both bullet and number formats will indent the items automatically when applied, you first need to remove the indent from the three tour features. Then you will try a numbered list format to see how it looks.

1 ● **Select the three tour features.**

   ● **Drag the First Line Indent marker on the ruler back to the margin boundary.**

   ● **Right-click on the selection and choose Bullets and Numbering.**

Another Method

The menu equivalent is Format/Bullets and Numbering.

   ● **Open the Numbered tab.**

Your screen should be similar to Figure 2.54

Figure 2.54

Additional Information

The None option is used to remove an existing numbering format.

The Bullets and Numbering dialog box displays examples of seven built-in numbered list formats. You can also change the appearance of the built-in formats using the Customize option. For example, you could change the color of the number for the entire list. You will use the second number format.

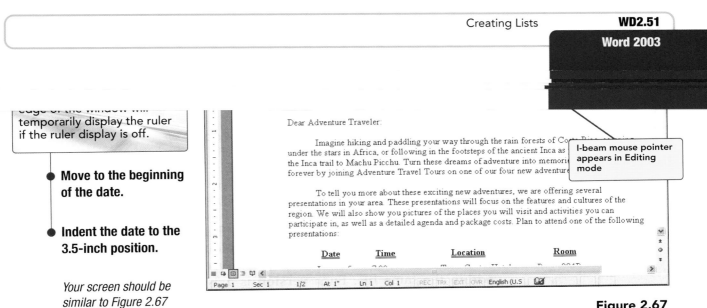

temporarily display the ruler if the ruler display is off.

   ● **Move to the beginning of the date.**

   ● **Indent the date to the 3.5-inch position.**

Your screen should be similar to Figure 2.67

Figure 2.67

1
- Return the zoom to Page Width.
- Press Ctrl + Home to move to the top of the document.
- Click 🔍 Print Preview.
- Click ⊞ Multiple pages and select 1x2 pages.

2
- Click OK to complete the command.
- Switch to the Tour Letter2 document.
- Click on the AutoShape (not the text) to select it.
- Click 📋 Copy.
- Switch back to the flyer and paste the banner at the bottom of the flyer.
- Position the banner appropriately.
- Choose File/Versions
- Click Save Now...
- Type Banner in the Comments text box.

Your screen should be similar to Figure 2.70

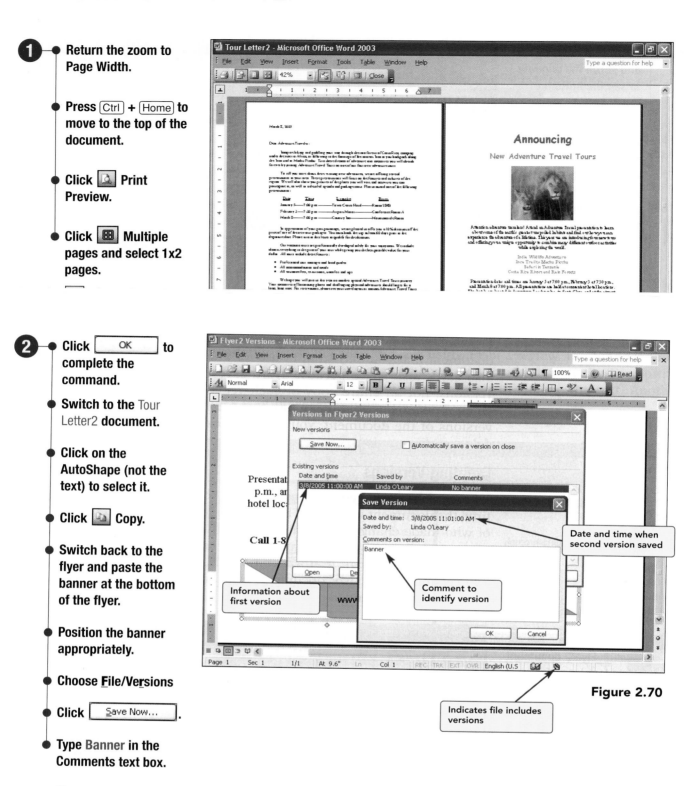

Figure 2.70

The first version you created is displayed in the Versions dialog box. The version information includes the date and time the version was saved, the name of the person who saved each version, and the comment. The second version will be added to this list when you complete the command. The most recent version always appears at the top of the list.

Opening a Version

Once a version has been created, you can go back and open, print, and delete earlier versions. You will open the "No banner" version.

1 ● Click [OK] to complete the command.

● Choose **File/Versions**.

● Select the "No banner" version from the list box.

● Click [Open].

● Scroll the windows to see the bottom of each document.

Your screen should be similar to Figure 2.71

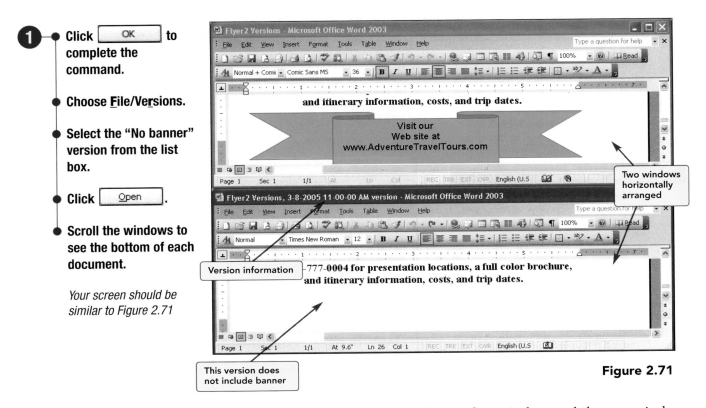

Two windows horizontally arranged

Version information

This version does not include banner

Figure 2.71

The "No banner" version is open in another window and the two windows are horizontally arranged on the screen. The version information appears in the title bar. You can view and print the version document. If you edit a document version, the revision needs to be saved as a new document file.

2 ● Close the "No banner" version window.

● Maximize and then close the Flyer2 Versions **window**.

● Close and save the Tour Letter2 **document**.

● Exit Word.

● If a question dialog box appears about a picture in the Clipboard, click [No].

Focus on Careers

EXPLORE YOUR CAREER OPTIONS

Assistant Broadcast Producer
Have you wondered who does the background research for a film or television broadcast? Or who is responsible for making sure a film production runs on schedule? Assistant producers are responsible for background research and the daily operations of a shooting schedule. They may also produce written materials for broadcast. These written materials are often compiled from multiple documents and sources. The typical salary range for an assistant broadcast producer is $27,000 to $38,000. Demand for those with relevant training and experience is expected to continue in this competitive job market.

lab review

key terms

active window   WD2.18

antonym   WD2.10

AutoFormat   WD2.59

AutoShape   WD2.55

bulleted list   WD2.50

case sensitive   WD2.24

destination   WD2.12

drag and drop   WD2.16

field   WD2.27

field code   WD2.27

field result   WD2.27

Format Painter   WD2.48

hard page break   WD2.20

hyperlink   WD2.58

indent   WD2.34

leader character   WD2.41

line spacing   WD2.43

numbered list   WD2.50

Office clipboard   WD2.12

outline numbered list   WD2.50

page break   WD2.20

page margin   WD2.30

soft page break   WD2.20

source   WD2.12

synonym   WD2.10

system Clipboard   WD2.12

tab stop   WD2.36

thesaurus   WD2.10

URL   WD2.58

version   WD2.64

mos skills

The Microsoft Office Specialist (MOS) certification program is designed to measure your proficiency in performing basic tasks using the Office 2003 applications. Getting certified demonstrates that you have the skills and provides a valuable industry credential for employment. After completing this lab, you have learned the following Microsoft Office Word Specialist skills:

Skill	Description	Page
Creating Content	Insert and edit text, symbols, and special characters	WD2.12
	Insert frequently used and predefined text	WD2.53
	Insert, position, and size graphics	WD2.55
	Navigate to specific content	WD2.22
Organizing Content	Create bulleted and numbered lists and outlines	WD2.50
	Insert and modify hyperlinks	WD2.58
Formatting Content	Format text	WD2.45
	Format paragraphs	WD2.33
	Modify document layout and page setup	WD2.29
Formatting and Managing Documents	Print documents, envelopes, and labels	WD2.64
	Preview documents and Web pages	WD2.61
	Change and organize document views and windows	WD2.18

command summary

Command	Shortcut Key	Button	Voice	Action
File/Page Set**u**p				Changes layout of page including margins, paper size, and paper source
File/Ve**r**sions				Saves, opens, and deletes document versions
Edit/Cu**t**	Ctrl + X	✂	Cut	Cuts selection to Clipboard
Edit/**C**opy	Ctrl + C	📋	Copy	Copies selection to Clipboard
Edit/**P**aste	Ctrl + V	📋	Paste	Pastes item from Clipboard
Edit/**F**ind	Ctrl + F			Locates specified text
Edit/R**e**place	Ctrl + H			Locates and replaces specified text
Insert/**B**reak/**P**age break	Ctrl + ↵Enter			Inserts hard page break
Insert/Date and **T**ime				Inserts current date or time, maintained by computer system, in selected format
Insert/**A**utoText				Enters predefined text
Insert/**A**utoText/AutoTe**x**t				Creates new AutoText entries
Insert/**P**icture/**A**utoShapes		AutoShapes ▾		Inserts selected AutoShape
F**o**rmat/**F**ont/Fon**t**/**U**nderline style/Single	Ctrl + U	U		Underlines selected text with a single line
F**o**rmat/**P**aragraph/**I**ndents and Spacing/Special/First Line	Tab			Indents first line of paragraph from left margin
F**o**rmat/**P**aragraph/**I**ndents and Spacing/Line Spacing	Ctrl + #	‡≡ ▾		Changes amount of white space between lines
F**o**rmat/Bullets and **N**umbering		≣ ≣		Creates a bulleted or numbered list
F**o**rmat /**T**abs				Specifies types and positions of tab stops
Format/**S**tyles and Formatting		🅰		Displays the Styles and Formatting task pane

command summary (continued)

Command	Shortcut Key	Button	Voice	Action
Tools/**S**pelling and Grammar	F7	ABC✓		Starts Spelling and Grammar Checker
Tools/**L**anguage/Thesaurus	⇧ Shift + F7			Starts Thesaurus tool
Window/Compare Side **b**y Side				Displays two document windows side by side to make it easy to compare content

matching

Match the item on the left with the correct description on the right.

1. field   _____   **a.** indents first line of paragraph

2. Tab   _____   **b.** mouse procedure that moves or copies a selection to a new
location

3. synonyms   _____   **c.** placeholder that instructs Word to insert information into a
document

4. destination   _____   **d.** automatically inserted by Word to start a new page when a
previous page is filled with text

5. drag and drop   _____   **e.** location of copied text

6. active window   _____   **f.** saved "snapshot" of a document

7. soft page break   _____   **g.** words with similar meaning

8. version   _____   **h.** document window displaying the insertion point

9. leader character   _____   **i.** vertical space between lines of text

10. line spacing   _____   **j.** solid, dotted, or dashed lines between tab stops

11. Ctrl + ←Enter

multiple choice

Circle the correct response to the questions below.

1. The _____ is a reference tool that provides synonyms and antonyms.
  a. find and replace feature
  b. AutoText feature
  c. thesaurus
  d. Clipboard

2. A _____ marks the point at which one page ends and another begins.
  a. leader character
  b. selection point
  c. field code
  d. page break

3. The _____ feature makes certain formatting changes automatically to your document.
  a. AutoText
  b. AutoComplete
  c. AutoFormat
  d. AutoCorrect

4. The field _____ contains the directions that tell Word the type of information to insert.
   a. results
   b. code
   c. placeholder
   d. format

5. The blank space around the edge of the page is called the _____ .
   a. gutter
   b. indent
   c. margin
   d. white space

6. The information that is displayed as a result of a field is called _____.
   a. a field code
   b. a field result
   c. case sensitive
   d. a wildcard

7. To convey a sequence of events in a document, you should consider using a _____ .
   a. bulleted list
   b. numbered list
   c. organization list
   d. paragraph list

8. A _____ is a Web site address.
   a. URL
   b. RUL
   c. WSL
   d. ULR

9. The feature most useful for copying or moving short distances in a document is _____ .
   a. drag and drop
   b. drop and drag
   c. move and place
   d. drag and place

10. _____ is a feature that applies the formats associated with a selection to another selection.
   a. Format Painter
   b. Find and Replace
   c. AutoFormat
   d. AutoShapes

true/false

Circle the correct answer to the following questions.

1. The spelling checker identifies synonyms for common words. True False
2. Formatting and text editing can be done in the Print Preview window. True False
3. Indents are used to set paragraphs off from the rest of the text. True False
4. The Find and Replace feature is used to locate misspelled words
   in a document. True False
5. A bulleted list conveys a sequence of events. True False
6. A source is the location from which text is moved or copied. True False
7. Soft page breaks are automatically inserted whenever the text reaches
   the bottom margin. True False
8. Using document versions creates separate files of different versions
   of a document. True False
9. AutoCorrect entries are used to insert commonly used words or
   phrases into a document. True False
10. A hyperlink is a connection to a location in the current document,
    another document, or to a Web site. True False

fill-in

1. As you add or remove text from a page, Word automatically _____ the placement of the soft
   page break.

2. A(n) _____ code instructs Word to insert the current date in the document using the selected
   format whenever the document is printed.

3. Standard single-sided documents have four _____: top, bottom, left, and right.

4. Double-sided documents with facing pages typically use _____ margins.

5. Text and graphic selections can be _____ to new locations in a document, saving time.

6. In a _____ style letter, all parts are aligned with the left margin. _____ and _____
   organize information and make your writing clear and easy to read.

7. Multiple _____ in a file provide "snapshots" of a document at specific times.

8. The _____ feature makes certain formatting changes automatically to your document.

9. Two types of page breaks that can be used in a document are: _____ and _____.

10. When a selection is moved or copied, the selection is stored in the _____ Clipboard, a
    temporary Windows storage area in memory.

Hands-On Exercises

step-by-step

Finalizing the Water Conservation Article ★

1. You are still working on the column for the utility company newsletter. You need to add information to the article and make several formatting changes to the document. Your completed article is shown here:

a. Open the document wd02_Conservation Tips.

b. Find and replace all occurrences of "H₂O" with "water." Spell and grammar-check the document.

c. Open the document Water Conservation you created in Step-by-Step Exercise 5 in Lab 1. Find and replace "%" with "percent." Display the document windows side-by-side. Copy the tips from the wd02_Conservation Tips document to the appropriate category in the Water Conservation article. Close the wd02_Conservation Tips document.

d. Change the line spacing of the tips to single spaced.

e. Save the document using the file name Water Conservation2.

f. Change the top and bottom margins to .75 inch. Change the right and left margins to 1 inch.

g. Apply three different bullet styles to the tips under the three categories. Indent the bulleted tips to the .75-inch position.

How Can I Conserve Water?

Nearly 75 percent of water used indoors is in the bathroom with baths, showers and toilet flushing account for most of this. If you have a lawn, chances are that this is your main water use. Typically, at least 50 percent of water consumed by households is used outdoors. The City's Water Conservation Program has many publications that offer suggestions to help you conserve water. Some of these suggestions include:

Personal Use Tips
o Take short showers instead of baths
o Run dishwashers and clothes washers with full loads only, or adjust water level to load size
o Turn the water off when brushing your teeth or shaving
o Keep a jug of cold water in the refrigerator instead of letting the tap run until cool

Repair Tips
➤ Install low-flow showerheads or flow restrictors
➤ Check your toilet for leaks by placing a few drops of food coloring in the tank. If it shows up in the bowl, replace the flapper
➤ Replace older toilets with new low-flow toilets or place a plastic jug filled with water in the tank to displace some of the water
➤ Repair dripping faucets by replacing washers
➤ Check for hidden leaks by monitoring your WATER meter
➤ Insulate your WATER pipes – you'll get hot WATER faster and avoid wasting WATER while it heats up

Outdoor Tips
• When washing the car, use soap and water from a bucket. Use a hose with a shut-off nozzle for the final rinse
• Plant low-WATER use and native plants instead of turf
• Clean your driveway with a broom, not a hose
• Adjust irrigation when the seasons change
• Adjust sprinkler so only the lawn is Watered, not the sidewalk or street
• Don't WATER on windy days
• When mowing, raise the blade level to its highest level. Close cut grass makes the roots work harder, requiring more WATER

Visit us for more water conservation tips at www.watertips.com

Student Name-2/3/2005

h. Use the thesaurus to find a better word for "biggest" in the first paragraph. Indent the first paragraph.

i. Below the last group of tips, add the text **Visit us for more water conservation tips at www.watertips.com**. Remove the hyperlink formatting. Format this line using the same format as the tip category headings. Add a color highlight to the line.

j. Replace the date in the last line with a date field.

k. Preview the document and, if necessary, reduce the size of the graphic to make the entire document fit on one page. Print the document.

l. Save the document using the same file name.

Expanding the Note-Taking Skills Handout ★

2. You are still working on the handout for your lecture on note-taking. You have several more tips you need to add to the document. You also want to rearrange the order of the tips and make several formatting changes to the document. Your completed document is shown here.

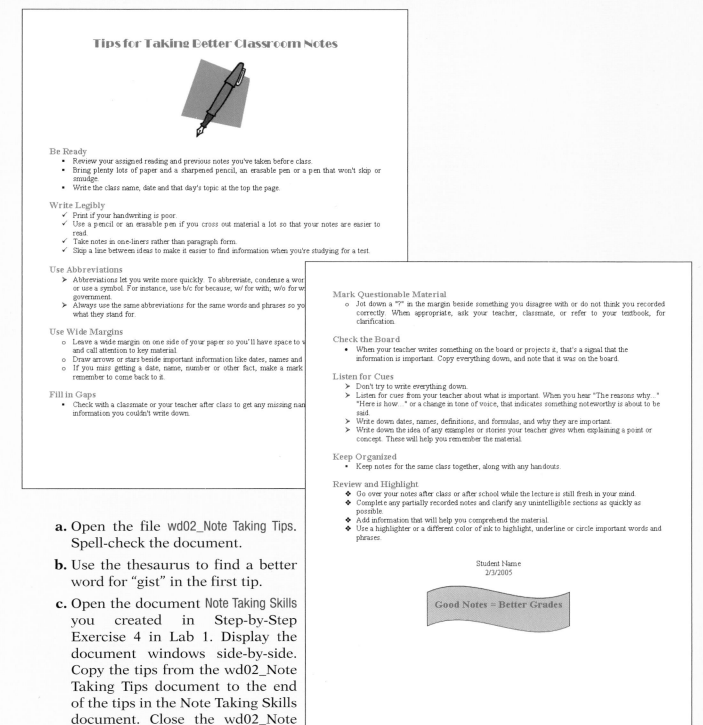

a. Open the file wd02_Note Taking Tips. Spell-check the document.

b. Use the thesaurus to find a better word for "gist" in the first tip.

c. Open the document Note Taking Skills you created in Step-by-Step Exercise 4 in Lab 1. Display the document windows side-by-side. Copy the tips from the wd02_Note Taking Tips document to the end of the tips in the Note Taking Skills document. Close the wd02_Note Taking Tips document.

d. Use Format Painter to change the format of the new headings to the same as the existing headings.

e. Move the Use Abbreviations tip below the Write Legibly tip. Move the Check the Board and Listen for Cues tips below the Mark Questionable Materials tip.

f. Change the left and right and top margins to.75 inch.

g. Break the tips under each topic heading into separate bulleted items using bullet styles of your choice. (A bulleted item may be more than one sentence if it contains an explanation or is a continuation of the same tip topic.)

h. Preview the document and insert a hard page break above the Mark Questionable Materials topic heading while previewing it.

i. Add the AutoShape "Wave" symbol from the Stars and Banners category to the document.

j. Add the text **Good Notes = Better Grades** to the shape. Bold, center, and size the text to 16 pt. Size the AutoShape to just large enough to display the text in a single line.

k. Add a fill color to the shape and color to the text to complement the colors you used in the document. Move the AutoShape to below your name. Delete the drawing canvas.

l. Replace the date in the last line with a date field using a format of your choice.

m. Save the document as Note Taking Skills2, preview and print it.

Promoting a Yoga Class ★ ★

3. The Lifestyle Fitness Club has just started a new series of yoga classes. You want to spread the word by creating a flyer for club members to pick up at the front desk. You have created a Word document with the basic information that you want to include in the flyer. Now you just need to make it look better. Your completed flyer is shown here:

a. Open the file wd02_Yoga Flyer.

b. Find each occurrence of "Yoga" and replace it with "yoga" wherever it is not at the beginning of a sentence or wherever it is not part of a class title. Find and replace all occurrences of "mins" with "minutes."

c. Use the spelling and grammar checker to correct the identified errors.

d. Bold, color, and center both title lines. Increase the font size of the main title line to 24 and the second title line to 18.

e. Set the right and left margins to 1 inch and the top and bottom margins to .7 inch.

f. Center the introductory paragraph. Set line spacing for the first paragraph to 1.5.

g. Bold, color, center and increase the font size to 14 of the three headings: Class Description, October Schedule, and Costs.

h. Use drag and drop to move the Yoga for Athletes class description below the Yoga for Beginners description. Adjust the line spacing as needed between descriptions. Highlight the three class names in yellow.

i. Add a bullet style of your choice to each of the three class description paragraphs.

j. Create a tabbed table of the schedule. Bold, underline, and add color to the table heads: Day, Time, Length, and Class. Use center tab styles for the Day and Class heads and center them over the columns. Add tab leaders of your choice between the Time, Length, and Class columns of data.

k. Create a tabbed table of the costs. Bold, underline, and add color to the two table heads, Series and Cost. Center tab the Series head over the column. Add a tab leader style of your choice between the Series and Cost columns of data.

l. Add the AutoShape "No" symbol from the Basic Shapes menu to the document.

m. Add the text **Stress** to the shape. Bold, center, and size the text to 18 pt. Center the text vertically in the shape by adding a blank line above it. Size the AutoShape to just large enough to display the text in a single line.

n. Add a red fill color to the shape and green color to the text. Move the AutoShape to the space to the left of the title lines. Delete the drawing canvas.

o. Add your name and the current date as a field on the last line on the page.

p. Save the document as Yoga Flyer. Print the document.

Orientation Meeting Schedule ★ ★ ★

4. The Animal Rescue Foundation is actively seeking volunteers to help support the organization. You are preparing an article to run in the newspaper promoting the organization and asking for volunteer help. In anticipation of attracting many new volunteers, the organization plans to hold extra Volunteer Orientation meetings for better convenience. You want to create a separate informational flyer about the schedule to give to volunteers. You also decide to include the orientation schedule in the article. Your completed document is shown here.

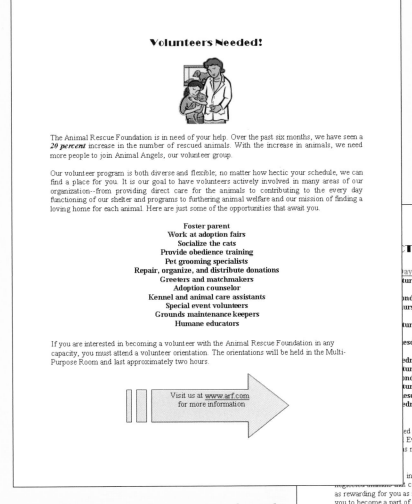

a. Open a new document and set the left and right page margins to 1 inch.

b. On the first line center the title **OCTOBER ORIENTATION SCHEDULE**. Apply formats of your choice to the title line.

c. Several lines below the title, type the following paragraphs:

If you are interested in becoming a volunteer with the Animal Rescue Foundation in any capacity, you must attend a volunteer meeting. The meetings will be held in the Multi-Purpose Room and last approximately two hours.

After you have attended a meeting, you will be called for a short interview in which you and our Volunteer/Special Events Coordinator can discuss your specific interests and availability. Additional meetings may be necessary depending on your interests (i.e., Animal Care/Handling).

d. Spell-check the document. Use the thesaurus to find a better word for "short" in the second paragraph.

e. Find and replace all occurrences of "meeting" with "orientation." Correct any identified grammar errors.

f. Set the line spacing of the paragraphs to double.

g. Several lines below the last paragraph, place center tab stops at 1½, 3⅛, and 4½ inches on the ruler.

h. Enter the word **Day** at the first tab stop, **Date** at the second tab stop, and **Time** at the third tab stop.

i. Using a left tab at 1¼ and 2¾ and a right tab stop at 5, enter the schedule information shown here into the table.

Saturday	October 5	10:00 A.M.
		1:00 P.M.
Monday	October 7	7:00 P.M.
Thursday	October 10	10:00 A.M.
		7:00 P.M.
Saturday	October 12	9:00 A.M.
		3:00 P.M.
Tuesday	October 15	10:00 A.M.
		7:00 P.M.
Wednesday	October 16	7:00 P.M.
Saturday	October 19	10:00 A.M.
Monday	October 21	7:00 P.M.
Saturday	October 26	1:00 P.M.
Tuesday	October 29	7:00 P.M.
Wednesday	October 30	10:00 A.M.
		7:00 P.M.

j. Change the font size of the table headings to 14 points, bold, and the same color as the title. Add an underline style of your choice to the table headings. Bold the text in the remainder of the table.

k. Move the second paragraph below the table.

l. Add your name and the current date as a field several lines below the last paragraph.

(continued on next page)

m. Save the document as Orientation Schedule.

n. Open the Volunteers Needed document you created in Lab 1, Step-by-Step Exercise 2. Set the left and right page margins to 1 inch.

o. Save the document as Volunteers Needed2.

p. Display the document windows side-by-side. Copy the text and the table from the Orientation Schedule document to below the list of volunteer jobs. Change the spacing of the copied paragraph to single spaced. Make any adjustments to the table as needed.

q. Apply the same formatting to the table title as you used in the article title. Insert a hard page break above the table title.

r. Move the paragraph that begins "If you are interested…" to the bottom of page one.

s. Create an AutoShape of your choice and add the text **Visit us at www.arf.com for more information**. Size the AutoShape appropriately. Remove the hyperlink format from the URL. Add color to the URL. Add a fill color to the AutoShape. Center the AutoShape at the bottom of the first page. Remove the drawing canvas.

t. Highlight the last line in the Volunteers Needed2 document.

u. Change the date to a date field. Save, preview, and print the Volunteers Needed2 document.

v. Create a version in the Orientation Schedule file with the comment "No AutoShape." Copy the AutoShape from Volunteers Needed2 to the bottom of the Orientation Schedule document. Center it. Save this version as "AutoShape." Preview and print the AutoShape version of the document (shown at right).

OCTOBER ORIENTATION SCHEDULE

If you are interested in becoming a volunteer with the Animal Rescue Foundation in any capacity, you must attend a volunteer orientation. The orientations will be held in the Multi-Purpose Room and last approximately two hours.

Day	Date	Time
Saturday	October 5	10:00 a.m.
		1:00 p.m.
Monday	October 7	7:00 p.m.
Thursday	October 10	10:00 a.m.
		7:00 p.m.
Saturday	October 12	9:00 a.m.
		3:00 p.m.
Tuesday	October 15	10:00 a.m.
		7:00 p.m.
Wednesday	October 16	7:00 p.m.
Saturday	October 19	10:00 a.m.
Monday	October 21	7:00 p.m.
Saturday	October 26	1:00 p.m.
Tuesday	October 29	7:00 p.m.
Wednesday	October 30	10:00 a.m.
		7:00 p.m.

After you have attended a orientation, you will be called for a brief interview in which you and our Volunteer/Special Events Coordinator can discuss your specific interests and availability. Additional orientations may be necessary depending on your interest (i.e., Animal Care/Handling).

Visit us at www.arf.com
for more information

Student Name

February 16, 2005

Advertising Weekly Specials ★ ★ ★

5. Now that the Downtown Internet Cafe has had its grand opening celebration, the owner wants to continue to bring in new and repeat customers by offering weekly specials. You want to create a flyer describing the roast coffee varieties and specials for the week. Your completed flyer is shown here.

a. Open a new document.

b. Enter the title **Downtown Internet Cafe** on the first line. Add three blank lines.

c. Enter **Roast Coffee** on line 4 followed by two blank lines.

d. Center the first line and change the font color to blue with a font size of 48 pt.

e. Center the second line and change it to blue with a font size of 22 pt.

f. On line 7, place a left tab stop at .5 and center tabs at 2.5 and 4.5 inches.

g. Enter the word **Coffee** at the first tab stop, **Description** at the second tab stop, and **Cost/Pound** at the third tab stop.

h. Enter the rest of the information for the table shown in the final document using left tabs at .5, 2, and 5.

i. Add tab leaders of your choice between the data in the table.

j. Increase the font of the table headings to 14 pt. Add bold, color, and an underline style of your choice to the table headings.

Open the file wd02_Coffee Flyer. Display the document windows side-by-side. Copy the first two paragraphs and insert them above "Roast Coffee" in the new document.

ell-check the document. Use the thesaurus to find better words for "desire" and "giant" in the paragraph.

ind and Replace to replace all occurrences of "java" with "coffee" (except the one following owered").

e words "Coffee Sale" below the title. Make them bold, font size 24 pt, and a color of e.

ragraph that begins with "Tired" bold, centered, and 14 pt, and set their line spacing d blue color to the URL.

Downtown Internet Café

Sale!

Coffee Sale

Tired of brewing a wimpy cup of coffee that just doesn't have the punch you crave? Then point your Web browser to *www.somecoffee.com* for our huge sale, and have our high-powered java delivered right to your front door. You'll never buy bland supermarket coffee again.

Through January, take $2 off the regular coffee prices shown below.

Roast Coffee

Coffee	Description	Cost/Pound
Colombian Blend	Classic body and aroma	$11
French Roast	Sophisticated taste	$10
Kenyan	Robust and deep flavor	$12
Arabian Blend	Strong yet subtle	$11

You can also order online at *www.somecoffee.com* today, and get coffee delivered right to your door! But hurry, our sale won't last forever.

Student Name
February 7, 2005

---

p. Increase the font size of the line above "Roast Coffee" to 18 pt. Center the text. Insert a blank line below it.

q. Copy the remaining paragraph from the wd02_Coffee Flyer document, and insert it at the bottom of the new document. Include two blank lines between the table and the paragraph.

r. Bold and center the final paragraph. Remove the hyperlink format from the URL. Format the URL as italic and blue.

s. Increase the top, left, and right margins to 1.5 inches.

t. Create the Explosion 1 AutoShape from Stars and Banners. Enter and center the word **Sale!** in red within it, size 22, and choose the gold fill color. Size the shape appropriately. Move the shape to the top left corner of the document. Delete the drawing canvas.

u. Add your name and a field with the current date several lines below the final paragraph. If necessary, adjust the formatting of the document so it fits on one page.

v. Save the document as Coffee Flyer2. Preview and print it.

on your own

Requesting a Reference ★

1. Your first year as a biology major is going well and you are looking for a summer internship with a local research lab. You have an upcoming interview and want to come prepared with a letter of reference from your last position. Write a business letter directed to your old supervisor, Rachel McVey, at your former lab, AMT Research. Use the modified block letter style shown in the lab. Be sure to include the date, a salutation, two paragraphs, a closing, and your name as a signature. Spell-check the document, save the document as Reference Letter, and print it.

Long Distance Rates Survey ★

2. American Consumer Advocates conducted a survey in October, 2002 comparing the costs of long distance rates. Create a tabbed table using the information shown below. Bold and underline the column heads. Add style 2 tab leaders to the table entries. Above the table, write a paragraph explaining the table contents.

Company	Per Minute	Monthly Fee	Customer Service Wait
Zone LD	3.5¢	$2.00	Less than 1 minute
Pioneer Telephone	3.9¢	none	1 minute
Capsule	3.9¢	none	17 minutes
ECG	4.5¢	$1.99	5 minutes
IsTerra	4.9¢	none	10 minutes

Include your name and the date below the table. Save the document as Phone Rates and print the document.

★ ★

3. Create a flyer to advertise something you have for sale (used car, stereo, computer, etc.). Integrate the following features into the flyer:

- Different fonts in different sizes, colors, and styles
- Bulleted or numbered list
- Indents
- An AutoShape
- A graphic
- A tabbed table with tab leaders

Include your name as the contact information. Save the document as For Sale Flyer and print it.

★ ★

4. You work for the City of New Orleans on a committee dedicated to attracting new residents. You have been asked to produce a relocation packet to aid people planning to move to the city. This packet includes information on local services, the weather, and the community at large. Use the information provided in the file wd02_New Orleans to create a one-page factsheet. Your completed project should include an introductory paragraph on relocation, graphics, table with the average weather statistics, a bulleted list of local attractions, and AutoShapes. Include your name as the contact and save the file as New Orleans2. Print the file.

★ ★ ★

5. Your political science class is studying the 2000 presidential election. Your instructor has divided the class into three groups and assigned each group a research project. Your group is to find out how Americans voted for the presidential candidates by age and sex. Use the Web to research this topic and write a one-page report on your findings. Include a table of the data you found. Use other features demonstrated in this lab, including AutoShapes, indents, bulleted lists, font colors, and so forth to make your report attractive and easy to read. Be sure to reference your sources on the Web for the data you located. Include your name and the current date below the report. Save the report as Election Results and print your report.

Creating Reports and Tables

LAB 3

Objectives

After you have completed this lab, you will know how to:

1 Create and modify an outline.

2 Hide spelling and grammar errors.

3 Use Click and Type, Document Map and Reading Layout.

4 Apply styles.

5 Create and update a table of contents.

6 Create a section break.

7 Center a page vertically.

8 Wrap text around graphics.

9 Add footnotes, captions, and cross-references.

10 Create and format a simple table.

11 Sort a list.

12 Add headers, footers, and page numbers.

13 Check formatting inconsistencies.

14 Print selected pages and save to a new folder.

Adventure Travel Tours

Adventure Travel Tours provides information on their tours in a variety of forms. Travel brochures, for instance, contain basic tour information in a promotional format and are designed to entice potential clients to sign up for a tour. More detailed regional information packets are given to people who have already signed up for a tour, so they can prepare for their vacation. These packets include facts about each region's climate, geography, and culture. Additional informational formats include pages on Adventure Travel's Web site and scheduled group presentations.

Part of your responsibility as advertising coordinator is to gather the information that

Adventure Travel will publicize about each regional tour. Specifically, you have been asked to provide information for two of the new tours: the Tanzania Safari and the Machu Picchu trail. Because this information is used in a variety of formats, your research needs to be easily adapted. You will therefore present your facts in the form of a general report on Tanzania and Peru.

In this lab, you will learn to use many of the features of Office Word 2003 that make it easy to create an attractive and well-organized report. A portion of the completed report is shown on the right.

© PhotoDisc

A table of contents listing can be created quickly from heading styles in a document

Page 1 (Table of Contents)

Tanzania and Peru

Table of Contents

Student Name
March 28, 2005

Page 1 (Tanzania)

Student Name 1

Tanzania

Geography and Climate

"In the midst of a great wilderness, full of wild beasts…I fancied I saw a summit…covered with a dazzlingly white cloud (qtd. in Cole 56). This is how Johann Krapf, the first outsider to witness the splendor of Africa's highest mountain, described Kilimanjaro. The peak was real, though the white clouds he "fancied" he saw were the dense layer of snow that coats the mountain.[1]

Tanzania is primarily a plateau that slopes gently downward into the country's five hundred miles of Indian Ocean coastline. Nearly three-quarters of Tanzania is dry savannah, so much so that the Swahili word for the central plateau is *nyika*, meaning "wasteland." Winding through these flatlands is the Great Rift Valley, which forms narrow and shallow lakes in its long path. Several of these great lakes form a belt-like oasis of green vegetation. Contrasting with the severity of the plains are the coastal areas, which are lush with ample rainfall. In the north the plateau slopes dramatically into Mt. Kilimanjaro.

Figure 1 - Giraffe in Serengeti

Ngorongoro Conservation Area

Some of Tanzania's most distinguishing geographical features are found in the Ngorongoro Conservation Area.[2] The park is composed of many craters and gorges, as well as lakes, forest, and plains. Among these features is the area's namesake, the Ngorongoro Crater. The Crater is a huge expanse, covering more than one hundred square miles. On the Crater's floor, grasslands blend into swamps, lakes, rivers, and woodland. Also within the Conservation Area's perimeter is the Olduvai Gorge, commonly referred to as the "Cradle of Mankind," where in 1931 the stone tools of prehistoric man were found. This find subsequently led to the discovery of the remains of humans who lived 1.75 million years ago.

Serengeti Plain

Adjacent to the western edge of the Ngorongoro Conservation Area is the Serengeti Plain. Its area is approximately 5,700 square miles, and its central savanna supports many grazing animals with plentiful water and lush grasses. Its southern portion is dry, receiving an average of only twenty inches of rainfall annually. The north is wooded grassland with watercourses and tributaries to larger rivers. Only two seasons occur on the Serengeti: dry and wet. The dry season occurs between June and October and the wet season between November to May.

---

[1] Mt. Kilimanjaro is 19,340 feet high, making it the fourth tallest mountain in the world.
[2] The Conservation Area is a national preserve spanning 3,196 square miles.

Created on 3/8/2005 1:00:00 PM

Wrapping text around graphics, adding figure captions, footnotes, headers, and footers are among many features that can be used to enhance a report

Page 3

Student Name 3

coming from the east. Some areas in the south are considered drier than the Sahara. Conversely, there are a few areas in this region where mountain rivers meet the ocean that are green with life and do not give the impression of being in a desert at all.

La Sierra

Inland and to the east is the mountainous region called La Sierra, encompassing Peru's share of the Andes mountain range. The southern portion of this region is prone to volcanic activity, and some volcanoes are active today. La Sierra is subject to a dry season from May to September, which is winter in that part of the world. Temperatures are moderate by day, and can be freezing in some areas during the night. The weather is typically sunny, with moderate annual precipitation. The former Incan capital Cuzco is in this region, as well as the Sacred Valley of the Incas. This region also contains Lake Titicaca, the world's highest navigable lake.[3]

La Selva

La Selva, a region of tropical rainforest, is the easternmost region in Peru. This region, with the eastern foot of the Andes Mountains, forms the Amazon Basin, into which numerous rivers flow. The Amazon River begins at the meeting point of the two dominant rivers, the Ucayali and Marañon. La Selva is extremely wet, with some areas exceeding an annual precipitation of 137 inches. Its wettest season occurs from November to April. The weather here is humid and extremely hot.

Region	Annual Rainfall (Inches)	Average Temperature (Fahrenheit)
La Costa	2	68
La Sierra	35	54
La Selva	137	80

Culture

Historical Culture

Peru is where the Incas built their homes and cities. They lived in the southern portion of La Sierra until around 1300 CE[4], when they moved north to the fertile Cuzco Valley. From here they built their empire, overrunning and assimilating neighboring lands and cultures. They organized into a socialist-type theocracy under an emperor—the Inca—whom they worshipped as a deity. The Inca Empire reached its maximum size by the late fifteenth and early sixteenth centuries.

In 1532 the Spanish explorer Francisco Pizarro landed in Peru. He saw great opportunity in seizing the empire because of the rich gold deposits in the Cuzco Valley, and did so with superior armament. This opened the door for masses of gold- and adventure-seeking conquistadors to join in the pursuit, who brought with them both modern weaponry and

---

[3] Lake Titicaca is 12,507 feet above sea level.
[4] Common Era (CE) is the period dating from the birth of Christ.

Created on 3/8/2005 1:00:00 PM

Including tables and using table formats make the report attractive and easy to read

Page 5

Student Name 5

Works Cited

Camerapix Publishers International. *Spectrum Guide to Tanzania*. Edison: Hunter, 1992.

Cole, Tom. *Geographic Expeditions*. San Francisco: Geographic Expeditions, 1999.

Hudson, Rex A., ed. "Peru: A Country Study." *The Library of Congress—Country Studies*. 1992. <http://lcweb2.loc.gov/frd/cs/petoc.html#pe0049> (11 Jan. 2001).

"The Living Edens: Manu—Peru's Hidden Rainforest." *PBS Online*. <http://www.pbs.org/edens/manu> (11 Jan. 2001).

Valdizan, Mónica V. "Virtual Peru." 9 Jan. 1999. http://www.xs4all.nl/~govertme/visitperu/ (11 Jan. 2001).

A list can be quickly sorted to appear in alphabetical order

The following concepts will be introduced in this lab:

1 **Style** Applying a style, a predefined set of formatting characteristics, to a selection allows you to quickly apply a whole group of formats in one simple step.

2 **Section** To format different parts of a document differently, you can divide a document into sections.

3 **Footnote and Endnote** A footnote is a source reference or text offering additional explanation that is placed at the bottom of a page. An endnote is also a source reference or long comment that typically appears at the end of a document.

4 **Text Wrapping** You can control the appearance of text around a graphic object by specifying the text wrapping style.

5 **Captions and Cross References** A caption is a numbered label for a figure, table, picture, or graph. A cross-reference is a reference from one part of a document to related information in another part.

6 **Splitting Windows** To view different parts of the document at the same time, you can create a split window by dividing the document window into two horizontal sections.

7 **Table** A table is used to organize information into an easy-to-read format of horizontal rows and vertical columns.

8 **Sort** Word can quickly arrange or sort text, numbers, or data in lists or tables in alphabetical, numeric, or date order based on the first character in each paragraph.

9 **Header and Footer** A header is a line or several lines of text in the top margin of each page. A footer is a line or several lines of text in the margin space at the bottom of every page.

Creating and Modifying an Outline

After several days of research, you have gathered many notes from various sources including books, magazines, and the Web. However, the notes are very disorganized and you are having some difficulty getting started writing the report. Often the best way to start is by creating an outline of the main topics.

Word 2003 allows you to create and view document content easily as an outline using Outline view. Outline view shows the hierarchy of topics in a document by displaying the different heading levels indented to represent their level in the document's structure, as shown in the example at right. The arrangement of headings in a hierarchy of importance

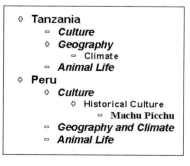

quickly shows the relationship between topics. You can use Outline view to help you create a new document or to view and reorganize the topics in an existing document.

Using Outline View

You will use Outline view to help you organize the main topics of the report.

1 ● **Start Office Word 2003.**

● **Close the task pane.**

● **Click** 📧 **Outline View.**

Your screen should be similar to Figure 3.1

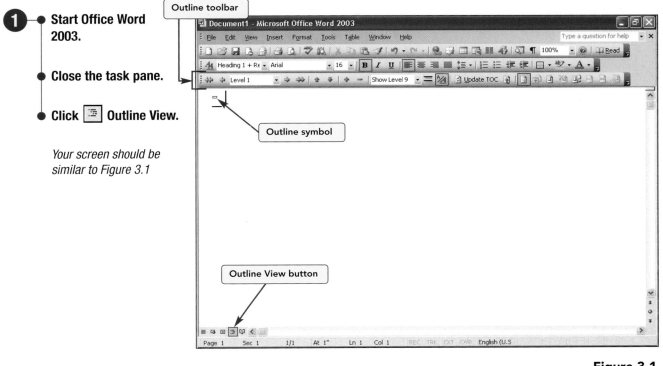

Figure 3.1

The Outline toolbar is displayed. It contains buttons that make it easy to modify the outline. The first line of the blank document displays an outline symbol. There are three outline symbols (□, ⊕, and ▫) that are used to identify the levels of topics in the outline and to quickly reorganize topics. You will begin by entering the main topic headings for the report.

2 • Type the following headings, pressing ⏎Enter after each except the last:

Tanzania

Climate

Geography

Animal Life

Peru

Culture

Historical Culture

Machu Picchu

Geography and Climate

Animal Life (**do not press** ⏎Enter)

• Correct any misspelled words and use Ignore All for any identified proper names.

Your screen should be similar to Figure 3.2

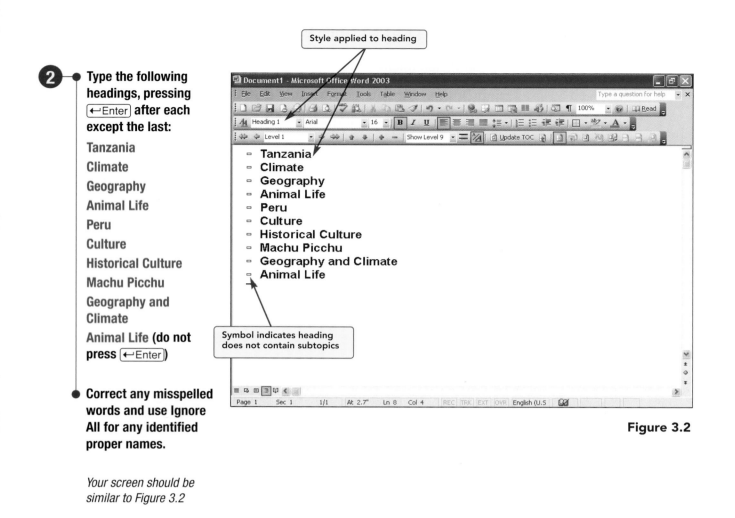

Figure 3.2

Each heading is preceded by the ⊡ outline symbol, which indicates that the heading does not contain subtopics. As you create a new document in Outline view, Word automatically applies styles to the text as it is entered in the outline.

Concept 1

Style

1 Applying a **style**, a predefined set of formatting characteristics, to a selection allows you to quickly apply a whole group of formats in one simple step. Word includes 75 predefined styles. Each style is assigned a name. You can also create your own custom styles. Many styles are automatically applied when certain features, such as footnotes, are used. Others must be applied manually to selected text.

Styles can be applied to characters, paragraphs, tables, and lists as described below.

Type of Style	Description
Character	Affects selected text within a paragraph, such as the font and size of text, and bold and italic formats.
Paragraph	Controls all aspects of a paragraph's appearance, such as text alignment, tab stops, and line spacing. It can also include character formatting. The default paragraph style is Normal, which includes character settings of Times New Roman, 12 pt, and paragraph settings of left indent at 0, single line spacing, and left alignment. In addition, many paragraph styles are designed to affect specific text elements such as headings, captions, and footnotes.
Table	Provides a consistent look to borders, shading, alignment, and fonts in tables.
List	Applies similar alignment, numbering or bullet characters, and fonts to lists.

The Style button indicates that the text is formatted as a Heading 1 style. **Heading styles** are one of the most commonly used styles. They are designed to identify different levels of headings in a document. Heading styles include combinations of fonts, type sizes, bold, and italics. The first four heading styles and the formats associated with each are shown in the table below:

Heading Level	Appearance
Heading 1	**Arial, 16 pt, bold, left align**
Heading 2	***Arial, 14 pt, bold, italic, left align***
Heading 3	**Arial, 13 pt, bold, left align**
Heading 4	**Times New Roman, 14 pt, bold, left align**

Additional Information

All Heading styles also includes 12 pt line spacing before the heading and 3 pt spacing after.

The first-level headings in a document should be assigned a Heading 1 style. This style is the largest and most prominent. The second-level headings (subheadings) should be assigned the Heading 2 style, and so on. Headings give the reader another visual cue about how information is organized in your document.

Changing Outline Levels

Next, you need to arrange the headings by outline levels. As you rearrange the topic headings and subheadings, different heading styles are applied based upon the position or level of the topic within the outline hierarchy. Headings that are level 1 appear as the top level of the outline and appear in a Heading 1 style, level 2 headings appear indented below level 1 headings and appear in a Heading 2 style, and so on.

The outline symbols are used to select and move the heading to a new location or level within the document. Dragging the outline symbol to the right or left changes the level. To demote a heading to a lower level, drag the symbol to the right; to promote a heading to a higher level, drag the symbol to the left. As you drag the symbol, a vertical solid gray line appears at each outline level to show where the heading will be placed.

First you will make the Climate topic heading a subtopic below the main heading of Tanzania.

① **Drag the ▭ symbol of the Climate heading to the right one level.**

Additional Information

The mouse pointer changes to ✛, indicating that dragging it will move the heading.

Your screen should be similar to Figure 3.3

Note that I am NOT replacing screens unless otherwise indicated.   cm

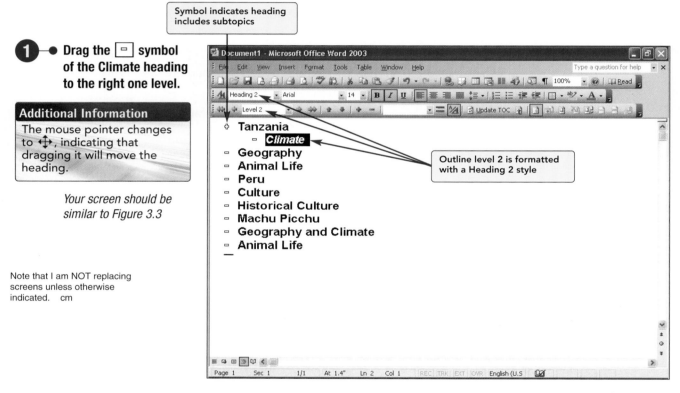

Figure 3.3

The Climate heading has changed to a Heading 2 style, and the heading is indented one level to show it is subordinate to the heading above it. The Tanzania heading now displays a ⊕ outline symbol, which indicates the topic heading includes subtopics. You can also click ⬅ Promote and ➡ Demote on the Outlining toolbar to change outline levels.

2 ● Click on the Geography topic.

● Click ➡ Demote 2 times.

● Demote the remaining topics to the heading levels shown below.

Animal Life	Level 2
Culture	Level 2
Historical Culture	Level 3
Machu Picchu	Level 4
Geography and Climate	Level 2
Animal Life	Level 2

Your screen should be similar to Figure 3.4

Figure 3.4

Another Method

You can also click ⬆ Move Up and ⬇ Move Down to move a topic.

Moving and Inserting Outline Topics

Next you want to change the order of topics. To move a heading to a different location, drag the outline symbol up or down. As you drag, a horizontal line shows where the heading will be placed when you release the mouse button.

1 ● Drag the Geography
heading up above the
Climate heading.

● Promote the
Geography heading to
a level 2.

● Demote the Climate
heading to a level 3.

*Your screen should be
similar to Figure 3.5*

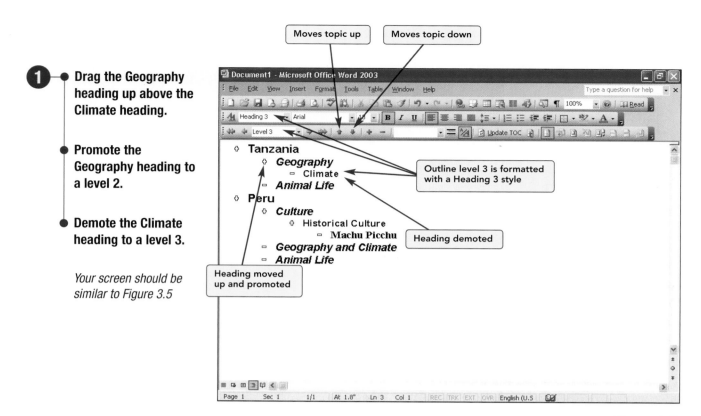

Figure 3.5

As you check the outline, you realize you forgot a heading for Culture
under Tanzania.

2 ● Move to the beginning
of the Geography
heading for Tanzania.

● Press ⏎Enter to
insert a blank topic
heading.

● Type Culture on the
blank heading line.

*Your screen should be
similar to Figure 3.6*

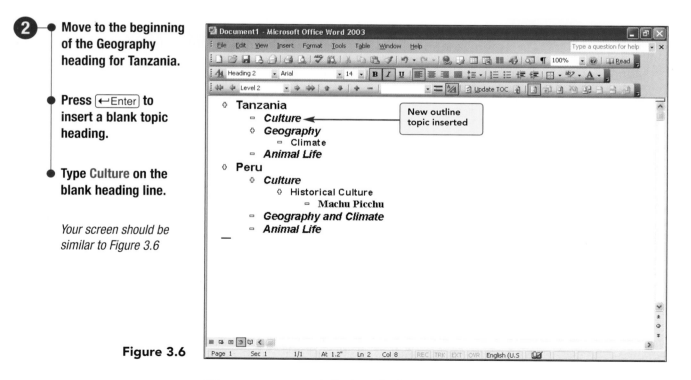

Figure 3.6

When you are satisfied with the organization, you can switch to Normal
view or Print Layout view to add detailed body text and graphics.

3 ● **Switch to Normal view.**

Your screen should be similar to Figure 3.7

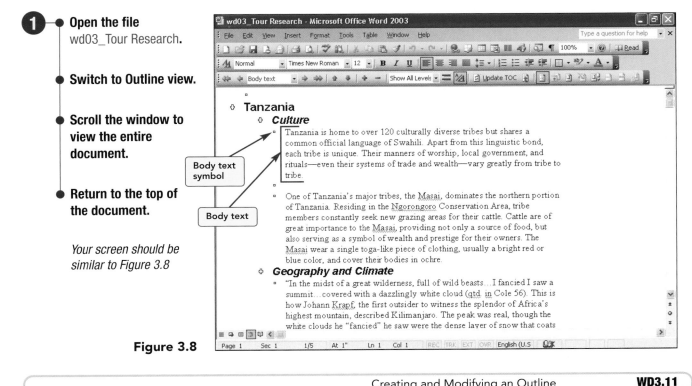

Outline topics in Normal view appear in heading style

Tanzania
Culture
Geography
Climate
Animal Life
Peru
Culture
Historical Culture
Machu Picchu
Geography and Climate
Animal Life

Figure 3.7

The topic headings appear left-aligned on the page in the style that was applied to the text as the outline was created.

Collapsing and Expanding the Outline

You have continued to work on the outline and report organization. Then you entered much of the information for the report and saved it. You will open the document to see the information that has been added to the report.

1 ● **Open the file** wd03_Tour Research.

● **Switch to Outline view.**

● **Scroll the window to view the entire document.**

● **Return to the top of the document.**

Your screen should be similar to Figure 3.8

Body text symbol

Body text

Tanzania
   Culture
    Tanzania is home to over 120 culturally diverse tribes but shares a common official language of Swahili. Apart from this linguistic bond, each tribe is unique. Their manners of worship, local government, and rituals—even their systems of trade and wealth—vary greatly from tribe to tribe.

    One of Tanzania's major tribes, the Masai, dominates the northern portion of Tanzania. Residing in the Ngorongoro Conservation Area, tribe members constantly seek new grazing areas for their cattle. Cattle are of great importance to the Masai, providing not only a source of food, but also serving as a symbol of wealth and prestige for their owners. The Masai wear a single toga-like piece of clothing, usually a bright red or blue color, and cover their bodies in ochre.

   Geography and Climate
    "In the midst of a great wilderness, full of wild beasts...I fancied I saw a summit...covered with a dazzlingly white cloud (qtd. in Cole 56). This is how Johann Krapf, the first outsider to witness the splendor of Africa's highest mountain, described Kilimanjaro. The peak was real, though the white clouds he "fancied" he saw were the dense layer of snow that coats

Figure 3.8

Page 1   Sec 1   1/5   At 1"   Ln 1   Col 1   REC TRK EXT OVR   English (U.S

The document is displayed as an outline with the topic headings indented appropriately. The body text appears below the appropriate heading. Any text not identified with a heading style is considered body text. The small square to the left of a paragraph identifies it as body text.

In Outline view, you can display as much or as little of the document text as you want. To make it easier to view and reorganize the document's structure, you can "collapse" the document to show just the headings you want. Alternatively, you can "expand" the document to display part of the body text below each heading or the entire body text. You can then easily move the headings around until the order is logical, and the body text will follow the heading. The table below shows how you can collapse and expand the amount of text displayed in Outline view.

To Collapse	Do This
Text below a specific heading level	Select the <u>lowest heading</u> you want to display from the [⧉] Show Level drop-down menu.
All subheadings and body text under a heading	Double-click [⊕] next to the heading.
Text under a heading, one level at a time	Click the heading text, and then click [−] Collapse.
All body text	Select the heading level you want to see from the [⧉] Show Level drop-down menu.
All body text except first line	Click [≡] Show First Line Only.
To Expand	**Do This**
All headings and body text	Select Show All Levels from the [⧉] Show Level drop-down menu.
All collapsed subheadings and body text under a heading	Double-click [⊕] next to the heading.
Collapsed text under a heading, one level at a time	Click the heading text, then click [+] Expand.

To change the amount of information displayed, you will collapse the display of the text under the Geography and Climate heading first. Then you will collapse everything below a level 3 heading so you can quickly check the report organization.

2
- Double-click ⊕ of the Geography and Climate heading.

- Open the [▾] Show Level drop-down list.

- Choose Show Level 3.

Your screen should be similar to Figure 3.9

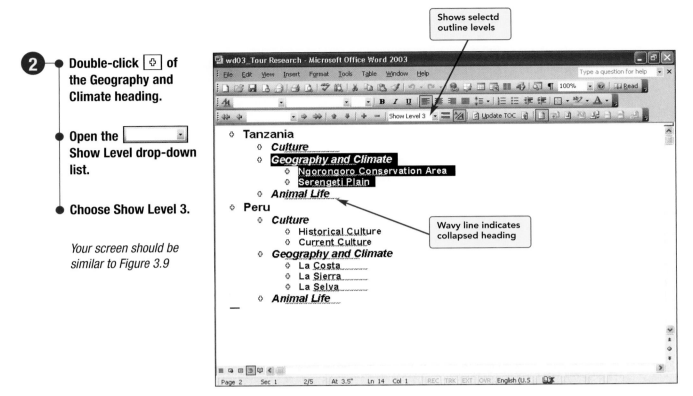

Shows selectd outline levels

Tanzania
  Culture
  Geography and Climate
    Ngorongoro Conservation Area
    Serengeti Plain
  Animal Life
Peru
  Culture
    Historical Culture
    Current Culture
  Geography and Climate
    La Costa
    La Sierra
    La Selva
  Animal Life

Wavy line indicates collapsed heading

Figure 3.9

Now only the three heading levels are displayed. The wavy line below a heading means the heading includes hidden or collapsed headings or body text.

As you look at the organization of the report, you decide to move the discussion of culture to follow the Geography and Climate section. Moving headings in Outline view quickly selects and moves the entire topic, including subtopics and all body text.

3 Drag the Culture heading in the Tanzania section down to above the Animal Life heading in the same section.

Drag the Culture heading in the Peru section down to above the Animal Life heading in the same section.

Choose **Show All Levels** from the [Show Level 3 ▾] Show Level drop-down list.

Scroll the report to see the top of the Peru Culture section on page 3.

Click in the document to deselect the text.

Your screen should be similar to Figure 3.10

◇ *Culture*
　　◇ **Historical Culture**
　　　　▫ Peru is where the Incas built their homes and cities. They lived in the southern portion of La Sierra until around 1300 CE, when they moved north to the fertile Cuzco Valley. From here they built their empire, overrunning and assimilating neighboring lands and cultures. They organized into a socialist-type theocracy under an emperor—the Inca—whom they worshipped as a deity. The Inca Empire reached its maximum size by the late fifteenth and early sixteenth centuries.

　　　　▫ In 1532 the Spanish explorer Francisco Pizarro landed in Peru. He saw great opportunity in seizing the empire because of the rich gold deposits in the Cuzco Valley, and did so with superior armament. This opened the door for masses of gold- and adventure-seeking conquistadors to join in the pursuit, who brought with them both modern weaponry and smallpox, which ultimately led to the demise of most of the Inca government. Civil disorder and rioting followed in what remained of the empire, and the Spanish used this as leverage to seal their victory.

Figure 3.10

The subtopics and body text appear below the heading you moved. When you move or change the level of a heading that includes collapsed subordinate text, the collapsed text is also selected. Any changes you make to the heading, such as moving, copying, or deleting it, also affect the collapsed text.

Saving to a New Folder

Next, you will save the outline and the research document with its changes in a folder that you will use to hold files related to the report. You can create a new folder at the same time you save a file.

Creates a new folder

1 • **Choose File/Save As.**

• **Change the Save In location to the appropriate location for your data files.**

• **Click Create New Folder.**

Your screen should be similar to Figure 3.11

wd03_Tour Research - Microsoft Office Word 2003

File Edit View Insert Format Tools Table Window Help

Type a question for help

Normal Times New Roman 12 B I U

Body text Show All Levels Update TOC

Save As

Save in: ZIP-100 (E:) Tools ▾

My Recent Documents
  wd03_Digital Camera
  wd03_Kayaking Flyer
  wd03_Tour Research
  wd03_Triple Crown
  wd03_Yoga Practice

Location where folder will be created

Desktop

New Folder

My Documents
  OK
  Name: Cancel

My Computer

Enter name of new folder

My Network Places

File name: wd03_Tour Research Save

Save as type: Word Document Cancel

the Spanish used this as leverage to seal their victory.

Page 3 Sec 1 3/5 At 4.9" Ln 21 Col 49 REC TRK EXT OVR English (U.S

Figure 3.11

Additional Information

See "Saving, Closing, and Opening Files" in Lab 1 for file-naming rules.

In the New Folder dialog box, you enter the folder name. The rules for naming folders are the same as for naming files, except they typically do not include an extension.

2 • **Type Report in the Name text box.**

• **Click** OK **.**

• **Enter the file name Tour Research.**

• **Click** Save **.**

• **Switch to Document1 containing the outline document.**

• **Save the outline to the Report folder with the file name Research Outline.**

• **Close the Research Outline document.**

Additional Information

You can also rename an existing folder by choosing Rename from the folder's shortcut menu and entering the new name.

The documents are saved in the newly created folder, Report.

Hiding Spelling and Grammar Errors

As you have been working on the report, you have noticed that many spelling and grammar errors are identified. You want to scroll the document to take a quick look at the types of errors identified. You have noticed that scrolling a larger document in Print Layout view takes more time because the view displays the extra blank (white) space on the page and the space allocated for the headers and footers. You can hide the display of this white space to make it faster to move through the document.

1 ● **Switch to Print Layout view.**

● **Click on the gray page separator space between any pages.**

● **Scroll to see the bottom of page 4 and the top of page 5.**

Your screen should be similar to Figure 3.12

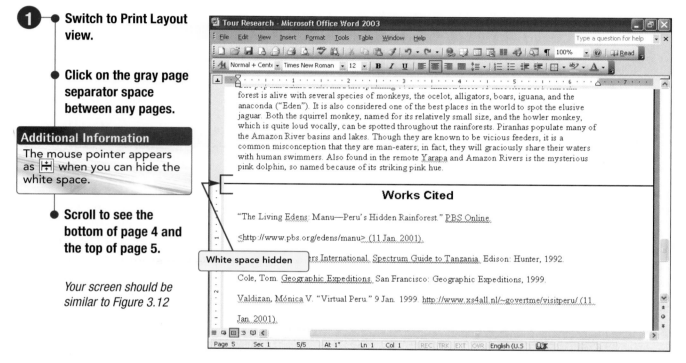

Figure 3.12

Any extra white space is eliminated, making scrolling much faster. As you scrolled the document you noticed that most of the identified errors are for proper names and words that are not in the dictionary. While working on a document, you can turn off the display of these errors so that they are not distracting.

2 ● **Choose Tools/Options.**

● **Open the Spelling & Grammar tab.**

Your screen should be similar to Figure 3.13

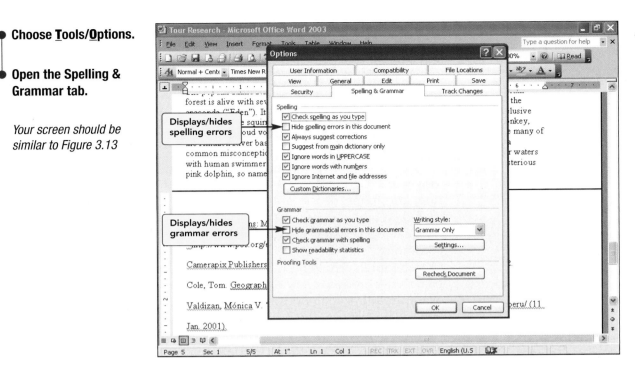

Figure 3.13

The Options dialog box is used to change the way many features in Word operate. The Spelling and Grammar tab displays options that control how these features operate. Checkmarks next to options indicate the setting is on. You want to turn off the display of spelling and grammar errors.

3 ● **Select Hide spelling errors in this document.**

● **Select Hide grammatical errors in this document.**

● **Click** OK .

● **Click on the gray page separator line to show the white space again.**

Additional Information

The mouse pointer appears as ⊞ when you can show white space.

● **Scroll up to see the top of page 4.**

Your screen should be similar to Figure 3.14

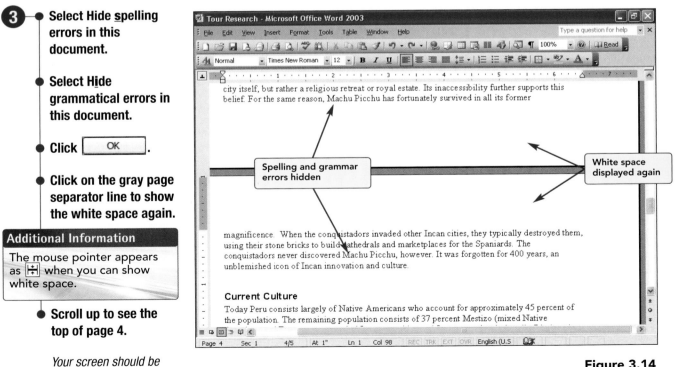

Figure 3.14

The red and green wavy lines are no longer displayed. You can still run spelling and grammar checking manually to check errors at any time. The extra blank space at the bottom of page 4 and the header and footer space are displayed again. Now that you know how to use this feature, you can turn it on and off whenever you want.

Formatting Documents Automatically

Now that you have finished reorganizing the report, you want to add a title page. Generally, this page includes information such as the report title, the name of the author, and the date. You also want this page to include a table of contents list.

When preparing research reports, two styles of report formatting are commonly used: MLA (Modern Language Association) and APA (American Psychological Association). Although they require the same basic information, they differ in how this information is presented. For example, MLA style does not include a separate title page, but APA style does. The report you will create in this lab will use many of style requirements of the MLA. However, because this report is not a formal report to be presented at a conference or other academic proceeding, some liberties have been taken with the style to demonstrate features in Word.

Using Click and Type

You will create a new page above the first report topic where you will enter the title information using the **Click and Type** feature. This feature, available in Print Layout and Web Layout views, is used to quickly insert text, graphics, and other items in a blank area of a document, avoiding the need to enter blank lines. This feature also applies the paragraph formatting needed to position an item at the location you clicked.

1 • Press `Ctrl` + `Home` to move to the top of the document.

• Press `Ctrl` + `←Enter` to insert a hard page break and create a blank page above it.

• Move to the top of the blank new page.

• Move the mouse pointer from left to right across the page and observe the change in the mouse pointer.

Your screen should be similar to Figure 3.15

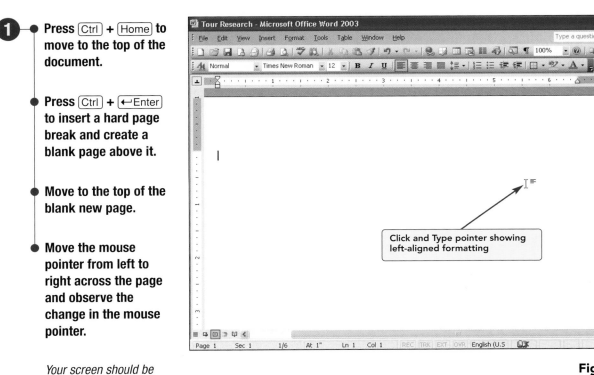

Click and Type pointer showing left-aligned formatting

Figure 3.15

Print Layout view includes formatting "zones" that control the formatting that will be applied. As you move the mouse pointer through the zones, the I-beam pointer displays an icon that indicates the formatting that will be applied when you double-click at that location. This is the Click and Type pointer. The pointer shapes and their associated formatting are described in the table below.

Pointer shape	Formatting applied
I ≡	Align left
I ≡	Align center
≡ I	Align right
I ≡	Left indent

To enable the Click and Type pointer, first click on a blank area, then as you move the mouse pointer, the pointer shape indicates how the item will be formatted. Double-clicking on the location in the page moves the insertion point to that location and applies the formatting to the entry. You will enter the report title centered on the page.

2

- Click on a blank area of the page to enable Click and Type.

- Double-click on the center of the page at the .5-inch vertical ruler position while the mouse pointer is a .

- Type the report title, **Tanzania and Peru.**

  Your screen should be similar to Figure 3.16

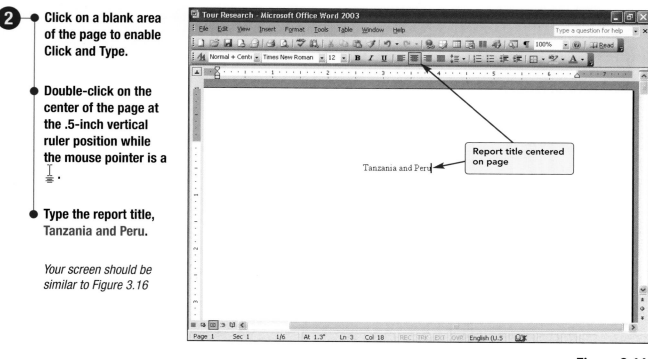

Figure 3.16

Next you will add a heading for the table of contents listing you will create. Then you will enter your name and date at the bottom of the title page.

3

- Double-click on the center of the page at the 1.5-inch vertical ruler position while the mouse pointer is a .

- Enter the title **Table of Contents.**

- In the same manner, enter your name centered at the 3-inch vertical ruler position.

- Press ⏎Enter.

- Enter the current date centered below your name.

  Your screen should be similar to Figure 3.17

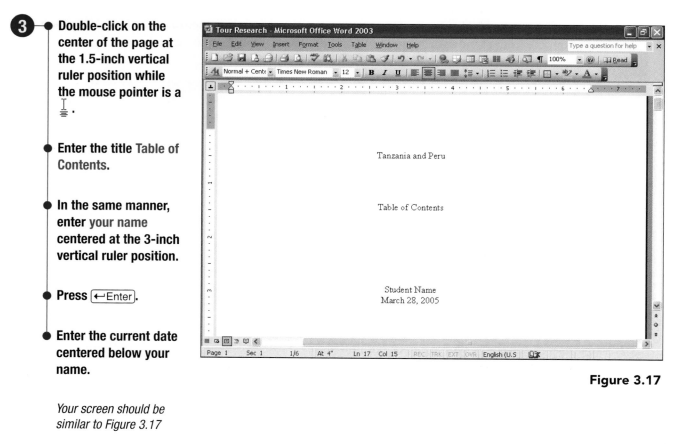

Figure 3.17

Applying Styles

Next you want to improve the appearance of the main title. You can do this quickly by applying a style to the title.

Move to anywhere in the Tanzania and Peru title.

Click [44] Styles and Formatting.

Your screen should be similar to Figure 3.18

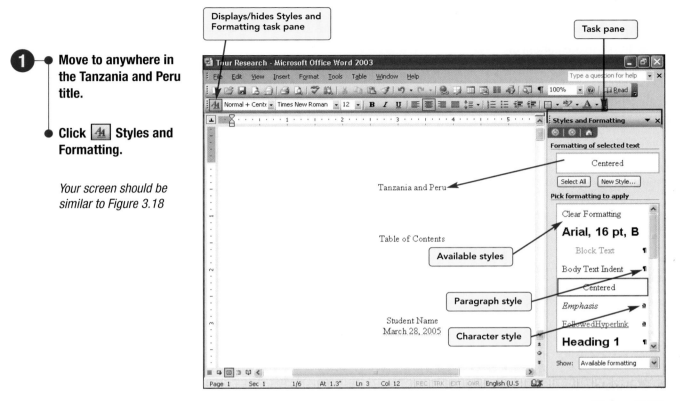

Figure 3.18

The Styles and Formatting task pane appears. The "Formatting of selected text" box shows that the text of the current selection is centered. The "Pick formatting to apply" list box displays the names of all available styles and formatting, including those that you have applied directly, in alphabetical order. The symbols to the right of the style name indicate the type of style, such as a paragraph style ¶ or a character style a . You want to display the complete list of styles and apply the Title style to the text.

2 ● **Select All styles from the Show drop-down list box.**

● **Scroll to the bottom of the "Pick formatting to apply" list and choose Title.**

Your screen should be similar to Figure 3.19

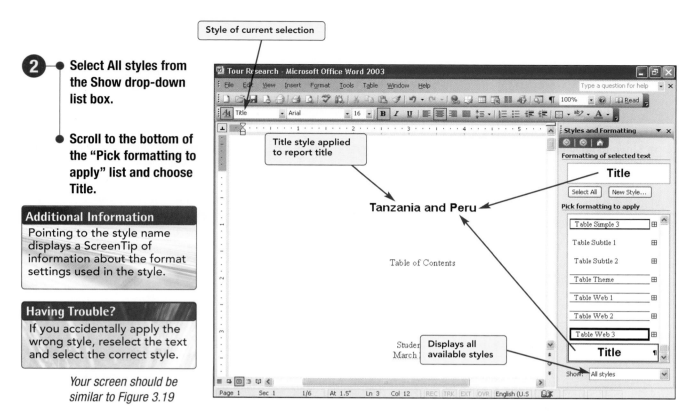

Figure 3.19

Notice that the entire title appears in the selected style. This is because a Title style is a paragraph style, affecting the entire paragraph at the insertion point. Also notice that the Style drop-down list button in the Formatting toolbar now displays "Title" as the style applied to the selection. This style includes formatting settings of Arial, 16 pt, and bold.

Next, you want to apply a Subtitle style to the Table of Contents heading. Another way to select a style is from the Style drop-down menu.

3 • Move the insertion point to anywhere in the Table of Contents heading.

• Open the Style drop-down menu.

Your screen should be similar to Figure 3.20

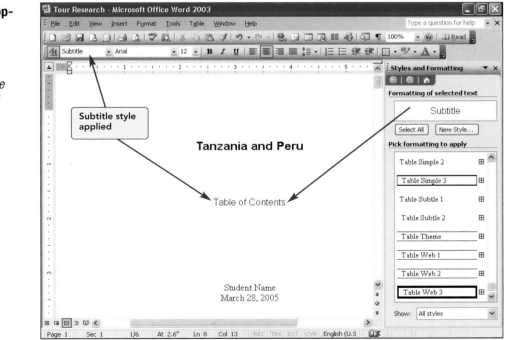

Figure 3.20

The Style drop-down menu displays all available styles. The style names are listed in alphabetical order and appear formatted in that style.

4 • Scroll the Style drop-down menu and choose Subtitle.

Your screen should be similar to Figure 3.21

Figure 3.21

Creating a Custom Style

Although the Title style looks good, you want to enhance it further using the shadow text effect. Then you will save the formatting associated with the title as a custom style so you can quickly apply the style in the future.

1 ● Select the report title.

● Choose **F**ormat/**F**ont.

● From the Font tab, select Shadow and click [OK].

● From the Styles and Formatting task pane, click [New Style].

Your screen should be similar to Figure 3.22

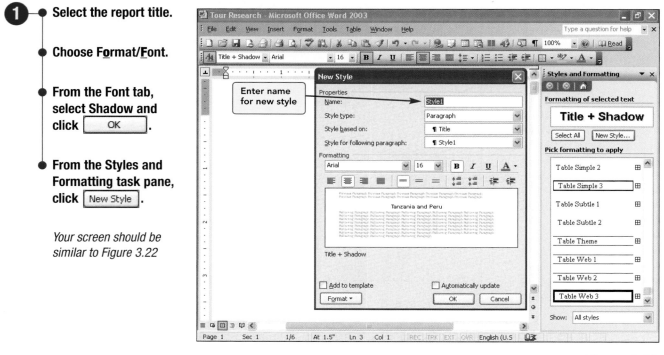

Figure 3.22

The New Style dialog box displays the settings associated with the selected text. The only action you need to take is give the style a more descriptive name.

2 ● In the Name text box, type Shadow Title.

● Click [OK].

Having Trouble?
If this style already exists on your computer, click [OK] and [Cancel] to continue.

Your screen should be similar to Figure 3.23

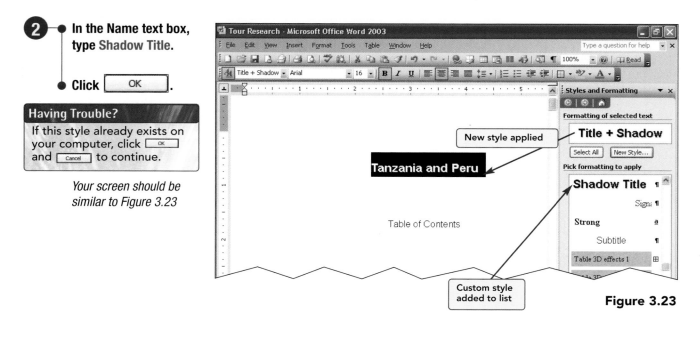

Figure 3.23

The new style name has been added to the list of available styles and can be applied like any other style. If you ever need to change a style back to the default document style, you can easily clear the style by moving to the text whose style you want removed and choosing Clear Formatting from the Style drop-down menu. You can also use **E**dit/Cle**a**r/**F**ormats to have the same effect.

Creating a Table of Contents

Now you are ready to create the table of contents. A table of contents is a listing of the topic headings that appear in a document and their associated page references (see the sample below). It shows the reader at a glance the topics that are included in the document and makes it easier for the reader to locate information. Word can generate a table of contents automatically after you have applied heading styles to the document headings.

Table of Contents

Generating a Table of Contents

You want the table of contents listing to be displayed several lines below the table of contents heading on the title page.

1 ● **Close the Styles and Formatting task pane.**

● **Move to the second blank line below the Table of Contents heading.**

Having Trouble?
If needed, use ¶ Show/Hide to help locate the position in the document.

● **Choose Insert/Reference/ Index and Tables.**

● **Open the Table of Contents tab.**

Your screen should be similar to Figure 3.24

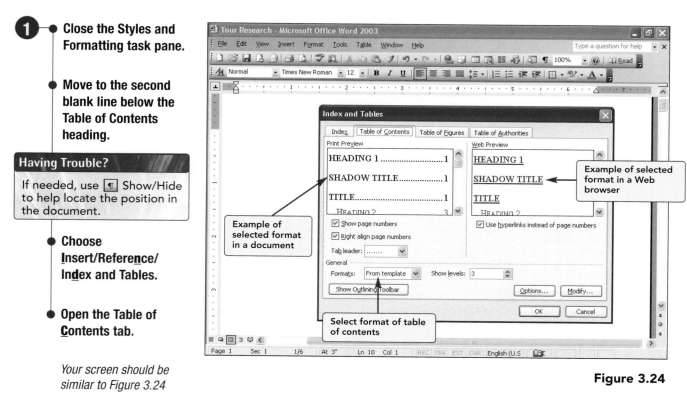

Figure 3.24

From the Table of Contents tab, you first need to select the format or design of the table of contents. There are seven predesigned table of contents formats available in the Formats drop-down list box. The default style is selected, and the Preview boxes display an example of how the selected format will look in a normal printed document or in a document when viewed in a Web browser. You will use one of the other predesigned formats.

2 ● **Open the Formats drop-down list box.**

● **Select several formats and look at the preview area to see an example of the selected format.**

● **Choose Distinctive.**

Your screen should be similar to Figure 3.25

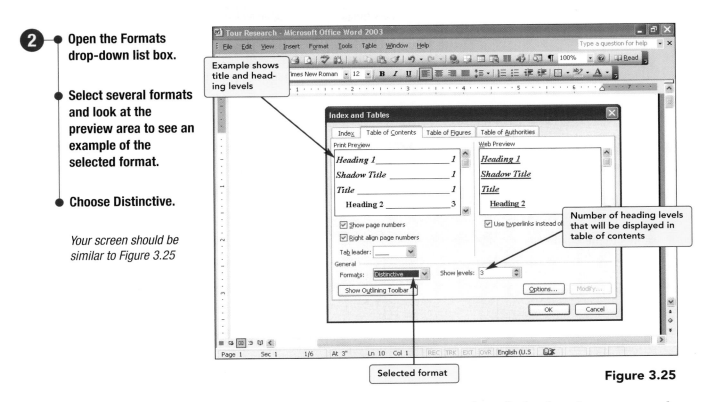

Example shows title and heading levels

Number of heading levels that will be displayed in table of contents

Selected format

Figure 3.25

The Print Preview area shows this style will display the page numbers flush with the right margin, and with a solid line tab leader between the heading entry and the page number. This format will display in the table of contents all entries in the document that are formatted with Headings 1, 2, and 3, as well as Title and Subtitle styles. You want the table of contents to include topics formatted with the Heading 4 style, but to exclude those formatted with the Title and Subtitle styles. You will modify the settings for the Distinctive format and turn off the use of these styles.

3 ● **Change the level number in the Show Levels text box to 4.**

● **Click** Options... .

Your screen should be similar to Figure 3.26

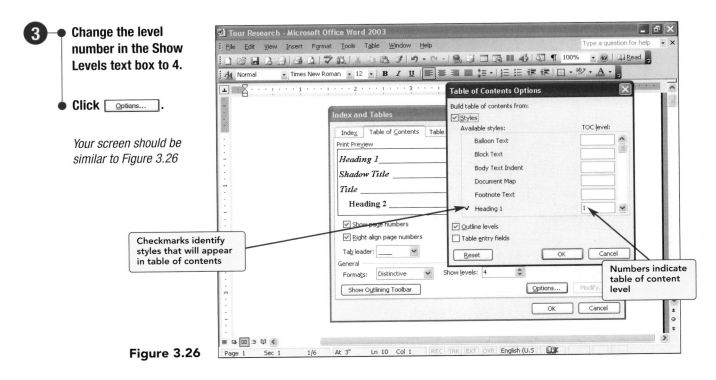

Checkmarks identify styles that will appear in table of contents

Numbers indicate table of content level

Figure 3.26

The Table of Contents Options dialog box shows the styles that are used to build the table of contents. The checkmark indicates the styles Word will look for in the document to use as items to include in the table of contents, and the number indicates the level at which they will be displayed. To clear a style selection, simply delete the number from the TOC level text box.

4 • Scroll to the bottom of the Available Styles list to see the Subtitle and Title selections.

• Delete the numbers from the Shadow Title, Subtitle, and Title text boxes to clear the checkmarks.

• Click [OK].

Your screen should be similar to Figure 3.27

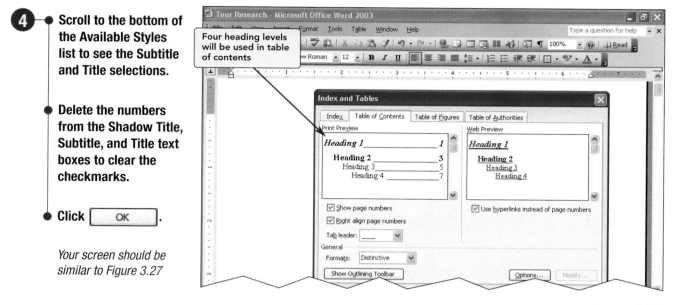

Figure 3.27

The Print Preview area now shows that four levels of headings will be used in the table of contents listing, and the title and subtitle will not be included. Now you are ready to generate the listing.

5 • Click [OK].

Your screen should be similar to Figure 3.28

Figure 3.28

Lab 3: Creating Reports and Tables

www.mhhe.com/oleary

Word searches for headings with the specified styles, sorts them by heading level, references their page numbers, and displays the table of contents using the Distinctive style in the document. The headings that were assigned a Heading 1 style are aligned with the left margin, and subordinate heading levels are indented as appropriate. The title and subtitle headings are not included. The table of contents that is generated is a field. This means it can be updated to reflect changes you may make at a later time in your document.

Navigating by Headings

In a large document, locating and moving to an area of text you want to view can take a lot of time. However, after headings have been applied to different areas of a document, there are several features that can make navigation easier. As a help when scrolling by dragging the scroll box, a ScreenTip identifies the topic heading in addition to the page number that will be displayed when you stop dragging the scroll box. If you have generated a table of contents, you can use the table of contents entries to quickly move to different areas. Even more convenient, however, is to use the Document Map feature to jump to a selected location.

Using a Table of Contents Hyperlink

Not only does the table of contents display the location of information in the report, but it can also be used to quickly move to a specific area. This is because each entry in the table is a separate field that is a hyperlink to the heading in the document. Because the table of contents is a field, it will appear shaded when selected. More importantly, it means that the table of contents can be easily updated to reflect changes you may make to the document after the list is generated.

A hyperlink, as you have learned, is a connection to a location in the current document, another document, or to a Web site. In this case, the table of contents hyperlinks are connections to locations in this document. Simply holding down [Ctrl] while clicking on a hyperlink in a Word document will move you directly to the selected location.

1 ● Click anywhere in the table of contents list.

● Hold down Ctrl and click the Peru table of contents line.

Your screen should be similar to Figure 3.29

Additional Information

Pointing to an entry in a table of contents displays a ScreenTip with directions on how to follow the hyperlink.

Additional Information

The mouse pointer shape changes to a 🖑 when holding down Ctrl and pointing to a hyperlink.

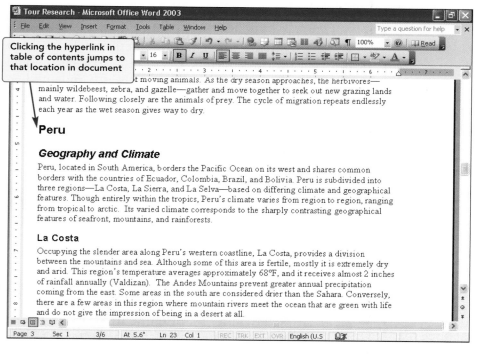

Figure 3.29

The insertion point jumps to the Peru heading in the document.

Using the Document Map

Now, however, the table of contents is no longer visible. If you wanted to move to a different topic, you would need to return to the top of the document and select another hyperlink. Another way to quickly move to different locations in the document is to use the Document Map feature. **Document Map** displays a list of the headings style in a document in a separate pane that is used to quickly navigate through the document and keep track of your location in it. When your document does not contain any headings formatted with heading styles, the program automatically searches the document for paragraphs that look like headings (for example, short lines with a larger font size) and displays them in the Document Map. If it cannot find any such headings, the Document Map is blank.

1 ● Click [icon] **Document Map.**

Another Method

The menu equivalent is **V**iew/**D**ocument Map.

Your screen should be similar to Figure 3.30

Document Map pane displays headings in your document

Indicates all subordinate levels are displayed

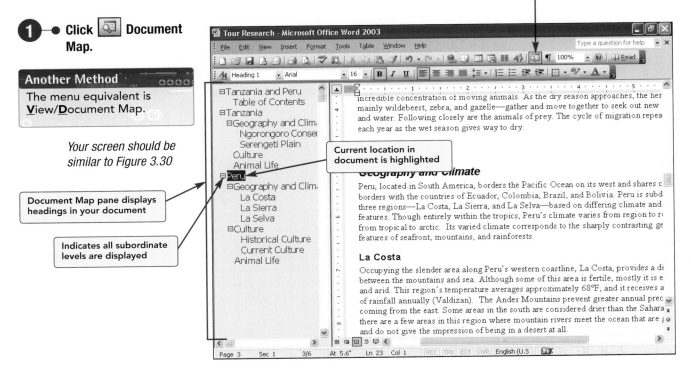

Displays/hides Document Map

Current location in document is highlighted

Figure 3.30

Additional Information

The Document Map pane can be resized by dragging the divider line between the panes.

The Document Map pane on the left edge of the window displays the headings in the document. All text that is formatted with a heading style is displayed in the Document Map pane. Notice the ⊟ symbol to the left of many of the headings in the Document Map; this symbol indicates that all subordinate headings are displayed. A ⊞ symbol would indicate that subordinate headings are not displayed. The highlighted heading shows your location in the document. Clicking on a heading in the Document Map quickly jumps to that location in the document.

2 ● Click on Culture (under Peru) in the Document Map.

● Click on Table of Contents.

Your screen should be similar to Figure 3.31

Takes you to the Table of Contents

Figure 3.31

You quickly moved from one topic location in the document to another. When using the Document Map, the selected topic heading is displayed at the top of the window and is highlighted in the Document Map.

The Document Map feature is available in all views and remains displayed in the view you are using until you turn it off. It must be turned on and off in each view independently.

Formatting Document Sections

You want to change the layout of the title page so that the text on the page is centered vertically between the top and bottom page margins. Because page layout settings affect entire documents, you need to create separate sections in the document to make this change to the title page only.

Concept 2

Section

2 To format different parts of a document differently, you can divide a document into **sections**. Initially a document is one section. To separate it into different parts, you insert section breaks. The **section break** identifies the end of a section and stores the document format settings, such as margins and page layout, associated with that section of the document.

The three types of section breaks, described in the following table, control the location where the text following a section break begins.

Type	Action	
Next Page	Starts the new section on the next page.	
Continuous	Starts the new section on the same page.	
Odd or Even	Starts the new section on the next odd or even numbered page.	

If you delete a section break, the preceding text becomes part of the following section and assumes its section formatting.

Creating a Section Break

Because the page layout you want to use on the title page is different from the rest of the document, you need to divide the document into two sections. You will delete the hard page break line you inserted and replace it with a section break.

1 ● **Switch to Normal view with 100% zoom.**

● **Scroll to see the bottom of page 1.**

● **Delete the hard page break line.**

Having Trouble?
To remove a hard page break, click on the page break line and press Delete.

● **Choose Insert/Break.**

Your screen should be similar to Figure 3.32

Hard page break removed

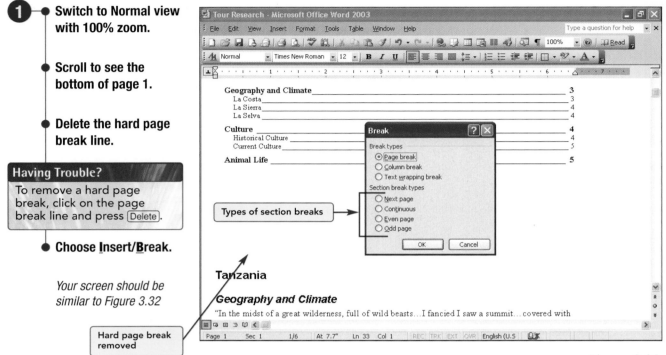

Types of section breaks

Figure 3.32

In the Break dialog box, you specify the type of section break you want to insert. In this case, you want the new section to start on the next page.

2 ● **Select Next page.**

● **Click** OK .

● **Delete the blank line above the Tanzania heading.**

Your screen should be similar to Figure 3.33

Type of section break

Section break line

Student Name
March 28, 2005

Section Break (Next Page)

Tanzania

Geography and Climate

"In the midst of a great wilderness, full of wild beasts...I fancied I saw a summit...covered with

Figure 3.33

A double dotted line and the words "Section Break" identify the type of document break that was inserted.

Centering a Page Vertically

Now that the title page is in a separate section, you can format it differently from the rest of the report. You want to change the layout of the title page to centered vertically. Vertical alignment determines the position of the text on a page relative to the top and bottom margins. The four vertical alignment settings are described in the following table.

Vertical Alignment	Effect	Vertical Alignment	Effect
Top	Aligns first line of text on page with the top margin. This is the default setting.	Center	Centers text between top and bottom margins.
Bottom	Aligns last line of text on page with the bottom margin.	Justified	Vertically justifies text so that it is spaced evenly down the page.

1 • **Switch back to Print Layout view.**

• **Move to anywhere in the title page.**

• **Click** **Document Map to turn off this feature.**

• **Zoom to Whole Page.**

• **Double-click on the vertical ruler to open the Page Setup dialog box.**

Another Method

The menu equivalent is File/Page Setup.

• **Open the Layout tab.**

Your screen should be similar to Figure 3.34

Figure 3.34

From the Vertical Alignment drop-down list box, you specify how the text is to be aligned on the page vertically. In addition, from the Apply To drop-down list box you need to specify the part of the document you want to be aligned to the new setting. Because you already divided the document into sections, this setting is already appropriately selected. You only need to specify the vertical alignment.

2 • **From the Vertical Alignment drop-down list, select Center.**

• **Click** [OK].

• **Delete all blank lines above the title.**

• **Click** **Save to save the changes you have made to the document.**

Your screen should be similar to Figure 3.35

Text vertically centered on page

Figure 3.35

Now you can see that the text on the title page is centered vertically between the top and bottom margins. Word required a section break at this location because a different page format, in this case vertical alignment, was used on this page than the rest of the document.

Including Source References

This document already includes parenthetical source references entered according to the MLA style for research papers. However, you still have several reference notes you want to include in the report as footnotes to help clarify some information.

Concept 3

Footnote and Endnote

3   Including source references or notes that explain or comment on information in the text as footnotes or endnotes is an essential element of a documented research paper. A **footnote** is a source reference or text offering additional explanation that is placed at the bottom of a page. An **endnote** is also a source reference or long comment that typically appears at the end of a document. You can have both footnotes and endnotes in the same document.

Footnotes and endnotes consist of two parts, the note reference mark and the note text. The **note reference mark** is commonly a superscript number appearing in the document at the end of the material being referenced (for example, text). It can also be a character or combination of characters. The **note text** for a footnote appears at the bottom of the page on which the reference mark appears. The footnote text is separated from the document text by a horizontal line called the **note separator**. Endnote text appears as a listing at the end of the document.

Note text can be of any length and formatted just as you would any other text. You can also customize the appearance of the note separators.

Adding Footnotes

The first footnote reference you want to add is the height of Mt. Kilimanjaro. This note will follow the reference to the mountain at the end of the first paragraph in the Geography and Climate section for Tanzania. To identify the location of the footnote number in the document, you position the insertion point at the document location first.

1
- Switch to Normal view and display the Document Map.
- Click on the Tanzania heading in the Document Map pane.
- Change the zoom to Page Width.
- Move to the end of the first paragraph after the word "mountain."
- Choose <u>I</u>nsert/ Refere<u>n</u>ce/Foot<u>n</u>ote.

Another Method

The keyboard shortcut to insert a footnote using the default settings is Alt + Ctrl + F.

Your screen should be similar to Figure 3.36

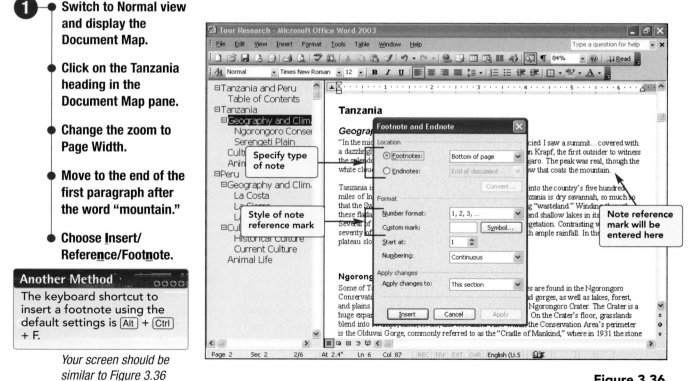

Figure 3.36

In the Footnote and Endnote dialog box, you specify whether you want to create footnotes or endnotes and the type of reference mark you want to appear in the document: a numbered mark or a custom mark. A custom mark can be any nonnumeric character, such as an asterisk, that you enter in the text box. You want to create numbered footnotes, so the default settings of Footnote and AutoNumber are acceptable.

2 Click [Insert].

Your screen should be similar to Figure 3.37

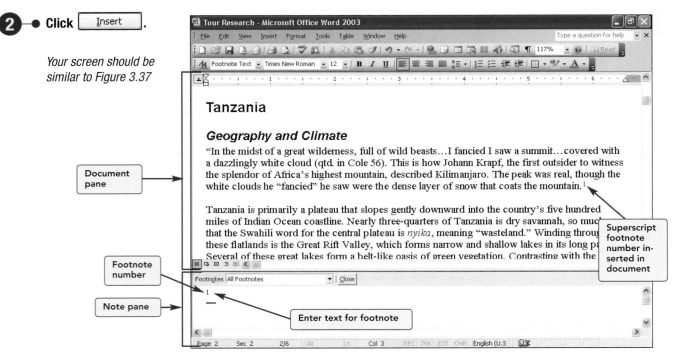

Figure 3.37

The document window is now horizontally divided into upper and lower panes. The Document Map pane is temporarily hidden while these two panes are displayed. When you close the lower pane, the Document Map pane will be displayed again.

The report is displayed in the upper pane. The footnote number, 1, appears as a superscript in the document where the insertion point was positioned when the footnote was created. The note pane displays the footnote number and the insertion point. This is where you enter the text for the footnote. When you enter a footnote, you can use the same menus, commands, and features as you would in the document window. Any commands that are not available are dimmed.

3 ● **Type** Mt. Kilimanjaro is 19,340 feet high, making it the fourth tallest mountain in the world.

Your screen should be similar to Figure 3.38

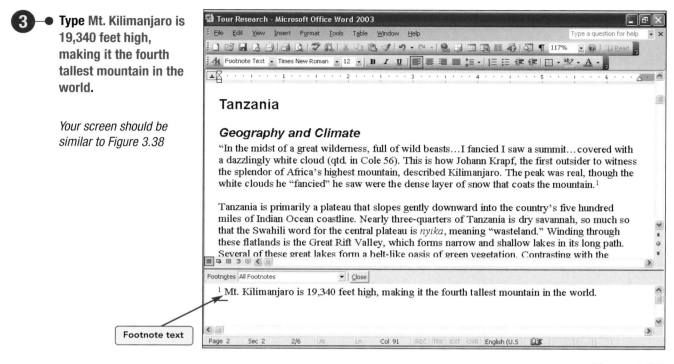

Footnote text

Figure 3.38

The second footnote you want to add is in the Geography and Climate section under Peru.

4 ● **Click** Close **to close the footnote pane and to redisplay the Document Map.**

● **Click on La Sierra in the Document Map.**

● **Click at the end of the paragraph following the word "lake."**

● **Choose Insert/ Reference/Footnote/ Insert .**

Your screen should be similar to Figure 3.39

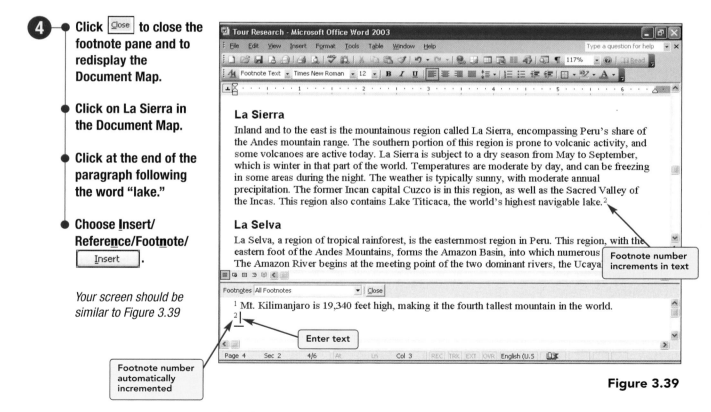

Footnote number increments in text

Enter text

Footnote number automatically incremented

Figure 3.39

The footnote number 2 is automatically entered at the insertion point location. The note pane is active again, so you can enter the text for the second footnote. You want to add a note about Lake Titicaca.

5 ● In the note pane, type Lake Titicaca is 12,507 feet above sea level.

Your screen should be similar to Figure 3.40

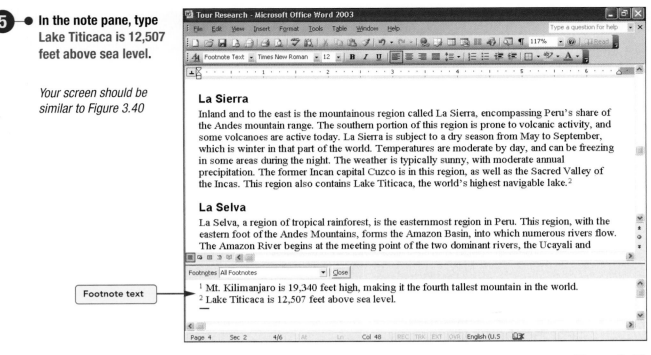

Footnote text

Figure 3.40

Now you realize that you forgot to enter a footnote earlier in the document, on page 2.

Additional Information

To delete a footnote or endnote, highlight the reference mark and press Delete. The reference mark and associated note text are removed, and the following footnotes are renumbered.

6 ● Close the note pane.

● Click Ngorongoro Conservation Area in the Document Map.

● Move to the end of the first sentence of the first paragraph, following the word "Area."

● Insert a footnote at this location.

Your screen should be similar to Figure 3.41

Footnote number inserted

Ngorongoro Conservation Area

Some of Tanzania's most distinguishing geographical features are found in the Ngorongoro Conservation Area.² The park is composed of many craters and gorges, as well as lakes, forest, and plains. Among these features is the area's namesake, the Ngorongoro Crater. The Crater is a huge expanse, covering more than one hundred square miles. On the Crater's floor, grasslands blend into swamps, lakes, rivers, and woodland. Also within the Conservation Area's perimeter is the Olduvai Gorge, commonly referred to as the "Cradle of Mankind," where in 1931 the stone tools of prehistoric man were found. This find subsequently led to the discovery of the remains of humans who lived 1.75 million years ago.

Serengeti Plain

Adjacent to the western edge of the Ngorongoro Conservation Area is the Serengeti Plain. Its area is approximately 5,700 square miles, and its central savanna supports many grazing animals

Footnotes | All Footnotes | Close

¹ Mt. Kilimanjaro is 19,340 feet high, making it the fourth tallest mountain in the world.
²
³ Lake Titicaca is 12,507 feet above sea level.

Page 2   Sec 2   2/6   At   Ln   Col 3   REC TRK EXT OVR English (U.S

Footnote number automatically adjusted for location in the text

Figure 3.41

7 **In the note pane, type** **The Conservation Area is a national preserve spanning 3,196 square miles.**

Your screen should be similar to Figure 3.42

Notice that this footnote is now number 2 in the document, and a blank footnote line has been entered in the note pane for the footnote text. Word automatically adjusted the footnote numbers when the new footnote was inserted.

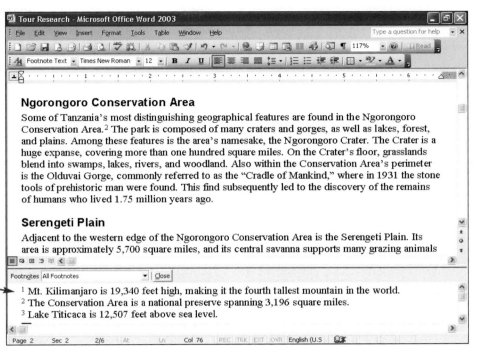

Footnote text

Figure 3.42

You are finished entering footnotes for now.

8 ● Close the note pane.

Additional Information

You can hide and display the note pane anytime by using the **V**iew/**F**ootnotes command or by double-clicking on a note reference mark.

● **If necessary scroll to see the bottom of this page.**

Your screen should be similar to Figure 3.43

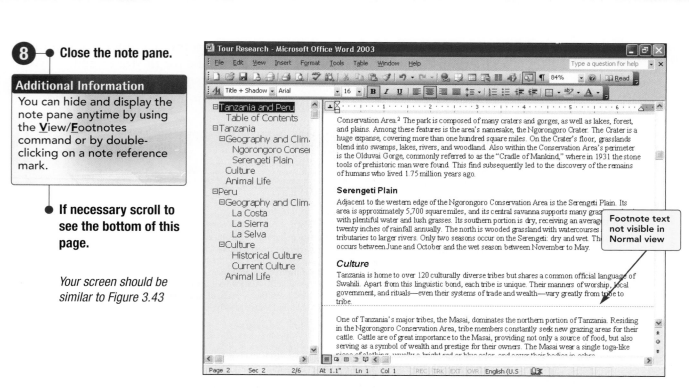

Figure 3.43

In Normal view, if the footnote pane is not open, you cannot see the footnote text.

Viewing Footnotes

To see the footnote text in Normal view, you point to the note reference mark and the footnote is displayed as a ScreenTip. Alternatively, you can switch to Print Layout view where the footnotes are displayed as they will appear when the document is printed.

1 ● Point to note reference
mark 2 in the
document.

The Conservation Area is a national
preserve spanning 3,196 square miles.

Footnote appears in ScreenTip

● Switch to Print Layout
view and set the zoom
to 75 percent.

● If necessary, scroll to
the bottom of page 2
to see the footnotes.

Additional Information

If the zoom percentage is too
small, the footnote numbers
will not display correctly.

*Your screen should be
similar to Figure 3.44*

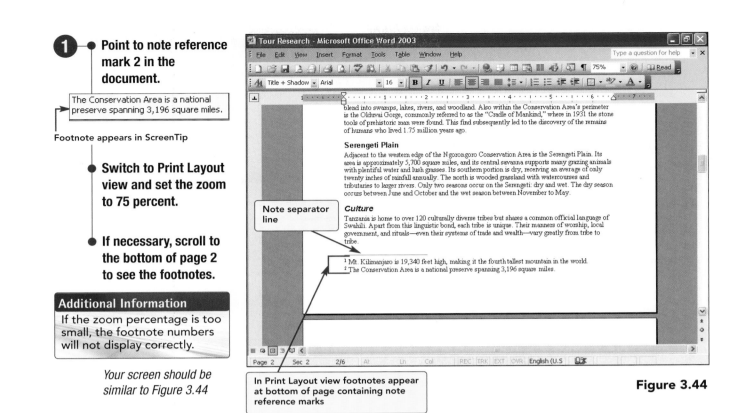

In Print Layout view footnotes appear
at bottom of page containing note
reference marks

Figure 3.44

The footnotes are displayed immediately above the bottom margin
separated from the text by the note separator line. They appear at the
bottom of the page containing the footnote reference mark.

Inserting a Footnote in Print Layout View

As you continue to check the document, you decide you want to explain
the CE abbreviation following the date 1300 in the Historical Culture
section. While in Print Layout view, you can insert, edit, and format
footnotes just like any other text. After using the command to insert a
footnote, the footnote number appears in the footnote area at the bottom
of the page, ready for you to enter the footnote text.

1 ● **Display the Document Map and move to the Historical Culture section.**

● **Move the insertion point after "CE" in the second sentence.**

● **Insert a footnote at this location.**

● **Type** Common Era (CE) is the period dating from the birth of Christ.

● **Click** 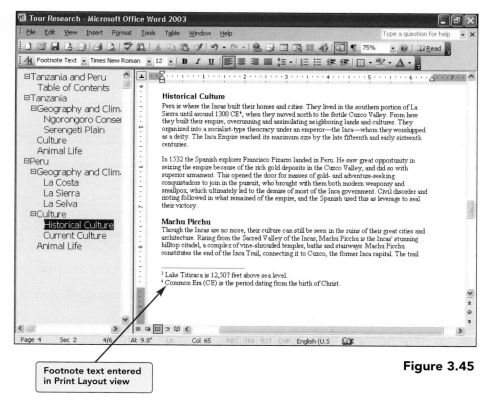 **Save to save the changes you have made to the document.**

Your screen should be similar to Figure 3.45

Footnote text entered in Print Layout view

Figure 3.45

Formatting Picture Layout

Next you want to add a picture in the report to complement the subject of the first topic. You want the text in the document where the picture will be inserted to wrap around the picture. To do this, you change the text-wrapping layout for the picture.

Concept 4
Text Wrapping

4 You can control the appearance of text around a graphic object by specifying the **text wrapping** style. The text in the paragraph may wrap around the object in many different ways as shown below.

Inline with Text	Square	Tight	Through	Top and Bottom	Behind Text	In Front of Text

When a picture is inserted into a Word document, it is an **inline object**. This means it is positioned directly in the text at the position of the insertion point. It becomes part of the paragraph, and any paragraph alignment settings that apply to the paragraph also apply to the picture.

By changing a graphic to a **floating object**, it is inserted into the **drawing layer**, a separate layer from the text that allows graphic objects to be positioned precisely on the page. You can change an inline object to a floating picture by changing the wrapping style of the object.

You will insert a picture of a giraffe next to the second paragraph on page 2.

1
- Use the Document Map to move to the Geography and Climate head under Tanzania.
- Move to the beginning of the second paragraph.
- Close the Document Map and change the zoom to Text Width.
- Insert the picture wd03_Giraffe **from your data files.**
- Reduce the size of the picture to approximately 2 by 2 inches.

Additional Information
Additional Information: Dragging the corner handle maintains the original proportions of the picture.

Your screen should be similar to Figure 3.46

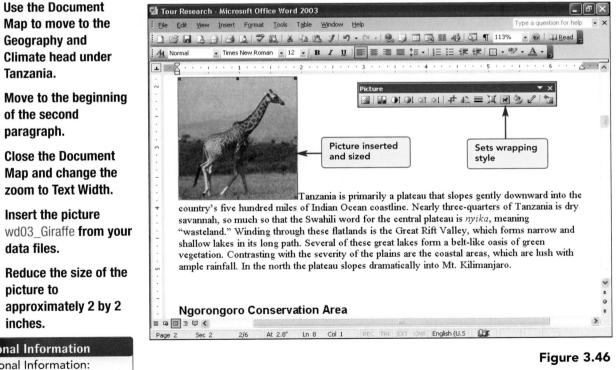

Figure 3.46

The picture has been inserted using the wrap default setting as an inline object and appears at the beginning of the paragraph like the first text characters of the paragraph. The text continues to the right of the picture.

The Picture toolbar is also automatically displayed. Its buttons (identified below) are used to modify the selected picture object. Your Picture toolbar may be floating or may be docked along an edge of the window, depending on its location when last used.

Wrapping Text Around Graphics

You want the text to wrap to the right side of the picture. To do this, you will change the wrapping style to Square.

1 ● Click [图] **Text Wrapping** on the Picture toolbar.

Another Method

The menu equivalent is F**o**rmat/**P**icture/Layout/ Wrapping Style.

default wrapping style

● Click [图] **Square.**

● If necessary, resize the picture until the text wraps around it as in Figure 3.47.

Your screen should be similar to Figure 3.47

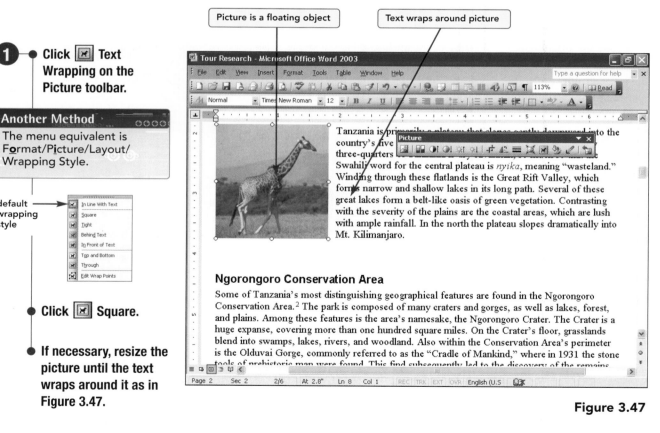

Figure 3.47

The picture is changed to a floating object that can be placed anywhere in the document, including in front of or behind other objects including the text.

Because the picture is aligned with the left margin, the text wraps to the right side of the object. If you moved the picture, because the wrapping style is Square, the text would wrap around the object on all sides.

2 ● Move the picture to the center of the paragraph to see how the text wraps around it.

Your screen should be similar to Figure 3.48

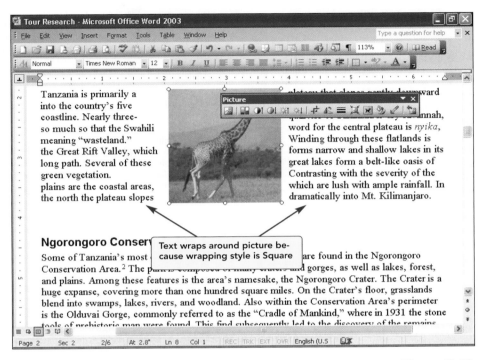

Figure 3.48

The text wraps on all sides of the object, depending on its location in the text. You will align this picture with the left margin again. Then you will add a second picture in the Peru Animal Life section.

3 ● Move the picture back to the left margin and aligned with the top of the paragraph (see Figure 3.47).

● Move to the beginning of the first paragraph in the Peru Animal Life section.

● Insert the picture wd03_Parrots to the left of the first paragraph.

● Change the wrapping style to Square.

● Position the picture as in Figure 3.49.

● Click 💾 to save the document.

Your screen should be similar to Figure 3.49

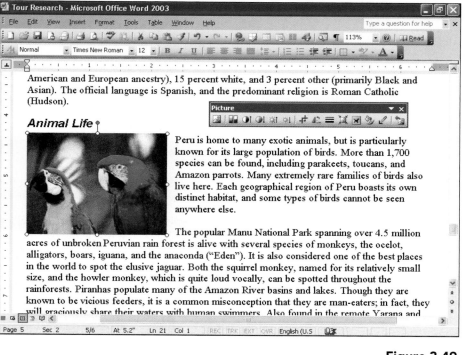

Figure 3.49

Referencing Figures

After figures and other illustrative items have been added to a document, it is helpful to include figure references to identify the items. Figure references include captions and cross-references. If the reader is viewing the document online, the captions and cross-references become hyperlinks to allow the reader to jump around in the document.

Concept 5
Captions and Cross-References

5 Using captions and cross-references in a document identifies items in a document and the helps the reader locate information quickly. A **caption** is a numbered label for a figure, table, picture, or graph. Word can automatically add captions to graphic objects as they are inserted, or you can add them manually. The caption label can be changed to reflect the type of object to which it refers, such as a table, chart, or figure. In addition, Word automatically numbers graphic objects and adjusts numbering when objects of the same type are added or deleted.

A **cross-reference** is a reference from one part of a document to related information in another part. Once you have captions, you can also include cross-references. For example, if you have a graph in one part of the document that you would like to refer to in another section, you can add a cross-reference that tells the reader what page the graph is on. A cross-reference can also be inserted as a hyperlink, allowing you to jump to another location in the same document or in another document.

Adding a Figure Caption

Next, you want to add a caption below the picture of the giraffe.

1 ● **Move to the blank line below the giraffe picture in the Tanzania section.**

Having Trouble?
If the blank line is not below the figure, make the figure smaller so the line does not wrap to the side of the figure.

● **Select the Giraffe picture.**

● **Choose Insert/ Reference/Caption.**

Your screen should be similar to Figure 3.50

Figure 3.50

The Caption options are described in the following table.

Option	Description
Label	Select from one of three default captions: Table, Figure, or Equation.
Position	Specify the location of the caption, either above or below a selected item. When an item is selected, the Position option is available.
New Label	Create your own captions.
Numbering	Specify the numbering format and starting number for your caption.
AutoCaption	Turns on the automatic insertion of a caption (label and number only) when you insert selected items into your document.

The default caption label, Figure, followed by the number 1 because it is the first figure in this document, appears in the Caption text box. You want to use this caption and to add additional descriptive text. The default setting of "Below selected item" is also correct.

2
● In the Caption text box, following "Figure 1," type - Giraffe in Serengeti.

● Click OK .

Your screen should be similar to Figure 3.51

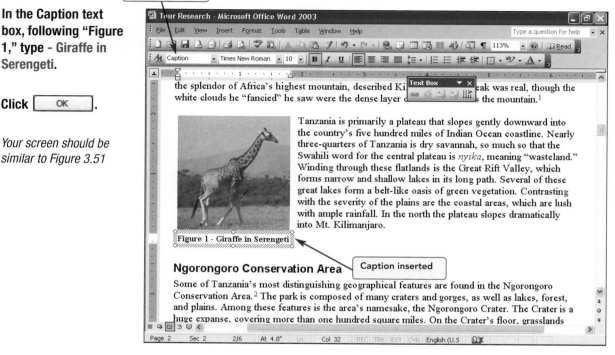

Style applied to caption text

Caption inserted

Figure 3.51

The caption label appears below the figure. It is inserted as a text box, a container for text and other graphic objects, that can be moved like any other object.

Adding a Cross-Reference

In the Animal Life section of the report, you discuss the animals found in the Serengeti. You want to include a cross-reference to the picture at this location.

While working in long documents, it is helpful to split the document window into two separate viewing areas.

Concept 6
Splitting Windows

6 To view different parts of the document at the same time, you can create a **split window** by dividing the document window into two horizontal sections. Each section is displayed in a pane that can be scrolled and manipulated independently. You can also display the document in different views in each pane. For example, you can display the document in Print Layout view in one pane and Normal view in the other.

Splitting the document window is most useful for viewing different sections of the document at the same time and allows you to quickly switch between panes to access information in the different sections without having to repeatedly scroll to the areas.

You will split the document window so you can see the figure you will reference in the upper pane and the text area where you will enter the cross-reference in the lower pane. When you create a split, the location of the split can be adjusted by dragging the pane divider line.

1 ● **Click outside the text box to deselect it.**

● **Choose Window/Split.**

● **Drag the split bar to the position shown in Figure 3.52.**

● **Click to position the split at that location.**

Another Method

You can also drag the split box located above the vertical scroll bar to create a split.

Your screen should be similar to Figure 3.52

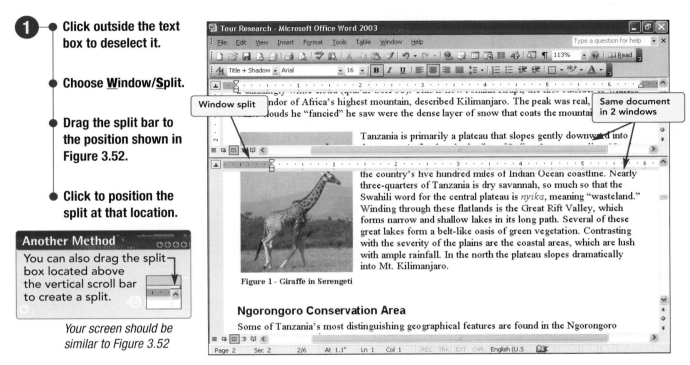

Figure 3.52

The document is divided into two horizontal panes. Next, you will scroll the document in the panes to display the areas you want to view. While using panes, the insertion point and the ruler are displayed in the active pane or the pane in which you are currently working.

2 ● Scroll the upper pane to display the Figure 1 caption below the giraffe picture.

● Scroll the lower pane to display the third paragraph in the Tanzania Animal Life section (page 3, section 2).

Your screen should be similar to Figure 3.53

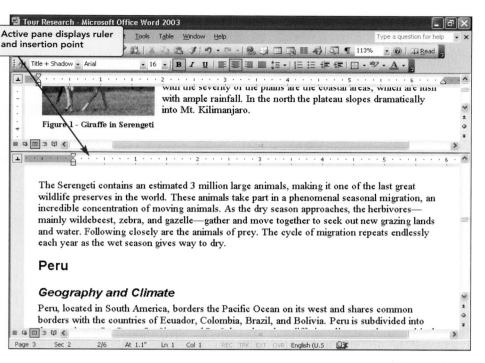

Active pane displays ruler and insertion point

Figure 1 - Giraffe in Serengeti

The Serengeti contains an estimated 3 million large animals, making it one of the last great wildlife preserves in the world. These animals take part in a phenomenal seasonal migration, an incredible concentration of moving animals. As the dry season approaches, the herbivores—mainly wildebeest, zebra, and gazelle—gather and move together to seek out new grazing lands and water. Following closely are the animals of prey. The cycle of migration repeats endlessly each year as the wet season gives way to dry.

Peru

Geography and Climate

Peru, located in South America, borders the Pacific Ocean on its west and shares common borders with the countries of Ecuador, Colombia, Brazil, and Bolivia. Peru is subdivided into

Figure 3.53

Now you can conveniently see both areas of the document while you enter the cross reference.

3 ● Move to after the word "water" (before the period) in the third paragraph in the Tanzania Animal Life section.

● Press [Spacebar].

● Type (see and press [Spacebar].

● Choose Insert/Reference/Cross-reference.

Your screen should be similar to Figure 3.54

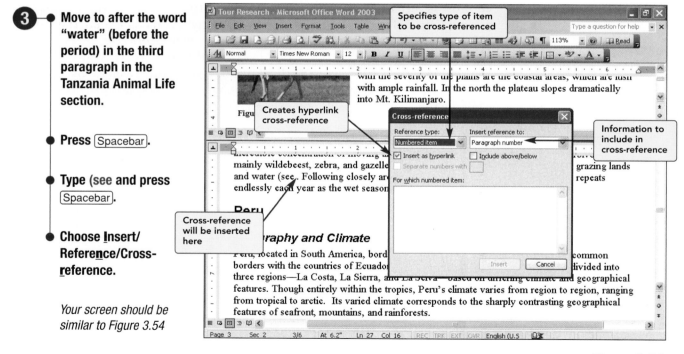

Specifies type of item to be cross-referenced

Creates hyperlink cross-reference

Information to include in cross-reference

Cross-reference will be inserted here

Figure 3.54

In the Cross-reference dialog box, you specify the type of item you are referencing and how you want the reference to appear. You want to reference the giraffe picture, and you want only the label "Figure 1" entered in the document.

4 • From the Reference Type drop-down list box, select Figure.

• From the Insert Reference To drop-down list box, select Only label and number.

Your screen should be similar to Figure 3.55

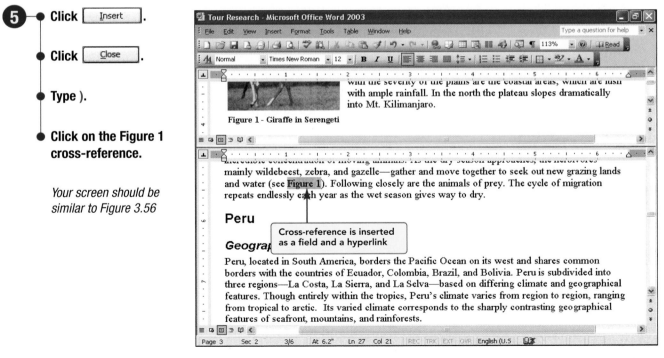

Figure 3.55

The For Which Caption list box lists all figure captions in the document. Because this document has only one figure caption, the correct figure caption is already selected. Notice that the Insert as Hyperlink option is selected by default. This option creates a hyperlink between the cross-reference and the caption. The default setting is appropriate.

5 • Click [Insert].

• Click [Close].

• Type).

• Click on the Figure 1 cross-reference.

Your screen should be similar to Figure 3.56

Figure 3.56

The cross-reference to Figure 1 is entered into the document as a field. Therefore, if you insert another picture or item that is cross-referenced, the captions and cross-references will renumber automatically. If you edit, delete, or move cross-referenced items, you should manually update the cross-references using Update Field. When you are working on a long document with several figures, tables, and graphs, this feature is very helpful.

Using a Cross-Reference Hyperlink

The cross-reference field is also a hyperlink, and just like a table of contents field, can be used to jump to the source it references.

1 ● Hold down Ctrl and click on the Figure 1 cross-reference.

Your screen should be similar to Figure 3.57

Clicking on cross-reference jumps to figure location in document

Figure 3.57

The document in the lower pane jumped to the caption beneath the figure. You will clear the split and save the document next.

2 ● Choose **W**indow/Remove **S**plit.

Another Method
You can also drag the split bar to the top of the document window or double-click on it to remove the split.

● Save the document.

The split is removed and the document window returns to a single pane.

Creating a Simple Table

Next, you want to add a table comparing the rainfall and temperature data for the three regions of Peru.

Concept 7
Table

7   A **table** is used to organize information into an easy-to-read format of horizontal rows and vertical columns. The insertion of a row and column creates a **cell** in which you can enter data or other information. Cells in a table are identified by a letter and number, called a **table reference**. Columns are identified from left to right beginning with the letter A, and rows are numbered from top to bottom beginning with the number 1. The table reference of the top leftmost cell is A1 because it is in the first column (A) and first row (1) of the table. The second cell in column 2 is cell B2. The fourth cell in column 3 is C4.

	A	B	C	D	E
1	(A1)	Jan	Feb	Mar	Total
2	East	7 (B2)	7	5	19
3	West	6	4	7	17
4	South	8	7 (C4)	9	24
5	Total	21	18	21	60

Tables are a very effective method for presenting information. The table layout organizes the information for readers and greatly reduces the number of words they have to read to interpret the data. Use tables whenever you can to make your documents easier to read.

The table you want to create will display columns for regions, rainfall, and temperature. The rows will display the data for each region. Your completed table will be similar to the one shown below.

Region	Annual Rainfall (Inches)	Average Temperature (Fahrenheit)
La Costa	2	68
La Sierra	35	54
La Selva	137	80

Inserting a Table

Word includes several different methods you can use to create tables. One method (Table/Convert/Text to Table) will quickly convert text that is arranged in tabular columns into a table. Another uses the Draw Table feature to create any type of table, but is most useful for creating complex tables that contain cells of different heights or a varying number of columns per row. The third method, which you will use, initially creates a simple table consisting of the same number of rows and columns.

1

- Click **La Selva** in the Document map.

- Close the Document map.

- Move to the second line of blank space below the paragraph on La Selva.

- Click 🔲 **Insert Table** (on the Standard toolbar).

Another Method ᵒᵒᵒᵒ
The menu equivalent is **T**able/**I**nsert/**T**able.

Your screen should be similar to Figure 3.58

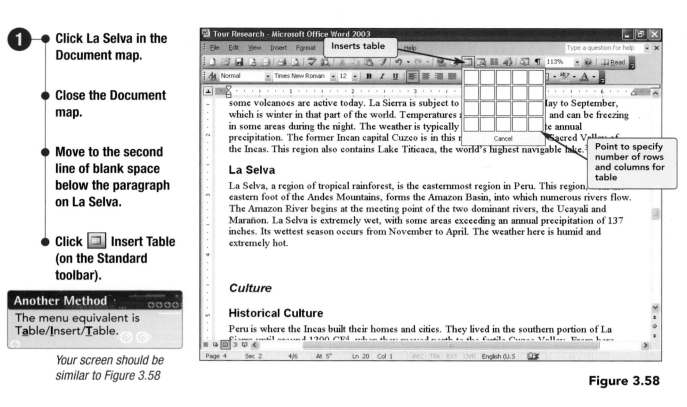

Figure 3.58

The Insert Table drop-down menu displays a grid in which you specify the number of rows and columns for the table. Moving the mouse pointer over the grid highlights the boxes in the grid and defines the table size. The dimensions are reflected in the bottom of the grid.

2

- Point to the boxes in Insert Table drop-down grid to highlight a 3-by-3 section.

- Click on the lower right corner of the selection.

Your screen should be similar to Figure 3.59

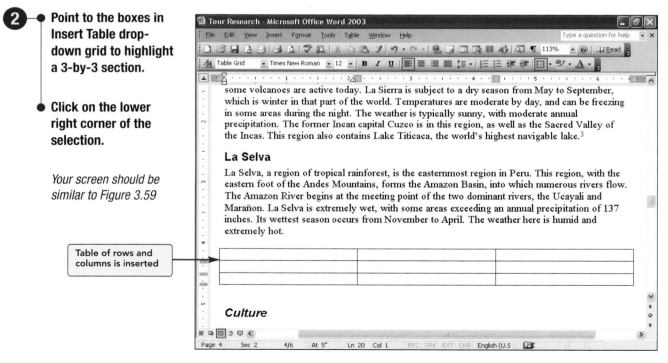

Figure 3.59

A table the full width of the page is drawn. It has equal sized columns and is surrounded by a black borderline.

Entering Data in a Table

Now you are ready to enter information in the table. Each cell contains a single line space where you can enter data. You can move from one cell to another by using the arrow keys or by clicking on the cell. In addition, you can use the keys shown in the table below to move around a table.

To Move To	Press
Next cell in row	[Tab ⇥]
Previous cell in row	[⇧ Shift] + [Tab ⇥]
First cell in row	[Alt] + [Home]
Last cell in row	[Alt] + [End]
First cell in column	[Alt] + [Page Up]
Last cell in column	[Alt] + [Page Down]
Previous row	[↑]
Next row	[↓]

Additional Information

Pressing [Tab ⇥] when in the last cell of a row moves to the first cell of the next row.

The mouse pointer may also appear as a solid black arrow when pointing to the table. When it is a ↓, you can click to select the entire column. When it is ↗, you can click to select a cell. You will learn more about this feature shortly.

You will begin by entering the information for La Costa in cells A1 through C1. You can type in the cell as you would anywhere in a normal document.

1

- If necessary, click cell A1.

- Type La Costa.

- Press Tab.

- In the same manner, type 2 in cell B1 and 68 in cell C1.

- Continue entering the information shown below, using Tab to move to the next cell.

Cell	Entry
A2	La Sierra
B2	35
C2	54
A3	La Selva
B3	137
C3	80

Your screen should be similar to Figure 3.60

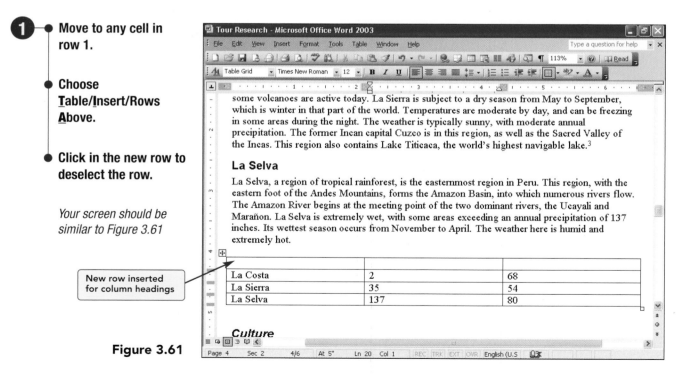

Figure 3.60

Inserting a Row

After looking at the table, you realize you forgot to include a row above the data to display the column headings.

1

- Move to any cell in row 1.

- Choose Table/Insert/Rows Above.

- Click in the new row to deselect the row.

Your screen should be similar to Figure 3.61

Figure 3.61

Now, you are ready to add the text for the headings.

2
- In cell A1 type **Region**.

- In cell B1 type **Annual Rainfall**.

- Press ←Enter to insert a second line in the cell.

- Type **(Inches)**.

- In cell C1 type **Average Temperature** on the first line and **(Fahrenheit)** on the second.

Your screen should be similar to Figure 3.62

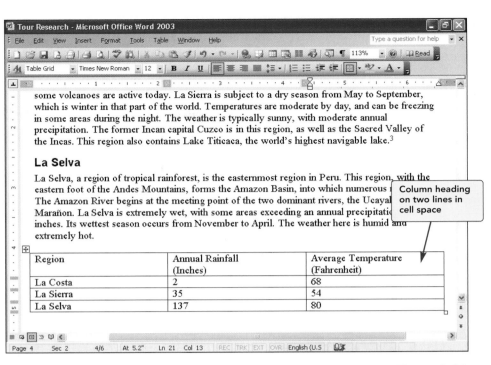

Figure 3.62

Sizing a Table

The table is much larger than it needs to be. To quickly reduce the overall table size, you can drag the resize handle □. This handle appears in the lower right corner whenever the mouse pointer rests over the table. Once the table is smaller, you will select the entire table by clicking the ⊞ move handle and center it between the margins.

1
- Drag the □ resize handle to decrease the width of the table to 5 inches (see Figure 3.63).

- Click ⊞ to select the entire table.

- Click ≡ Center.

Additional Information

You can also drag the ⊞ Move handle to move the table to any location.

Your screen should be similar to Figure 3.63

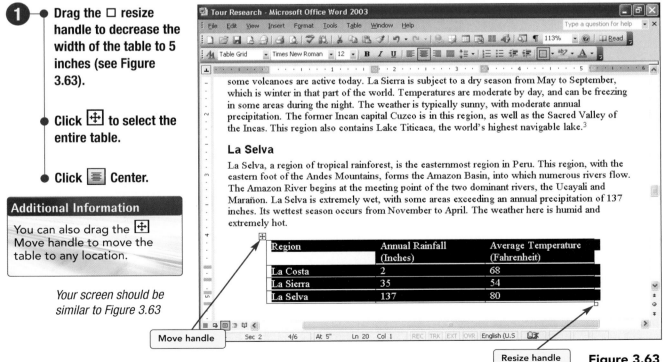

Figure 3.63

Formatting a Table

To enhance the appearance of the table, you can apply many different formats to the cells. This process is similar to adding formatting to a document, except that the formatting affects the selected cells only.

You want the entries in the cells A1 through C1, and B2 through C4, to be centered in their cell spaces. As you continue to modify the table, many cells can be selected and changed at the same time. You can select areas of a table using the Select command on the Table menu. However, it is often faster to use the procedures described in the table below.

Area to Select	Procedure
Cell	Click the left edge of the cell when the pointer is ◢.
Row	Click to the left of the row when the pointer is ◿.
Column	Click the top of the column when the pointer is ↓.
Multiple cells, rows, or columns	Drag through the cells, rows, or columns when the pointer is ↓, or select the first cell, row, or column and hold down ⇧Shift while clicking on another cell, row, or column.
Contents of next cell	Press Tab⇥.
Contents of previous cell	Press ⇧Shift + Tab⇥.
Entire table	Press Alt + 5 (on the numeric keypad with NumLock off) or click ⊞.

1 • Select cells A1 through C1.

• Click ▤ Center.

• In the same manner, center cells B2 through C4.

• Click on any cell of the table.

Your screen should be similar to Figure 3.64

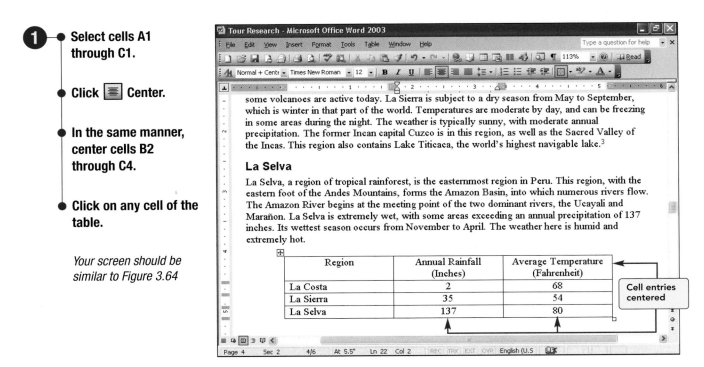

Figure 3.64

A quicker way to apply formats to a table is to use the table AutoFormat feature. This feature includes built-in combinations of formats that can be applied to a table. The AutoFormats consist of a combination of fonts, colors, patterns, borders, and alignment settings.

2 • Choose T**a**ble/Table Auto**F**ormat.

Your screen should be similar to Figure 3.65

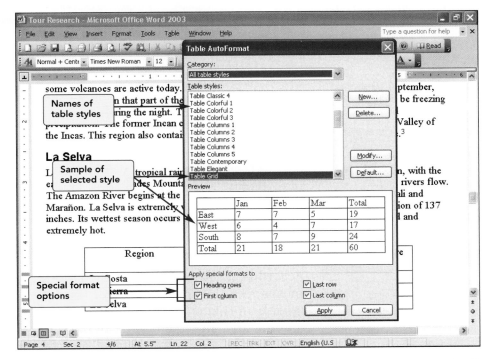

Figure 3.65

From the AutoFormat dialog box, you select the format design you want to apply to the table. The Table Grid style is the default selection. In addition, all the sections of the table that will receive special formatting, such as the heading row and last row, are selected. These settings allow you to emphasize different areas of the table, such as the last row and column where total values are frequently displayed. The Preview area shows how the selected format will look.

Since this table does not include any special information in the last column or the last row, you do not want any special formats applied to them.

3 • Clear the **L**ast Row and Last Col**u**mn special format options.

• Select several names from the Table styles list and look at the samples in the Preview box.

• Select Table Colorful 1.

• Click [Apply].

• Select the table and center it again.

• Click outside the table to deselect it.

• Click 🖫 Save.

Your screen should be similar to Figure 3.66

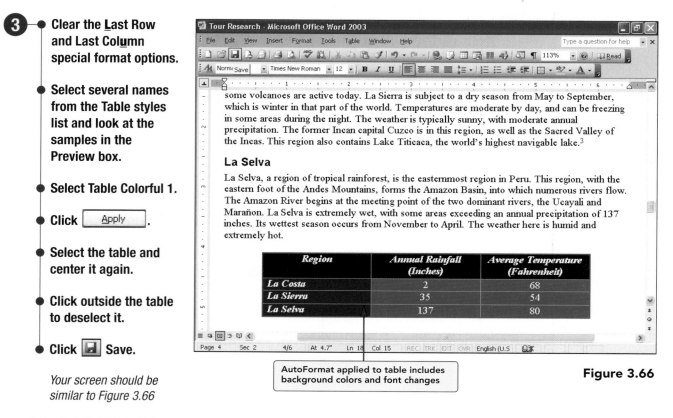

AutoFormat applied to table includes background colors and font changes

Figure 3.66

Additional Information
Use the Table Normal AutoFormat style to restore the default table style.

The table is reformatted to the new design. Different color backgrounds are applied to the entire table along with a change in the text color and italics. Using AutoFormat was much faster than applying these features individually.

Sorting a List

Additional Information
MLA formatting for the Works Cited page also requires that the page is a separate numbered page with the title "Works Cited" centered one inch from the top margin. It should also be double-spaced, as is the entire report.

The last page of the report contains the list of works cited in the report. According to the MLA style, each work directly referenced in the paper must appear in alphabetical order by author's last name. Additionally, they must be formatted as hanging indents—the first line is even with the left margin, and subsequent lines of the same work are indented .5 inch. This page needs to be alphabetized and formatted. To quickly arrange the references in alphabetical order, you can sort the list.

Concept 8

Sort

8 Word can quickly arrange or **sort** text, numbers, or data in lists or tables in alphabetical, numeric, or date order based on the first character in each paragraph. The sort order can be ascending (A to Z, 0 to 9, or earliest to latest date) or descending (Z to A, 9 to 0, or latest to earliest date). The following table describes the rules that are used when sorting.

Sort By	Rules
Text	First, items beginning with punctuation marks or symbols (such as !, #, $, %, or &) are sorted.
	Second, items beginning with numbers are sorted. Dates are treated as three-digit numbers.
	Third, items beginning with letters are sorted.
Numbers	All characters except numbers are ignored. The numbers can be in any location in a paragraph.
Date	Valid date separators include hyphens, forward slashes (/), commas, and periods. Colons (:) are valid time separators. If unable to recognize a date or time, Word places the item at the beginning or end of the list (depending on whether you are sorting in ascending or descending order).
Field results	If an entire field (such as a last name) is the same for two items, Word next evaluates subsequent fields (such as a first name) according to the specified sort options.

When a tie occurs, Word uses the first nonidentical character in each item to determine which item should come first.

First you will change the format of the list of works to hanging indent and then you will rearrange the order. You will use the default Sort Text settings that will sort by text and paragraphs in ascending order.

1
- Move to the last page of the document.
- Select the list of references.
- Drag the ⌂ Hanging Indent marker on the ruler to the .5 inch position.

Having Trouble?
Click and drag on the triangle section of the Hanging Indent marker.

Another Method
You could also apply the Body Text Indent style or press Ctrl + T to create hanging indents.

- Choose Table/Sort.
- Click [OK].
- Deselect the list of references.

Your screen should be similar to Figure 3.67

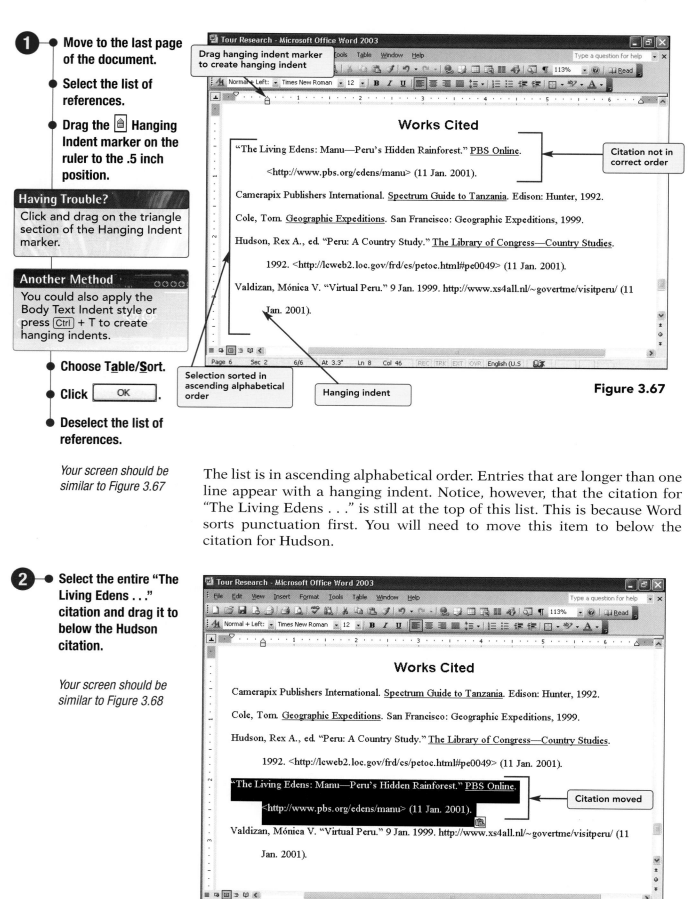

Figure 3.67

The list is in ascending alphabetical order. Entries that are longer than one line appear with a hanging indent. Notice, however, that the citation for "The Living Edens . . ." is still at the top of this list. This is because Word sorts punctuation first. You will need to move this item to below the citation for Hudson.

2
- Select the entire "The Living Edens . . ." citation and drag it to below the Hudson citation.

Your screen should be similar to Figure 3.68

Figure 3.68

Creating Headers and Footers

Next you want to add information in a header and footer to the report.

Concept 9
Header and Footer

9 Headers and footers provide information that typically appears at the top and bottom of each page in a document and helps the reader locate information in a document. A **header** is a line or several lines of text in the top margin of each page. The header usually contains the title and the section of the document. A **footer** is a line or several lines of text in the margin space at the bottom of every page. The footer usually contains the page number and perhaps the date. Headers and footers can also contain graphics, such as a company logo.

    The same header and footer can be used throughout a document, or a different header and footer can be used in different sections of a document. For example, a unique header or footer can be used in one section and a different one in another section. You can also have a unique header or footer on the first page, or omitted entirely from the first page, or use a different header and footer on odd and even pages.

Adding a Header

You want the report header to display your name and the page number.

1 ● Move to the Tanzania heading on page 2.

● Choose **V**iew/**H**eader and Footer.

Your screen should be similar to Figure 3.69

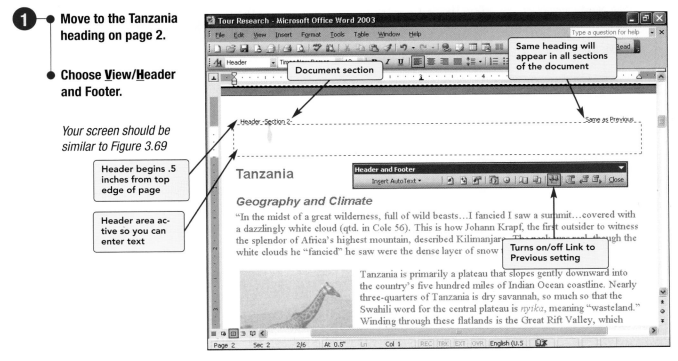

Figure 3.69

The document dims, and the header area becomes active. The Header and Footer toolbar is automatically displayed. Its buttons, identified below, are used to add items to the header and footer and to navigate between headers and footers.

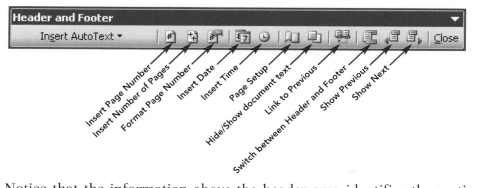

Notice that the information above the header area identifies the section location of the document where the insertion point is positioned, in this case, section 2. In addition, in the upper right corner the message "Same as Previous" is displayed. When this setting is on, the header in the sections before and after the section in which you are entering a header will have the same header. Because you do not want the title page in section 1 to have a header, you will break the connection between sections by turning off this option.

2 ● Click 📇 **Link to Previous.**

Your screen should be similar to Figure 3.70

Additional Information

MLA style requires that headers and footers be placed .5 inch from the top and bottom of the page. This is the default layout for the normal document. The header includes the page number preceded by the author's name.

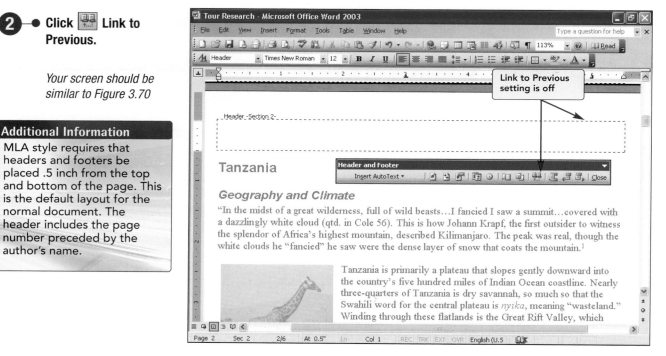

Figure 3.70

You type in the header as if it were a mini-document. The header and footer text can be formatted just like any other text. In addition, you can control the placement of the header and footer text by specifying its alignment: left-aligned, centered, or right-aligned in the header or footer space. You will enter your name followed by the page number, right-aligned.

3
- Type **your name**.
- Press **Spacebar**.
- Click **#** **Insert Page Number**.
- Click **≡** **Align Right**.

Your screen should be similar to Figure 3.71

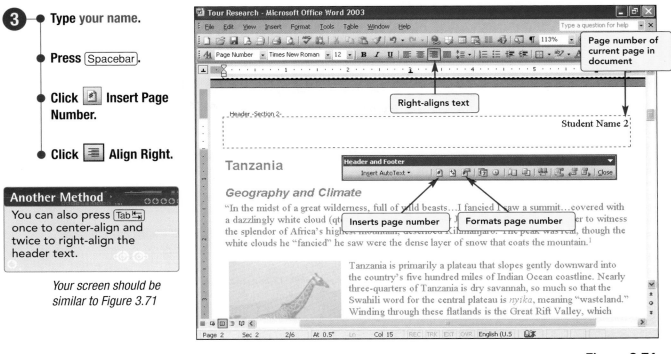

Figure 3.71

The page number "2" is displayed, because that is the current page in the document. You do not want the title page included in the page numbering, but instead want to begin page numbering with the first page of section 2.

4
- Click **#** **Format Page Number**.

Your screen should be similar to Figure 3.72

Figure 3.72

The Page Number Format dialog box is used to change the format of page numbers, to include chapter numbers, and to change the page numbering sequence. The default page numbering setting continues the numbering from the first section. You will reset the page number sequence to begin section 2 with page 1.

5 ● Choose Start **A**t.

Additional Information
The default Start At setting begins numbering with 1.

● Click [OK].

Your screen should be similar to Figure 3.73

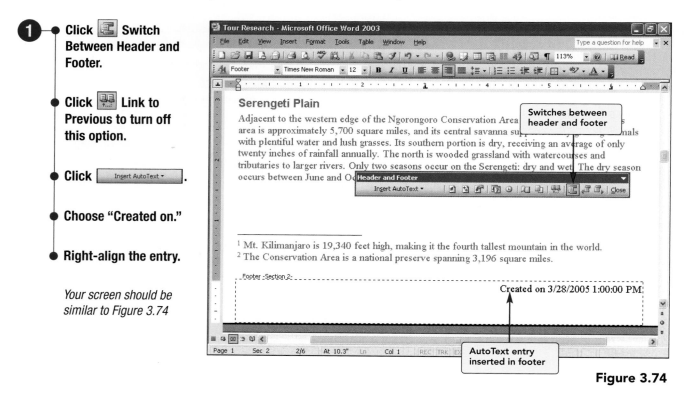

Figure 3.73

The header now displays "1" as the current page number.

Adding a Footer

You want to display the date in the footer. To quickly add this information, you will use an AutoText entry.

1 ● Click Switch Between Header and Footer.

● Click Link to Previous to turn off this option.

● Click [Insert AutoText ▾].

● Choose "Created on."

● Right-align the entry.

Your screen should be similar to Figure 3.74

Figure 3.74

The AutoText entry is displayed followed by the date and time.

2 ● **Close the Header and Footer toolbar.**

● **In section 2, scroll down to see the bottom of page 1 and the top of page 2.**

Your screen should be similar to Figure 3.75

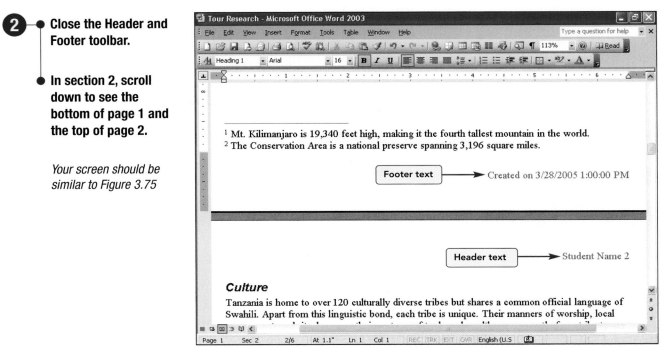

Figure 3.75

The document area is active again, and the header and footer text appears dimmed. The header and footer can only be seen in Print Layout view and when the document is printed.

Checking the Document

Before you print the report, you want to quickly read the entire document. You will do this using the Reading Layout view. Then you will do a final check for spelling and grammar errors in the document, including the footnotes, header, and footer. You also want to check the formatting of the document for consistency. Many times when creating a long document, it is easy to format areas differently that should be formatted the same. For example, if your headings are mostly formatted as Heading 2 styles, but you accidentally format a heading with a Heading 3 style, Word can locate the inconsistent formatting and quickly make the appropriate correction for you. Using the formatting consistency checker can give your documents a more professional appearance.

Using Reading Layout View

To make documents easier to read, Word includes a Reading Layout view that displays the document like pages in a book.

1 ● Click 🕮 Read .

Another Method

You can also check ▣ in the scrollbar or press [Alt] + R to switch to Reading Layout view.

● If necessary, click ▣ **Allow Multiple Pages to display two screen pages.**

● If the Document Map is displayed, click 🔍 Document Map to close it.

Your screen should be similar to Figure 3.76

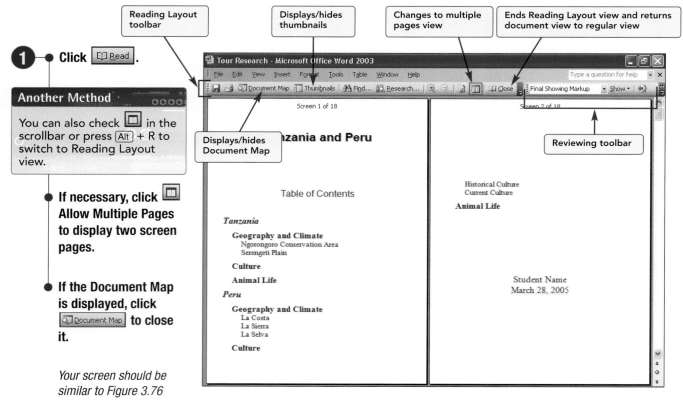

Reading Layout toolbar

Displays/hides thumbnails

Changes to multiple pages view

Ends Reading Layout view and returns document view to regular view

Displays/hides Document Map

Reviewing toolbar

Figure 3.76

The body of the document is displayed as screen pages that are sized to fit your screen and that are easy to browse. These pages do not represent the pages you would see when you print the document. Because Reading Layout view is not designed for editing and creating a document, unnecessary features, such as the Standard and Formatting toolbars and the status bar, are hidden to provide more space on the screen to display the document in pages.

The Reading Layout toolbar is displayed and contains buttons to access reading-related activities. In addition the Reviewing toolbar is displayed and includes features to help you to annotate the document with comments and highlighting.

Using Reading Layout view you can quickly review the entire manuscript as if reading a book. You can use the scroll bar to browse the document two screen pages at a time. To jump quickly to different sections of the document you can display the Document Map. You can also display thumbnail images of each screen page in a separate pane and click on the thumbnail to display that page. A single page is displayed when thumbnails or the Document Map are displayed.

2 ● Click the ▼ scroll arrow several times to read several pages of the document.

● Click [⊞ Thumbnails].

● Click on thumbnail image 8.

Your screen should be similar to Figure 3.77

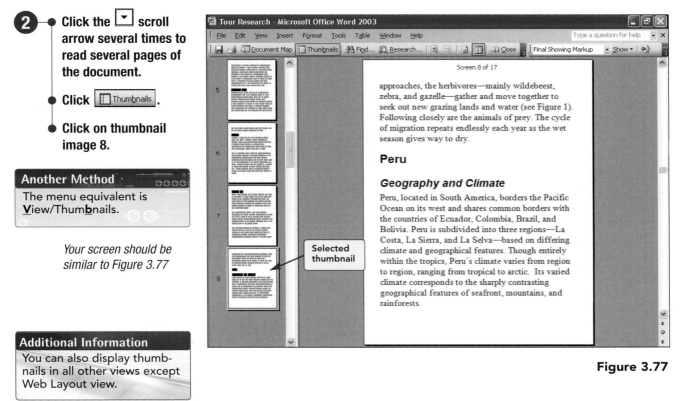

Additional Information
You can also display thumbnails in all other views except Web Layout view.

Figure 3.77

The selected thumbnail is surrounded by a gold border and the selected screen page is displayed.

3 ● Click [⊞ Thumbnails] to turn off this feature.

● Click [▣ Close] to close Reading Layout view and return to the previous screen view.

Another Method
You could also press [Esc] or [Alt] + C to exit Reading Layout view.

Redisplaying Spelling and Grammar Errors

Now you will turn on the display of spelling and grammar errors again and then spell and grammar check the document.

1 Move to the top of page 1 of section 2.

• Choose **Tools/Options/Spelling and Grammar**.

• Clear the checkmark from Hide **s**pelling errors in this document.

• Clear the checkmark from H**i**de grammatical errors in this document.

• Click OK .

• Click Spelling and Grammar.

• Choose **I**gnore All for all proper names, special terms and abbreviations. Respond appropriately to any other located errors.

• Click OK to end spelling and grammar checking.

Your screen should be similar to Figure 3.78

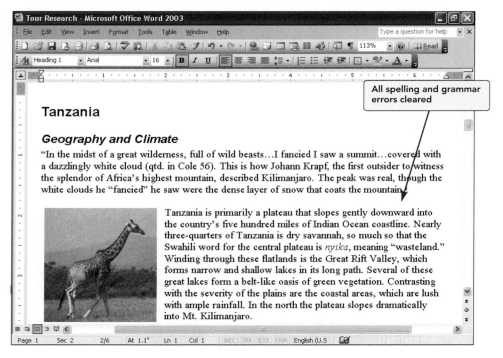

All spelling and grammar errors cleared

Figure 3.78

The Spelling and Grammar Checker first checked the document text for errors, then footnotes, and finally headers and footers.

Checking Formatting Inconsistencies

Next, you will turn on the Formatting Consistency Checker feature to check for formatting inconsistencies. Word identifies inconsistencies with a blue wavy underline.

- Choose **T**ools/**O**ptions.

- From the Edit tab, select Mark **f**ormatting inconsistencies.

- Click [OK].

- Right-click on the word Nyika in the second paragraph.

Your screen should be similar to Figure 3.79

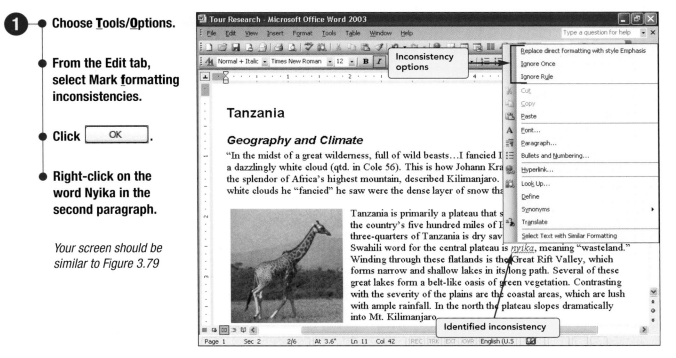

Figure 3.79

The first identified formatting inconsistency is for the italics applied to the word "nyika." When checking for formatting inconsistencies, Word looks for occurrences of similar formatting that you have applied directly to text, of styles that contain additional direct formatting, and of direct formatting that matches styles that are applied elsewhere in the document. If two occurrences of formatting are markedly different, then they are not identified as inconsistent. However, in cases where the formatting is very similar, they are identified as inconsistent. In this case, the identified inconsistency is because the formatting was applied directly to the word using the italics feature, and the same result could be obtained by using the style Emphasis. Because changing this formatting will not affect the appearance of the word, you will ignore the suggestion.

2 • Choose Ignore Once.

• Scroll to page 4 to see the next located occurrence in the Machu Picchu heading.

• Right-click on Machu Picchu.

Your screen should be similar to Figure 3.80

Figure 3.80

The suggested change is to replace the direct formatting of this text (14 points and bold) with the equivalent heading style. Because you want the topic to appear in the table of contents, you will replace the formatting with the Heading 4 style. Then you will move to the last located inconsistency.

3 • Choose Replace direct formatting with style Heading 4.

• Move to the Works Cited page.

• Right-click on the Works Cited title.

• Right-click on any of the referenced works.

Your screen should be similar to Figure 3.81

Figure 3.81

The suggested change for all the cited works is to use the Body Text Indent style. You will not make this change since it will not affect the appearance of the text. The suggested style change for the title was to use the Title style. In this case, you want to change it to a Heading 1 style so it will appear in the table of contents. You will need to make this change directly.

4 ● Apply the **Heading 1** style to the Works Cited heading.

● Click **≡** Center.

● Choose **T**ools/**O**ptions/ Edit/Mark formatting inconsistencies to turn off this feature.

● Click **OK**.

Your screen should be similar to Figure 3.82

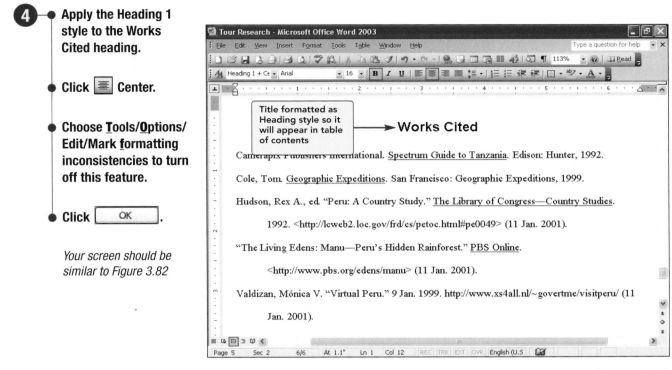

Figure 3.82

Updating a Table of Contents

You have made many modifications to the report since generating the table of contents, so you want to update the listing. Because the table of contents is a field, if you add or remove headings, rearrange topics, or make other changes that affect the table of contents listing, you can quickly update the table of contents. In this case, you have added pictures and a table that may have affected the paging of the document, and you changed two headings to heading styles. You will update the table of contents to ensure that the page references are accurate and that all headings are included.

1 ● Move to the top of the document.

● Right-click on the table of contents to display the shortcut menu.

● Choose <u>U</u>pdate Field.

Another Method

You can also press [F9] to quickly update a field.

● Choose Update <u>e</u>ntire table.

● Click [OK].

● Click outside the table of contents to deselect it.

● Scroll the window to see the entire table of contents.

Your screen should be similar to Figure 3.83

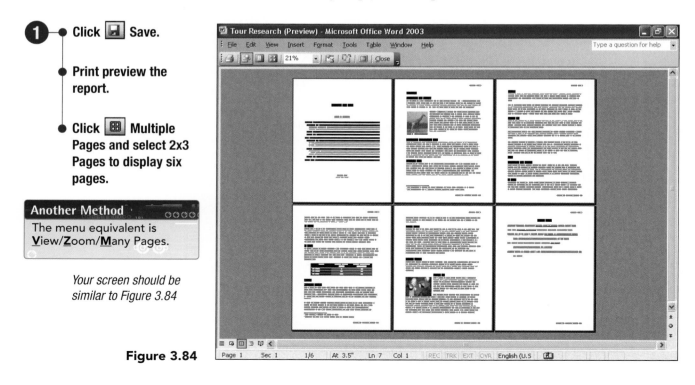

Figure 3.83

The page numbers referenced by each table-of-contents hyperlink have been updated as needed and the two new topics are listed.

Printing Selected Pages

You are now ready to print the report.

1 ● Click 💾 Save.

● Print preview the report.

● Click 📄 Multiple Pages and select 2x3 Pages to display six pages.

Another Method

The menu equivalent is <u>V</u>iew/<u>Z</u>oom/<u>M</u>any Pages.

Your screen should be similar to Figure 3.84

Figure 3.84

You would like to print only the first, second, fourth, and sixth pages of the document. To do this, you use the Print dialog box to select the pages you want to print. When printing pages in different sections, the page number and section number (p#s#) must be identified in the page range.

2 ● Choose **File/Print**.

● If necessary, select the appropriate printer for your computer system.

● Type **p1s1, p1s2, p3s2, p5s2** in the Pages text box.

● Click [OK] .

● Click [■] One Page to return the preview display to a single page.

● Close Print Preview.

● Change to Normal view, if necessary, turn off Document Map, and set the zoom to 100%.

● Close the file and exit Word.

Your printed output should be similar to that shown in the Case Study at the beginning of the lab.

Focus on Careers

EXPLORE YOUR CAREER OPTIONS

Market Research Analyst
Have you ever wondered who investigates the market for new products? Ever thought about the people who put together phone surveys? Market research analysts are responsible for determining the potential sales for a new product or service. They conduct surveys and compile statistics for clients or their employer. These reports usually include report features like a table of contents, cross-references, headers and footers, and footnotes for references. Market research analysts may hold positions as faculty at a university, work for large organizations, or hold governmental positions. The salary range for market research analysts is $37,000 to $52,000 and demand is high in a strong economy.

lab exercises

matching

Match the item on the left with the correct description on the right.

1. split window _____
2. table reference _____
3. inline image _____
4. Document Map _____
5. tight wrap _____
6. section break _____
7. cross-reference _____
8. note pane _____
9. Click and Type _____
10. heading style _____
11. footnote

a. combination of fonts, type sizes, bold, and italics used to identify different levels of headings in a document
b. divides document into two areas you can view and scroll independently
c. graphic positioned directly in the text
d. feature used to quickly insert items in a blank area of a document
e. letter and number used to identify table cells
f. uses headings to navigate through the document
g. text closely follows contours around a graphic
h. reference from one part of the document to another part
i. instructs Word to end one set of format settings and begin another
j. additional explanatory information at the bottom of a page

multiple choice

Circle the correct response to the questions below.

1. A(n)_____ displays information in horizontal rows and vertical columns.
   a. Document Map
   b. cell reference
   c. object
   d. table

2. _____ are lines of text at the top and bottom of a page outside the margin lines.
   a. characters and paragraphs
   b. headers and footers
   c. tables and text wrappers
   d. styles and sections

3. A _____ allows you to see two parts of the same document at the same time.
   a. divided window
   b. split window
   c. sectioned window
   d. note pane

4. A _____ is inserted automatically when a new page is created in a document.
   a. hard page break
   b. section break
   c. soft page break
   d. page division

5. You can control how text appears around a graphic with _____ styles.
   a. sorting
   b. text wrapping
   c. section
   d. caption

6. A(n) _____ is a predesigned set of formats that can be applied to characters and paragraphs.
   a. AutoFormat
   b. effect
   c. style
   d. font

7. A _____ is a title or explanation for a table, picture, or graph.
   a. statement
   b. cross-reference
   c. caption
   d. footnote

8. A _____ is a reference from one part of a document to related information in another part of the same document.
   a. Document Map
   b. note
   c. heading
   d. cross-reference

9. Text sorted in _____ order appears alphabetically from A to Z.
   a. ordered
   b. descending
   c. ascending
   d. rescending

10. _____ displays a document like pages in a book.
   a. Reading Layout view
   b. Print preview
   c. Print Layout
   d. Multiple page view

lab exercises

true/false

Circle the correct answer to the following questions.

1. Paragraph styles are a combination of any character formats and
    paragraph formats that affect all text in a paragraph.   True   False
2. Word automatically applies styles to the text in an outline as it is entered.   True   False
3. AutoCaption selects one of three default captions.   True   False
4. The Document Preview pane displays the headings in your document.   True   False
5. The drawing layer is separate from the text in a document.   True   False
6. A section break identifies the end of a section and stores the document
    format settings.   True   False
7. When a tie occurs in a sort, Word sorts text by numerical characters.   True   False
8. A style is a combination of character formats.   True   False
9. A cross-reference can be placed within a document to refer back to a
    figure or other reference in the document.   True   False
10. An endnote is a source reference that typically appears
    at the end of a document.   True   False

fill-in

1. The _____ identifies the end of a section and stores the document format settings.

2. A(n) _____ is a set of formats that is assigned a name and can be quickly applied to a selection.

3. The _____ for a footnote appears at the bottom of the page on which the reference mark appears.

4. By changing a graphic to a(n) _____ it is inserted into the drawing layer.

5. The intersection of a row and column creates a(n) _____.

6. You can arrange, or _____, numbers or data in lists or tables in Word.

7. A(n) _____ is a line or several lines of text at the top of each page in a document.

8. A(n) _____ is used to organize information into horizontal rows and vertical columns.

9. _____ are source references or long comments that usually appear at the end of a document.

10. Specifying _____ controls how text appears around a graphic object.

Hands-On Exercises

step-by-step

Creating a Table ★

1. You work for the Animal Rescue Foundation and are putting together a list of the donation sites to give to local pet stores along with a map showing the location of each site. You would like to put the donation site list in a table. Your completed table is shown here.

   a. Open a new document and use Click and Type to enter the title **Animal Rescue Foundation Donation Sites** at the top of the document. Apply the Title style. Include a blank line below the title.

   b. Insert a simple table with 3 columns and 10 rows. Enter the following information into the table:

3	Pets 'R Us	Sally Lee
1	Reptile House	Suhas Daftuar
6	Exotic Bird Co.	Chirag Shah
5	Animal House	James Smith
4	Aimee's Pets	AJ Guerin
2	Aquarium Emporium	Mendi Gault
7	Cats & Kittens	Alicia McKellan
8	Fancy Fins	William Hertzler
10	Bird's the Word	Helen Bunch
9	Ma's Paws	Susanna Dickson

   c. Change the order of the list so that it is sorted by the numbers in ascending order.

   d. Insert a new row above the first entry and enter the following headings:

Map Location	Donation Site	Contact Information

   e. Apply a table AutoFormat of your choice to the table.

   f. Center the table.

   g. Color the title to match colors used in the table.

   h. Include a footnote, "See map for site locations" with the reference mark next to the Map Locations table heading.

   i. Add a header to the document that displays your name left-aligned and the current date right-aligned.

   j. Save the document as Donation Sites.

   k. Preview and print the document.

Student Name 4/13/2005

Animal Rescue Foundation Donation Sites

Map Location[1]	Donation Site	Contact Information
1	Reptile House	Suhas Daftuar
2	Aquarium Emporium	Mendi Gault
3	Pets 'R Us	Sally Lee
4	Aimee's Pets	AJ Guerin
5	Animal House	James Smith
6	Exotic Bird Co.	Chirag Shah
7	Cats & Kittens	Alicia McKellan
8	Fancy Fins	William Hertzler
9	Ma's Paws	Susanna Dickson
10	Bird's the Word	Helen Bunch

[1] See map for site locations.

Creating and Modifying an Outline ★

2. The Downtown Internet Café provides handouts to customers on different topics related to coffee. You are just starting work on a new handout about selecting the right beans. To help organize your thoughts, you decide to create an outline of the main topics to be included. Your completed outline is shown here.

a. Open a new blank document. Switch to Outline view. Turn on formatting marks.

b. The topics you want to discuss are shown below. Enter these topics at the outline level indicated, pressing ⏎Enter at the end of each.

Aroma (Level 1)

Traditional Blends (Level 2)

Colombian Supremo (Level 3)

French Roast (Level 3)

Sumatra French Roast (Level 4)

Viking French Blend (Level 4)

Espresso Roast (Level 3)

Guatemala Antigua (Level 3)

Brazil Santos (Level 3)

Body (Level 1)

African Coffees (Level 2)

Ethiopian Yirgacheffe (Level 2)

Ethiopian Harrar (Level 2)

Tanzanian Peaberry (Level 3)

Acidity (Level 1)

Asian Coffees (Level 2)

Sumatra Mandheling (Level 3)

Hawaiian Coffees (Level 2)

Hawaiian Kona Fancy (Level 3)

Maui Kaanapali (Level 3)

Flavor (Level 1)

Central and South American Coffees (Level 2)

Costa Rican Tarrazzu (Level 3)

Jamaican Blends (Level 3)

Jamaican Blue Mountain (Level 4)

Jamaica Prime (Level 4)

Student Name—November 12, 2005

Aroma

Traditional Blends

French Roast

Sumatra French Roast

Viking French Blend

Colombian Supremo

Espresso Roast

Brazil Santos

Body

African Coffees

Ethiopian Yirgacheffe

Ethiopian Harrar

Tanzanian Peaberry

Flavor

Central and South American Coffees

Costa Rican Tarrazzu

Jamaican Blends

Jamaican Blue Mountain

Jamaica Prime

Acidity

Asian Coffees

Sumatra Mandheling

Celebes Kalossi Toraja

Student Name—November 12, 2005

Hawaiian Coffees

Hawaiian Kona Fancy

Maui Kaanapali

c. Move the Flavor topic and all subtopics above the Acidity topic.

d. In the Body topic, change the subtopics Ethiopian Yirgacheffe and Ethiopian Harrar to level 3.

e. In the Aroma topic, move Colombian Supremo below Viking French Blend.

f. Insert a new level 3 line, **Celebes Kalossi Toraja** as the last subtopic under Asian Coffee.

...e Guatemala Antigua topic under Aroma.

... formatting marks. Switch to Normal view.

...our name and the date centered in a header.

...age 1 of the outline.

...he outline as Coffee Outline in a new folder name Cafe. Close the file.

a Flyer ★ ★

...ports Company is introducing a new line of kayaking and equipment. It is holding a weekend promotional event to familiarize the community with paddling equipment. You have already started designing a flyer to advertise the event, but it still needs additional work. Your completed flyer is shown below.

a. Open the file wd03_Kayaking Flyer.

b. Change the left and right margins to 1 inch.

c. Create the following table of data below the ". . . boat giveaway!" paragraph.

TIME	EVENT
12:00 p.m.	Freestyle Whitewater Panel Discussion
1:15 p.m.	Kids Canoe Relay Race
1:30 p.m.	Becky Andersen & Brad Ludden Autographed Boats Charity Auction
2:30 p.m.	Drawing for Extrasport Joust Personal Flotation Device
3:00 p.m.	Team Dagger Autograph Session
5:00 p.m.	Free BBQ dinner

d. Use Table/AutoFit/AutoFit to Contents to size the table to the cell contents.

e. Apply an AutoFormat of your choice to the table. Center the table.

f. Insert the picture wd03_Kayacker from your data files to the right of the text "Meet Team Dagger." If necessary, size the graphic as shown in the example. Apply the Tight wrapping style and right horizontal alignment.

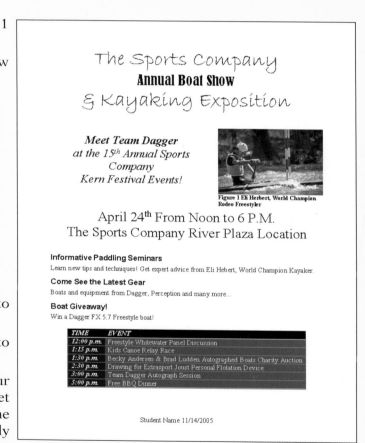

g. Add a caption of **Eli Herbert, World Champion Rodeo Freestyler** below the image.

h. Add formatting and styles of your choice to the document. Center the page vertically.

i. Preview the document. Make any editing changes you feel are appropriate.

j. Enter your name and the date centered in the footer.

k. Save the document as Kayaking Flyer.

l. Preview and print the document.

Writing a Report ★ ★ ★

4. As a senior trainer at Lifestyle Fitness Club, you are responsible for researching new fitness and sharing your findings with other trainers and clients. You have written a Beginner's Gui Yoga to distribute to club members. Pages two through three contain the body of your rep Several pages of your completed report are shown here. Use the features presented in this lab to ad the following to the report.

a. Open the file wd03_Yoga Practice.

b. Create a new page at the beginning of the document to be used as a title page. Enter the report title, **Beginner's Guide to Yoga**, your name, and the date centered on separate lines. Format the report title using the Title style.

c. Apply a Heading 1 style to the five topic headings.

d. Create a table of contents on the title page below the date with a style of your choice.

e. Remove the hard page break and replace it with a next page section break, then center the title page vertically.

f. Insert the graphics wd03_History and wd03_Yoga Pose as shown in the example. Wrap the text around the graphics using a text wrapping method of your choice. Include captions below the graphic.

What is Yoga?

If you are beginning to think that Americans everywhere "do yoga"—you are right! Celebrities, the young, and the old, are spending time in the yoga studio. Over 18 million Americans practice one of the many styles of yoga for health, fitness, and spiritual well-being. Perhaps it seems like a new fad—the latest in a long line of abdominal crunch machines, aerobic dance routines, or martial arts hybrids. But yoga is not another dance routine requiring leg warmers; yoga has been a powerful mind and body therapy for thousands of years. While it first made an appearance in the United States in the 1800s, but it took the peace loving youth of the 1960s to bring it to popular attention. Today you can find yoga classes at the local YMCA, or as an extension of the New Age community, in nearly every city in the US.

There are many types of yoga, but yoga practice usually consists of a series of poses. These poses, called asanas, are designed to stretch and strengthen the body; most asanas are practiced in pairs to balance opposites. Yoga practice usually emphasizes breathing exercises and meditation in addition to series of asanas. Many consider yoga meditation in action. However, most Americans do not practice yoga as part of a specific spiritual tradition, rather they seek stress reduction, relaxation, and general health benefits of yoga. Regardless of your spiritual beliefs, yoga practice is designed to strengthen the link between mind and body.

Figure 1--Yoga emphasizes breathing and meditation.

History of Yoga

The roots of yoga are found in India, more than 5000 years ago, before written language even existed. Ceramics from this period include images of yoga poses.[1] Many people mistakenly attribute the origins of yoga to Hinduism, but Yoga actually predates Hindu practices. In fact, the term "yoga" is a Sanskrit, one of the world's oldest languages, meaning to connect the mind, body, and spirit.

The main branches of yoga as we know them today began to appear in India at approximately the same time as the Christian era began in the Middle East. In the 1960s when Western celebrities, like the Beatles, sought out the magnetic yogis like Maharishi Mahesh Yogi, yoga reconnected with the West.

Figure 2--Yoga's roots lie in ancient India.

Benefits

As alternative therapies, like acupuncture, massage, and meditation, have become more popular options for those with chronic pain, interest in yoga has also increased. However, Western medicine has only recently begun to

[1] Ancient ceramics found in the caves of Mojendro-Daro and Harappa depict recognizable yoga positions.

Student Name   10/23/2005

Beginner's Guide to Yoga

Student Name
October 23, 2005

Table of Contents

Student Name   10/23/2005

g. Apply additional formats of your choice to the report.

h. Under the section History of Yoga, move to the end of the second sentence in the first paragraph after the word "poses" and add the following text as a footnote:

Ancient ceramics found in the caves of Mojendro-Daro and Harappa depict recognizable yoga positions.

i. In the Ashtanga (Power Yoga) description, move to the end of the second sentence after the word "style" and add the following text as a footnote:

Vinyasa is a flow or sequence of poses.

j. At the end of the document, create a Works Consulted page following the example in the lab. Apply a Heading 1 style to the page title. Sort the list and use a .5 inch hanging indent. Enter the following four reference sources:

Iyengar, B.K.S. *Yoga: The Path to Holistic Health.* Los Angeles: DK Publishing, 2001.

Sparrowe, Linda. *Yoga.* New York: Hugh Lautner Levin Associates, 2002.

Phillips, Kathy. *The Spirit of Yoga.* Los Angeles: Barrons Educational Series, 2002.

Wilber, Ken. The *Yoga Tradition: History, Religion, Philosophy and Practice Unabridged.* Philadelphia: Hohm Printers, 2001.

k. Update the table of contents and adjust any formatting as necessary.

l. In the header, add right-aligned page numbers. Do not number the title page. Add your name and the date centered in the footer.

m. Use Reading Layout view to review the document. Run a style consistency check.

n. Save the document as Yoga Guide in a new folder. Preview the document. Print the table of contents and pages one and four of the report.

Writing a Report ★ ★ ★

5. The marketing coordinator at Adventure Travel Tours has recently completed a study of market trends. She has concluded backpacking tours are a growing specialty. You have been asked to compose a report on some new tours and lightweight backpacking for distribution to some key customers. You have already started working on the report and just have some finishing touches to add. The table of contents will appear on the first page of the document. Pages two through four contain the body of your report. Several pages of your completed report are shown here. Use the features presented in this lab to add the following to the report.

a. Open the file wd03_Triple Crown.

b. Create a new page at the beginning of the document to be used as a title page. Enter the report title, **Lightweight Backpacking Adventures**, your name, and the date centered on separate lines. Format the report title only using the Title style.

c. Apply level 1 headings to the six topic headings.

d. On the title page below the date enter the text **Table of Contents** and format it using the Subtitle style. Create a table of contents using the Formal style. Display one level of headings and exclude the Title style.

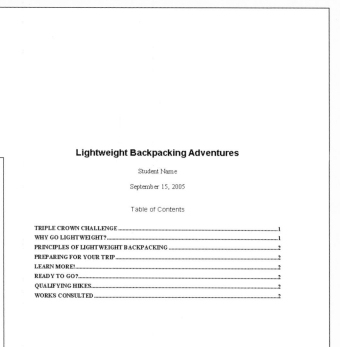

Lightweight Backpacking Adventures

Student Name

September 15, 2005

Table of Contents

Student Name - September 15, 2005

1

Triple Crown Challenge

Adventure Travel Tours, your premier active adventure vacation planner, is proud to announce three new adventure tours: Lightweight Backpacking Expeditions on the Pacific Coast Trail, Appalachian Trail, and Continental Divide Trail. Beginning in 2004 Adventure Travel Tour Guides will begin leading expeditions to complete each of these long distance hiking undertakings. At over 2000 miles long each, these three trails represent some of the greatest adventures available in the United States![1]

Figure 1 Hiking the PCT

In order to guarantee your success on these challenging adventures, Adventure Travel Tours is embarking on several qualifying lightweight backpacking trips. We invite you to join us on these exciting adventures and find out if the Triple Crown is the quest for you! Tracey Lynne, our Continental Divide Trail expert, has composed this introduction to lightweight backpacking to whet your appetite for the adventures ahead. (See Figure 4 ATT Guide Tracey Lynne) Please feel free to contact Tracey at Adventure Travel Tours to learn more about lightweight backpacking and the upcoming hikes!

Why Go Lightweight?

Any hiker will tell you: cutting weight is of utmost importance when you plan on hiking miles in the wilderness with all of your possessions strapped to your back. Accordingly, there are many "tricks of the trade" diehard backpackers use to cut weight from their packs. Some cut the handles from their toothbrushes, others trim the margins from their maps, and other hikers have been known to hike 2000 miles on granola and candy bars to avoid the weight of a cook stove and fuel. Yet most hikers don't flinch when it comes to buying the latest heavyweight hiking boots. Marketers have convinced those who love the outdoors that it is a dangerous world out there and we will need the heaviest and most durable backpacks, clothing, shoes, and equipment to survive. Traditional backpacking gear is designed to survive everything you can put it through—and more. Most gear is heavy and heavy duty, but all of this durability adds weight to our gear.

Figure 2 Jack Denae Goes "Lightweight"

Backpackers have begun to rethink their actual needs when out in the wilderness with an eye on reducing weight. Even with all the

[1] The Pacific Coast Trail is 2,650 miles long. The Appalachian Trail is 2,155 miles long. The Continental Divide Trail is approximately 2,800 miles long.

Student Name - September 15, 2005

e. Remove the hard page break and replace it with a next page section break, then center the title page vertically.

f. In this step you will be inserting several graphics. For each of these, size the graphic appropriately and add captions of your choice. Wrap the text around the picture using whatever text wrapping method you prefer. Insert the following pictures at the specified location:

- Insert the graphic wd03_PCT to the right of the first paragraph of the report.
- Insert the graphic wd03_Lightweight to the left of the first paragraph of the Why Go Lightweight? section.
- Insert the graphic wd03_Backpack to the right of the second paragraph in the Principles of Lightweight Backpacking section.
- Insert wd03_Tracey to the left of the last paragraph in the last section of the report.

g. In the second paragraph of the Triple Crown Challenge section, after the word "Lynne," add a cross-reference, with the Figure number and caption, for the photo of Tracey. Use the split window feature to add the cross-reference.

h. Apply additional formatting of your choice to the report. An example may be adding color to the title and headings.

i. Under the section Triple Crown Challenge in the last sentence of the first paragraph, after the word "States!," add the following text as a footnote: **The Pacific Coast Trail is 2,650 miles long. The Appalachian Trail is 2,155 miles long. The Continental Divide Trail is approximately 2,800 miles long.**

j. Under the section Principles of Lightweight Backpacking after the fourth sentence of the first paragraph, after the word "weight," add the following text as a footnote: **For example, a lightweight titanium stove weighs approximately three ounces, where the traditional stove may weigh as much as three times that weight.**

k. Add a new section titled **Qualifying Hikes**, with the following information in a table following the last paragraph in the Ready to Go? section:

Hike	Location	Distance	Date	Guide
Death Valley	California	35 miles	August 29, 2005	Logan Thomas
Paria Canyon	Page, Arizona	40 miles	September 12, 2005	Logan Thomas
Bryce To Zion	N. Arizona	120 miles	October 15, 2005	Tracey Lynne
Brian Head	Utah	95 miles	November 5, 2005	Jack Denae
Capitol Reef Park	Utah Desert	65 miles	February 23, 2006	Jack Denae

l. Apply formatting of your choice to the new table. Apply a Heading 1 style to the title.

m. At the end of the document, create a works consulted page following the example in the lab with a hanging indent. Enter the following five reference sources:

Jardine, Ray. *Beyond Backpacking: Ray Jardine's Guide to Lightweight Hiking. Arizona: AdventureLore Press, 1992.*

Berger, Karen. *Hiking the Triple Crown: Appalachian Trail — Pacific Crest Trail — Continental Divide Trail — How to Hike America's Longest Trails.* NY: Mountaineers Books, 2000.

Gibson, John. *Go Light: The Complete Guide to Lightweight Equipment for Hiking and Backpacking Eastern America!* New York, Thorndike Press, 2002.

Ridley, Tom. *Power Packing: Principles of Lightweight Long Distance Backpacking.* New York: Puffin, 1999.

Bryson, Bill. *A Walk in the Woods: Rediscovering America on the Appalachian Trail.* New York: Broadway Books, 1999.

n. Sort the list of references. Apply a Heading 1 style to the page title.

o. Update the table of contents and adjust formatting as needed.

p. In the header, add right-aligned page numbers. Do not number the title page. Enter your name and the date centered in the footer.

q. Use Reading Layout view to review the document. Run a style consistency check.

r. Save the document as ATT Triple Crown in a new folder. Preview the document. Print the table of contents and pages 1, 4, and 5 of the report.

on your own

Creating an Information Sheet ★

1. You work for a small camera repair and retail shop. You have fielded many different questions about digital cameras lately and have decided to compile these questions in an information sheet. Your completed document will offer your customers answers to the most common questions about digital technology and help them make informed choices when they buy new cameras. Use the features presented in this lab to add the following to your information sheet:

- Open the file wd03_Digital Cameras.

- Use the Document Map to locate the headings in the document and apply appropriate heading levels.

- Create a bulleted list in the Advantages of Digital Cameras section. Use Format Painter to add bold and underlines to the beginning of each sentence, before the semicolon. Do the same for the Disadvantages of Digital Cameras section.

- Use the following information to create a simple table. Apply an AutoFormat of your choice to the table.

Number of Pixels	Print Size
Less than 1 megapixel	Good for e-mail
1 megapixel	4X6-inch prints
2 megapixels	5X7-inch prints
3 megapixels	8X10-inch prints
4 megapixels	11X14-inch prints
5 megapixels	16X20-inch prints

- Add graphics of your choice to the document. Wrap the text around each image and use alignments of your choice. Add captions to the images.

- Display a page number at a position of your choice in the footer.

- Include your name and the date in the header.

- Save the document as Digital Cameras. Preview and print the document.

Using an Outline to Create a Report ★ ★

2. You are continuing your work on the Downtown Internet Café coffee bean flyer. Your outline includes the main characteristics of coffee beans, with examples of different beans that emphasize these characteristics. Create a report using this outline that discusses the four characteristics of coffee beans: acidity, flavor, aroma, and body. Discuss the different regions coffee comes from and the characteristics regional coffee emphasizes. Include the following features in your report:

- Open the file Coffee Outline you created in Step-by-Step Exercise 2 of this lab.
- Create a title page and table of contents. Center the title page vertically.
- The body of the report should include at least three footnotes and two cross-referenced images.
- Include a works cited page with an alphabetical list of your reference sources.
- Add page numbers to the report, excluding the title page.
- Include your name and the date in the footer.
- Save the report as Coffee Report in a new folder. Preview and print the title page, the first page, and the works cited page.

Preparing for a Job Search ★ ★

3. You are graduating next June and want to begin your job search early. To prepare for getting a job, locate three sources of information on this topic. Use your school's career services department, the library, newspaper, and magazine articles as sources. Begin by creating an outline of the topics you will include in the report. Using the outline, write a brief report about your findings. Include the following features in your report:

- A title page that displays the report title, your name, the current date, and a table of contents. Center the page vertically. Use appropriate text formatting.
- The body of the paper should include at least two levels of headings and a minimum of three footnotes.
- The report layout should include page numbers on the top right corner of every page (excluding the title page). The title page should be vertically aligned.
- Include at least one picture with a caption and cross-reference.
- Include a table that compares the jobs you are interested in.
- Include a works cited page with an alphabetical list of your reference sources.
- Save the report as Job Search in a new folder. Preview and print the document.

Writing a Research Paper ★ ★ ★

4. Create a brief research report (or use a paper you have written in the past) on a topic of interest to you. The paper must include the following features:

- A title page that displays the report title, your name, the current date, and a table of contents.
- The body of the paper should include at least two levels of headings and a minimum of three footnotes.
- The report layout should include page numbers on the top right corner of every page (excluding the title page). The title page should be vertically aligned.
- Include at least one picture with a caption and cross-reference.

- Include a table of information.
- Include a works cited page with an alphabetical list of your reference sources.
- Save the document as Research in a new folder. Preview and print the title page and last page of the report.

Creating a Research Report ★ ★ ★

5. Computer viruses can strike at any time and can cause serious problems. Use the Web as a resource to learn more about them, then write a brief report defining computer viruses. Describe three viruses, what they do, and the effect they could have on a large company. The paper must include the following features:

- A title page that displays the report title, your name, the current date, and a table of contents.
- The body of the paper should include at least two levels of headings and a minimum of three footnotes.
- The report layout should include page numbers on the top right corner of every page (excluding the title page). The title page should be vertically aligned.
- Include at least one picture with a caption and cross-reference.
- Include a table of information.
- Include a works cited page with an alphabetical list of your reference sources.
- Save the document as Computer Viruses. Preview and print the document.

Working Together 1: Word 2003 and Your Web Browser

Case Study

Adventure Travel Company

Adventure Travel Tours has a World Wide Web (WWW) site through which it hopes to be able to promote its products and broaden its audience of customers. In addition to the obvious marketing and sales potential, it wants to provide an avenue for interaction between the company and the customer to improve customer service. The company also wants the Web site to provide articles of interest to customers. The articles, with topics such as travel background information and descriptions, would change on a monthly basis as an added incentive for readers to return to the site.

You believe that the flyer you developed to promote the new tours and presentations could be used on the Web site. Office Word 2003 includes Web-editing features that help you create a Web page quickly and easily. While using the Web-editing features, you will be working with Word and with a Web browser application. This capability of all Office 2003 applications to work together and with other applications makes it easy to share and exchange information between applications. Your completed Web pages are shown here.

Note: The Working Together tutorial is designed to show how two applications work together and to present a basic introduction to creating Web pages.

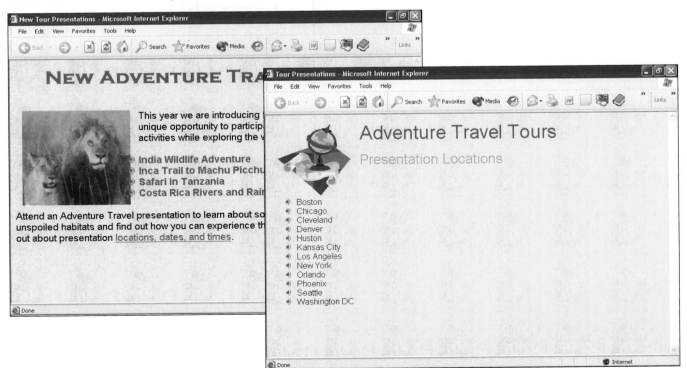

Saving a Word Document as a Web Page

You want to create a Web page to be used on the company's Web site. A **Web page** is a document that can be used on the WWW. The Web page you create will provide information about the tour presentations. Word offers three ways to create or **author** Web pages. One way is to start with a blank Web page and enter text and graphics much as you would a normal document. Another is to use the Web Page Wizard, which provides step-by-step instructions to help you quickly create a Web page. Finally, you can quickly convert an existing Word document to a Web page.

Because the tour flyer has already been created as a Word document and contains much of the information you want to use on the Web page, you will convert it to a Web page document. You made a couple of changes to the flyer, giving it a title that is more appropriate for the Web page and removing the AutoShape banner. You will use the modified version of the flyer as the basis for the Web page.

1 ● **Start Office Word 2003.**

● **Open the file** wdwt_Presentations **from the appropriate location.**

● **Close the Getting Started task pane.**

Your screen should be similar to Figure 1

Revised flyer document

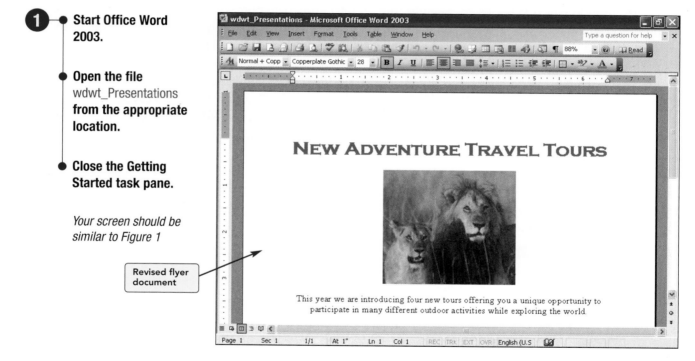

Figure 1

Word converts a document to a Web page by adding HTML coding to the document. **HTML (HyperText Markup Language)** is a programming language used to create Web pages. HTML commands control the display of information on a page, such as font colors and size, and the way an item will be processed. HTML also allows users to click on hyperlinks and jump to other locations on the same page, other pages in the same site, or other sites and locations on the WWW. HTML commands are interpreted by the browser software you are using. A **browser** is a program that connects you to remote computers and displays the Web pages you request.

When a file is converted to a Web page, the HTML coding is added and it is saved to a new file with an .html file extension.

2 ● Choose File/Save as Web Page.

Your screen should be similar to Figure 2

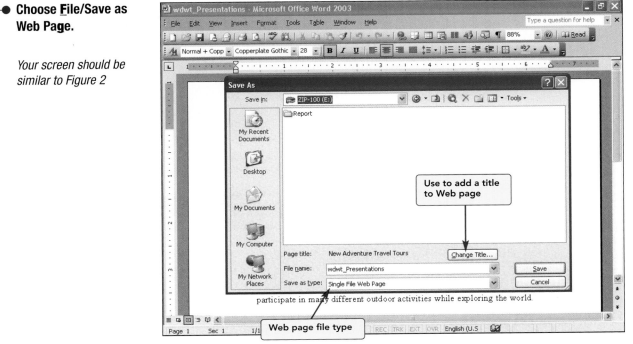

Figure 2

The file type of Web Page is automatically specified. You want to save the Web page using the file name New Tour Presentations in a new folder. You also need to provide a title for the page. This is the text that will appear in the title bar of the Web browser when the page is displayed. You want the title to be the same as the file name.

3 If necessary, change the location to save to the appropriate save location.

● Create a new folder named ATT Web Page.

● Change the file name to New Tour Presentations.

● Click | Change Title... |.

● Change the title to New Tour Presentations.

● Click | OK |.

● Click | Save |.

● If an informational box appears, click | Continue |.

Your screen should be similar to Figure 3.

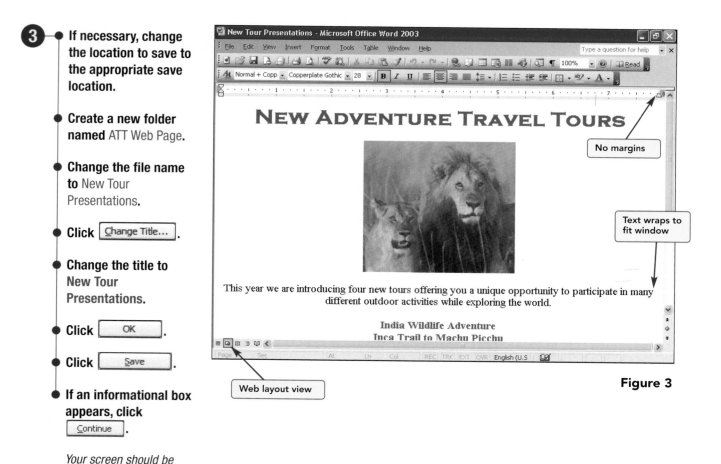

Figure 3

The flyer has been converted to an HTML document and is displayed in Web Layout view. Although the menu bar contains the same menus, Word customizes some menus, commands, and options to provide the Web page authoring features. This view displays the document as it will appear if viewed using a Web browser. This document looks very much like a normal Word document. In fact, the only visible difference is the margin settings. A Web page does not include margins. Instead, the text wraps to fit into the window space. However, the formatting and features that are supported by HTML, in this case the paragraph and character formatting such as the font style, type size, and color attributes, have been converted to HTML format.

Web Layout view does not display the HTML codes that control the formatting of the Web page. To view these codes, you will switch to HTML Source view.

4 Choose **V**iew/HTML
Sourc**e**.

Having Trouble?
If the HTML Script Editor is
not installed on your system,
you will not be able to use
this feature.

● If necessary, maximize
the window.

HTML tags

*Your screen should be
similar to Figure 4*

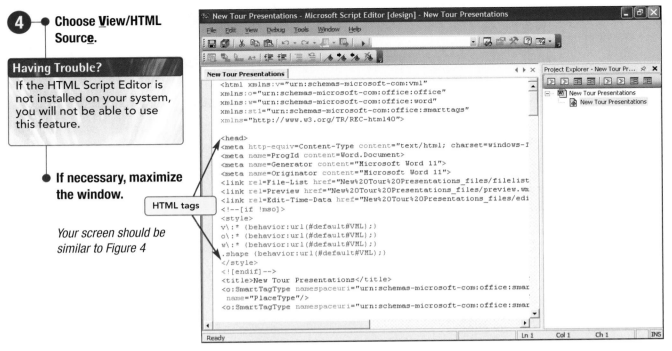

Figure 4

Every item on a Web page has properties associated with it that are
encoded in HTML tags. **Tags** are embedded codes that supply information
about the page's structure, appearance, and contents. They tell your
browser where the title, headings, paragraphs, images, and other
information should appear on the page. Converting this document to
HTML format using Word was much easier than learning to enter the
codes yourself.

5 ● Click ✕ in the title bar to close the Microsoft Script Editor window.

The Web page is displayed in Web Layout view again.

Making Text Changes

Next, you want to change the layout of the Web page so that more
information is displayed in the window when the page is viewed in the
browser. To do this, you will delete any unnecessary text and change the
paragraph alignment to left-aligned.

1
- Delete the last two paragraphs in the flyer.

- Select all the text below the picture.

- Click ▤ Left.

- Add bullets preceding the list of four tours.

- Move to the top of the document.

Your screen should be similar to Figure 5

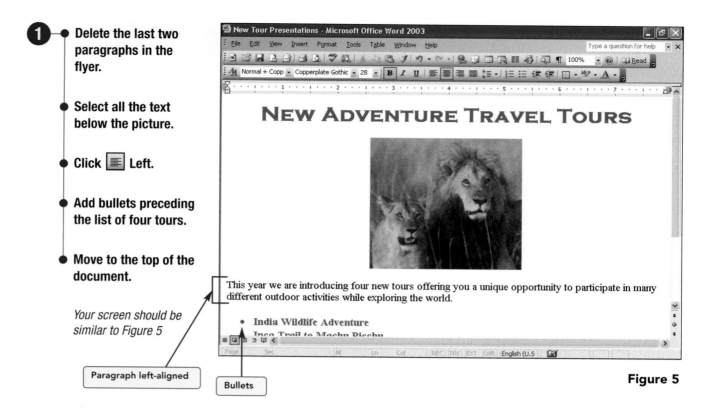

Paragraph left-aligned

Bullets

Figure 5

Changing the Picture Layout

You still cannot view all the information in a single window. To make more space, you will move the picture to the left edge of the window and wrap the text to the right around it. Unlike a normal Word document, a Web page document does not have pictures and other graphic elements embedded in it. In an HTML file, each graphic object is stored as a separate file that is accessed and loaded by the browser when the page is loaded. In an HTML file, each graphic object is stored as a separate file that is accessed and loaded by the browser when the page is loaded. Word creates a link to the object's file in the HTML file. The link is a tag that includes the location and file name of the graphic file.

Additionally, graphics are inserted into a Web page document as inline objects. You can change the wrapping style and move, size, and format graphic objects in a Web page just like embedded objects in a Word document.

1

- Click on the picture to select it.

- If necessary, display the Picture toolbar.

- Drag the graphic to the "T" in "This" at the beginning of the first paragraph.

- Click 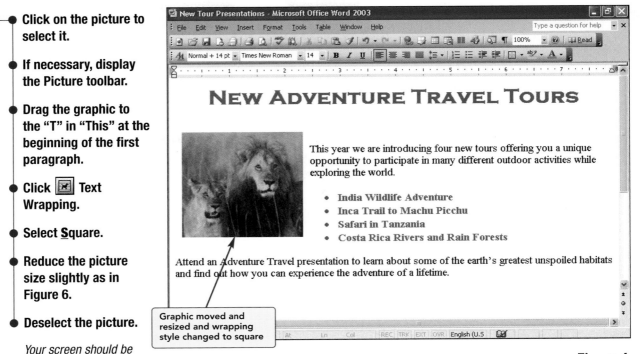 Text Wrapping.

- Select **S**quare.

- Reduce the picture size slightly as in Figure 6.

- Deselect the picture.

Your screen should be similar to Figure 6

Figure 6

Now all the information is visible. Next, you will make a few other adjustments to improve the appearance.

Applying a Theme

Because color and design are important elements of Web pages, you can add a background color and other special effects to a Web page. Many of these special effects are designed specifically for Web pages and cannot be used in printed pages. Like styles, Word includes many predesigned Web page effects, called **themes**, which you can quickly apply to a Web page.

1 ● Choose
   Format/Th**e**me.

   *Your screen should be
   similar to Figure 7*

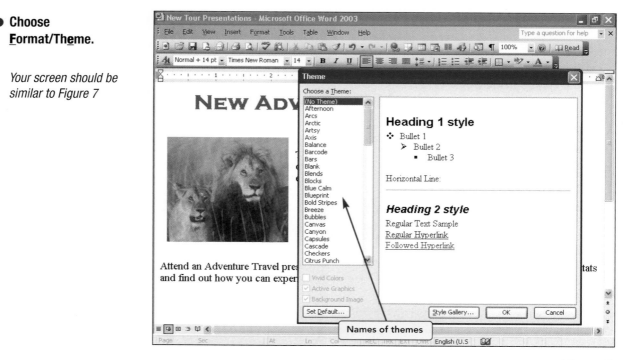

Figure 7

The Choose a Theme list displays the names of all the themes that are provided with Word. The preview area displays a sample of the selected theme showing the background design, bullet and horizontal line style, and character formats that will be applied to headings, normal text, and hyperlinks.

2 ● **Select several themes
   to preview them.**

● **Select the Tabs and
   Folders theme.**

Having Trouble?

If the Tabs and Folders theme is not available, try Expedition or Artsy.

● **Click** [OK] .

● **If necessary, readjust
   the picture.**

● **Click** 🖫 **Save to save
   the changes you have
   made to the Web page.**

   *Your screen should be
   similar to Figure 8*

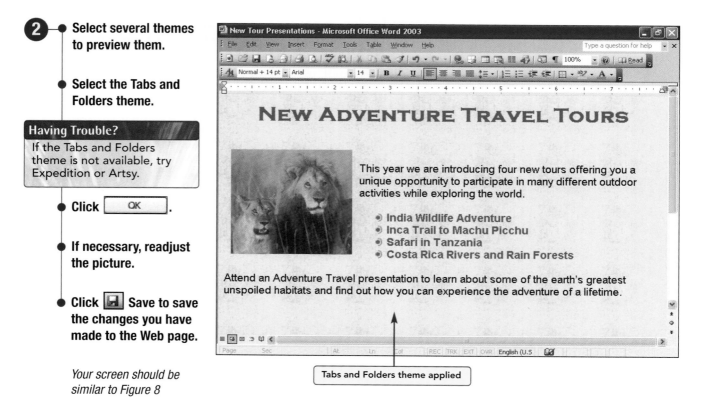

Tabs and Folders theme applied

The formatting settings associated with the selected theme are applied to the Web page. The two obvious changes are the addition of a background design and graphical bullets.

Creating a Hyperlink

Next, you want to create another Web page that will contain a list of presentation locations. You will then add a hyperlink to this information from the New Tour Presentations page. As you have learned, a hyperlink provides a quick way to jump to other documents, objects, or Web pages. Hyperlinks are the real power of the WWW. You can jump to sites on your own system and network as well as to sites on the Internet and WWW.

The list of tour locations has already been entered as a Word document and saved as a file.

1 ● Open the file wdwt_Locations.

● Save the document as a Web page to the ATT Web Page folder with the file name Locations and a page title of Tour Presentation Locations.

● Apply the same theme to this page.

● Save the page again.

Your screen should be similar to Figure 9

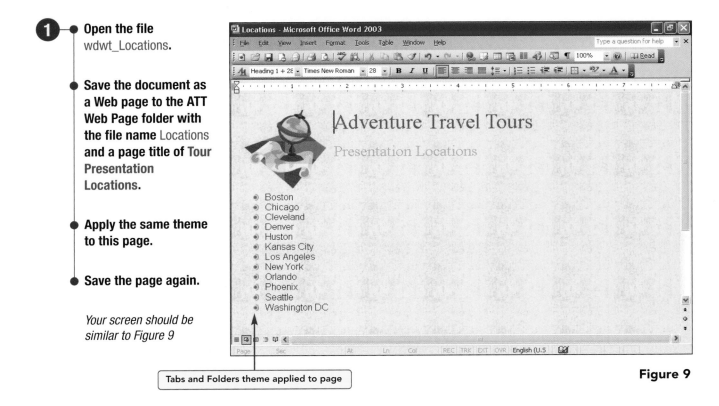

Tabs and Folders theme applied to page

Figure 9

Now you are ready to create the hyperlink from the New Tour Presentations page to the Locations page.

2 • Switch to the New Tour Presentations window.

• Add the following text to the end of the last paragraph: **Find out about presentation locations, dates, and times.**

• Select the text "locations, dates, and times."

• Click **Insert Hyperlink** (on the Standard toolbar).

Another Method
The menu equivalent is Insert/Hyperlink and the keyboard shortcut is Ctrl + K.

Your screen should be similar to Figure 10

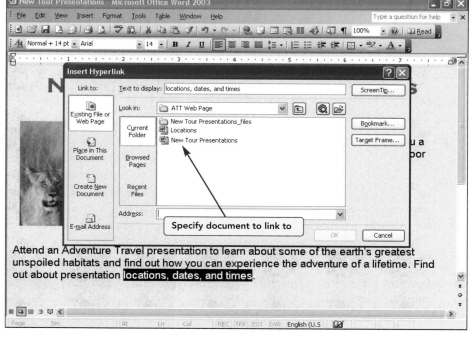

Figure 10

From the Insert Hyperlink dialog box, you need to specify the name of the document you want the link to connect to.

3 • Select Locations from the file list.

• Click OK.

Your screen should be similar to Figure 11

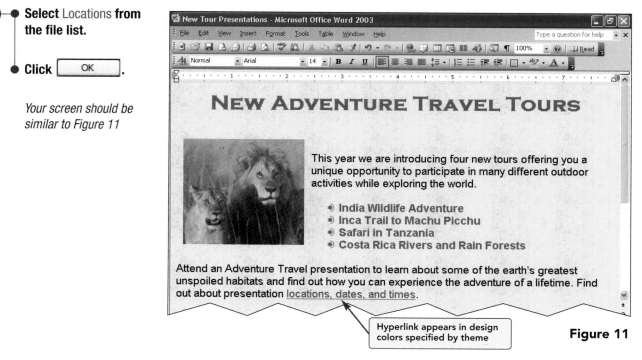

Figure 11

The selected text appears as a hyperlink in the design colors specified by the theme.

4 ● **Hold down** `Ctrl` **and
click the hyperlink.**

*Your screen should be
similar to Figure 12*

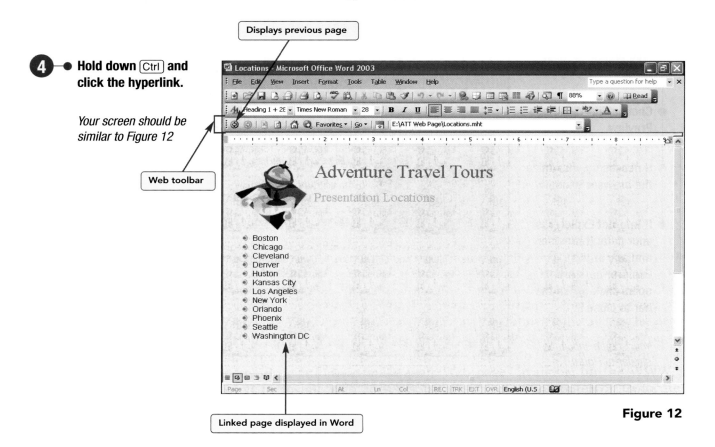

Displays previous page

Web toolbar

Linked page displayed in Word

Figure 12

Because the Locations document is already open in a window, clicking the
hyperlink simply switches to the open window and displays the page. In
addition, the Web toolbar is displayed. Its buttons are used to navigate
and work with Web pages.

You plan to add hyperlinks from each location to information about
dates and times for each location at a later time.

Previewing the Page

To see how your Web page will actually look when displayed by your
browser, you can preview it.

key

author   WDWT1.2

browser   WDWT1.3

HTML (Hypertext Markup Language)   WDWT1.2

tag   WDWT1.5

theme   WDWT1.7

Web page   WDWT1.2

mos skills

The Microsoft Office Specialist (MOS) certification program is designed to measure your proficiency in performing basic tasks using the Office 2003 applications. Getting certified demonstrates that you have the skills and provides a valuable industry credential for employment. After completing this lab, you have learned the following Microsoft Office Word Specialist skills:

Skill	Description	Page
Organize Content	Insert and modify hyperlinks	WDWT1.9
Formatting and Managing Documents	Preview documents and Web pages	WDWT1.11
	Save documents in appropriate formats for different uses	WDWT1.3

command summary

Command	Shortcut Keys	Button	Action
File/Save as Web Page			Saves file as a Web page document
File/Web Page Preview			Previews Web page in browser window
View/HTML Source			Displays HTML source code
Insert/Hyperlink	Ctrl + K	🔗	Inserts hyperlink
Format/Theme			Applies a predesigned theme to Web page

step-by-step

Adding a New Web Page ★

1. You want to continue working on the Web pages about the new tour presentations for the Adventure Travel Web site. Your next step is to create links from each location to information about each location's presentation date and times. Your completed Web page for the Los Angeles area is shown here.

   a. In Word, open the Web page file Locations you created in this lab.

   b. Open the document wdwt_LosAngeles. Save the document as a Web page to the ATT Web Page folder with the file name LosAngeles and a page title of **Los Angeles Presentation Information**.

   c. Apply the Tabs and Folders design theme to the new page. Change the first title line to a Heading 1 style and the second title line to a Heading 2 style. Change the title lines color to the same colors used on the Locations page. Add color to the table headings. Enhance the Web page with any features you feel are appropriate.

   d. Two lines below the table add and bold the text **Contact [your name] at (909) 555-1212 for more information.**

   e. On the Locations page, create a link from the Los Angeles text to the Los Angeles page. Test the link.

   f. Resave both Web pages and preview them in your browser. Print the Los Angeles Web page.

   g. Exit the browser and Word.

Adventure Travel Tours

The Adventure Travel Tours manager is very pleased with the research you did on Tanzania and Peru. The company plans to feature tours to these areas in the next few months and wants to provide its clients with much of the information you gathered. A good way to present this type of information is through a monthly newsletter. Newsletters allow businesses to present timely information. Unlike a flyer, whose purpose is to quickly attract attention and provide a small amount of information, a newsletter is designed to provide detailed information. Because newsletters are generally several pages long, you have enough space to paint a picture and tell a story.

After discussing the plans for the upcoming newsletters with the Adventure Travel Tours manager, you have decided to make the African safari in Tanzania the focus of the next month's newsletter. In addition to using several topics from the material in the report on Tanzania, the newsletter will include various tips and facts about the country. You will also include some information about other upcoming tours and events.

In a newsletter, information must be easy to read and, more important, visually appealing. In this lab, you will use the WordArt and desktop publishing tools in Word 2003 to create the newsletter shown on the following page.

© Getty Images

Use the WordArt feature to create an attractive headline.

Newsletter-style columns make newsletters easy to read as well as attractive.

Text boxes, graphics, color, and borders enhance the appearance of the newsletter.

The following concepts will be introduced in this lab:

1 **WordArt** WordArt is used to enhance your documents by changing the shape of text and adding special effects such as 3-D and shadows.

2 **Collect and Paste** Collecting and pasting is the capability of the program to store multiple copied items in the Office Clipboard and then paste one or more of them into another document.

3 **Newsletter-Style Columns** Newsletter-style columns display text so that it flows from the bottom of one column to the top of the next.

4 **Hyphenation** The hyphenation feature inserts a hyphen in long words that fall at the end of a line, splitting the word between lines.

5 **Text Box** A text box is a graphic object that is a container for text or graphics.

Creating a Newsletter Headline

A newsletter commonly consists of two basic parts: the headline and the body (see the following figure). The headline, also called the nameplate or banner, is the top portion of the newsletter. It generally contains the name, issue or volume number, and publication date. It may also include a company logo, a line that announces the main subject or article included in the newsletter, and a brief table of contents. The body, which is the text of the newsletter, is commonly displayed in a two- or three-column format. Article headings often include subheadings that help organize the newsletter topics. The headline is often visually separated from the body by horizontal lines, called rules. Your sample newsletter will include many of these features.

The first thing you want to do is to create a headline for the newsletter. The headline will display the name of the newsletter, "The Adventure Traveler," the date of publication, and the volume number. The text for the headline has already been entered for you.

1 ● Start Office Word 2003.

● If necessary, maximize the Word application window.

● To see the headline text, open the file wd04_Headline.

● If necessary, change to Print Layout view.

Your screen should be similar to Figure 4.1

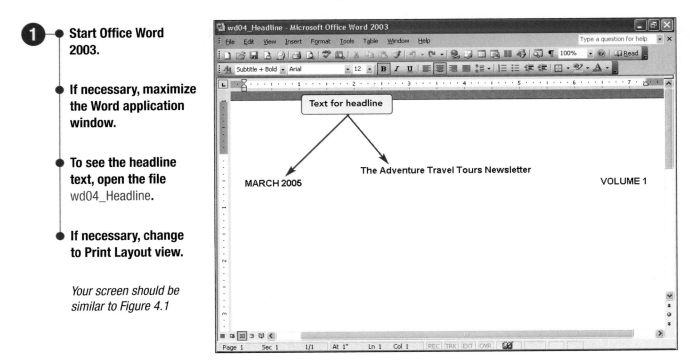

Figure 4.1

Using WordArt

You need to add the newsletter name above the headline text. You will use the WordArt feature to make this name unique and more interesting.

Concept 1

Word Art

1 WordArt is used to enhance your documents by changing the shape of text and adding special effects such as 3-D and shadows. You can also rotate, flip, and skew WordArt text. The text that is added to the document using WordArt is a graphic object that can be edited, sized, or moved to any location in the document. In addition, it can be changed using the Drawing toolbar buttons.

You can use WordArt to add a special touch to your documents. However, you should limit its use to headlines in a newsletter or to a single element in a flyer. You want the WordArt to capture the reader's attention. Here are some examples of WordArt.

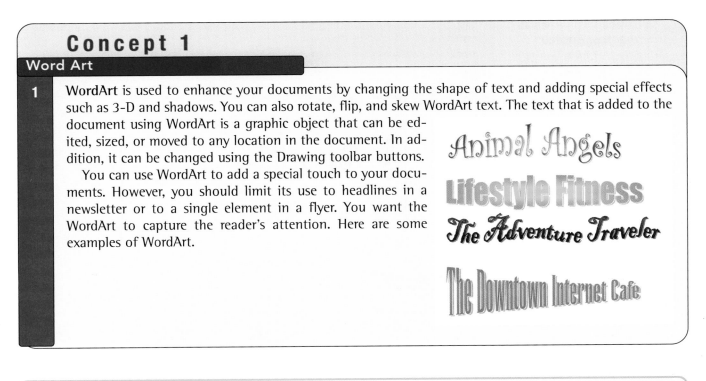

You will create a WordArt object consisting of the newsletter name for the headline. The Drawing toolbar is used to access the WordArt feature.

1 • **If necessary, display the Drawing toolbar.**

Having Trouble?

Click 🔲 Drawing to display the Drawing toolbar.

• **Click** 🔲 **Insert WordArt.**

Your screen should be similar to Figure 4.2

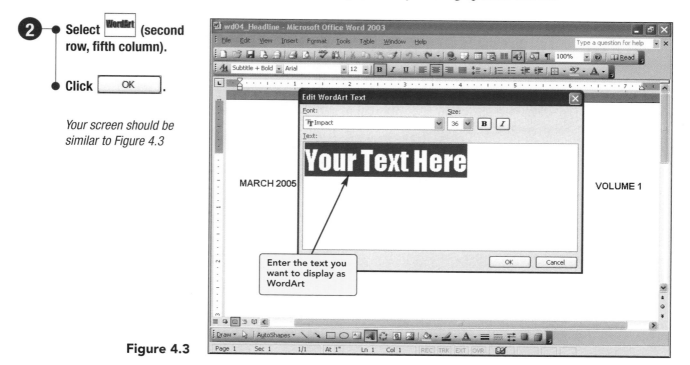

Figure 4.2

In the WordArt Gallery dialog box, you first select one of the 30 styles or designs of WordArt you want to use for the headline. The styles consist of a combination of fonts, colors, and shapes and are just a starting point. As you will soon see, you can alter the appearance of the style by selecting a different color or shape, and by adding special effects.

2 • **Select** 🔲 **(second row, fifth column).**

• **Click** OK .

Your screen should be similar to Figure 4.3

Figure 4.3

Next, in the Edit WordArt Text dialog box, you need to replace the sample text with the text you want displayed using the selected WordArt design.

3 ● Type **The Adventure Traveler.**

● Click OK .

Your screen should be similar to Figure 4.4

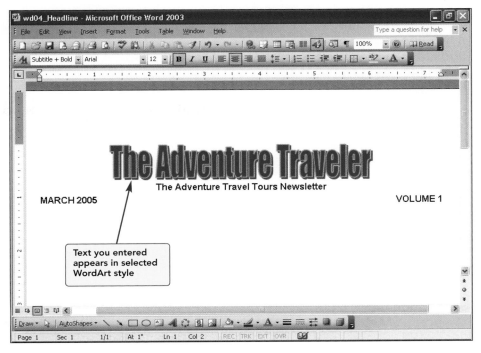

Figure 4.4

Another Method
To review these features, refer to Concept 4: Text Wrapping, in Lab 3.

Now the words you entered are displayed in the selected WordArt style in the document. When a WordArt object is first inserted in the document, it has a default wrapping style of In Line with Text, assuming the formatting of the line into which it was inserted, in this case, centered.

Changing the WordArt Shape and Size

Now that you can see how the selected style looks in the headline, you decide to change the WordArt shape to another. You can select from 40 different shapes provided in the WordArt palette and apply the shape to the selected object.

Whenever a WordArt object is selected, the WordArt toolbar is displayed. The WordArt toolbar buttons (identified below) are used to modify the WordArt.

1 ● Select the WordArt object.

● Click WordArt Shape.

● Choose 🔲 Inflate Top (fourth row, fifth column).

Your screen should be similar to Figure 4.5

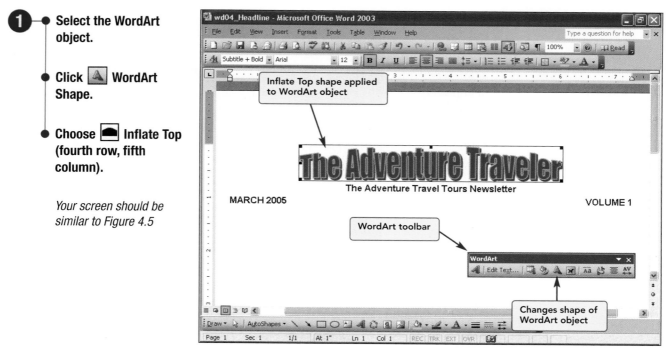

Figure 4.5

The selected shape is applied to the WordArt object. You also want the WordArt object to extend the full width of the text space between the margins. To do this you will increase its width.

2 ● Drag the sizing handles of the WordArt shape to increase the height and width as shown in Figure 4.6.

Another Method

You can also adjust the size to exact measurements using Format/WordArt/Size and entering values to specify an exact height and width.

Your screen should be similar to Figure 4.6

Figure 4.6

The WordArt is now the full text width of the page.

Changing the WordArt Fill and Line Color

Next you want to change the color of the WordArt characters. You can easily do this using some of the special effects options that can be applied to graphic objects.

Special drawing effects, such as shadows and 3-D effects, can easily be added to text and graphics, including WordArt objects, to enhance the appearance of your document. When you draw an object, a border automatically appears around it. You can change the thickness and color of the border. You also can fill a drawing object with a solid color, a gradient color, texture, or a picture. Adding shadows or 3-D effects gives depth to an object.

Use these effects in moderation. You want to capture the reader's interest with your graphics but not detract from your message.

1 ● Click 🔳 Format WordArt on the WordArt toolbar.

● Open the Colors and Lines tab.

Another Method ○○○○

The menu equivalent is Format/**W**ordArt/Colors and Lines.

Your screen should be similar to Figure 4.7

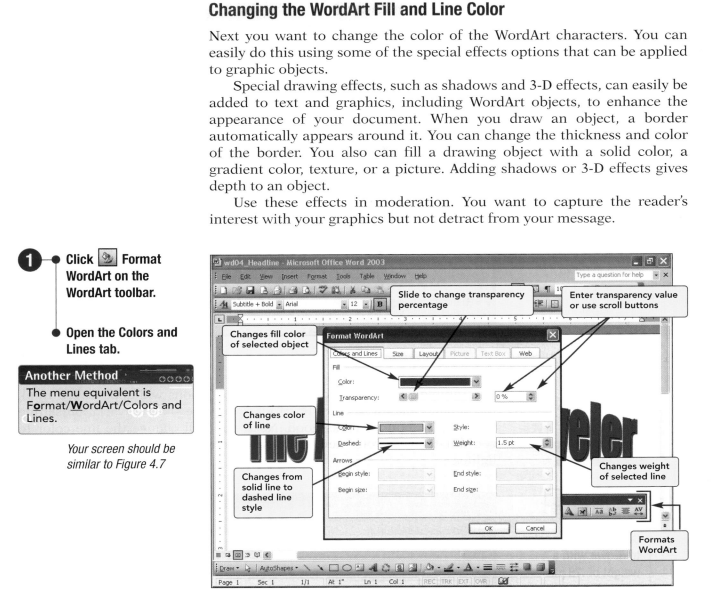

Figure 4.7

The default color and line settings for the selected WordArt design style are a blue fill color set to 0 percent transparency with a light blue line color. When set, the transparency option makes the selected fill color less opaque, allowing the shadow color to bleed through. When set to zero, the color is solid or opaque. You want to change the WordArt color to a light orange and gold color combination. You can combine colors using a gradient fill.

2
- Select the subtitle line of text below the newsletter title.
- Choose F**o**rmat/**F**ont.
- Increase the font size to 14.
- Open the Cha**r**acter Spacing tab.

Your screen should be similar to Figure 4.11

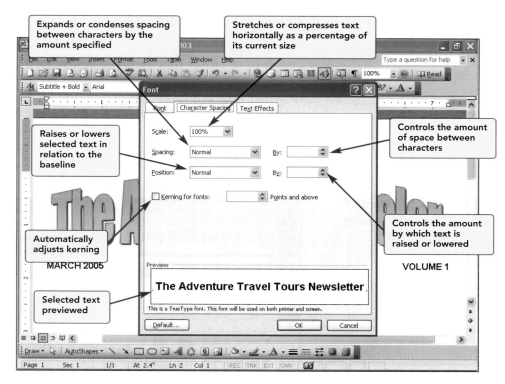

Expands or condenses spacing between characters by the amount specified

Stretches or compresses text horizontally as a percentage of its current size

Raises or lowers selected text in relation to the baseline

Automatically adjusts kerning

Selected text previewed

Controls the amount of space between characters

Controls the amount by which text is raised or lowered

MARCH 2005

VOLUME 1

Figure 4.11

The Character Spacing tab is used to expand or condense the space between characters by a specified amount. You can also kern characters above a specified point size. Expanding or condensing characters changes the space by an equal amount regardless of the font design. You can also specify the amount of space by which you want to expand or condense the spacing. The default setting is 1 point.

3
- From the **S**pacing drop-down list box, select Expanded.
- Increase the **By** amount to 1.5 pt.
- Click ▭ OK ▭.
- Click on the subtitle line to deselect it.

Your screen should be similar to Figure 4.12

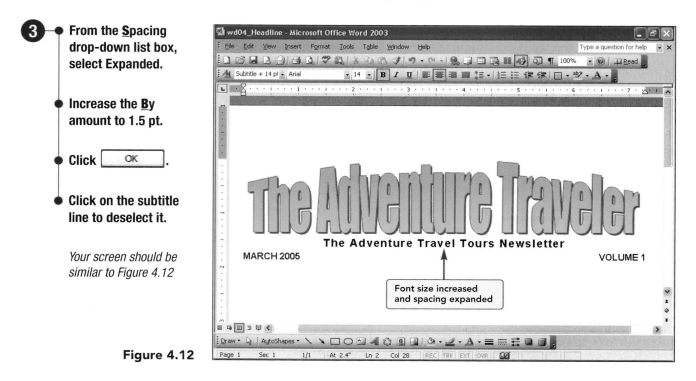

The Adventure Travel Tours Newsletter

MARCH 2005

VOLUME 1

Font size increased and spacing expanded

Figure 4.12

The spacing between characters has increased, making the headline subtitle more prominent.

Creating Horizontal Rules

Next you want the newsletter's issue identification information, which in this newsletter is the publication date and issue number, to be displayed between two horizontal lines or rules. Rules can be added to any side of a selected paragraph or object.

1 ● **Move to anywhere within the line of text containing the publication date and issue number.**

● **Choose Format/Borders and Shading.**

● **Open the Borders tab if necessary.**

Your screen should be similar to Figure 4.13

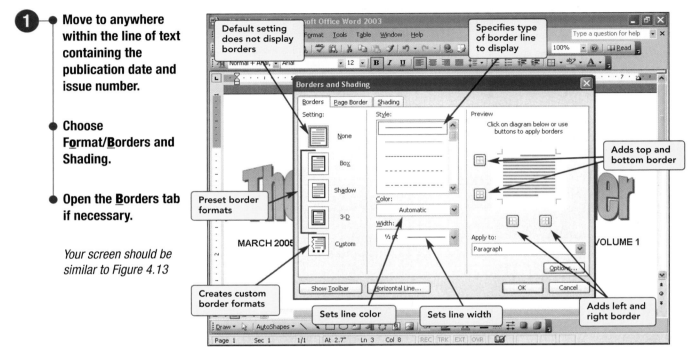

Figure 4.13

From the Borders and Shading dialog box, you can specify the style, color, weight, and location of the border. You can apply either a preset box border by selecting from the Setting options, or a custom border. You want to create a custom border that will display a 1.5-point single-line border in brown above the text, and a 3-point double-line border in brown below the text. As you specify the line settings, the Preview area will reflect your selections.

2 ● Click 🖾 Custom.

Another Method

You can also specify border settings using the Tables and Borders toolbar.

● From the **W**idth drop-down list box, select 1½ pt.

● Open the **C**olor palette and select Brown.

● Click 🖾 Top Border.

Your screen should be similar to Figure 4.14

Figure 4.14

The Preview area of the dialog box shows how a top border line using the settings you specified will appear. Next you will add a double-line bottom border.

3 ● From the St**y**le list box, select ☐.

● From the **W**idth drop-down list, select 3 pt.

● From the **C**olor drop-down list, select Brown.

● Click 🖾 Bottom Border.

Having Trouble?

Use the None option to remove all border lines, or remove individual lines by selecting the border location again.

● Click ☐ OK ☐.

● Save the headline as Newsletter Headline.

Your screen should be similar to Figure 4.15

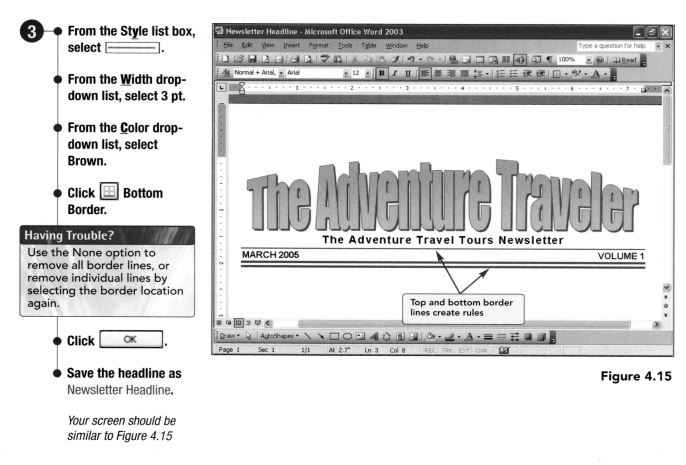

Figure 4.15

The horizontal lines extend between the margins above and below the text in the color, style, and point size you specified. The newsletter headline is now complete and can be used with any newsletter.

Researching Information on the Web

You have created a file of facts about Tanzania and still need to add the Tanzania Embassy address and Web site to the document. You will get this information using the Research task pane to access the Web.

Note: You need an Internet connection, and the Online Services feature must be activated. Click Research Options in the Research task pane and select the services you want to access. If you do not have this feature available, type the information shown in Figure 4.18 and skip to step 4.

1 ● **Open the file**
wd04_Tanzania Facts.

● **Click** ⬛ **Research.**

● **Type Tanzania embassy in U.S.** in the Search for text box.

● **Select MSN Search from the Show Results From list box.**

Your screen should be similar to Figure 4.16

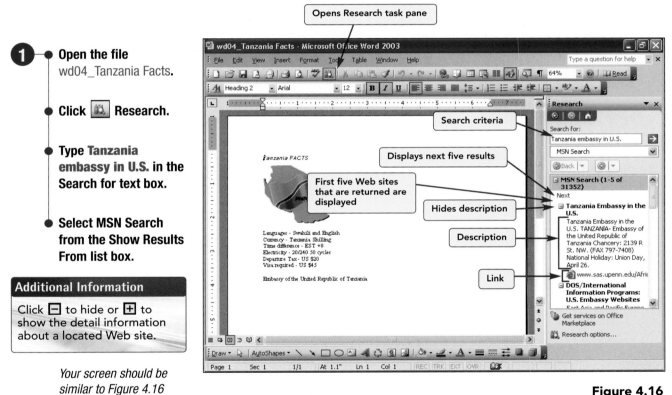

Figure 4.16

The results area of the Research task pane displays the first five Web sites that meet your search criteria. Each result includes a link to the Web site. You will locate a Web site that looks like it will have the information you need and then click on the link to that site.

2 ● Scroll the results list to locate "All of the Embassies of Washington D.C." result.

Having Trouble?
If necessary, click Next to see the next five results.

● Click the www.embassy.org/ embassies link.

Having Trouble?
If this Web site is not available, select a link to another located site to find this information.

Your screen should be similar to Figure 4.17

Web site opened in Internet Explorer browser

Research task pane displayed

Figure 4.17

The Web site opens for the selected page. If your browser is Internet Explorer, the Research task pane is displayed along the left side of the screen to allow you to select and view other sites. You will use the Quick Index to locate the Tanzania embassy information and then copy the address from the Web page to your Word document.

3

- Click **T** in the Quick Index list.

- Click the **Tanzania** link.

- Select (highlight) the address on the Web page.

- Press Ctrl + C to copy it to the Clipboard.

- Close the browser window.

- Paste the address as the last line in the document.

- From the Paste Options menu, select **Match Destination Formatting**.

Your screen should be similar to Figure 4.18

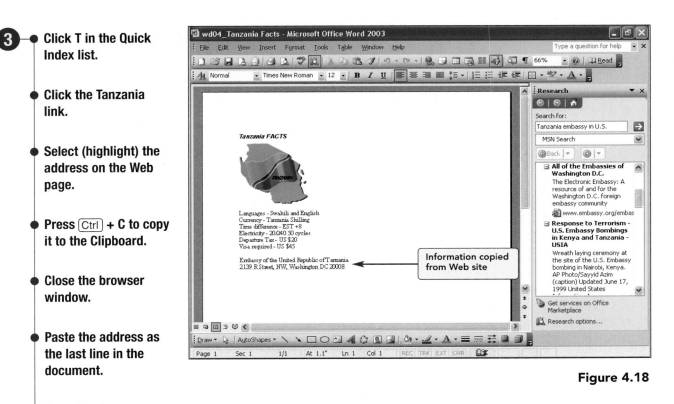

Figure 4.18

The information you located on the Web is inserted into the document.

4

- Close the Research task pane.

- Save the document as Tanzania Facts **to your data file location.**

Assembling the Newsletter from a Variety of Sources

Now that your research is complete, you are ready to assemble the newsletter. Following your manager's suggestions, you modified the report you wrote about Tanzania and Costa Rica by shortening the topic coverage and dividing the topics into several brief articles to be used in this and future newsletters. You saved the articles on different topics in separate files.

In this month's newsletter, you will use the articles about the African Safari. You also have two other short topics to include in this month's newsletter saved in separate files. You will open all of the documents and then combine the articles to create the content for the newsletter.

1 ● **Open the file** wd04_Newsletter Articles.

● **If necessary, change the view to Print Layout and the zoom to Page Width.**

● **Scroll through the text to view the contents of the document.**

● **Open the files** wd04_Be an Adventure Traveler **and** wd04_Costa Rica Adventure.

Additional Information

Hold down Ctrl while selecting multiple file names to open multiple files at the same time.

Having Trouble?

The Wd04_Costa Rica Adventure document may be displayed depending upon the order in which you opened the files.

Having Trouble?

Your screen may show taskbar buttons in a group if the Properties settings of the taskbar have been changed.

Your screen should be similar to Figure 4.19

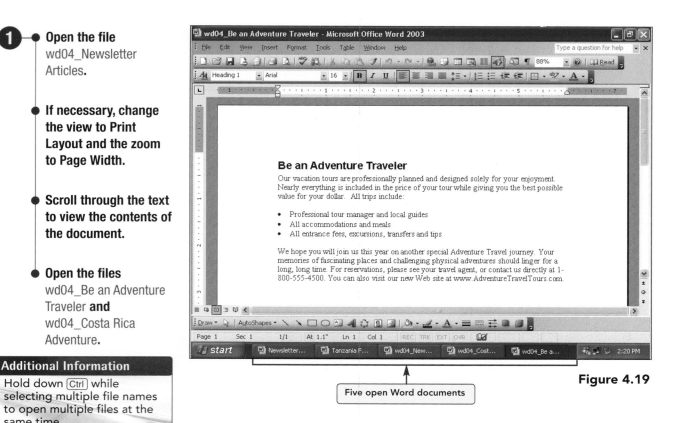

Figure 4.19

Five open Word documents

Using the Office Clipboard

You now have five open documents. You want to copy the newsletter banner into the document containing the lead article about the African Safari. In addition, you want to copy the information from the other three documents, Tanzania Facts, Costa Rica Adventure, and Be an Adventure Traveler, into this same file containing the lead article. You can copy and paste the selections one after the other, or you can use the Office Clipboard to collect multiple items and paste them into the document as needed.

Concept 2

Collect and Paste

2   **Collecting and pasting** is the capability of the program to store multiple copied items in the Office Clipboard and then paste one or more of them into another document. For example, you could copy a chart from Excel, then switch to Word and copy a paragraph, then switch to PowerPoint and paste the two stored items into a slide in one easy step. This saves you from having to switch back and forth between documents and applications.

The Office Clipboard and the system Clipboard are similar but separate features. The major difference is that the Office Clipboard can hold up to 24 items whereas the system Clipboard holds only a single item. When the Office Clipboard feature is closed, any cut or copied item is copied to both the system and Office Clipboards. The next cut or copied item replaces the existing item in both Clipboards. When the Office Clipboard is open, each successive cut or copied item is added to the Office Clipboard, while it replaces the last item stored in the system Clipboard. When you use the Office Clipboard, you can select the items in any order to paste from any of the items stored.

The Office Clipboard is available for all Office 2003 applications and non-Office programs if the Cut, Copy, and Paste commands are available. You can copy from any program that provides copy and cut capabilities, but you can only paste into Word, Excel, Access, PowerPoint, and Outlook.

Copying Multiple Objects to the Office Clipboard

First you will copy the headline to the Office Clipboard. You will open the Office Clipboard before copying the item so you can see the item as it is added.

1 • Switch to the **Newsletter Headline** document window.

• Choose **Edit/Office Clipboard**.

• Choose **Edit/Select All** to select the entire headline.

• Click [icon] **Copy**.

Another Method

You can also use [Ctrl] + A to select the entire document and [Ctrl] + C to copy the selection to the Clipboard.

Your screen should be similar to Figure 4.20

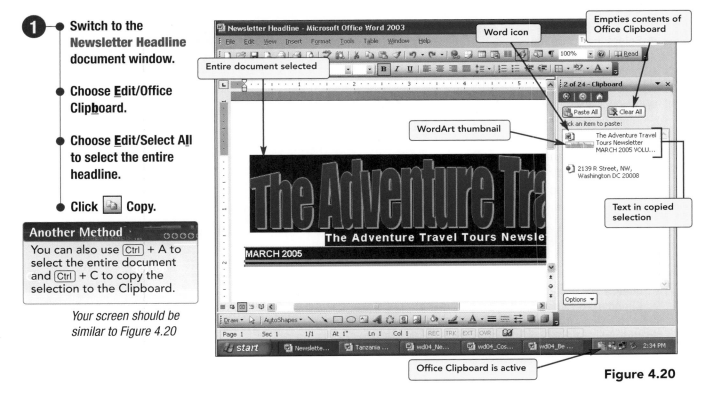

Figure 4.20

The Clipboard task pane is displayed automatically when the Office Clipboard is opened. The task pane is used to view the items in the Office

Clipboard and to select and paste items into other documents. The Office Clipboard icon appears in the system taskbar to show that the Clipboard is active. It also briefly displays a ScreenTip showing the number of items collected out of a possible 24 items as each selection is copied.

As items are added to the Office Clipboard, an entry for each item is displayed in the Office Clipboard gallery in the Clipboard task pane. Each entry includes an icon representing the source Office program of the item and a portion of the copied text or a thumbnail of a copied graphic. The item you just copied appears at the top of the gallery. The second item, the Embassy address, was added to the Office Clipboard when you copied it earlier before you opened the Office Clipboard.

Next you will copy the contents of the other three documents into the Office Clipboard. When the Office Clipboard is open in the Clipboard task pane in one program or document, the Clipboard task pane does not automatically appear when you switch to another program or document. However, it is still active and will continue to store copied items.

2 ● **Switch to the** wd04_Be an Adventure Traveler **document.**

● **Select the entire file.**

● **Click** 📋 **Copy.**

● **In a similar manner, copy the entire contents of the** Tanzania Facts **and** wd04_Costa Rica Adventure **files to the Office Clipboard.**

● **Double-click** 📋 **Clipboard in the system taskbar to display the Office Clipboard task pane.**

Your screen should be similar to Figure 4.21

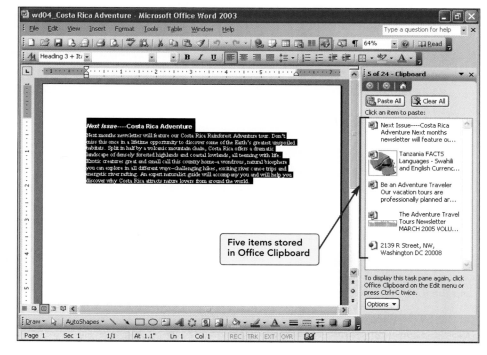

Five items stored in Office Clipboard

Figure 4.21

The Office Clipboard now contains five entries. The most recently added item is displayed at the top of the gallery.

Since you do not need the embassy address entry, you will delete it before continuing.

3 ● **Point to the embassy entry and click the drop-down list button.**

Having Trouble?
If the embassy address is not displayed, skip Step 3.

● **Click Delete from the shortcut menu.**

Another Method
You can also right-click on the item to open the shortcut menu

Your screen should be similar to Figure 4.22

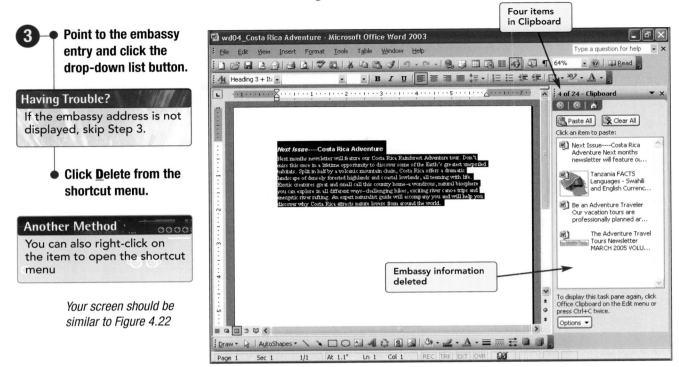

Four items in Clipboard

Embassy information deleted

Figure 4.22

There are now four items in the Office Clipboard gallery.

Pasting Multiple Objects from the Office Clipboard

Now you are ready to paste the items into the main article document. You want to paste the headline first.

1
- **Switch to the** wd04_Newsletter Articles **document.**

- **If necessary, move to the beginning of the Featured Tour heading at the top of the document.**

- **Display the Clipboard task pane.**

- **Click on the newsletter headline item to paste it into the top of the document.**

Another Method

You could also select Paste from the item's shortcut menu.

Additional Information

The Office Clipboard Paste All option inserts the contents of all copied items in the order in which they were added to the Office Clipboard.

Your screen should be similar to Figure 4.23

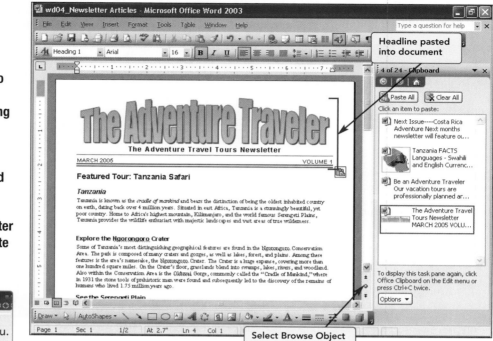

Figure 4.23

Another Method

The menu equivalent is **E**dit/**G**o To (or Ctrl + G), select the object type you want to go to (in this case Heading) and click Next or Previous to move to the next or previous occurrence. You can also type the name or number of the item in the Enter text box to move specifically to that item.

Next you want to insert the information from the Be an Adventure Traveler file before the article about Animal Life. A quick way to move to specific elements in a document is to use the Select Browse Objects feature and select the type of object by which you want to browse through the document. Then you use the Browse Objects scroll buttons to move to the next or previous located element of the specified type.

2
- Click 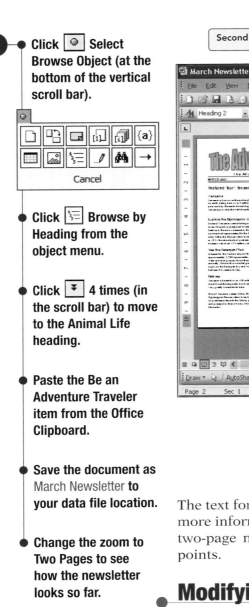 Select Browse Object (at the bottom of the vertical scroll bar).

- Click ⧉ Browse by Heading from the object menu.

- Click ⎓ 4 times (in the scroll bar) to move to the Animal Life heading.

- Paste the Be an Adventure Traveler item from the Office Clipboard.

- Save the document as March Newsletter to your data file location.

- Change the zoom to Two Pages to see how the newsletter looks so far.

Your screen should be similar to Figure 4.24

Figure 4.24

The text for the newsletter already fills almost two pages and you still have more information to add to the document. To make the articles fit into the two-page newsletter format better, you decide to reduce the font to 11 points.

Modifying Styles

Because you plan to add more articles to this document, you will make the font change by modifying the Normal style for this document. Then, as new information is added, it will automatically be formatted using the settings associated with the modified style.

1
- **Return the zoom to Page Width.**

- **Move to a line of text that is formatted with the Normal style.**

Having Trouble?

Normal will appear in the Style toolbar button.

- **Click** 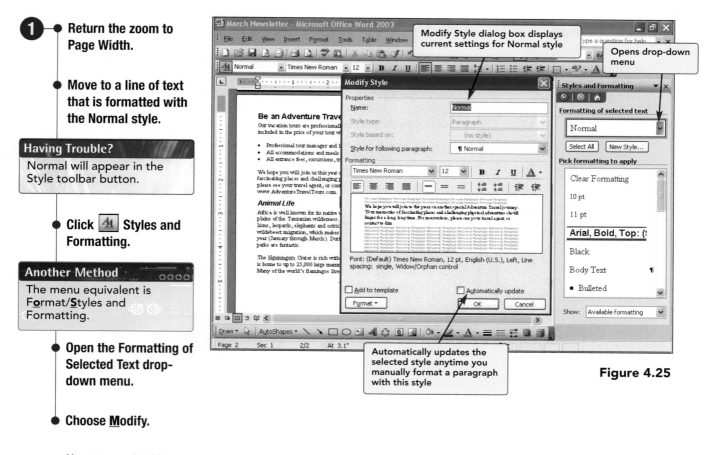 **Styles and Formatting.**

Another Method

The menu equivalent is Format/Styles and Formatting.

- **Open the Formatting of Selected Text drop-down menu.**

- **Choose Modify.**

Your screen should be similar to Figure 4.25

Additional Information

You will learn about templates in Lab 5.

Figure 4.25

The current settings for the selected style are displayed in the Modify Style dialog box. The Add to Template option adds the modified style to the template used to create the document. If you do not select this option as you will do, the Normal style is changed for the current document only. The Automatically Update option will automatically redefine the selected style whenever you manually format a paragraph with this style. It then applies the updated style to the entire document. You want to change the font size to 11 points for the current document only.

2 • Select 11 from the size drop-down list box.

• Click [OK].

Your screen should be similar to Figure 4.26

Modified Normal style applied

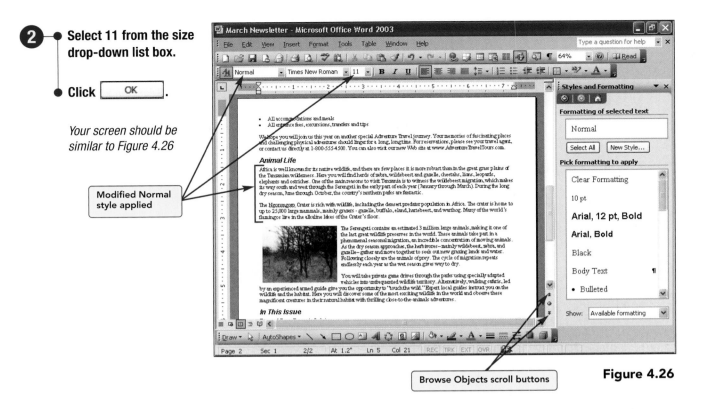

Browse Objects scroll buttons

Figure 4.26

The modified Normal style is applied to all paragraphs in the document that are formatted with the Normal style. Now you will insert the Costa Rica Adventure text above the Natives section in the document. Because you last specified Heading as the element to go to, you can quickly scroll the document by headings using the Browse Objects scroll buttons. These buttons scroll based on the last selected element type.

3 • Click [±] Previous Heading 2 times (in the scroll bar) to move to the Natives heading on page 1.

• Display the Clipboard task pane.

• Paste the Next Issue— Costa Rica Adventure item from the Office Clipboard.

• Close the Clipboard task pane.

• Save the document.

• Change the zoom to Two Pages again.

Your screen should be similar to Figure 4.27

New text pasted in document automatically converted to modified Normal style

Figure 4.27

Modifying Styles   **WD4.25**

The article content is pasted into the document and automatically converted to the new modified Normal style associated with this document. Reducing the font size slightly keeps the document to within its two-page limit.

Inserting Hidden Text

As you look at the newsletter, you feel it would benefit greatly from the addition of a picture near the top of the document. You know that one of the guides has several pictures that would be suitable. Until you get the pictures, however, you want to add a reminder in the document to do this. But you do not want the reminder to display or affect the layout of the document. To do this, you will hide the reminder text.

1

● **Move to the beginning of the first paragraph of the newsletter.**

● **Change the zoom to Page Width.**

● **Type Reminder: Add picture here..**

● **Press ←Enter.**

● **Select the entire line containing the reminder text.**

● **Choose F_ormat/_Font.**

● **Open the Fo_n_t tab and select _H_idden.**

● **Click [OK].**

Your screen should be similar to Figure 4.28

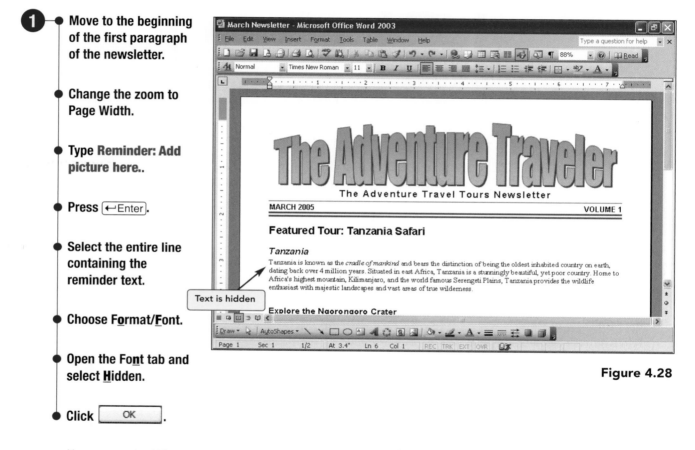

Figure 4.28

The text is hidden and does not affect the layout of the document. Then, when you want to see hidden text, you display formatting marks.

2 ● Click ¶ Show/Hide¶.

Your screen should be similar to Figure 4.29

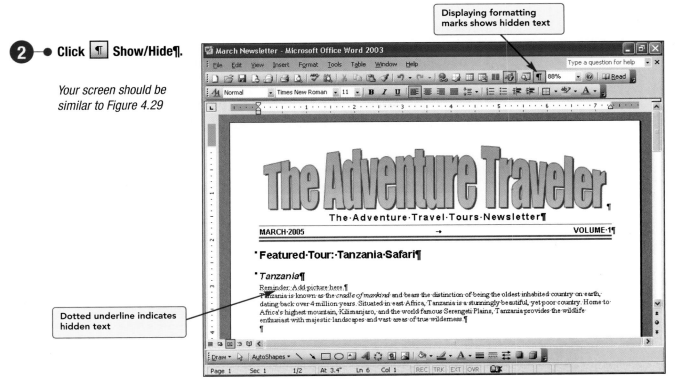

Displaying formatting marks shows hidden text

Dotted underline indicates hidden text

Figure 4.29

The dotted lines below the text indicate the text is hidden. Because it is easy to display hidden text, do not use this feature to hide confidential information.

Creating Newsletter-Style Columns

Now you are ready to format the newsletter to display in newsletter-style columns.

Concept 3
Newsletter-Style Columns

3 **Newsletter-style columns** display text so that it flows from the bottom of one column to the top of the next. The default document setting is one column the full width of the margins, so the text appears to flow continuously from one page to the next. On occasion, the layout for your document may call for two or more columns on a page.

Newspapers, magazines, and newsletters are common applications for newsletter-style columns. The optimum column width for reading comfort is 4.5 inches. In a newsletter, narrow columns help the reader read the articles more quickly, and you as the writer can fit information on a page in a visually pleasing arrangement. Note, however, that if you use more than four columns on an 8½-by-11-inch page, the columns will be too narrow and the page will look messy.

When you change the format of a document to display multiple columns, the entire document changes to the new format. To affect only a portion of a document, you need to divide the document into sections. Because you do not want the headline to appear in column format, you will create a section break below the headline.

1 • Move to the beginning of the Featured Tour heading.

• Choose <u>I</u>nsert/<u>B</u>reak/Con<u>t</u>inuous.

• Click [OK].

Having Trouble?

Refer to Lab 3, Concept 2, to review section breaks.

Your screen should be similar to Figure 4.30

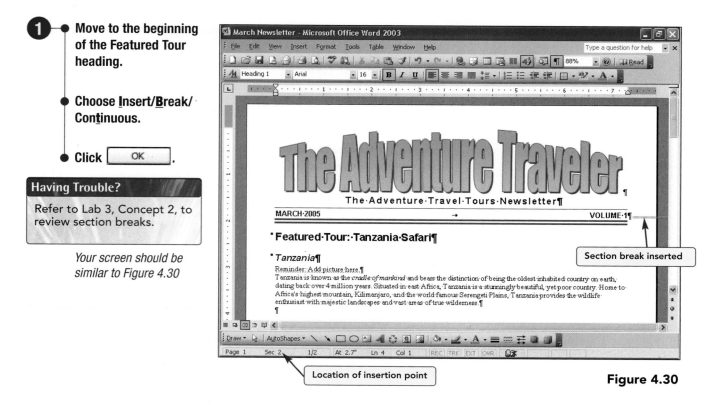

Figure 4.30

Because formatting marks are still displayed, you can see the section break line in Print Layout view. Additionally, the status bar shows that the insertion point is positioned in section 2. The new section continues to the end of the document unless another section break is inserted.

Applying a Two-Column Layout

You want the newsletter to have two columns of text on the first page.

1
- Click ¶ Show/Hide¶.

- Choose Format/Columns.

- Select Two from the Presets area.

Your screen should be similar to Figure 4.31

Figure 4.31

Using the Presets area, you can select up to three evenly spaced columns or two unevenly spaced columns. If none of the preset styles is appropriate, you can enter a number in the Number of Columns text box to create up to 14 columns.

The Number of Columns text box displays 2 as the selected number of columns. Based on the number of columns you specify and your document's left and right margin settings, Word automatically calculates the size of the columns and the spacing between them. Using the default setting, the two columns will be 3.4 inches wide, separated by 0.5 inch. The Preview box shows how text will appear on the page using the specified column settings.

2
- Click [OK].

- Change the zoom to Two Pages.

Having Trouble?
Do not be concerned if the text in your columns wraps differently than in Figure 4.32. This is a function of the selected printer on your system.

Your screen should be similar to Figure 4.32

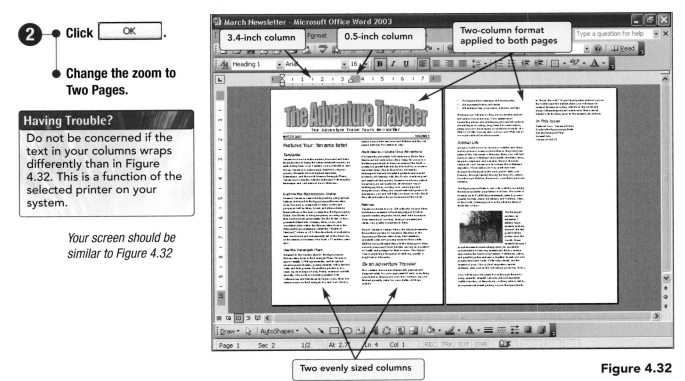

Figure 4.32

The text is displayed as two evenly sized newsletter-style columns, with 0.5 inch of space between. The text at the bottom of the first column continues at the top of the second column. The column markers on the horizontal ruler show the size and spacing of each column.

Applying a Three-Column Layout

Next you would like the second page of the newsletter to be in three-column format. You want a second page to begin at the "Be an Adventure Traveler" heading. To force a new page and section, you will insert a New Page section break. Then you will format the section to three columns. Another way to specify columns is to use the 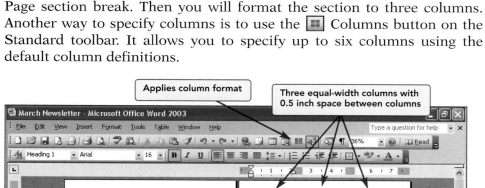 Columns button on the Standard toolbar. It allows you to specify up to six columns using the default column definitions.

1

- Move to the beginning of the Be an Adventure Traveler heading.

- Choose Insert/Break/ Next Page/ [OK].

- Click 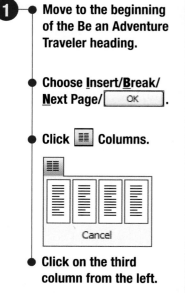 Columns.

- Click on the third column from the left.

Your screen should be similar to Figure 4.33

Applies column format

Three equal-width columns with 0.5 inch space between columns

Figure 4.33

The text on the second page now appears in three equally sized columns while the text on the first page remains formatted as two columns.

Sizing Columns

The default width of 0.5 inch between the columns was appropriate for two columns, but seems too wide for three columns. You want to reduce the space between columns to 0.3 inch and maintain equal column widths.

1 • Change the zoom to Page Width.

• Choose **F**ormat/**C**olumns.

• In the Width and Spacing section of the dialog box, reduce the **S**pacing to 0.3" for column 1.

• Select **E**qual Column Width.

• Click [OK].

• Save the document.

Another Method
You can also drag the column marker in the ruler to adjust the column size and spacing between columns.

Your screen should be similar to Figure 4.34

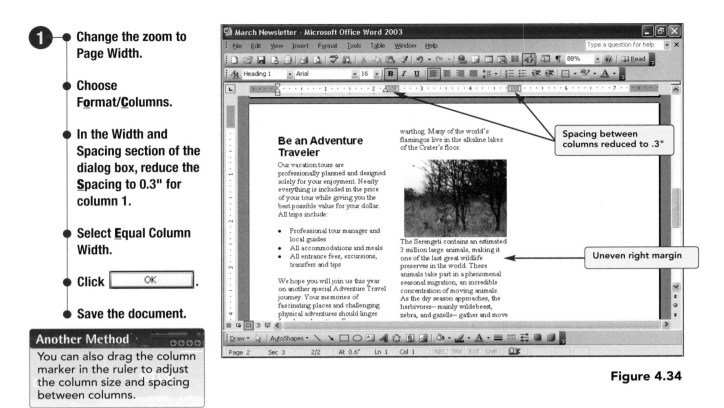

Figure 4.34

The columns are equally sized with 0.3 inch between them. Because the columns are wider, allowing more text to fit on a line, there are now only two full columns of text.

Using Hyphenation and Justification

Now that the layout is in columns, you notice that the lines have very uneven right margins. On lines of text where there are several short words, wrapping the text to the next line is not a problem. However, when long words are wrapped to the next line, a large gap is left on the previous line. To help solve this problem you will hyphenate the document.

Concept 4

Hyphenation

4 The **hyphenation** feature inserts a hyphen in long words that fall at the end of a line, splitting the word between lines. Because Word automatically moves long words that fall at the end of a line to the beginning of the next line, uneven right margins or large gaps of white space commonly occur in a document. Using hyphenation reduces the amount of white space and makes line lengths more even, thereby improving the appearance of a document. The program inserts **optional hyphens**, which break the word only if it appears at the end of a line. Then, as you edit the document, the hyphenation is adjusted appropriately.

1 — Choose Tools/Language/Hyphenation.

Your screen should be similar to Figure 4.35

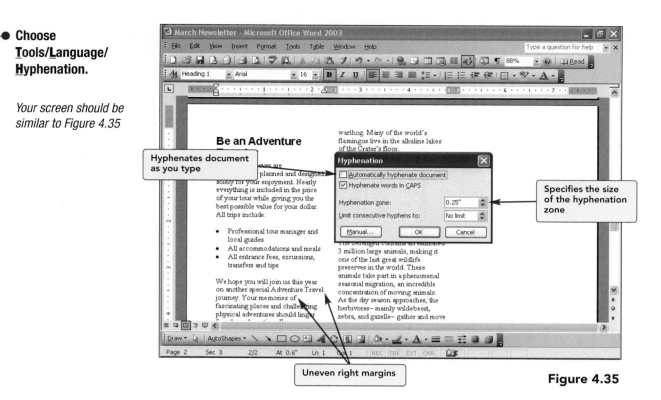

Figure 4.35

Additional Information

Use the [Manual...] button only if you want to be able to accept, reject, or change the proposed hyphenation of each word that Word is considering hyphenating.

From the Hyphenation dialog box you can select the Automatically Hyphenate Document option, which lets Word set hyphenation for the entire document. You can also specify the size of the **hyphenation zone**, an unmarked space along the right margin that controls the amount of white space in addition to the margin that Word will allow at the end of a line. Making the hyphenation zone narrower (a smaller number) reduces the unevenness of lines by hyphenating more words, while making the zone wider (a larger number) hyphenates fewer words. Finally, you can specify whether words appearing in all capital letters should be hyphenated.

2
- Select **Automatically Hyphenate Document.**
- If necessary, specify a hyphenation zone setting of 0.25".
- Click [OK].

Your screen should be similar to Figure 4.36

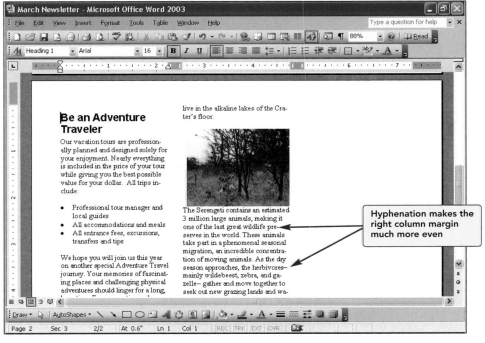

Hyphenation makes the right column margin much more even

Figure 4.36

Word has examined each line and determined where it is possible to hyphenate a word. Hyphenating the newsletter has made the column margins much less uneven. Word generally proposes accurate hyphenation. If you do not agree with how a word is hyphenated after it has been done, you can select the word and hyphenate it manually.

To further improve the appearance of the columns, you decide to change the text alignment to justified.

3
- Select all the text that is formatted in columns.
- Click ▤ **Justify.**
- Scroll the document to check the layout.
- Change the Be an Adventure Traveler heading alignment back to left-aligned.
- Save the document.

Your screen should be similar to Figure 4.37

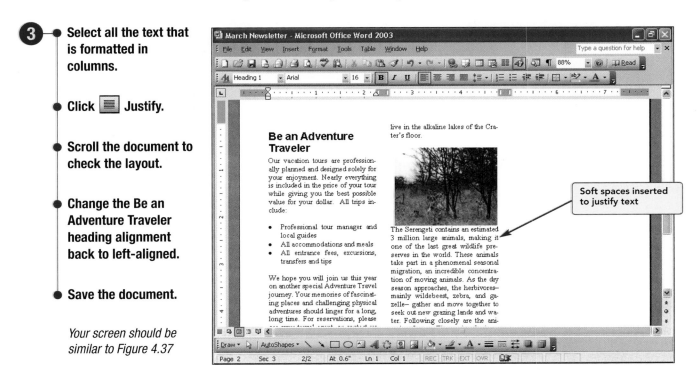

Soft spaces inserted to justify text

Figure 4.37

All full lines now end with the right edge of each column. To do this, soft spaces were inserted between words to push the text to the right edge of each column. The soft spaces adjust automatically whenever additions or deletions are made to the text.

Creating Sidebars

You would like to set the Next Issue—Costa Rica Adventure article on the first page of the newsletter apart from the rest of the newsletter articles by adding a border and shading to the paragraph. An article you want to keep separate from other articles or information, and that highlights an article next to it, is called a **sidebar**. You can use a sidebar for such things as a list of contributors, addresses or contact information, a small self-contained story, a preview of the next issue, or a calendar or schedule.

Adding Borders and Shading to Paragraphs

First you will add the border around the article. To do this, you first select the text you want to include in the sidebar. When text is formatted into columns, you can use the mouse to move and select text just as in a document formatted with a single column. When you drag to select text in column layout, however, the selection moves from the bottom of one column to the top of the next.

1 ● **Move to the Next Issue—Costa Rica Adventure heading (on the first page).**

● **Select the text from the heading to the end of the paragraph.**

● **Open the** ⊞▾ **Border drop-down menu (on the Formatting toolbar).**

● **Choose** ⊞ **Outside Border.**

Another Method
The menu equivalent is Format/**B**orders and Shading/**B**orders/Box.

Your screen should be similar to Figure 4.38

Figure 4.38

The last-used border style, in this case a double, 3-pt weight, brown line, surrounds the selection. You want to change the border style to a single line in a lighter weight. Then, to make the sidebar stand out even more, you will add a shading color to the box.

2
- Choose **F**ormat/**B**orders and Shading/**B**orders.

- Change the line style to the single-line style and 1½ pt. weight.

- Open the **S**hading tab.

Your screen should be similar to Figure 4.39

Figure 4.39

The Shading tab includes a color palette of fill colors. Selecting No Fill removes a previously selected fill. The name of the selected color appears in the text box to the right of the palette, and the preview area shows how the selection will appear. The More Colors option opens another dialog box of Standard and Custom colors from which you can select. The Apply To option allows you to apply the color to the paragraph or selected text. The default is to apply it to the paragraph containing the insertion point. If a selection is made, the color is applied to the entire selection.

3
- Select light yellow (last row, third column).

- Click .

- Click on the selection to deselect it.

Your screen should be similar to Figure 4.40

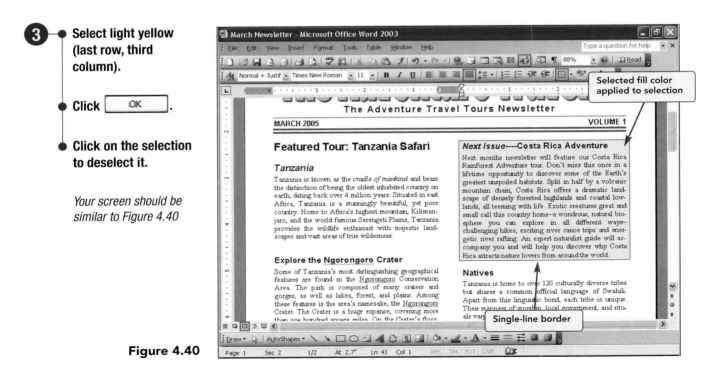

Figure 4.40

You also want to add the same border and shading to the Be an Adventure Traveler article on the second page. You can easily repeat the previous formatting by using the Repeat command.

4 ● **Move to the Be an Adventure Traveler heading.**

● **Select the text from the heading to the end of the article.**

● **Choose Edit/Repeat Borders and Shading.**

Another Method

The keyboard equivalent is Ctrl + Y.

● **Click on the selection to deselect it.**

Your screen should be similar to Figure 4.41

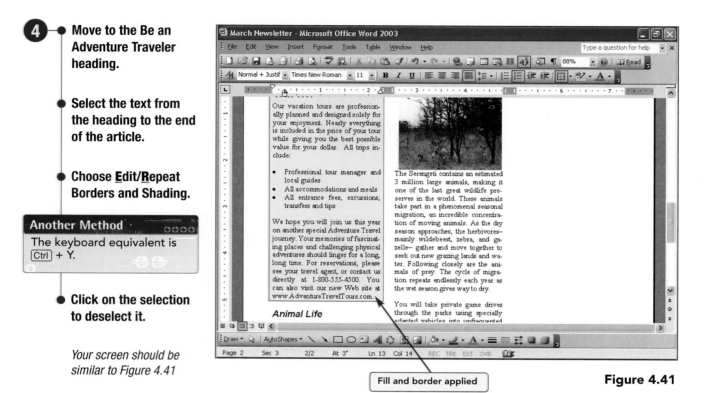

Fill and border applied

Figure 4.41

Creating Text Boxes

Next you want to add the information about the Tanzania Facts to the newsletter. Again, you would like to make this information stand out by displaying it as a sidebar. Another way to display information as a sidebar is to insert it in a text box.

Concept 5

Text Box

5
A **text box** is a graphic object that is a container for text or graphics. Because text boxes are graphic objects, you can place them on the page as you would a picture or WordArt, and move and resize them. You can also add drawing features to text boxes to enhance their appearance.

When using newsletter-style columns, the text scrolls from the bottom of one column to the top of the next. If you want your newsletter to have specific objects in fixed places on the page, it is best to use text boxes and link those that need to flow from one page to the next. When you link text boxes together, the large articles will automatically flow into the correct text boxes on the other pages in the newsletter. Text that is contained in a single text box or linked text boxes is called a **story**.

Generally, the first page of a newsletter should contain the beginnings of a main article and a secondary article, a sidebar with the newsletter contents, and perhaps a quote pulled from the article to capture the interest of someone just skimming the first page. The remainders of the articles are usually found on another page.

You will create a text box on the last page to contain the Tanzania facts information.

1 ● Display the Clipboard task pane.

● Paste the Tanzania Facts item at the end of the second column on the last page.

● Click ✖ Clear All to clear the contents of the Office Clipboard.

Additional Information

Additional Information: The system Clipboard is cleared also.

● Close the Clipboard task pane.

● Scroll to the top of page 2 and select the text beginning with the heading Tanzania FACTS to the end of the article.

● Click 🔲 Text Box on the Drawing toolbar.

Another Method

The menu equivalent is Insert/Text Box.

● Scroll to the bottom of page 2 and move the text box by dragging it to the top of the third column.

Your screen should be similar to Figure 4.42

Figure 4.42

The selected text is placed in a text box. The text is inserted using the modified Normal font size of 11 points. In addition, the Text Box toolbar may be displayed. Its buttons (identified below) are used to link text boxes together so that text flows from one to the next. You will use this feature shortly.

Notice that when you moved the text box, all the objects inside the text box moved too. This is because the text box is a graphic object and is considered one graphic element. However, you can still format the text and size the graphic as separate items.

Formatting a Text Box

You will enhance the appearance of the text and text box next.

1 ● Reduce the text size (excluding the heading) to 10 points and bold the text.

● Click [⬛ ▾] Fill Color and select Gold from the color palette.

Additional Information
Because a text box is a drawing object, the Drawing toolbar buttons can be used to make these changes.

● Click [✎ ▾] Line Color and change the line color to Orange.

● Center the entire contents of the text box.

● Deselect the text box.

Your screen should be similar to Figure 4.43

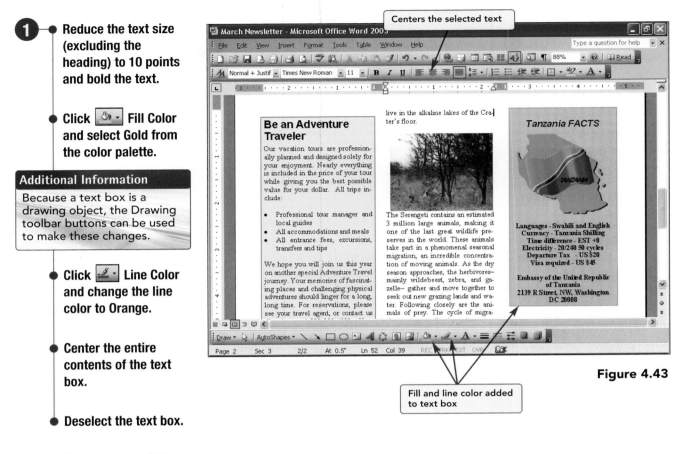

Centers the selected text

Fill and line color added to text box

Figure 4.43

Next you want to include the listing of newsletter contents in a text box and move it to the first page of the newsletter.

2
- Move to the In This Issue heading at the bottom of page 2.
- Select the heading and the five lines of text that follow.
- Apply a text box to the selection.
- Fill the box with a Light Orange color.
- Add a Brown 1½ pt. border to the text box.
- Move the text box to the bottom of column 2 on page 1 as shown in Figure 4.44.
- Click outside the text box to deselect it.

Your screen should be similar to Figure 4.44

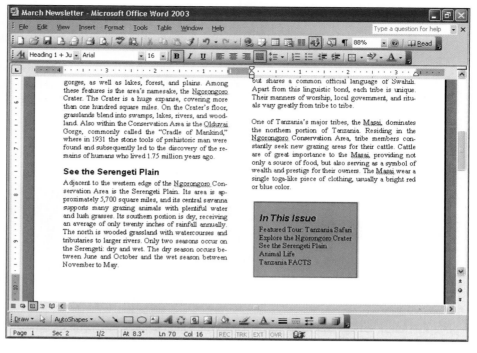

Figure 4.44

Now you would like to see the effects your changes have made to the layout and design of your newsletter.

3
- Save the document again.
- Change the zoom to Two Pages.

Your screen should be similar to Figure 4.45

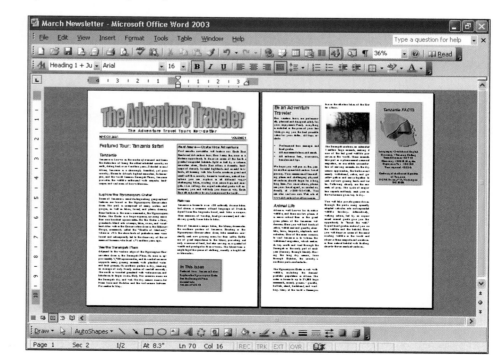

Figure 4.45

The first page of the newsletter is full and the second page has a lot of empty space. Because you still want to add a picture to the first page, some of the text on the first page needs to be moved to the second page.

Linking Text Boxes

As you look at the layout, you decide to make space on the first page by creating a linked text box for the two topics about the Ngorongoro Crater and the Serengeti Plain.

1 ● Change the zoom to Page Width.

● Move to the heading **Explore the Ngorongoro Crater** and select the text through the end of the **See the Serengeti Plain** article.

● Click ▣ **Text Box**.

● Add a Light Turquoise fill color and Orange border to the text box.

● Reduce the size of the text box until only the first article is displayed in it.

● Change the zoom to Two Pages.

Your screen should be similar to Figure 4.46

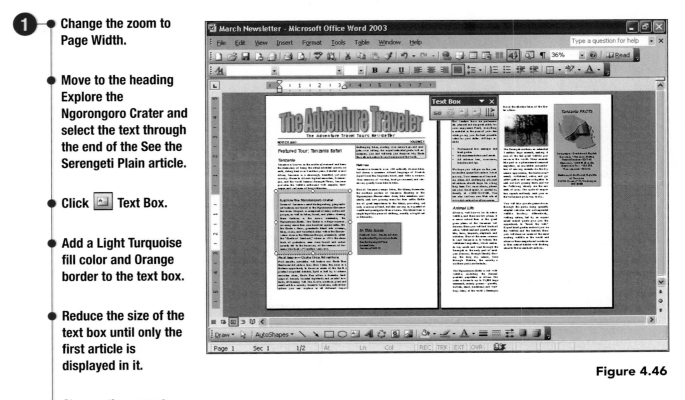

Figure 4.46

Now you will create the second text box on page 2 where the remainder of the story will be displayed.

2 • Move to the bottom of column 2 of page 2.

• Change the zoom to Page Width.

• Click 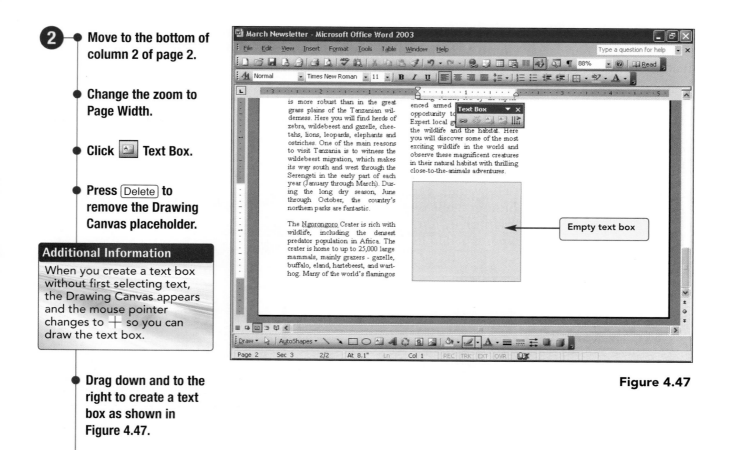 Text Box.

• Press Delete to remove the Drawing Canvas placeholder.

Additional Information

When you create a text box without first selecting text, the Drawing Canvas appears and the mouse pointer changes to ╋ so you can draw the text box.

• Drag down and to the right to create a text box as shown in Figure 4.47.

• Add a Light Turquoise fill color and Orange border to the text box.

Your screen should be similar to Figure 4.47

Figure 4.47

A text box created in this manner is inserted as a floating object. You want to change the wrapping style to Square. Then you will create a link between the two text boxes so that the overflow information from the first text box will flow into the empty text box. The text boxes to which you link must be empty—they cannot contain text. To make it easier to work, you will change to Two Page Zoom and to Full Screen view. In Full Screen view, everything is hidden on the screen except for the document. You can, however, display the menu bar by pointing to the top of the screen to work in this view.

3 ● Change the zoom to Two Pages.

● Choose **V**iew/F**u**ll Screen.

● Choose F**o**rmat/Text B**o**x/Layout/S**q**uare/ [OK].

Another Method

You can also right-click the text box border and select Format Text B**o**x from the shortcut menu.

● Click on the Ngorongoro Crater text box on page 1 to select it.

● Click 🔗 Create Text Box Link (in the Text Box toolbar).

Another Method

You can also select Create Text Box Link from the object's shortcut menu.

Your screen should be similar to Figure 4.48

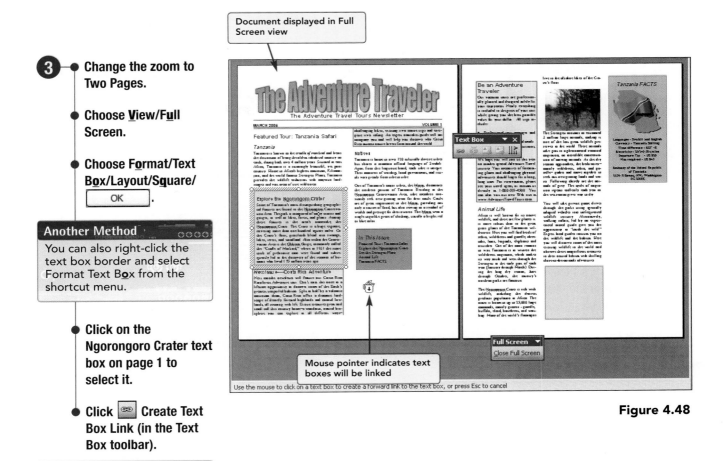

Document displayed in Full Screen view

Mouse pointer indicates text boxes will be linked

Use the mouse to click on a text box to create a forward link to the text box, or press Esc to cancel

Figure 4.48

The mouse pointer changes to an upright pitcher, which indicates there is text that is not showing that can flow into another text box. The next step is to link the boxes.

4 ● Click on the blank text box on page 2.

● Select the text box on page 2 and drag the top sizing handle to increase the height of the text box to fully display the text.

● If necessary, adjust the height of the first text box on page 1 to fully display the first article.

● If necessary, resize the linked text box to fully display the second article.

Your screen should be similar to Figure 4.49

Figure 4.49

The overflow text from the first text box flows into the linked text box. To indicate to the reader that the article is continued on another page, you will add a "Continued on" line to the bottom of the first text box and a "Continued from" line to the top of the second text box. You plan to use Roman numerals for the newsletter's page numbers and want the page reference to reflect this style.

5
- Move to the end of the topic in the first text box and press [←Enter].

Having Trouble?

If necessary, increase the length of the text box on page 1 to display the new line.

- Type **Continued on page II**.

- Press [←Enter] and type **Continued from page I**.

- Click [Close Full Screen] and return the zoom to Page Width.

Another Method

You can also press [Esc] to close the Full Screen view.

- Change the font style to italic and right-aligned for both "Continued" lines.

- Deselect the text box.

- Save the newsletter again.

Your screen should be similar to Figure 4.50

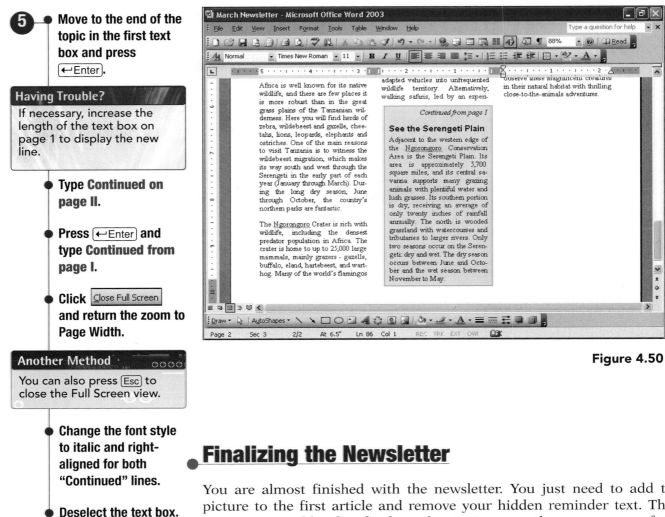

Figure 4.50

Finalizing the Newsletter

You are almost finished with the newsletter. You just need to add the picture to the first article and remove your hidden reminder text. Then you want to add a few final touches to improve the appearance of the newsletter. First, however, you want to check the word count of the document.

Checking Word Count

Now that the newsletter content is about complete, you want to check the word count. This way, when you work on the next month's newsletter, you will have a general idea as to the amount of text that is needed to fill two pages using the same layout.

1 ● Choose **T**ools/**W**ord Count.

● Click [S̲how Toolbar].

Another Method

You can also open the Word Count toolbar from the toolbar shortcut menu.

Having Trouble?

Your Word Count toolbar may be floating or docked, depending on where it was when last used.

Your screen should be similar to Figure 4.51

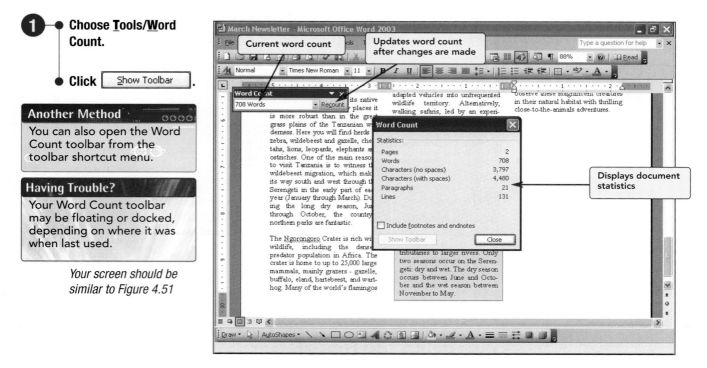

Figure 4.51

The Word Count dialog box displays the same statistics for the document as in the File Properties dialog box. The Word Count toolbar also displays the word count statistics by default, but can display other document statistics by selecting the type from the Word Count Statistics drop-down menu. As soon as you make a change in the document that affects the statistics, the number in the Word Count Statistics box clears. To update the statistics, the button is used. You will see how this works as you continue to work on the newsletter. Now, however, because you displayed the Word Count toolbar, you can close the dialog box and continue to monitor these statistics in the toolbar as you work.

2 ● Click [C̲lose].

● If necessary, dock the Word Count toolbar below the Formatting toolbar.

Removing Hidden Text

Next, you want to insert a picture where you added a hidden reminder to include it. To see where you planned to add the picture, you will display the hidden text.

1

- Click **¶** Show/Hide to display formatting marks.

- Display the top of the newsletter.

- Select the line of hidden text.

- Choose **Format/Font/Font/Hidden/** OK .

- Deselect the text.

- Click Recount on the Word Count toolbar to update the word count.

Your screen should be similar to Figure 4.52

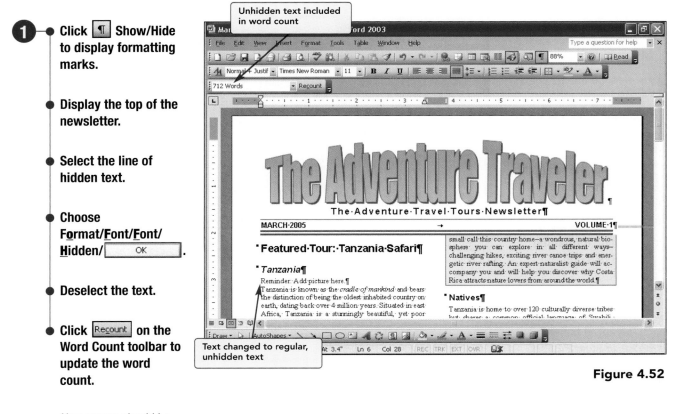

Figure 4.52

Additional Information

You could also delete the hidden text without unhiding it first.

The reminder text is now regular text and is included in the word count of the document. Since you do not need the reminder anymore, you will delete the text to remove it. Then you will insert the picture.

2 • Select and delete the reminder text.

• Insert the picture wd04_Giraffe from your data files at this location.

• Reduce the size of the picture to slightly larger than half the column width.

• Change the wrapping style to Square.

• Click ¶ Show/Hide to hide formatting marks again.

• Change to Whole Page zoom and adjust the layout of the elements as in Figure 4.53.

Having Trouble?
If necessary, increase the size of the picture to force the Next Issue topic to the top of the column 2.

• Click Recount on the Word Count toolbar to update the count.

Your screen should be similar to Figure 4.53

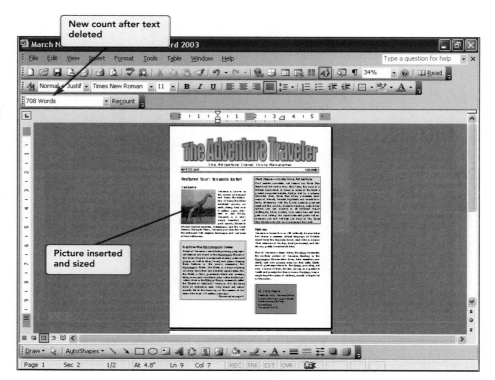

New count after text deleted

Picture inserted and sized

Figure 4.53

The addition of the picture makes the first page much more interesting. As you edited the document, the word count in the toolbar cleared. Now, after updating the count, the new count reflects the deletion of the four words.

Customizing Bullets

As you look at the information on the first page, you decide the article titles in the "In This Issue" box would stand out more if they were bulleted. In addition to the standard bullets, you can use a unique symbol or a graphic as a bullet. You can also change the size of the indent from the margin and the spacing between the bullet and the text. You will add a custom picture bullet.

1 • Return the zoom to Page Width.

• Select the five article titles in the In This Issue box.

• Choose F̲ormat/Bullets and N̲umbering.

• Select the first bullet style.

• Click Cus̲tomize... and then click Picture....

Your screen should be similar to Figure 4.54

Figure 4.54

From the Picture Bullet dialog box, you select the graphic bullet you want to use. You will use the blue box bullet with shading.

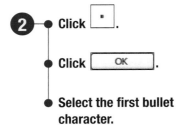

2 • Click ▪.

• Click OK.

• Select the first bullet character.

Your screen should be similar to Figure 4.55

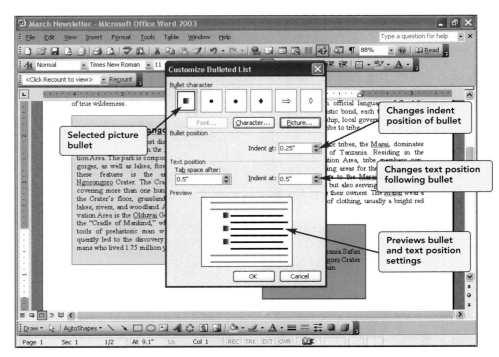

Figure 4.55

Then, from the Customize Bulleted List dialog box, you will decrease the indent for the bullet position and the text position. The preview area will display the effects of your selections.

3 • Reduce the Bullet Position indent amount to 0.1".

• Decrease both the Text Position settings to 0.3".

• Click [OK].

• Deselect the text.

• If necessary, increase the width of the text box to display the items on a single line.

Your screen should be similar to Figure 4.56

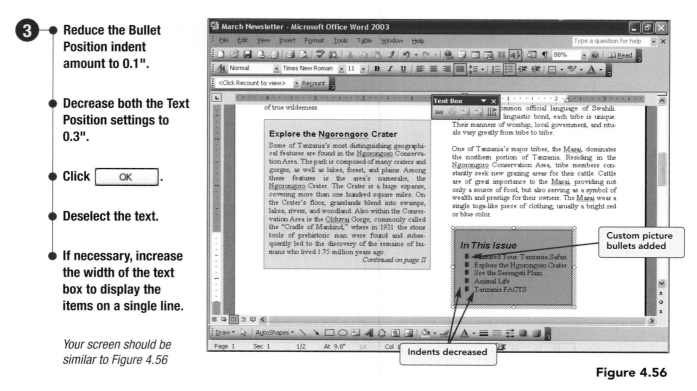

Figure 4.56

The graphic bullets add much more impact to the listing of articles.

Using Special Characters and Symbols

The next change you want to make is to replace the four dashes in the title of the Next Issue box with a single long dash line, called an **em dash**.

1 • Select the four dashes in the Next Issue title.

• Choose **I**nsert/**S**ymbol.

• Open the **S**pecial Characters tab and select Em Dash from the list.

• Click [Insert].

• Move the dialog box to see the Next Issue heading.

Your screen should be similar to Figure 4.57

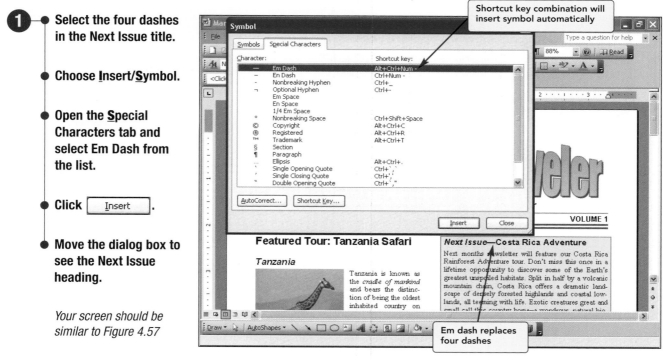

Figure 4.57

The four dashes are replaced with the em dash character, and the Symbol dialog box remains open for you to make additional selections. Those symbols that are frequently used include a shortcut key combination that can be used to insert the symbol automatically for you. You can also specify your own shortcut key combination for any of the characters or have the special character automatically entered whenever a specified character string is typed.

Another change you want to make to customize the newsletter is to place a small symbol at the end of each article to let the reader know that the article is finished and will not continue onto another page. You will add a symbol at the end of the article on page 1 and another at the end of the article on page 2.

2 ● With the Symbol dialog box still open move to immediately after the period at the end of the text in the second column on page 1.

● Open the **S**ymbols tab and select Symbol from the **F**ont drop-down list.

● Scroll the list and select the diamond symbol (see Figure 4.58).

● Click [Insert].

Your screen should be similar to Figure 4.58

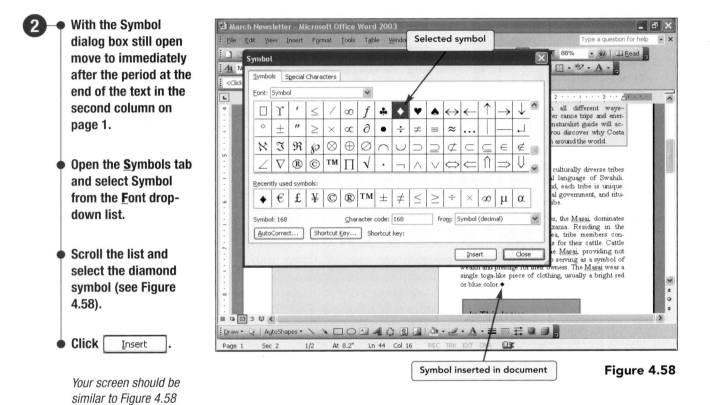

Figure 4.58

You want to change the diamond symbol color to orange and then add the same symbol to the end of the article on page 2.

3 • Click [Close] to close the dialog box.

• Select the diamond symbol.

• Change the font color to Orange.

Additional Information

You can use the same procedure to change the formatting, such as the color, of bullets and numbering in lists.

• Copy the diamond symbol to the end of the text in column 3 on page 2.

Your screen should be similar to Figure 4.59

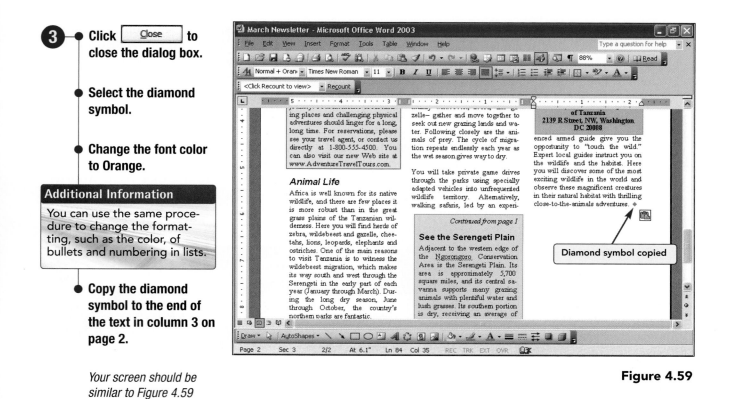

Figure 4.59

Adding a Drop Cap

Finally, you would like to make the first letter of the first paragraph of the newsletter a drop cap. A **drop cap**, used most often with the first character in a paragraph, appears as a large uppercase character with the top part of the letter even with the line and the rest of the letter extending into the paragraph below it. The character is changed to a graphic object in a frame, and the text wraps to the side of the object.

1 ● Move to the top of the newsletter and select the "T" in "Tanzania" (first letter of word in first paragraph).

● Choose F**o**rmat/**D**rop Cap/**D**ropped.

● Decrease the **L**ines to drop to 2.

● Click [OK].

● If necessary, position the drop cap graphic appropriately at the beginning of the paragraph.

● Add the same style and size drop cap to the "A" of "Africa" at the beginning of the article under Animal Life and position it appropriately.

Your screen should be similar to Figure 4.60

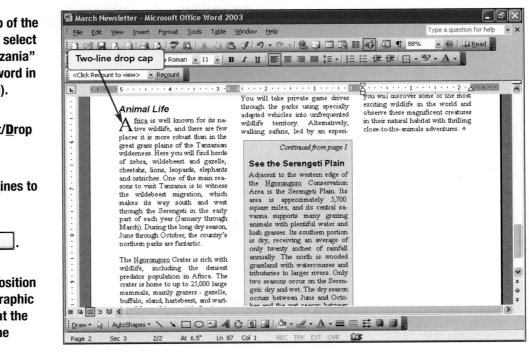

Figure 4.60

The drop-cap effect emphasizes the beginning of the paragraph and makes the columns appear more like those in a magazine.

Refining the Layout and Position of Graphics

The picture and text boxes on page 2 appear too close to the surrounding text. Also, you want to make sure that they are the same width as the column width, 2.23 inches. You will increase the spacing above and below these objects and exactly size their width to the same as the column width.

1 • Switch to Two Pages zoom and check the layout of the newsletter.

• Double-click on the photo of the lions on page two to display the Format Picture dialog box.

• Open the Layout tab and click [Advanced...].

• Open the Text Wrapping tab.

• Set the top and bottom distance from the text to 0.1".

• Click [OK].

• Open the Size tab and change the Width to 2.23".

Having Trouble?
You may need to type the size in the width text box.

• Click [OK].

• Make the same adjustment to the two text boxes on this page.

Your screen should be similar to Figure 4.61

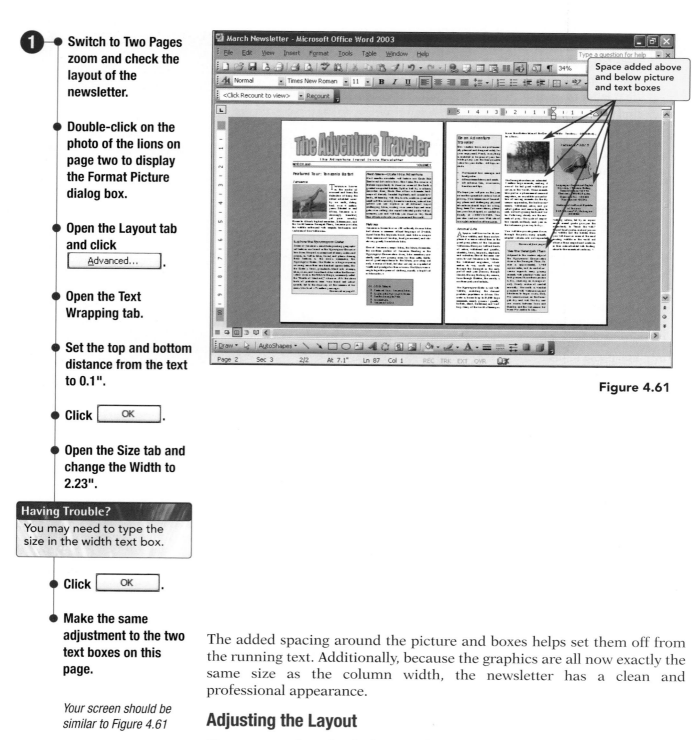

Figure 4.61

The added spacing around the picture and boxes helps set them off from the running text. Additionally, because the graphics are all now exactly the same size as the column width, the newsletter has a clean and professional appearance.

Adjusting the Layout

Now you need to check the newsletter layout and move text and graphic elements around on the page until the newsletter has an orderly yet interesting appearance.

1 • Move the photo of lions to the top of column 2 on the second page.

• Increase the length of the linked text box to fully display the text.

• Position and size the other graphic elements so your newsletter is similar to that shown in Figure 4.62.

• Add your name and the current date below the text box on page 2.

• Move to page 1 and insert a right-aligned page number using the uppercase Roman numeral format in the footer.

Your screen should be similar to Figure 4.62

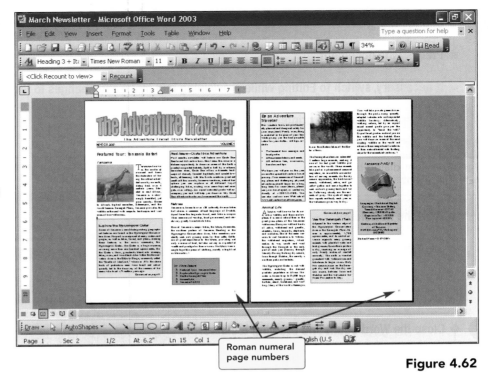

Roman numeral page numbers

Figure 4.62

Printing the Newsletter

As a final check before printing, it is a good idea to display the document in the Print Preview window to make sure that elements will print correctly using the specified printer setting.

lab exercises

matching

Match the item on the right with the correct description on the left.

1. A graphic object composed of text.
2. Holds only a single cut or copied item.
3. Displays text that flows from the bottom of one column to the top of the next
4. Breaks a word only if it falls at the end of a line.
5. Text in a single text box or linked text boxes.
6. Character that extends into the paragraph below.
7. Displays hidden text.
8. A separate but related story, placed near an article.
9. A graphic object that is a container for text or graphics.
10. Shadows and 3-D effects added to graphics.
11. Hides the menu bar, toolbar, ruler, and status bar.

_____ **a.** hyphenation

_____ **b.** sidebar

_____ **c.** system Clipboard

_____ **d.** text box

_____ **e.** drop cap

_____ **f.** special drawing effects

_____ **g.** WordArt

_____ **h.** full screen view

_____ **i.** newsletter-style

_____ **j.** story

multiple choice

Circle the correct response to the questions below.

1. Text that is _____ is not included in the word count.
   a. in text boxes
   b. hidden
   c. in headers and footers
   d. hyphenated

2. _____ are graphic objects that are used to contain text or graphics.
   a. Text boxes
   b. List boxes
   c. Phrase boxes
   d. Display boxes

3. Text that flows from the bottom of one column to the top of the next is displayed in _____ column format.
   a. adjusted
   b. fixed
   c. newspaper
   d. newsletter-style

4. _____ adjusts the spacing between particular pairs of letters depending on the font design to improve the appearance of the text.
   a. Floating
   b. Kerning
   c. Anchoring
   d. Locking

5. _____ appear as large uppercase characters that extend into the paragraph below it.
   a. Drop caps
   b. Character objects
   c. Enlarged characters
   d. Declining characters

6. Information you want to separate from other articles or information that highlights an article next to it is called a _____.
   a. sidetrack
   b. sidestep
   c. sideline
   d. sidebar

7. You can specify the size of the _____ zone, an unmarked space along the right margin that controls the amount of white space at the end of a line.
   a. tab
   b. border
   c. margin
   d. hyphenation

8. Word inserts a/an _____ hyphen, which breaks the word only if it falls at the end of a line.
   a. optional
   b. adjusted
   c. floating
   d. fixed

9. _____ is the capability of the program to store multiple copied items and paste one or more into another document.
   a. Gathering and pasting
   b. Collecting and pasting
   c. Hyphenating and adding
   d. Copying and pasting

10. Horizontal lines, or _____, can be added to any side of a paragraph or object.
   a. tabs
   b. vertical lines
   c. rules
   d. headlines

Hiking Newsletter ★ ★ ★

5. Adventure Travel Tours publishes a monthly newsleter to highlight upcoming trips and keep clients informed on unique travel opportunities. This month the newsletter features information on the Triple Crown hike and explains lightweight backpacking principles.

a. Start Word 2003 and open the file wd04_ Hike Triple Crown.

b. Create a WordArt headline with the text **The Adventure Traveler**. Adjust the size to fit between the margins.

c. Enter, center, and bold the text **The Adventure Travel Tours Newsletter** below the WordArt. Increase the character spacing of the line by 2 points.

d. Enter and bold the text **March 2005** and **Volume IV** on the next line. Add a right tab at the right margin and indent "Volume IV" to this position.

e. Add borders of your choice above and below the date and volume line.

f. Insert a blank line and a continuous section break before the first paragraph of the newsletter.

g. Select all the text, excluding the headline, and format it to two columns with 0.3-inch spacing and equal column width.

h. Save the document as ATT Hiking Newsletter.

i. Insert the graphic wd04_Trail at the top of the first column. Change the wrapping style to Top and Bottom and horizontal alignment to Center. Set the bottom distance to text to .1".

j. Insert a page break following the end of the text.

k. Create a text box in the second column of page one.

Low-Impact Adventuring

Traveling light doesn't just refer to the weight we carry on our backs, it's also about treading lightly and treating nature with care and respect. The following tips are designed to lessen our impact on the natural world when we are out adventuring:

◆ Pack it in, Pack it Out! Nothing is more discouraging than to encounter someone else's garbage during your adventure in the pristine wilderness. Make sure that everything you bring into the wild goes back out with you. Be a Good Samaritan and carry out any refuse you find during your travels.

◆ Fires Smarter. Never cut living trees for firewood! Always use an existing fire ring in areas where camp fires are allowed. Finally, absolutely **do not** leave a camp fire untended.

◆ Leave only footprints, take only photographs! The only thing you

ways clean up your garbage! Report any contact with animals, especially injured or lost wildlife to your Ranger. ®

continued from page 1

shoes, sleep under the stars, and dehydrate their own high energy food.

eight ight nt. To ker

the gear.

are-you ht

The Adventure Traveler

The Adventure Travel Tours Newsletter

March 2005   Volume IV

and find out if the Triple Crown is the quest for you!

Triple Crown Challenge

Adventure Travel Tours, your premier active adventure vacation planner, is proud to announce three new adventure tours: Lightweight Backpacking Expeditions on the Pacific Coast Trail, Appalachian Trail, and Continental Divide Trail. At over 2000 miles long each, these three trails represent some of the greatest adventures available in the United States!

In order to guarantee your success on these challenging adventures, Adventure Travel Tours is embarking on several qualifying lightweight backpacking trips to Death Valley, Paria Canyon, Bryce to Zion, Brian Head and Capitol Reef Park. We invite you to join us on these exciting adventures

Why Go Lightweight?

Any hiker will tell you: cutting weight is of utmost importance when you plan on hiking miles in the wilderness with all of your possessions strapped to your back. Accordingly, there are many "tricks of the trade" diehard backpackers use to cut weight from their packs. Some cut the handles from their toothbrushes, others trim the margins from their maps, and other hikers have been known to hike 2000 miles on granola and candy bars to avoid the weight of a cook stove and fuel. Yet most hikers don't flinch when it comes to buying the latest heavyweight hiking boots, pack, or tent.

Most gear is heavy and heavy duty, but all of this durability adds weight to our gear. Backpackers have begun to rethink their actual needs when out in the wilderness with an eye on reducing weight. These adventurers hike in tennis continued on page 2

Student Name   I

l. Open the files wd04_Lightweight and wd04_Low Impact. Copy the contents of both files into the Office Clipboard. Close both files.

m. Paste the "Why Go Lightweight" article in the text box. Paste the "Low-Impact" article to the first column of page two.

n. Create a second text box at the top of the second column of the second page. Link the text boxes.

o. Add the text **Continued on page 2** and **Continued from page 1** to the text boxes. Right align and italicize the lines. Add borders and shading of your choice to the boxes.

p. Save the file.

q. Use the Research task pane to search the encyclopedia for "Conservation Ethics." Use the information you find to create an additional bulleted item. Replace the bullets with custom bullets of your choice.

r. Move the second text box to the bottom of page two.

s. Insert the graphic wd04_Forest after the last bulleted item on page two. Change the text wrapping style to Top and Bottom.

t. Add automatic hyphenation to the document. Apply styles of your choice to the headlines in the newsletter.

u. Add symbols of your choice to the end of the "Why Go Lightweight?" and "Low Impact Adventuring" stories. Add color to the symbols.

v. Adjust the layout of the newsletter as needed to match the layout of the example.

w. Add your name and a roman numeral page number to the footer.

x. Save the file and print the document.

on your own

Activity Newsletter ★

1. Prepare a two-page newsletter on an activity or club of interest to you. The newsletter should include the following features: WordArt, column format, linked text boxes, clip art and/or pictures. When you are finished, add your name and the current date to the the footer. Check the layout of your document and make adjustments as necessary. Save the newsletter as Activity Newsletter and print the document.

Creating a Newsletter ★ ★

2. You are a physical education major and have written a report on water exercises. Open the file wd04_Water Exercise. Use this file to create a newsletter for students who use the pool at your school's recreation center. Use the features you have learned in Word, including WordArt, clip art, borders, colors, and text boxes, to create a newsletter that is both informative and visually appealing. When you are finished, add your name, the current date, and page numbers to the footer. Check the layout of your document and make adjustments as necessary. Save your file as Water Exercise Newsletter and print the document.

lab exercises

PTA Newsletter ★ ★ ★

3. You are a member of the PTA at the local elementary school. The budget for the year has just been released and the parents are trying to accommodate requests from the teachers and staff for equipment and supplies. The parents decide that a fund raiser will be necessary. In order to fund the purchases, the school has decided to hold an old-fashioned ice cream social. You have volunteered to put together a newsletter to be distributed to the students advertising the event. Your completed newsletter should include WordArt, column format, and other graphic features. Add your name, the date, and page numbers to the footer. Save the newsletter as PTA Newsletter, and print the document.

Garden Newsletter ★ ★ ★

4. The neighborhood that you live in has begun construction of a public garden in a previously vacant lot. You are the chairperson of the committee that raised the funds for the park. You and the other committee members have decided to distribute a newsletter updating the contributors and community on the park's progress. Your newsletter should have great visual appeal. Be sure to include WordArt and other graphic features, as well as photos of the garden. Add your name, the current date, and roman numeral page numbers to the footer. Save the document as Garden Newsletter and print it.

Creating a Personal Newsletter ★ ★ ★

5. Create a monthly newsletter with small articles on a topic of your choice. Use the Web or other resources to obtain information on your topic. Use the features you have learned in Word to create a newsletter that is both informative and visually appealing. Include features such as WordArt, clip art, borders, colors, and text boxes. When you are finished, add your name, the current date, and page numbers to the footer. Check the layout of your document and make adjustments as necessary. Save the document as My Newsletter and print it.

Creating Memos, Complex Tables, Charts, and Diagrams

LAB 5

Objectives

After completing this lab, you will know how to:

1 Use and modify a template.

2 Group objects.

3 Create and enhance a complex table.

4 Change text and page orientation.

5 Perform calculations in a table.

6 Create and modify a chart.

7 Create an outline-style numbered list.

8 Create a diagram.

9 E-mail a memo.

Case Study

Adventure Travel Tours

In addition to the four new tours, Adventure Travel Tours offers many established adventure tours. The four most popular tours are the Amazon River Expedition, the Yukon Bicycling Tour, the Australian Outback Adventure, and the Continental Divide Hike. You need to prepare a memo for the regional manager that contains a table showing the sales figures for these four major tours for the past three years. In addition, you want to include a strategy to increase sales for the four tours.

Your next project is to create a memo to announce the creation of a new department at Adventure Travel Tours. A new group of employees has been created to handle the Adventure Travel Tours Web site. Your memo will include an organization chart to introduce the new department and staff.

Chase Jarvis/Getty Images

Using the Draw Table feature, you can create complex table layouts.

Microsoft Graph quickly creates charts from table data.

Organization charts can illustrate any type of concept that consists of a hierarchal organization.

Concept Preview

The following concepts will be introduced in this lab:

1   **Template**   A template is a document file that includes predefined settings that control the design and structure of a document.

2   **Stacking Order**   Stacking order is the order objects are positioned in the drawing layer.

3   **Group**   A group is two or more objects that are combined so that you can work with them as you would a single object.

4   **Formulas and Functions**   Formulas and functions are used to perform calculations in tables.

5   **Chart**   A chart, also called a graph, is a visual representation of numeric data.

6   **Diagram**   A diagram is a graphic object that can be used to illustrate concepts and enhance your documents.

Using a Template

You would like to create the sales-figure memo using one of the document templates included with Word.

Concept 1

Template

1   A **template** is a document file that includes predefined settings that control the design and structure of a document. Every Word document, including the blank default document, is based on a document template.

The default document settings are stored in the **Normal template** file. Whenever you create a new document using this template, the same default settings are used. The Normal document template is referred to as a **global template** because it contains settings that are available to all documents.

Word includes many different templates that are designed to help you create professional-looking business documents such as letters, faxes, memos, reports, brochures, press releases, manuals, newsletters, resumes, invoices, purchase orders, and Web pages. Many of the templates are available within Word. Many more are available at the Microsoft Office Online Templates Web page. Unlike global templates, the settings included in these specialized templates are available only to documents based on that template. You can also design and save your own document templates.

All template files have a .dot file extension and are stored in the Templates folder. The Normal document template, for example, is named Normal.dot. When a template file is opened, the file type changes to a Word document (.doc). This prevents accidentally overwriting the template file when the file is saved.

You will use one of Word's memo templates as the basis for your sales-figure memo. Then you will change different elements in the memo template to give it your own personal style.

1
- **Start Office Word 2003.**
- **If necessary, display the Drawing toolbar and ruler.**
- **Display the New Document task pane.**

Additional Information

Word displays the last used templates in the Recently Used Templates section on the task pane.

- **In the Templates section, click** [On my computer...] **.**
- **Open the Memos tab.**
- **Select** [Contemporary Memo] **.**

Your screen should be similar to Figure 5.1

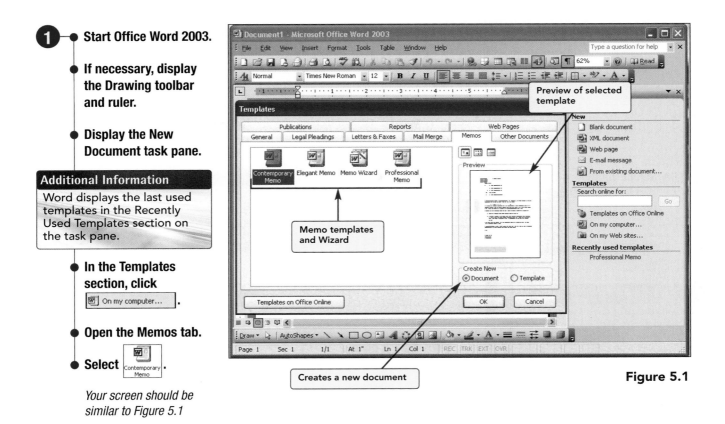

Figure 5.1

Word has several memo templates and a Memo Wizard that guides you step by step through creating a memo. The Preview area displays how the selected memo template looks. You will use the Professional Memo template to create your memo. The Create New section allows you to create a new document file from the template or a new template file. You want to create a new document.

2
- **If necessary, select Document from the Create New section.**
- **Double-click** [Professional Memo] **.**
- **Change the zoom to Page Width.**

Your screen should be similar to Figure 5.2

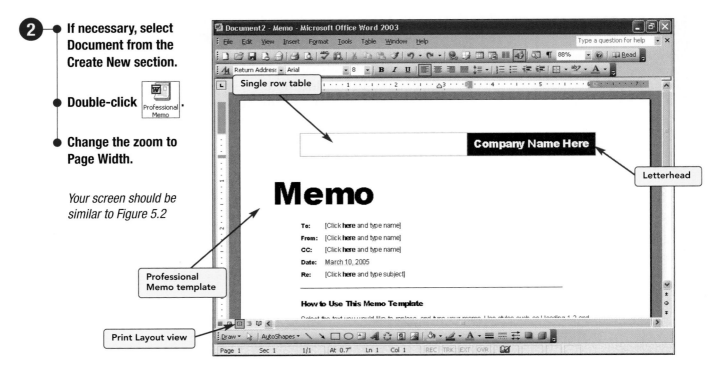

Figure 5.2

The memo template is opened as a Word document and is displayed in Print Layout view.

Replacing Placeholders

The template uses a single-row table to control the layout of the company letterhead. You will replace the sample text in the table cell with the company name.

1 ● Select (highlight) the text Company Name Here.

● Type Adventure Travel Tours.

Having Trouble?
If the table gridlines are not displayed, choose Table/Show Gridlines.

Your screen should be similar to Figure 5.3

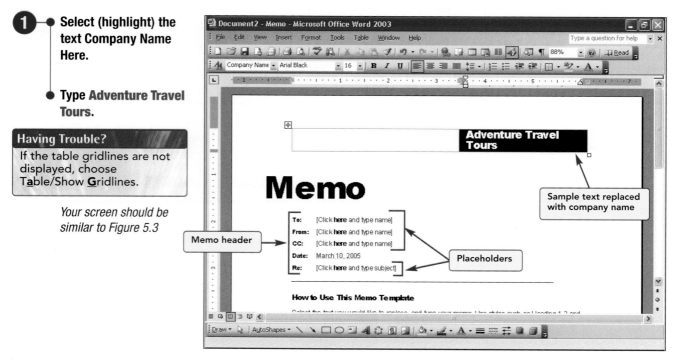

Figure 5.3

Additional Information
You can delete unwanted items from the memo template by selecting the object and pressing Delete.

The next area in the memo template you need to modify is the memo header, which includes the name of the recipient, the sender's name, a carbon or courtesy (CC) copy recipient, the date, and a subject line. The text in brackets is a field that is a **placeholder** for the information that needs to be entered at that location. The placeholder displays instructions about the text you are to enter. This feature is found in most templates. Notice that the date is the current system date. This is because the date entry is a date field.

You will enter the appropriate information in the memo header.

2 • Click the To: placeholder.

• Type **Maria Salverez, Manager.**

• Replace the remaining four placeholders with the following:

From: **Your Name**

CC: **Ed Munson, Sales Coordinator**

Re: **Tour Sales Analysis**

Your screen should be similar to Figure 5.4

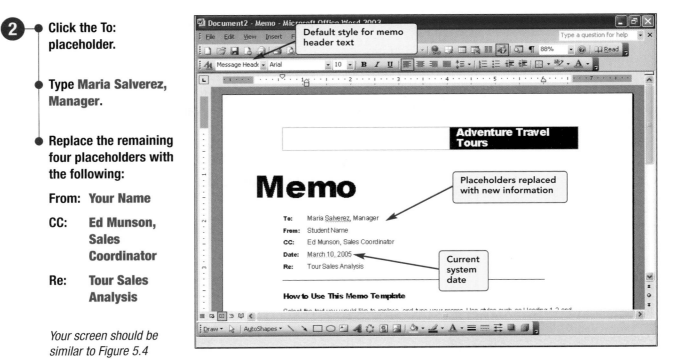

Figure 5.4

The four fields are deleted and replaced with the information you entered. Notice that the Style list box displays "Message Header." This is the default style associated with the header text and sets the font to Arial and the size to 10 points.

Modifying Field Formats

The date in the memo template is a field that displays the current system date. You want to change the date format to include the day of the week. To do this, you need to edit the field format.

1 • Right-click on the Date field.

• Choose **E**dit Field.

Your screen should be similar to Figure 5.5

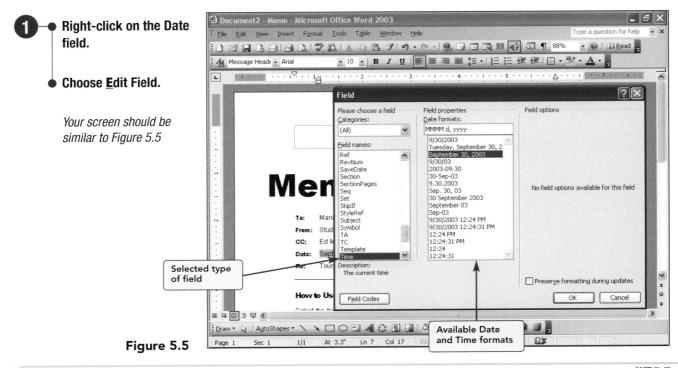

Figure 5.5

The Field dialog box displays a list of field names and formats for the selected field. Because the Date field is selected, the Time category is open and the available formats for date and time are displayed in the Field Properties area.

2 ● **From the Date Formats list, select the format that includes the day of the week.**

● **Click** [OK].

Your screen should be similar to Figure 5.6

Additional Information

If you type over the Date field with text, you will delete the field code from the document and the date will not update automatically.

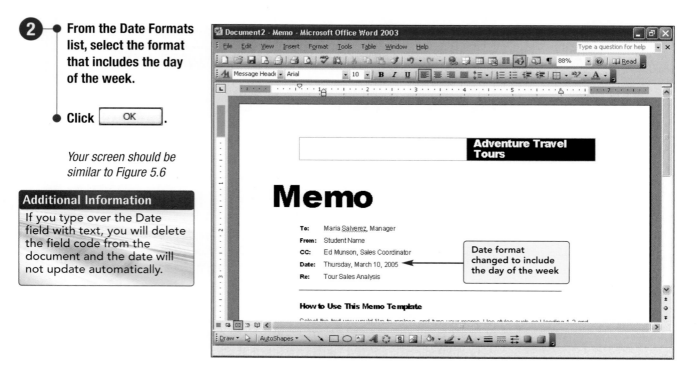

Figure 5.6

Entering Body Text

Next you want to enter the body of the memo. The memo template also includes sample text containing instructions on how to use the template in the body of the memo. You will replace the sample text with the information you want to include in the memo. However, because the sample text is not a field, you first need to select the text to be deleted before typing the replacement text.

1

- Click ¶ Show/Hide to turn on formatting marks.

- Scroll the window to see the sample text in the body of the memo.

- Select the heading, the instructions paragraph, and the three blank lines below the paragraph.

- Type the following text: **On the following page is a table showing sales revenue for the four major tours for the past three years. I have also included the number of tour participants for each year..**

- Press ←Enter twice.

- Save the document as Sales Analysis Memo **to your data file location.**

Your screen should be similar to Figure 5.7

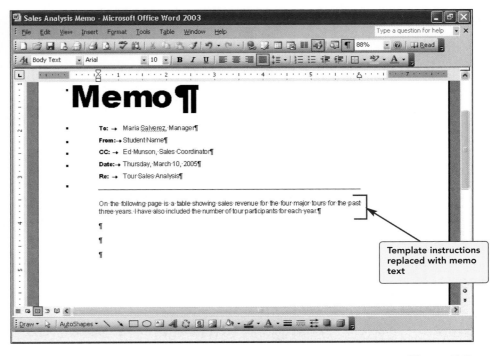

Figure 5.7

The template instructions are replaced with your own memo text. The memo is automatically saved as a document file with a .doc file extension. The template file is unchanged on your computer so you can use it again to create another memo.

Creating a Company Logo

Next, you want to create a graphic to use as the company logo to display next to the company name in the letterhead. The logo will consist of a picture of a mountain and a WordArt object of the company slogan, "Be an Adventure Traveler."

Grouping Objects

Additional Information

See Concept 4: Text Wrapping in Lab 3 to review this concept.

You have saved the two graphic objects you will use to create the logo in a file. You will combine the two graphics objects into one object to use as the logo. To do this, you first need to change them from inline objects to floating objects by changing their wrapping style.

1 • **Open the file** wd05_Logo Elements.

• **Scroll the document to see both the picture and the WordArt.**

• **Change the wrapping style of the mountain picture to square.**

Your screen should be similar to Figure 5.8

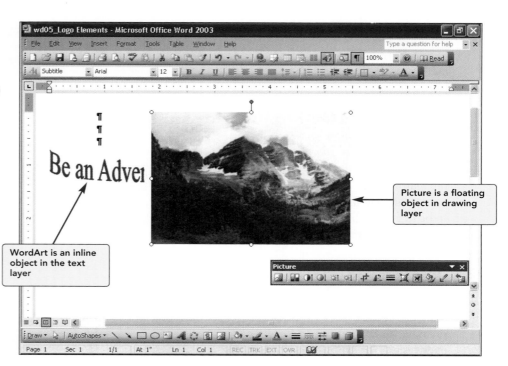

Figure 5.8

Because the mountain picture has been added to the drawing layer and is a floating object, it appears over the WordArt object which is still an in line object.

2 • **Click on the WordArt object to select it.**

• **Change the WordArt object wrapping style to Square.**

Your screen should be similar to Figure 5.9

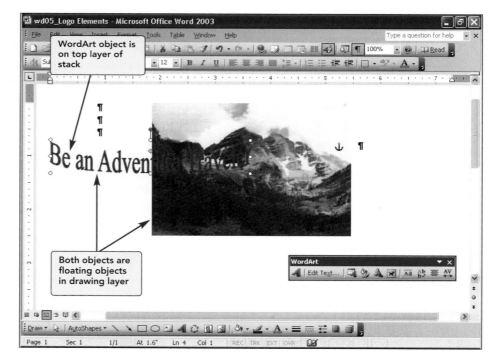

Figure 5.9

Now both objects are floating objects in the drawing layer, and the WordArt object covers a portion of the mountain picture. This is because as objects are added to the drawing layer, they automatically stack in individual layers and may overlap.

Concept 2

Stacking Order

2   **Stacking order** is the order objects are positioned in the drawing layer. As each object is added to the drawing layer, it is added to the top layer. Adding objects to separate layers allows each object to be positioned precisely on the page, including in front of and behind other objects, including the text layer. You can cycle between objects in the stack and move objects to different levels within a stack.

Sometimes it is easy to lose an object behind another. If this happens, you can press `Tab ⇆` to cycle forward or `⇧ Shift` + `Tab ⇆` to cycle backward through the stacked objects until the one you want is selected. To actually change the stacking order, open the Draw menu on the Drawing toolbar and select Order. To see how this works, you will move the WordArt object back one position in the stack.

3 ● Click `Draw ▾` and choose Order/Send to Bac**k**.

● Press `Tab ⇆` to cycle forward through the stack.

Your screen should be similar to Figure 5.10

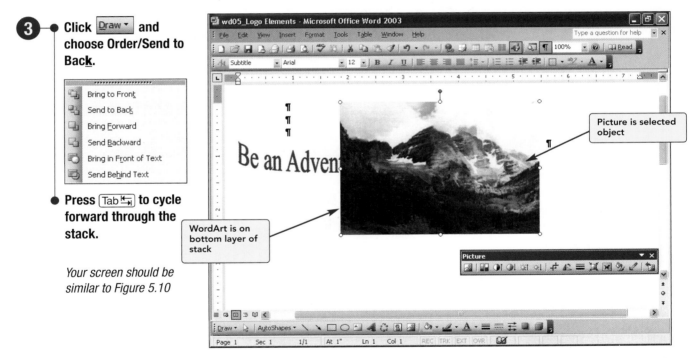

Figure 5.10

The WordArt object is now the first object in the stack and moved behind the picture. The picture is selected because using `Tab ⇆` cycles forward one object at a time through objects in the stack.

You decide you want the WordArt to appear on top of the picture, so you will reorder the objects. You also want the WordArt centered at the bottom of the picture. Finally, you want to group the two objects to create a single object.

Concept 3

Group

3 A **group** is two or more objects that are combined so that you can work with them as you would a single object. For example, multiple objects in a group can be rotated, flipped, or resized as if they were a single object. You can also change the attributes associated with the grouped object. **Attributes** are features such as line color and fill color that can be changed using drawing tools and menu commands. When an object is grouped, you can change the fill color of all objects in the group at the same time.

Many clip art images are composed of several different pieces that are grouped together. Sometimes you may want to ungroup an object so that the individual parts can be manipulated independently. Other times you may want to combine several objects to create your own graphic object that better suits your needs.

Selected drawing objects (ungrouped)

Selected drawing objects (grouped)

---

4 ● Select the WordArt object.

● Click `Draw ▾` and choose O**r**der/**B**ring to Fron**t**.

● Hold down ⇧Shift and click on the picture.

● Click `Draw ▾` and choose **A**lign or Distribute/Align **B**ottom.

● Click `Draw ▾` and choose **A**lign or Distribute/Align **C**enter.

● Click `Draw ▾` and choose **G**roup.

Another Method
You could also choose Grouping from the shortcut menu and select Group.

Your screen should be similar to Figure 5.11

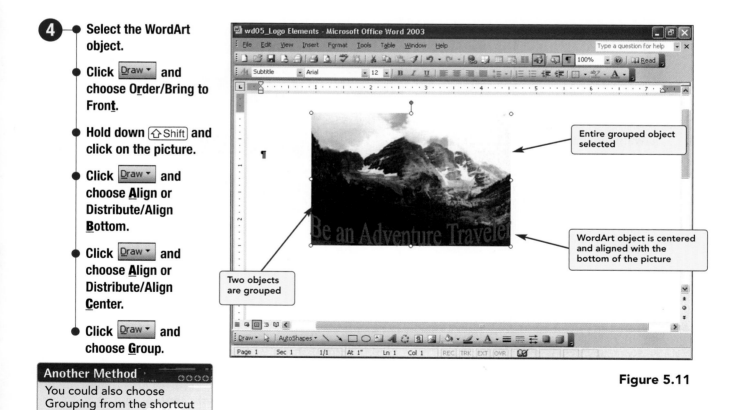

Figure 5.11

The WordArt is centered and aligned with the bottom of the picture and the two objects are grouped as a single object.

Modifying an Object Within a Group

Now that the WordArt is on top of the picture, it does not show up well because it is too dark. You want to make the text color a lighter blue so that it will stand out better. To do this, you can modify the attributes associated with the individual WordArt object while it is still grouped.

Notice the sizing handles are clear circles surrounding the object. This indicates that the entire grouped object is selected. When the entire grouped object is selected, you can then modify the grouped object using the F**o**rmat/**O**bject menu command.

You can select any single object within the group by first selecting the group and then clicking on the individual object. When an object within a group is selected the sizing handles are gray circles with an 'X' in the middle. The toolbars and features that are available depend on the type of object within the group that is selected. You will cycle through selecting the different elements of the grouped object, and then you will modify the WordArt object.

5 ● Click outside the grouped object to deselect it.

● Click the grouped object to select it.

● Click the picture object to select it.

● Click the WordArt object to select it.

● Click 🖌 Format WordArt on the WordArt toolbar.

● Change the fill color to pale blue.

● Click [OK].

Your screen should be similar to Figure 5.12

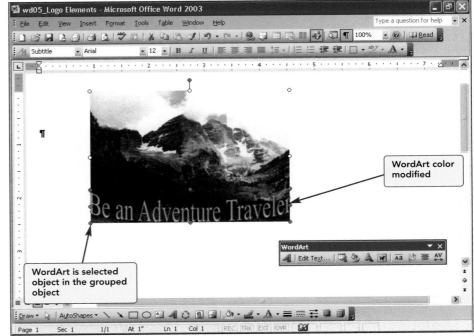

Figure 5.12

The text stands out better on the dark background now that the text color is lighter.

Sizing and Copying a Grouped Object

Next you will reduce the size of the grouped object and copy it to the memo. Because the objects are grouped, when you size and copy the object it will act as a single object. You also need to change it back to an in line image so that when you copy it to the memo, it will be inserted as part of the text.

1
- Press Tab ⇆ to cycle to select the grouped object.

- Choose **F**ormat Object from the object's shortcut menu.

- From the Layout tab, select **I**n line with text.

- Click [OK].

- Reduce the size of the object to approximately 1 inch high by 2.5 inches wide.

Having Trouble?
You can adjust the size exactly by using the Size tab in the Format Object dialog box.

- Save the file as Logo Grouped **to your data file location.**

Your screen should be similar to Figure 5.13

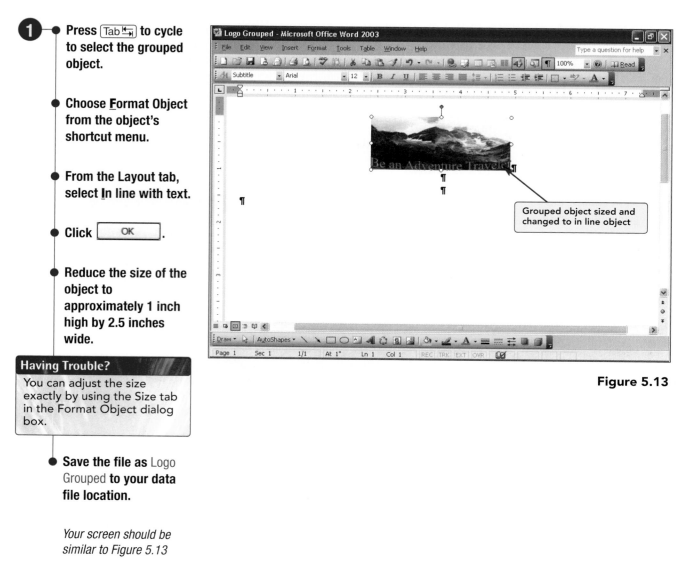

Grouped object sized and changed to in line object

Figure 5.13

The grouped object is now ready to be copied into the table containing the company letterhead of the memo.

2 • Copy the grouped object into the left cell of the table in the memo.

• Size and right-align the letterhead table similar to that shown in Figure 5.14.

Having Trouble?

Refer to Lab 3, page WD 3.59 to review sizing and moving tables.

• Save the document.

Your screen should be similar to Figure 5.14

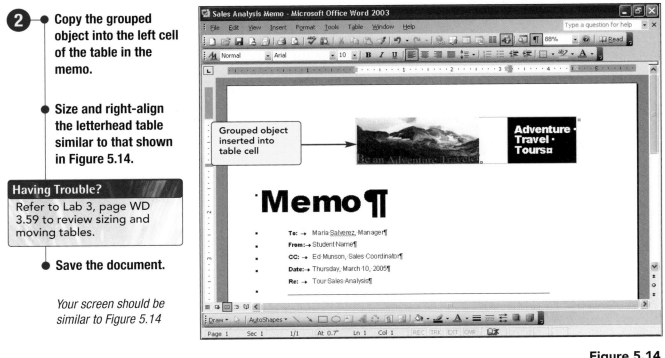

Figure 5.14

You will continue to refine the appearance of the letterhead later. You will continue to work on the memo content next.

Creating a Complex Table

Having Trouble?

Refer to Lab 3, Concept 7, to review tables.

Next you want to create a table to display the tour sales data below the memo text. The table will display the data vertically (in columns) for the three years and horizontally (in rows) for the four tours and a total. Your completed table will be similar to the one shown below.

ANNUAL TOUR SALES						
		2002		2003		2004
		#	Sales	#	Sales	#	Sales
Tours	Amazon River Expedition	44	$192,940	50	$219,250	56	$245,560
	Yukon Bicycling Tour	60	189,600	68	214,880	73	230,680
	Australian Outback Adventure	98	673,750	112	770,000	120	825,000
	Continental Divide Hike	20	174,500	24	209,400	32	279,200
TOTAL			$1,230,790		$1,413,530		$1,580,440

Using Draw Table

You will use the Draw Table feature to create this table. The Draw Table feature can be used to create any type of table, but is particularly useful for creating a complex table like this.

1 ● **Move to the first blank line below the paragraph in the body of the memo.**

Your screen should be similar to Figure 5.15

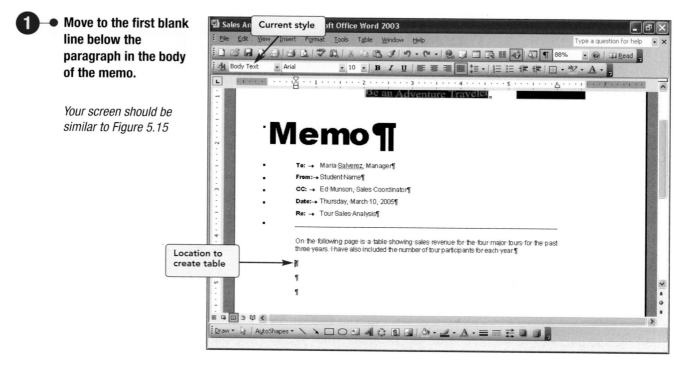

Figure 5.15

Notice that the Style list box displays "Body Text." The Body Text style includes formatting settings that will adversely affect the table that you are about to create at this location. You will change the style to Normal for the body text before creating the table. Then you will display the Tables and Borders toolbar to help you create the table.

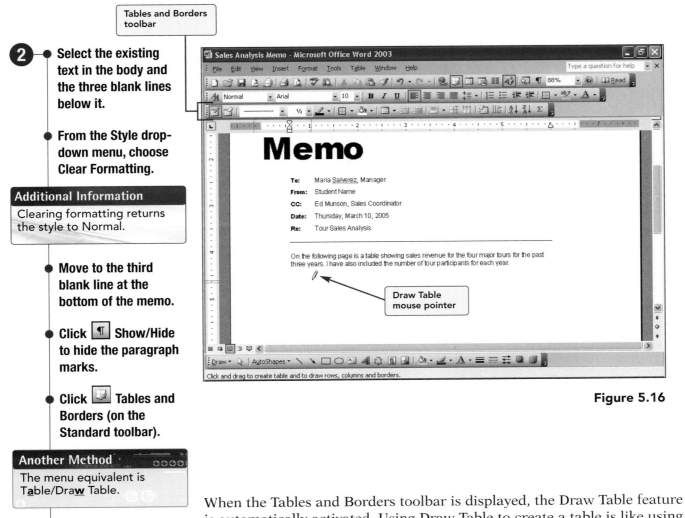

2

- Select the existing text in the body and the three blank lines below it.

- From the Style drop-down menu, choose Clear Formatting.

Additional Information

Clearing formatting returns the style to Normal.

- Move to the third blank line at the bottom of the memo.

- Click ¶ Show/Hide to hide the paragraph marks.

- Click 🔲 Tables and Borders (on the Standard toolbar).

Another Method

The menu equivalent is Table/Draw Table.

- If necessary, dock the Tables and Borders toolbar below the Formatting toolbar.

Your screen should be similar to Figure 5.16

Figure 5.16

When the Tables and Borders toolbar is displayed, the Draw Table feature is automatically activated. Using Draw Table to create a table is like using a pen to draw a table. The mouse pointer changes to ✎ when positioned in the text area, and a dotted line appears to show the boundary or lines you are creating as you drag. First you define the outer table boundaries; then you draw the column and row lines.

The Tables and Borders toolbar buttons (identified below) are used to modify table settings.

3 • Click below the paragraph and drag downward and to the right to create an outer table boundary of approximately 3 inches high by 6 inches wide (refer to Figure 5.14).

• Drag the right indent marker on the ruler to the right margin of the table.

Your screen should be similar to Figure 5.17

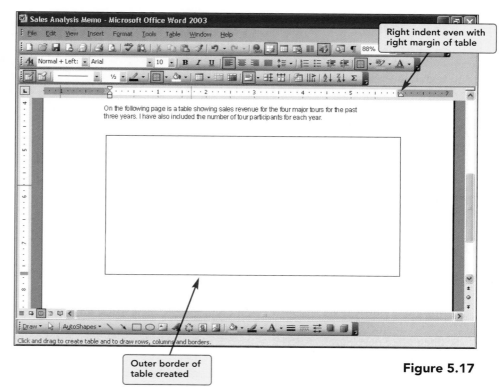

Figure 5.17

The outer border of the table is created. Next you need to add lines to create the columns and rows. When creating row or column lines, drag from the beginning boundary to the end to extend the line the distance you want. A dotted line appears in the ruler to show your position in the table as you draw. If you make an error, click [↻] Undo or [☒] Eraser and drag over the line.

As you create the row and columns in the next step, refer to Figure 5.18 for placement. Do not be concerned if your table does not look exactly like Figure 5.18 when you are done as you will learn all about adjusting table rows and columns in following steps.

4 ● Add four vertical column lines at positions 0.5, 3, 4, and 5 on the ruler (see Figure 5.18).

● Draw seven horizontal lines to create the rows as shown in Figure 5.18. (Lines 4, 5, and 6 begin at the first column.)

● Click 📝 to turn off Draw Table.

Having Trouble?

Do not be concerned if your rows are not evenly sized, you will adjust them shortly.

Another Method

Typing in any cell will also turn off Draw Table.

Your screen should be similar to Figure 5.18

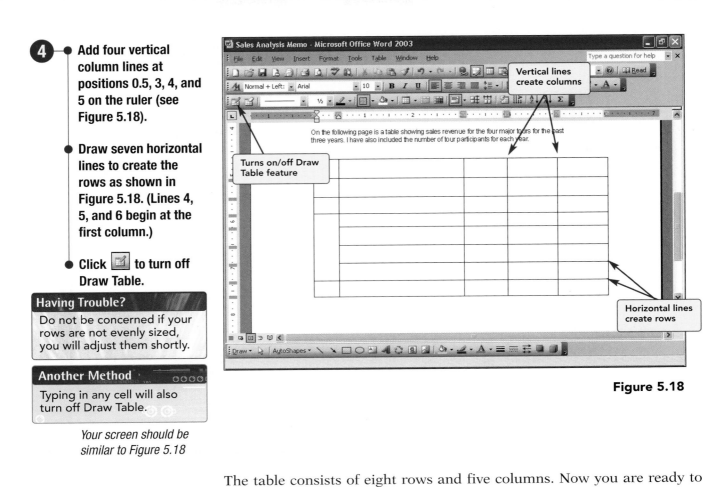

Figure 5.18

The table consists of eight rows and five columns. Now you are ready to enter information in the table.

5 ● Enter the labels and data in the cells as shown in Figure 5.19. Include $ symbols in row 4 Sales Values only.

Your screen should be similar to Figure 5.19

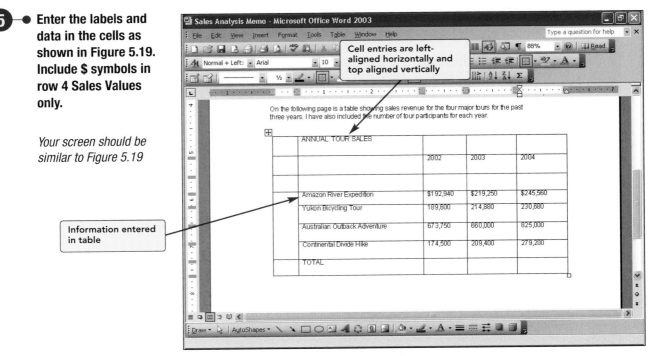

Figure 5.19

By default, entries in cells are left-aligned horizontally and top-aligned vertically in the cell space. You want to center the year headings horizontally and right-align the sales values.

6
- Select cells C2 through E2, containing the year headings.

- Click ☰ Center.

- Select the cells containing the sales values and right-align the values.

- Click in the table to deselect the cells.

- Save the document.

Your screen should be similar to Figure 5.20

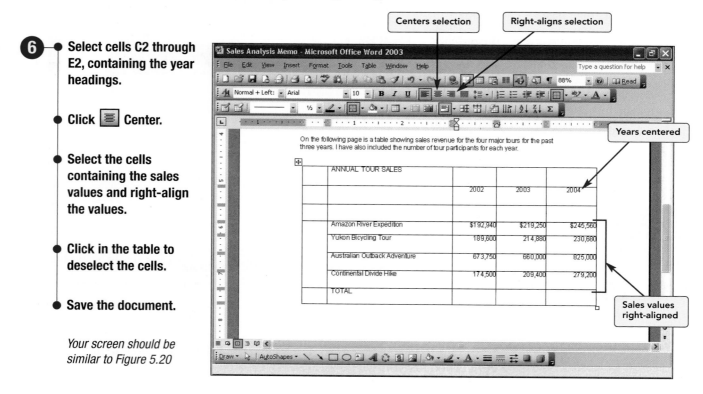

Figure 5.20

You will continue to add more formatting changes to improve the appearance of the table shortly.

Inserting a Column

You realize that you forgot to include columns for the number of people who took the tours in each year. To add this information, you need to insert three new columns to the left of the sales values. You can do this quickly using the Draw Table feature again.

1 • Click [icon] **Draw Table.**

• **Using Figure 5.21 as a reference, drag to add three new columns at the 3.25, 4.25, and 5.25 positions extending from row 3 through row 7.**

• **Turn off the Draw Table feature.**

Another Method

The Ta̲ble/I̲nsert/Columns to the L̲eft command will add a full height column to the left of the current column.

Your screen should be similar to Figure 5.21

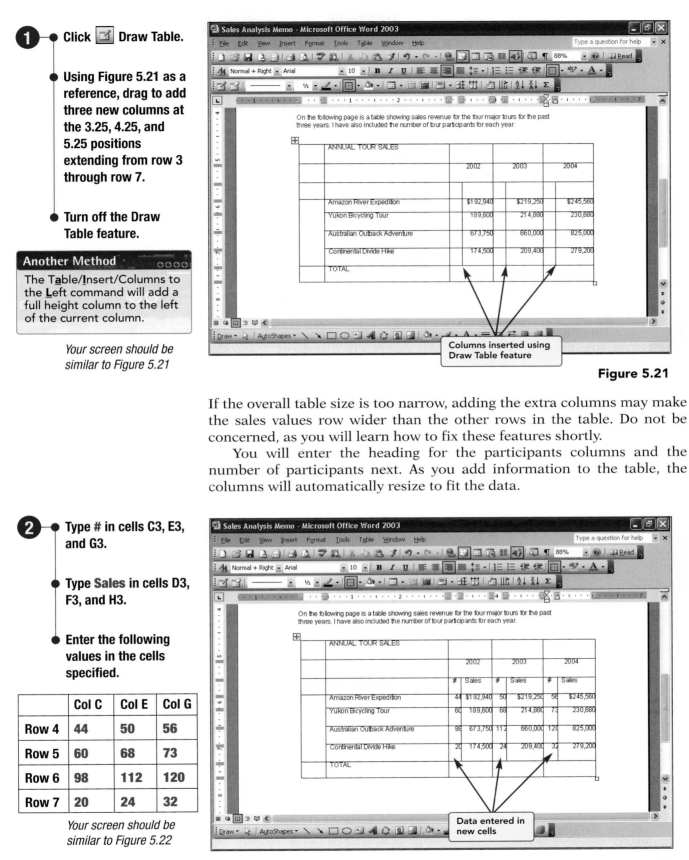

Columns inserted using Draw Table feature

Figure 5.21

If the overall table size is too narrow, adding the extra columns may make the sales values row wider than the other rows in the table. Do not be concerned, as you will learn how to fix these features shortly.

You will enter the heading for the participants columns and the number of participants next. As you add information to the table, the columns will automatically resize to fit the data.

2 • **Type # in cells C3, E3, and G3.**

• **Type Sales in cells D3, F3, and H3.**

• **Enter the following values in the cells specified.**

	Col C	Col E	Col G
Row 4	44	50	56
Row 5	60	68	73
Row 6	98	112	120
Row 7	20	24	32

Your screen should be similar to Figure 5.22

Data entered in new cells

Figure 5.22

Performing Calculations in a Table

Now you want to calculate the sales revenue totals. Rather than adding the values for each column of data and entering them in the Total row, you can enter a formula to make this calculation for you.

Concept 4
Formulas and Functions

4 **Formulas** and **functions** are used to perform calculations in tables. A **formula** is an expression that contains any combination of numbers, fields resulting in numbers, table references, and operators. **Operators** specify the type of calculation to perform. The most common operators are + (add), − (subtract), * (multiply), and / (divide).

To use the operators, follow the common arithmetic laws: multiply and divide before adding and subtracting, and calculate whatever is in parentheses first. For example, the formula, 125 + D3 * D5 will multiply the value in cell D3 by the value in cell D5 and then add 125. If you want to add 125 to D3 and then multiply the result by D5, put 125 and D3 in parentheses: (125 + D3) * D5.

A **function** is a prewritten formula. One function you may use frequently is the SUM function. SUM calculates the total of a column of numbers. Other functions include:

Function	Description
AVERAGE	Calculates the average of a column of numbers
COUNT	Totals the number of cells in the column
MAX	Displays the maximum value in the column
MIN	Displays the minimum value in the column

To reference cells in formulas and functions, use a comma to separate references to individual cells and a colon to separate the first and last cells in a range of cells. For example C1, C5 references the values in cells C1 and C5, whereas C1:C5 references the values in the range of cells C1, C2, C3, C4, and C5.

The calculated result of a formula or function is displayed in the table cell containing the formula or function. The result of the calculation is a field. Therefore, if the data in the referenced cells of the formula or function changes, updating the field quickly recalculates the result.

The formulas and functions in Word let you create simple tables and spreadsheets for your documents. For larger, more complex spreadsheets, use Excel and then paste the spreadsheet into your document.

Calculating a Sum

You will enter a formula to sum the sales revenue values in the 2002 column of data.

1 ● **Move to the Total cell for the 2002 year.**

● **Choose Table/Formula.**

Your screen should be similar to Figure 5.23

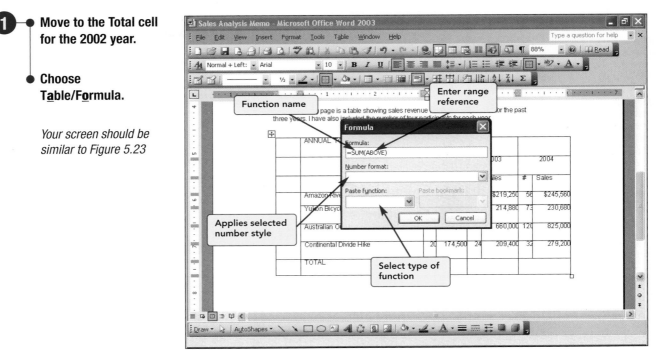

Figure 5.23

In the Formula dialog box, you enter the type of formula and the table cell references for the formula in the Formula text box. The function =SUM(ABOVE) is displayed by default because that is the only location of cells containing values to sum. The range reference ABOVE will calculate a sum for all values directly above the current cell. The Paste Function list box is used to select a different type of function if needed. You can also type the function or formula directly in the Formula text box. From the Number Format drop-down list box, you can select a number style.

You want to sum the values in the range of cells D4 through D7 (D4:D7) and will replace ABOVE with the specific table cell references.

In the Formula text box, replace the word ABOVE in the parentheses with D4:D7.

Double-click the word ABOVE to quickly select it.

The cell reference is not case sensitive. You could type D or d.

● **Click** | OK |.

Your screen should be similar to Figure 5.24

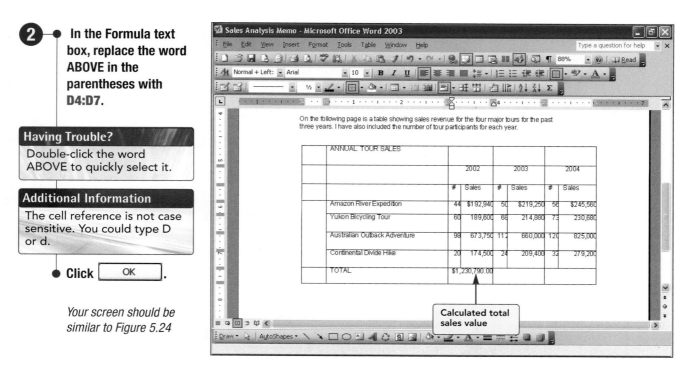

Figure 5.24

Using the values in the specified cells of the table, the formula correctly calculates the result of $1,230,790.00. The value is automatically displayed in currency number format style. This is because the first value in the range displays a currency symbol and Word reflects this format by applying the currency number format to the calculated value.

Because the SUM function is the most frequently used function, it has its own shortcut button. You will use the shortcut to calculate the sales total for 2003.

3

Move to the Total cell for the 2003 year.

● **Click** Σ **AutoSum.**

Your screen should be similar to Figure 5.25

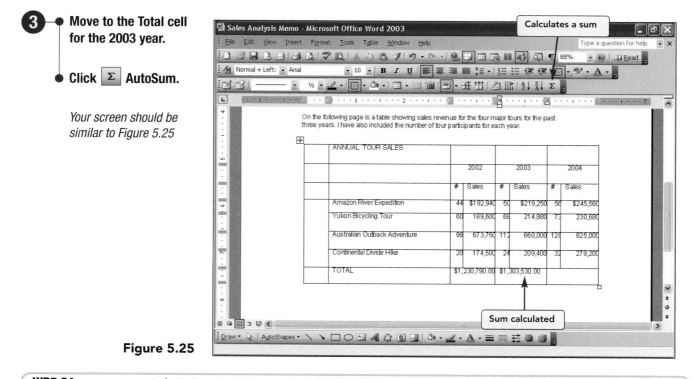

Figure 5.25

Using the Σ AutoSum button enters a SUM function that calculates the sum of all the numbers above the current cell. The calculated value of $1,303,530.00 is displayed in cell D8. It is also formatted as currency.

Updating a Calculation

As you look at the total, you think it seems a little low and decide to check the values you entered for the year. You see that the Australian Outback Adventure value was entered incorrectly. It should be 770,000. Because the calculated result is a field, after changing the value in the cell, you can quickly update the calculation.

1 ● **Change the entry in cell F6 to 770,000.**

● **Click on the value in the 2003 Total cell and press F9 to update the field.**

Another Method

You can also select Update Field from the field's shortcut menu.

Your screen should be similar to Figure 5.26

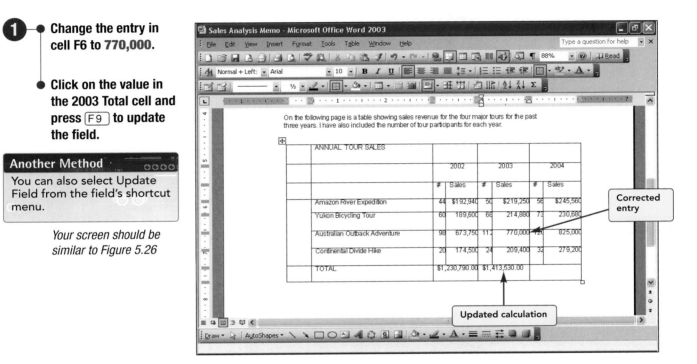

Figure 5.26

The correct calculated value of $1,413,530.00 is displayed in the cell. Next you need to enter the function to calculate the total value for 2004. Additionally, you decide you do not want the two decimal places displayed for the three totals and will delete them.

2 ● Enter the function to calculate the total for 2004.

● Click in the field and delete the decimal and two decimal places from each of the three calculated results.

● Right-align the TOTAL label and total values.

● Save the document again.

Your screen should be similar to Figure 5.27

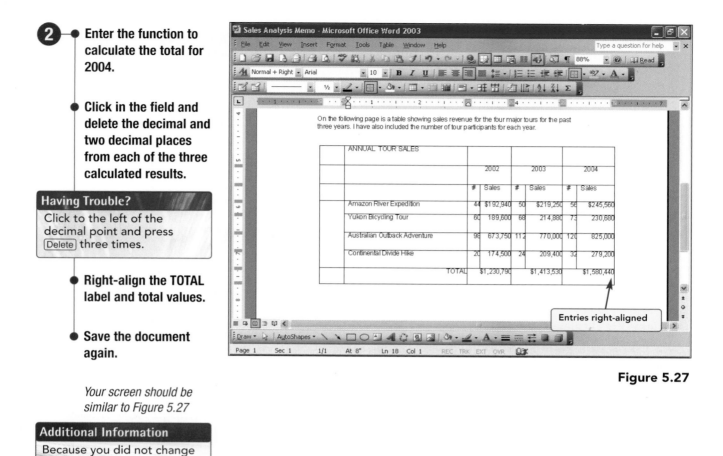

Figure 5.27

Enhancing a Complex Table

The table is really taking shape. Now that the content of the table is complete, you want to improve its appearance by enhancing the title, adding color, increasing the text size, and modifying the border lines.

Merging Cells

After looking at the table, you decide to display the title centered over all columns of the table. To do this, you will combine the cells in the first row to create a single cell and then center the label within the cell.

1 • **Select row 1.**

Having Trouble?

Click at the left edge of the row to select the entire row.

• **Click** 📑 **Merge Cells.**

Another Method

The menu equivalent is Table/Merge Cells.

• **Click** ▤ **Center.**

• **Click in the cell to deselect it.**

Your screen should be similar to Figure 5.28

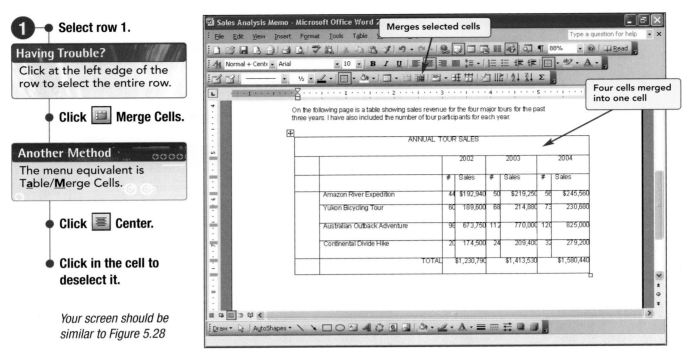

Figure 5.28

The four column dividers are eliminated, and the top row is one cell. The entry is centered in the cell space.

Changing Text Orientation

In cell A4 you want to display the heading "Tours." You also want the heading to appear centered and the orientation to be vertical within the cell space.

1 • **Enter Tours in cell A4.**

• **Click** 📊 **Change Text Direction twice.**

Another Method

The menu equivalent is Format/Text Direction/Orientation.

• **Click** 📊 **Center.**

Additional Information

Notice the graphic in the alignment buttons changed to reflect the text orientation of the selection.

Your screen should be similar to Figure 5.29

Figure 5.29

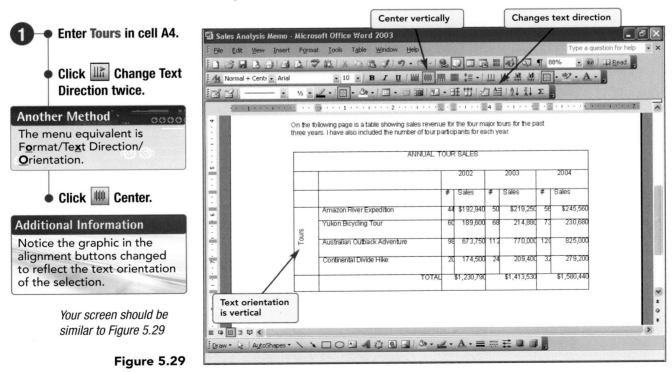

Adding Cell Shading

To differentiate the areas of the table, you will add color shading.

1 ● Select the entire table.

● Open the 🎨 ▾ Shading Color drop-down menu.

● Click ⌈ More Fill Colors... ⌋.

● If necessary, open the Standard tab.

Your screen should be similar to Figure 5.30

Figure 5.30

From the Colors dialog box, you can select from standard colors or create a custom color. The Standard tab palette includes many shade variations of the same colors that are included in the drop-down color palette list.

2 ● Select a color of your choice from the standard color palette.

● Click ⌈ OK ⌋.

● Select the tour names and sales values, and apply another shading color to the cells in this range.

● Deselect the range.

Your screen should be similar to Figure 5.31

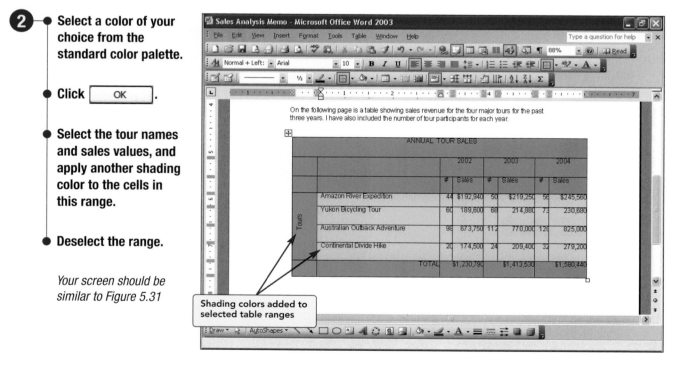

Figure 5.31

Next you want to enhance the text of the headings and the table data.

3 • Select the table title and increase the font size to 16 points, and add bold with a color of your choice.

• Select the year headings and increase the font size to 14 points, add bold and the same color as the title. Apply the same formats to the Tours label.

• Select the remaining text in the table and increase the font size to 12 points.

• Center and apply the same font color to the # and Sales headings.

• Apply the same font color and bold to the TOTAL label and values.

Your screen should be similar to Figure 5.32

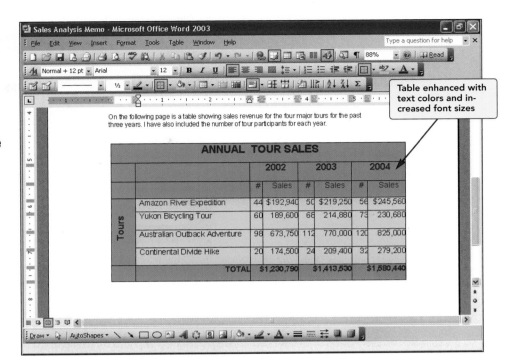

Figure 5.32

Changing Page Orientation

Because the increased point size makes the table contents look crowded, you decide to make the entire table larger.

1
- Select the table.

- Drag the sizing handle to the right to increase the width of the table to the 7-inch position on the ruler.

Your screen should be similar to Figure 5.33

ANNUAL TOUR SALES

Tours		2002		2003		2004	
		#	Sales	#	Sales	#	Sales
	Amazon River Expedition	44	$192,940	50	$219,250	56	$245,560
	Yukon Bicycling Tour	60	189,600	68	214,880	73	230,680
	Australian Outback Adventure	98	673,750	112	770,000	120	825,000
	Continental Divide Hike	20	174,500	24	209,400	32	279,200
	TOTAL		$1,230,790		$1,413,530		$1,580,440

On the following page is a table showing sales revenue for the four major tours for the past three years. I have also included the number of tour participants for each year.

Table too wide to fit on page

Figure 5.33

Now the table is too wide to fit easily within the width of the page. When text is wider than the width of the page, you can change the orientation of the page from **portrait**, in which text is printed across the width of the page, to **landscape**, in which text is printed across the length of the page.

Because the memo will look better in the current orientation of portrait, you decide to display the table on a separate page that will print in landscape orientation. To have different orientations within a document, you need to insert a section break first, and then apply the orientation to the section you want affected.

2
- If necessary, insert a blank line above the table.

- Move to the blank line above the table.

- Insert a **N**ext Page section break.

- Choose **F**ile/Page Set**u**p/Land**s**cape.

- Click OK .

- Change the zoom to Two Pages.

Your screen should be similar to Figure 5.34

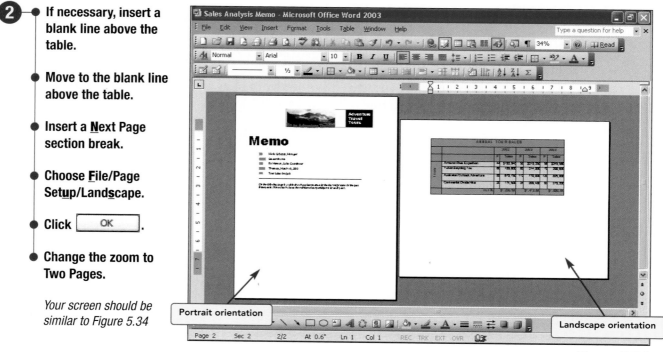

Portrait orientation

Landscape orientation

Figure 5.34

The entire table now easily fits across the width of the page.

Sizing Rows and Columns

Next, you want to decrease the width of column A. To change the width of a column or row, point to the column divider line and drag it to the right or left to increase or decrease the column width, or up or down to increase or decrease the row height. A temporary dotted line appears to show your new setting.

1 ● Return the zoom to Page Width.

● Point to the right border of column A and drag to the left to decrease the column width to the minimum amount possible.

● If necessary, increase the width of column B to display the tour names on a single line.

● If the last column in the four tours rows is uneven, drag the border line to make it even with the rest of the outside edge of the table.

Additional Information

The mouse pointer appears as ╂ when you can drag to size a row or column.

Your screen should be similar to Figure 5.35

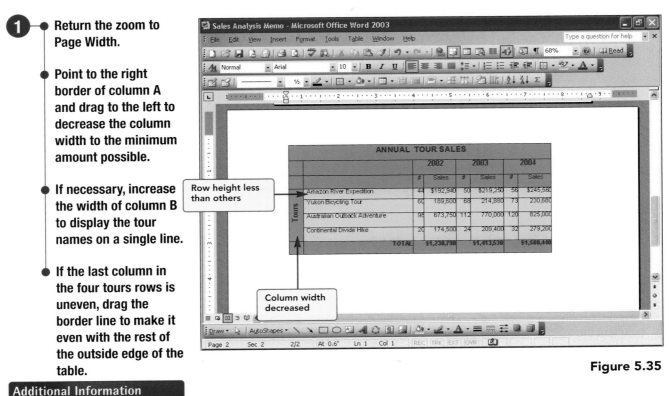

Figure 5.35

You also want to adjust the height of the rows to be equally sized.

2 ● Select the entire table.

● Click Distribute Rows Evenly.

Another Method ○○○○
The menu equivalent is Table/**A**utofit/Distribute Rows Eve**n**ly.

Your screen should be similar to Figure 5.36

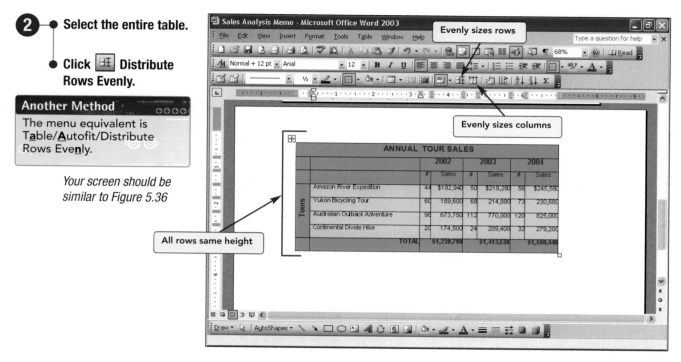

Figure 5.36

You also want the widths of the # columns to be the same and the widths of the Sales columns to be the same. However, because these columns are not adjacent, you cannot use the Distribute Columns Evenly feature. Instead, you need to specify the exact width for each column.

3 ● Select the 2002 # column.

● Choose T**a**ble/Table P**r**operties/Col**u**mn.

● Select Preferred **W**idth.

● Enter .5 in the text box.

Your screen should be similar to Figure 5.37

Figure 5.37

You can continue specifying settings for the other columns by using the ⎡ Next Column ▸▸ ⎤ and ⎡ ◂◂ Previous Column ⎤ buttons to move from one column to another and making the appropriate selections. You will move to each of the # columns first and set their width to .5 inch. Then you will set the width of the sales value columns to 1 inch. The new settings are applied to the table as you make your selections.

4 • Click [Next Column ►►] twice to move to column 5.

• Select Preferred **W**idth and set the width to 0.5 inch.

• Move to column 7 and set the width to 0.5 inch.

• In a similar manner, set the column widths for columns 8, 6, and 4 to 1 inch.

• Click [OK].

• Click on the table to deselect the column.

Your screen should be similar to Figure 5.38

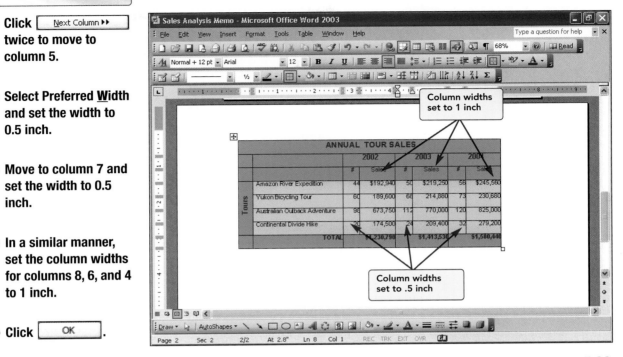

Figure 5.38

Changing Cell Margins and Centering Vertically

Although you have adjusted the size of the columns and rows, the table content still looks a little crowded. This is because entries in the cells that were right-aligned are touching the right cell border line. You will increase the cell margin space to increase the space between the boundary of the cell and the text inside the cell. You also want to vertically center the data in the table to further improve the readability of the table content.

1

- Select the entire table.

- Choose T**a**ble/Table Pr**o**perties/C**e**ll.

- Click [**Options...**].

- Click **S**ame as the whole table to clear the selection.

- Increase the **R**ight margin setting to .15.

- Click [OK].

- Click **C**enter.

- Click [OK].

- Click in the table to deselect it.

Your screen should be similar to Figure 5.39

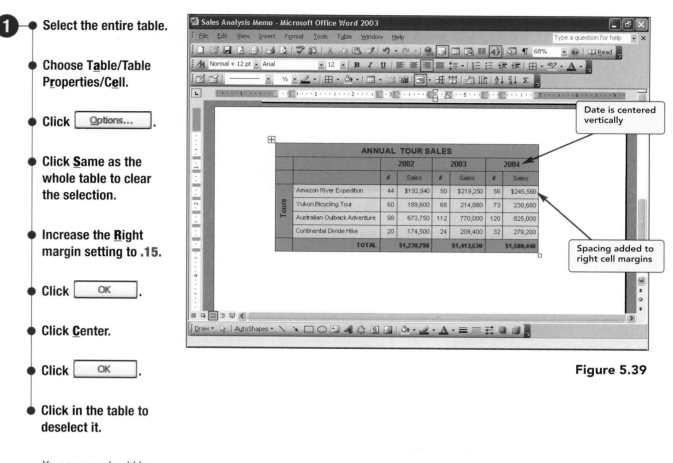

Figure 5.39

The extra margin padding on the right side of the cell makes the data much easier to read.

Removing Border Lines

When a table is created, single, black, 0.5-point solid-line borders are added by default around each cell. Once color and other formatting has been added to a table, you may no longer need all the border lines to define the spaces. You will remove the border line below row 1 first.

1 Move to row 1.

• Open the Border drop-down menu.

Additional Information

The ⬚▾ button in either the Standard or Tables and Borders toolbar can be used.

• Click ⬛ Bottom Border to clear the border line.

Additional Information

The Border drop-down menu identifies the border lines that are used in a selected cell by highlighting them.

Your screen should be similar to Figure 5.40

Changes cell borders

Bottom border line is removed and gray gridline is visible

ANNUAL TOUR SALES						
	2002		2003		2004	
	#	Sales	#	Sales	#	Sales
Amazon River Expedition	44	$192,940	50	$219,250	56	$245,560
Yukon Bicycling Tour	60	189,600	68	214,880	73	230,680
Australian Outback Adventure	98	673,750	112	770,000	120	825,000
Continental Divide Hike	20	174,500	24	209,400	32	279,200
TOTAL		$1,230,790		$1,413,530		$1,580,440

Figure 5.40

The border line is removed, but a gray gridline is still displayed. Gridlines are used to help you see the cell boundaries; however, they are not printed.

2 Remove the border lines from the cells as shown in Figure 5.41.

Additional Information

The Inside Border option quickly removes all inside border lines from a selection.

Your screen should be similar to Figure 5.41

Table with many border lines removed

ANNUAL TOUR SALES						
	2002		2003		2004	
	#	Sales	#	Sales	#	Sales
Amazon River Expedition	44	$192,940	50	$219,250	56	$245,560
Yukon Bicycling Tour	60	189,600	68	214,880	73	230,680
Australian Outback Adventure	98	673,750	112	770,000	120	825,000
Continental Divide Hike	20	174,500	24	209,400	32	279,200
TOTAL		$1,230,790		$1,413,530		$1,580,440

Figure 5.41

Finally, you want the table centered on the page.

3
- Select the entire table.
- Click 🔳 Center.

Another Method
The menu equivalent is
Table/Table Properties/
Table/Center.

- Deselect the table.
- Close the Tables and Borders toolbar.
- Save the document again.

Your screen should be similar to Figure 5.42

Table centered between margins

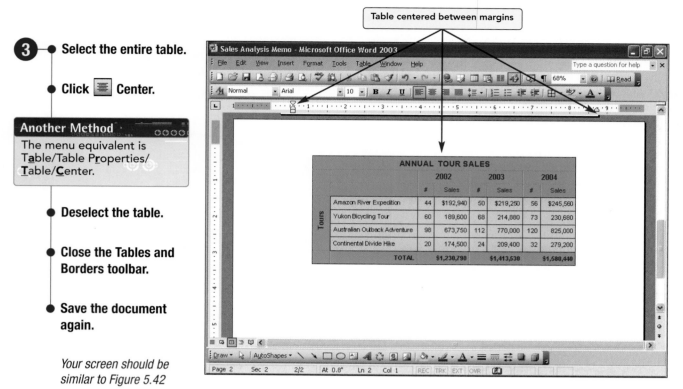

Figure 5.42

Note: If you are running short on time, this is an appropriate place to end this session.

Creating a Chart

As you look at the data in the table, you decide to include a chart of the data below the table, to illustrate the trends in sales.

Concept 5

Chart

5   A **chart**, also called a graph, is a visual representation of numeric data. Presenting data as a chart provides more impact than the data alone and makes it easier to see trends and comparisons. Office Word 2003 includes a separate program, Microsoft Graph, designed to help you create 14 types of charts with many different formats for each type.

Each type of chart represents the data differently and has a different purpose. It is important to select the type of chart that will provide the right emphasis to support the data. The basic chart types are described below.

Type of Chart		Description
	Area	Shows the relative importance of a value over time by emphasizing the area under the curve created by each data series.
	Bar	Displays categories vertically and values horizontally, placing more emphasis on comparisons and less on time. Stacked-bar charts show the relationship of individual items to a whole by stacking bars on top of one another.
	Column	Similar to a bar chart, except categories are organized horizontally and values vertically.
	Line	Shows changes in data over time, emphasizing time and rate of change rather than the amount of change.
	Pie	Shows the relationship of each value in a data series to the series as a whole. Each slice of the pie represents a single value in a data series.

Most charts are made up of several basic parts, as described in the following table.

Part	Description
X axis	The bottom boundary of the chart, also called the category axis, is used to label the data being charted; the label may be, for example, a point in time or a category.
Y axis	The left boundary of the chart, also called the value axis, is a numbered scale whose numbers are determined by the data used in the chart. Each line or bar in a chart represents a data value. In pie charts there are no axes. Instead, the data that is charted is displayed as slices in a circle or pie.
Legend	A box containing a brief description identifying the patterns or colors assigned to the data series in a chart.
Titles	Descriptive text used to explain the contents of the chart.

Pasting Data from a Table

To specify the data in the table to use in the chart, you will copy the sales labels in row 3, the four tour names in column B, and the sales values for the three years in columns D, F, and H.

1 ● Select cells B3 through H7.

● Click 🖹 Copy.

● Move to the blank line below the table.

● Press ⏎Enter.

● Choose Insert/Object/ Microsoft Graph Chart.

● Click [OK].

● If necessary, display the toolbars on two rows again.

Your screen should be similar to Figure 5.43

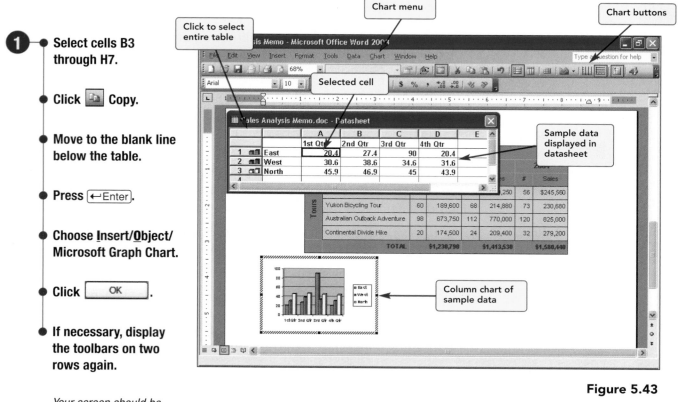

Figure 5.43

The Graph feature is activated and a table, called a **datasheet**, containing sample data is displayed in a separate window. A column chart using the sample data from the datasheet is inserted in the document. Notice that the datasheet displays the column letters A through E and row numbers 1 through 4 to label the cells in the table. The cell that is surrounded by the border is the selected cell and is the cell you can work in.

In addition to displaying sample data, the datasheet also contains placeholders for the row labels, which are used as the legend in the chart, and for the column labels, which are used as X-axis labels. The menu bar now includes a Chart menu and the Standard toolbar includes buttons for working with charts.

Specifying the Chart Data

You need to replace the sample data in the datasheet with the data you copied from the table.

1 • Click in the cell in the top left corner of the Datasheet window to select the entire table.

• Click 📋 Paste and click [OK] in response to the advisory box.

• Click in the datasheet to deselect it.

• Increase the size of the datasheet window to view all the data.

Your screen should be similar to Figure 5.44

Figure 5.44

The data in the datasheet is updated to include the data from the table, and the chart reflects the change in data. Next you need to remove the three columns of data containing the number of participants and change the remaining column headings to reflect the three years.

2 • Right-click the column A heading and choose **D**elete.

• Delete the other two columns with # in the heading row.

• In the first row of column A, replace "Sales" with **2002**.

• In the same manner, change the "Sales" headings in columns B and C to **2003** and **2004**.

Your screen should be similar to Figure 5.40

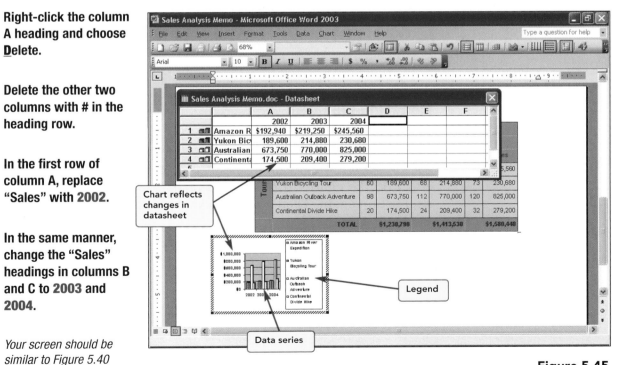

Figure 5.45

Each group of related data that is plotted in the chart is a **data series**.

Each data series has a unique color or pattern assigned to it so that you can identify the different series. The legend identifies the color or pattern associated with each data series. As you can see, the values and text in the chart are directly linked to the datasheet, and any changes you make in the datasheet are automatically reflected in the chart.

Sizing the Chart

Now that the data is specified, you can close the datasheet. Then you will increase the size of the chart.

1 • **Close the Datasheet window.**

• **Drag the right-corner and right-center sizing handles to increase the height and width of the chart.**

• **Click outside the chart to deselect it.**

Having Trouble?

If the chart moves to page 3, reduce its height so that it stays on page 2.

Your screen should be similar to Figure 5.46

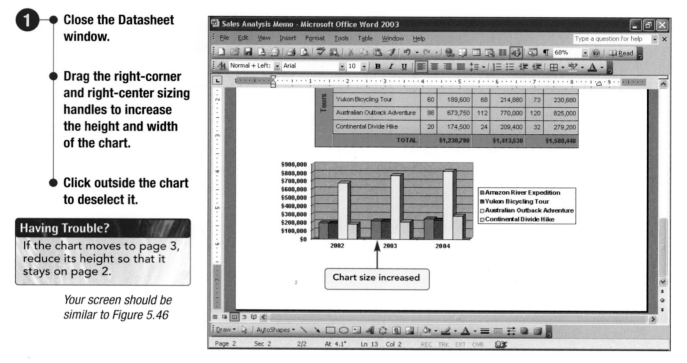

Figure 5.46

Modifying the Chart

The initial chart that is created is a 3-D column chart. As you look at the chart, you decide you want to change the default colors to colors that coordinate with the table in the memo. You also want to remove the 3-D effect on the chart. To modify the chart, you need to activate the Chart application again. Then you can use the features on the Chart menu and toolbar to edit the chart. First you will change the background color of the plot area.

1 • Double-click on the chart.

Another Method ○○○○
The menu equivalent is **E**dit/Chart **O**bject/**E**dit.

• If necessary, close the datasheet.

• Right-click on the area behind the columns of data.

• Choose F**o**rmat Walls.

Another Method ○○○○
The menu equivalent is **Fo**rmat/**Se**lected Walls and the keyboard shortcut is Ctrl + 1.

• From the Area color palette, select a similar color to that you used behind the sales values in the table.

• Click [OK] .

Your screen should be similar to Figure 5.47

Figure 5.47

You also want to change the background color of the chart area.

2 • Right-click on the white background of the chart.

• Choose F**o**rmat Chart Area.

• From the Area color palette, select a similar color to that used in the table.

• Click [OK] .

Your screen should be similar to Figure 5.48

Figure 5.48

Next you will change the color of the columns.

3 ● **Right-click on any one of the Australian Outback Adventure columns.**

● **Choose F_ormat Data Series.**

● **If necessary, open the Patterns tab.**

Another Method

The menu equivalent is F_ormat/S_elected Data Series and the keyboard shortcut is Ctrl + 1.

● **From the Area color palette, select a color that coordinates with the table.**

● **Click** OK .

Your screen should be similar to Figure 5.49

Figure 5.49

Next you want to change the type of column chart to display flat columns rather than 3-D columns.

4 ● **Right-click on any one of the columns.**

● **Choose Chart T_ype.**

● **Select Clustered Column (row 1 column 1).**

● **Click** OK .

Another Method

The menu equivalent is C_hart/Chart T_ype.

Your screen should be similar to Figure 5.50

Figure 5.50

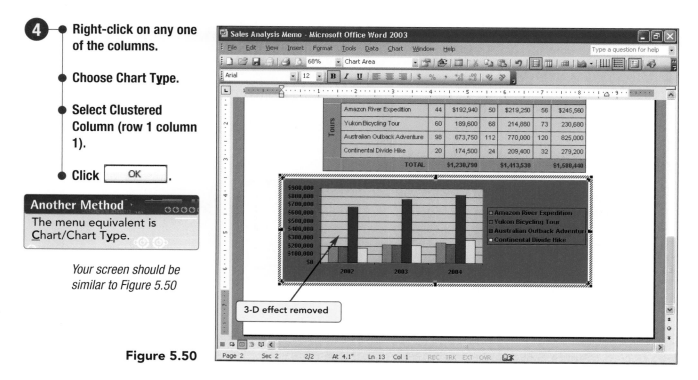

The 3-D effect has been removed from the columns. You also want to reduce the number of values that display on the Y Value axis. Currently because the values increment by 100,000, there are nine values displayed. To reduce the number of values, you increase the incremental value.

5 • **Right-click anywhere on the Y Value axis.**

• **Choose Format Axis.**

Another Method

The menu equivalent is **F**ormat/**Se**lected Axis and the keyboard shortcut is `Ctrl` + 1.

• **If necessary, open the Scale tab.**

• **Type 200000 in the Major Unit text box.**

• **Click** OK .

Your screen should be similar to Figure 5.51

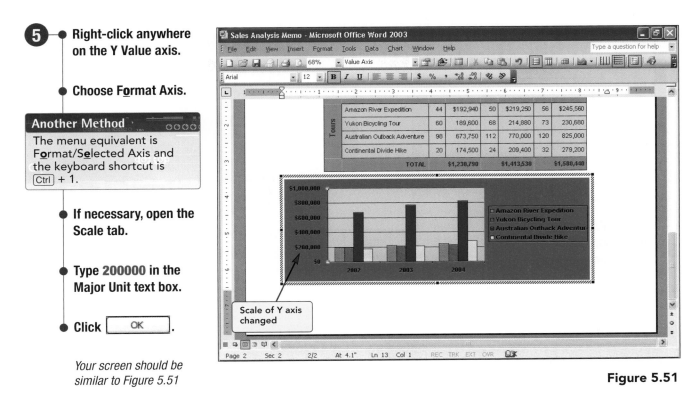

Figure 5.51

There are now only five values displayed along the Y-axis.

The last two changes you want to make are to reduce the font size of the text in the legend and to center the chart object.

6
- **Right-click on the legend.**
- **Choose Format Legend.**

- **Open the Font tab and select 10 pt as the font size.**
- **Click** OK .
- **Click outside the chart to exit the Graph application.**
- **Select the chart object.**
- **Click ≡ Center.**
- **If necessary, adjust the width of the chart to the same as the table.**
- **Deselect the chart object.**
- **Save the document again.**
- **Change to Whole Page zoom.**
- **If necessary, delete any blank lines above the table.**

Your screen should be similar to Figure 5.52

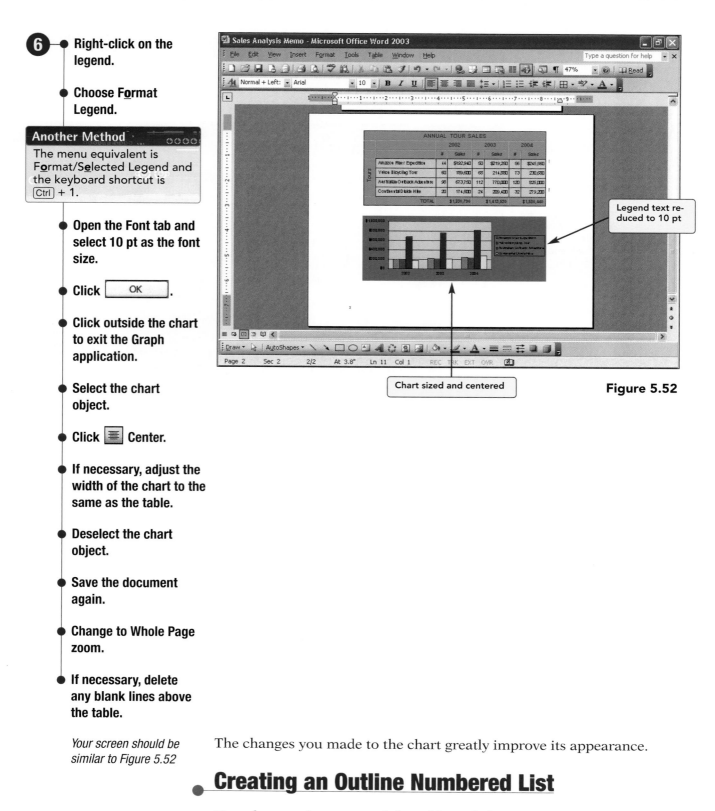

Legend text reduced to 10 pt

Chart sized and centered

Figure 5.52

The changes you made to the chart greatly improve its appearance.

Creating an Outline Numbered List

Now that you have created the table and chart, you want to include in the memo a strategy on how to increase sales for the four major tours. First you will add a lead-in paragraph, and then you will enter the proposed strategy to increase sales.

1

- Set the zoom to Page Width.

- Click ¶ to display paragraph marks.

- Move to the end of the first paragraph in the memo before the section break.

- Press ←Enter twice.

- Type: You will notice that sales have steadily increased over the past three years. The following strategy has been developed to ensure further increases in future sales.

- Press ←Enter three times.

- Type Strategy to Increase Sales.

- Press ←Enter.

Your screen should be similar to Figure 5.53

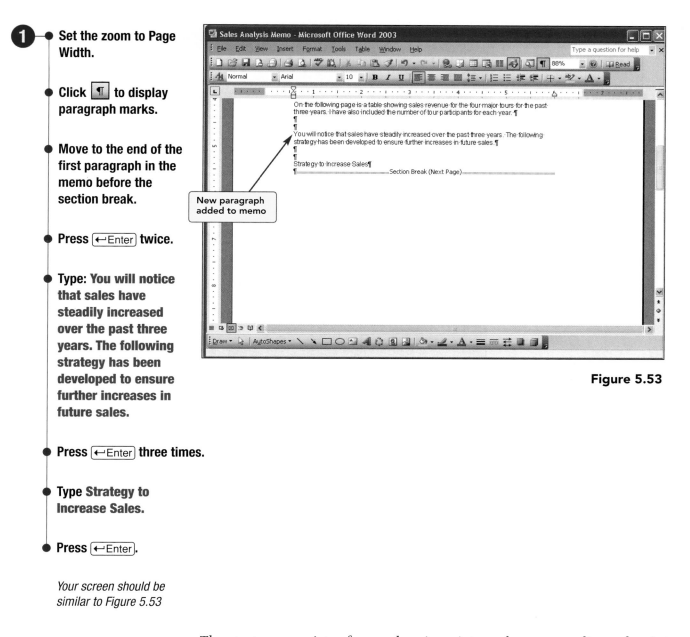

New paragraph added to memo

Figure 5.53

The strategy consists of several main points and corresponding subpoints. The best way to add this information to your memo is to use an **outline numbered list** which applies a hierarchal structure to a list, similar to creating an outline. Unlike an outline, built-in heading styles are not applied to the items in the list. Up to nine levels can be included in an outline numbered list.

2 ● **Click** ¶ **to turn off**

1 ● **Choose File/Save As.**

● **Select Document Template as the file type.**

● **Enter ATT Memo as the file name.**

Your screen should be similar to Figure 5.62

Figure 5.62

Templates are saved by default to the Templates folder on your system. You can also save templates to other locations just like any other document. You cannot save a document as a template by typing the file extension .dot as part of the file name.

2 ● **Click** Save .

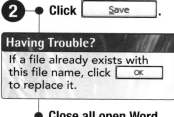

Having Trouble?
If a file already exists with this file name, click OK to replace it.

● **Close all open Word files.**

Another Method
You could also create a new template by choosing Template from the Create New section of the Templates dialog box when opening a template. The revised document is automatically saved with the template file format.

Using the Template

Now you will use the new ATT Memo template to create the memo announcing the new Web Development department at Adventure Travel Tours. Custom templates appear by default in the General tab of the Templates dialog box.

1

- From the New Document task pane, click "On my computer" from the Templates area.

- Open the General tab.

- Select ATT Memo.

- Click [OK].

- Replace the placeholder text with the following information:

  To: Adventure Travel Tours Staff

  Re: Web Development Department

- Delete the CC line in the header.

Your screen should be similar to Figure 5.63

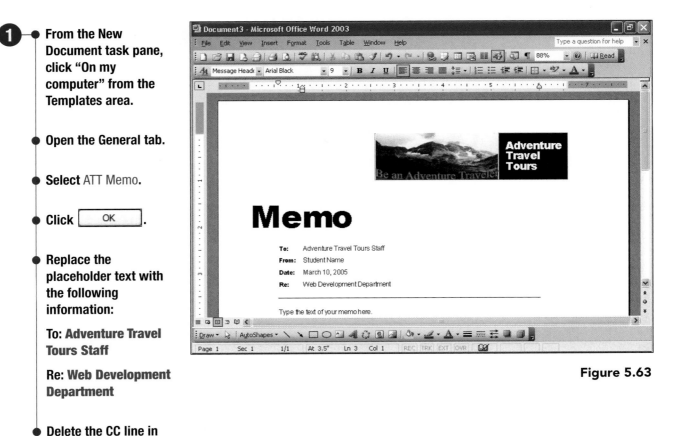

Figure 5.63

Your custom template file works just like the Professional Memo template you used earlier. Now, however, because you have added the logo and modified many of the other settings, it saves even more time.

The body of the memo will explain the new department and introduce the employees in the department.

2 • Replace the template directions with the following text: **Announcing the New ATT Web Development Department.**

• Press ←Enter twice and type the following text: **Adventure Travel Tours is proud to announce the creation of our Web Development Department. We are very excited about this new addition to Adventure Travel Tours and are looking forward to a new, revitalized Web site in the near future.**

• Apply a Heading 1 style to the first line.

• Save the document as New Department Memo to your data file location.

Your screen should be similar to Figure 5.64

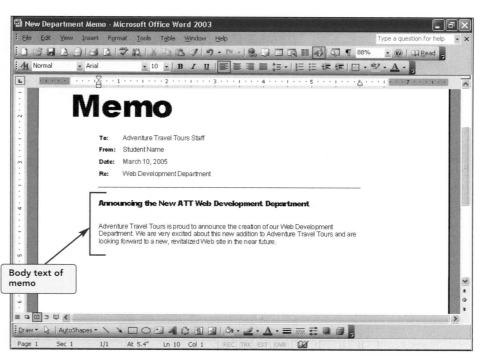

Figure 5.64

Creating a Diagram

Now you are ready to create a diagram showing the organization of the new department and staff.

6 A **diagram** is a graphic object that can be used to illustrate concepts and enhance your documents. Unlike charts, diagrams are based on text rather than numeric information. Word has six predesigned diagrams you can use. The type of diagram you choose depends on the purpose of the diagram and the type of concept you want to illustrate. The table below describes the diagram types and uses.

Type		Use
	Cycle	Shows a process that has a continuous cycle.
	Target	Shows steps toward a goal.
	Radial	Shows relationships of elements to a core element.
	Venn	Shows areas of overlap between and among elements.
	Pyramid	Shows foundation-based relationships.
	Organization	Shows hierarchical-based relationships.

Additionally, you can create flowcharts (or flow diagrams) using a combination of AutoShapes on the Drawing toolbar, including flowchart shapes and connectors. Flowcharts show a process that has a beginning and an end.

Inserting the Diagram

You will enter an introductory paragraph on the new department and then create an organization chart diagram to display the department organization. The completed diagram you will create is shown below.

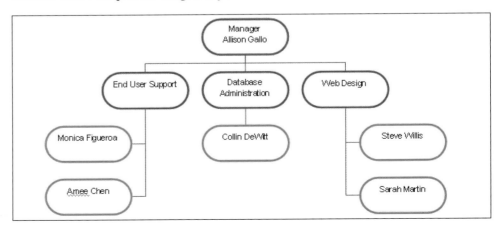

1

- Move to the end of the paragraph and press ⏎Enter twice.

- Type **The organization chart below identifies the names and positions of the employees in this department.**

- Press ⏎Enter twice.

- On the Drawing toolbar, click [icon].

Another Method

The menu equivalent is Insert/Diagram.

Your screen should be similar to Figure 5.65

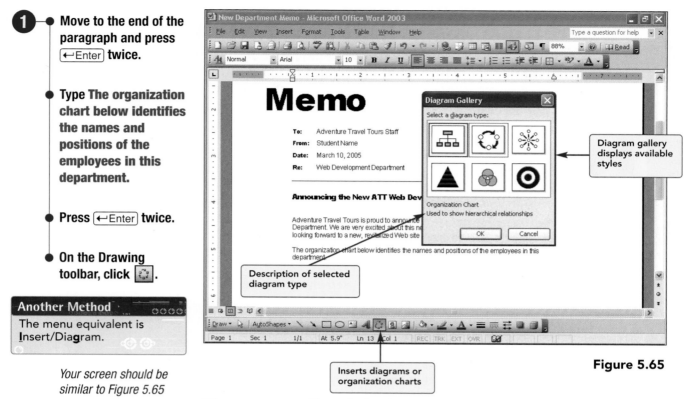

Figure 5.65

The Diagram Gallery dialog box asks you to select a type of diagram. The best type of diagram to represent the new department is an organization chart. Typically, organization charts are used to illustrate a working unit within a company; however, they can also be used to illustrate any type of concept that consists of a hierarchal organization.

2

- Select each of the diagram types and read the description.

- Select [icon] Organization Chart.

- Click ⟨ OK ⟩.

Your screen should be similar to Figure 5.66

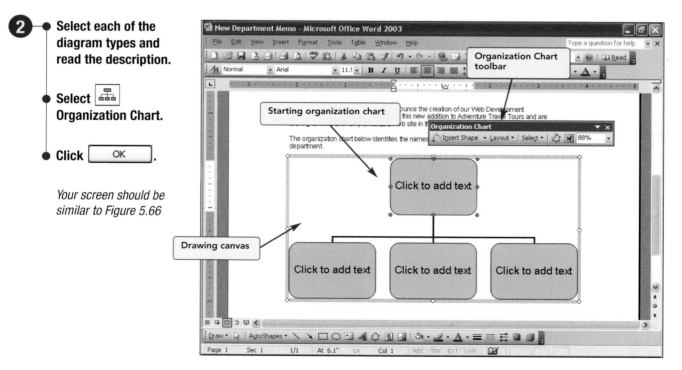

Figure 5.66

A starting organization chart consisting of four boxes arranged in a hierarchy is displayed. A drawing canvas surrounds the entire chart and keeps all pieces of the chart together as a unit. The position of the boxes or shapes in an organization chart and what they represent are described below.

	Shape	Represents
	Superior	Placed above and connected to any other shape, such as an employee (subordinate or co-worker shape) or assistant shape.
	Assistant	Placed below and connected to any other shape with an elbow connector. This shape is placed above any additional subordinate shapes for the particular superior shape it is attached to.
	Subordinate	Placed below and connected to a superior (or manager) shape.
	Co-worker	Placed next to another shape that is connected to the same superior (or manager) shape.

Additionally, the Organization Chart toolbar is automatically opened. It contains buttons to add shapes, modify the layout, and enhance the chart.

Entering Text in the Diagram

You will enter text for the first two levels.

1 ● Click in the top box and type **Manager**.

Your screen should be similar to Figure 5.67

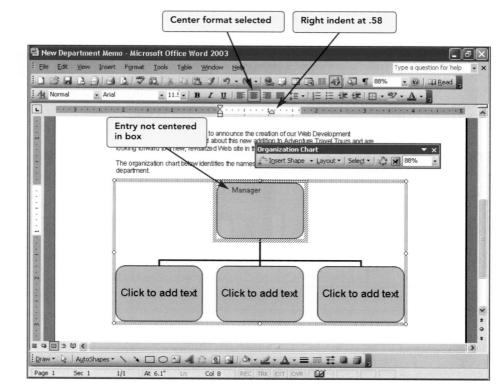

Center format selected

Right indent at .58

Entry not centered in box

Figure 5.67

Notice the alignment setting for the text box is centered, but because the right indent in the box is set at .58 inches, the same as the modified Normal style setting used in the memo body, it does not appear centered. You need to clear the indent setting for all boxes in the organization chart. Then, you will continue entering the text for the other levels.

2 • Click outside the box but inside the drawing canvas.

• Choose F**o**rmat/ **P**aragraph and reduce the right indentation setting to 0".

• Click [OK].

• Click at the end of "Manager" in the top box and press [←Enter].

• Type **Allison Gallo.**

• Click in the second level box on the left.

• Type **End User Support.**

• In the middle box, type **Database Administration.**

• In the end box, type **Web Design.**

Your screen should be similar to Figure 5.68

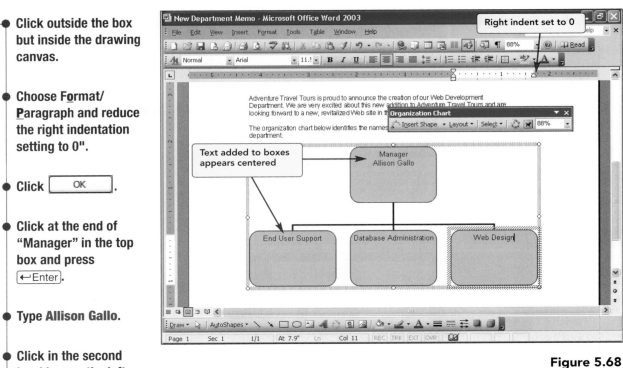

Figure 5.68

Now that the right indent setting for all boxes in the chart is zero, the text appears centered within each box.

Adding Subordinate Shapes

Next you need to add two subordinate shapes below the End User Support shape to contain the names of the employees. As you add shapes, the diagram will automatically resize to fit the drawing canvas. If you do not want the diagram to resize, you can expand the drawing canvas before adding more shapes by dragging the drawing canvas handles.

You will let the chart resize to the current drawing canvas size, as there is still plenty of space.

1 • **Click on the End User Support box.**

• **Open the** ⏚ Insert Shape ▾ **drop-down list.**

• **Click Subordinate.**

• **Click** ⏚ Insert Shape ▾ **to insert a second subordinate shape.**

Additional Information

The default selection for ⏚ Insert Shape ▾ is Subordinate.

Your screen should be similar to Figure 5.69

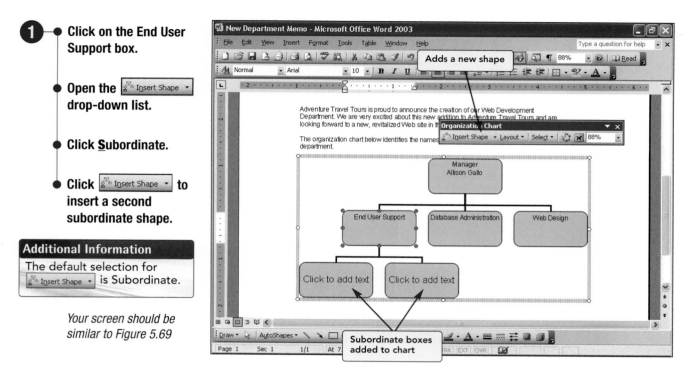

Adventure Travel Tours is proud to announce the creation of our Web Development Department. We are very excited about this new addition to Adventure Travel Tours and are looking forward to a new, revitalized Web site in t...

The organization chart below identifies the names... department.

Manager
Allison Gallo

End User Support   Database Administration   Web Design

Click to add text   Click to add text

Adds a new shape

Subordinate boxes added to chart

Figure 5.69

Changing the Diagram Layout

The two new shapes are added in a horizontal line subordinate to the selected shape. You decide to change the layout of this grouping so the subordinate shapes line up in a column below the superior shape. The four types of layouts are described in the following table.

	Layout	Description
	Standard	Subordinate shapes line up horizontally below the superior shape.
	Both Hanging	Subordinate shapes hang in columns both to the left and right of the superior shape.
	Left Hanging	Subordinate shapes hang in columns to the left of the superior shape.
	Right Hanging	Subordinate shapes hang in columns to the right of the superior shape.

When changing the layout, the superior shape above the shapes whose layout you want to change must be selected.

1 • If necessary, click on the End User Support box.

• Open the drop-down list.

• Select **L**eft Hanging.

Your screen should be similar to Figure 5.70

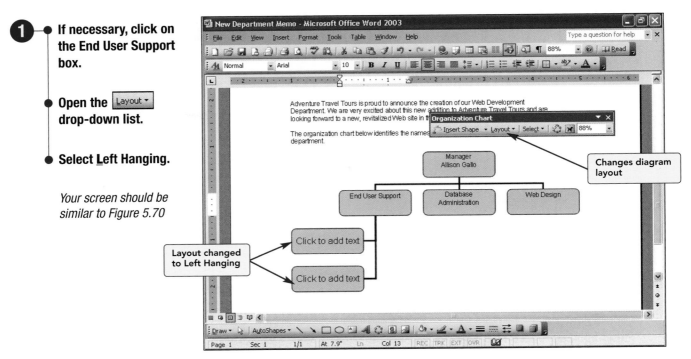

Figure 5.70

Now you will add the employee names to the two new subordinate shapes. Then you will add subordinate shapes for the other two areas.

2 • In the first subordinate shape below End User Support, type **Monica Figueroa.**

• Enter **Amee Chen** in the second subordinate shape.

• Add a subordinate shape below Database Administrator and enter **Collin DeWitt.**

• Insert two subordinate shapes below Web Design using the **R**ight Hanging layout, and enter the names **Steve Willis** and **Sarah Martin.**

Your screen should be similar to Figure 5.71

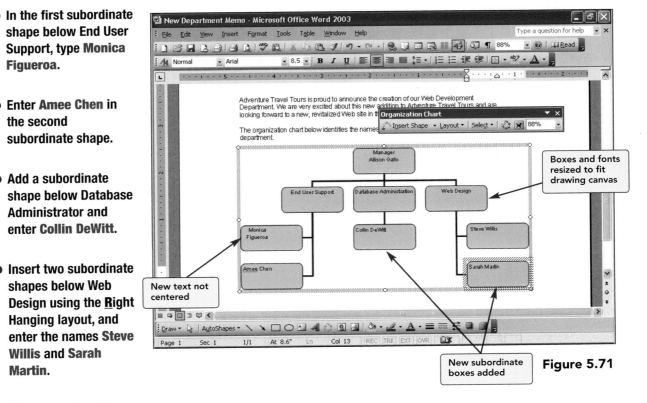

Figure 5.71

As more subordinate shapes were added to the chart, the boxes resized to fit within the drawing canvas and the font size within the boxes decreased as well.

Changing the Diagram Style

The text in the newly added boxes needs to be centered correctly by changing the right margin indent to zero. You also want to increase the font size slightly to make it easier to read. Finally, you want to change the style of the organization chart. There are 15 different AutoFormat styles consisting of different shape designs and colors from which you can select.

1

- Hold down ⇧Shift and click on the five new subordinate boxes to select them.

- Choose Format/ Paragraph and reduce the right indentation to 0".

- Click OK .

- Click on the chart background to clear the selection.

- Change the font size to 9 pt.

- Click 🗗 AutoFormat.

- Select Outline.

- Click OK .

- Click outside the diagram to close the drawing canvas.

- Save, preview, and print the memo.

Your screen should be similar to Figure 5.72

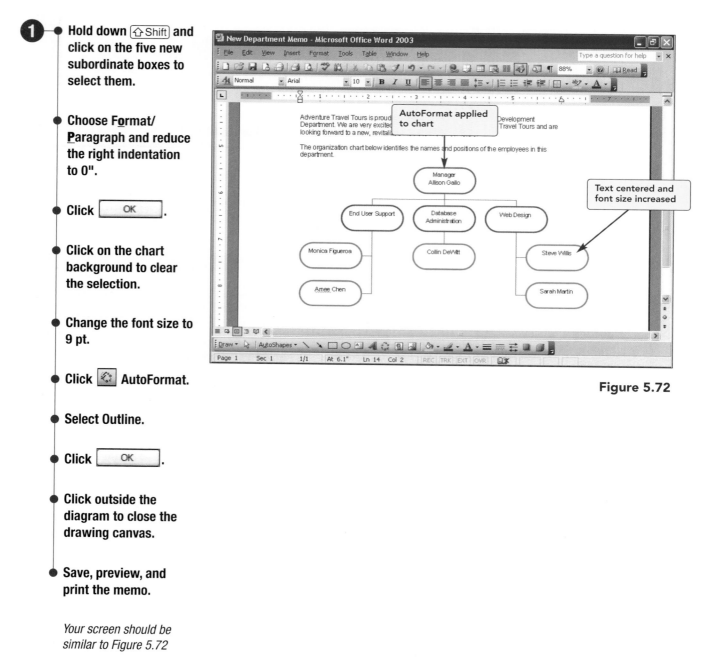

Figure 5.72

E-Mailing the Memo

Having Trouble?

If you do not have an e-mail program installed, the button is not displayed and you will need to skip this section.

You decide to give a copy of the memo to your supervisor for his review before sending it to the Adventure Travel Tours staff. The quickest way to do this is to send the memo in an e-mail message. All the Office System applications have the capability to access and send e-mail using an e-mail program on your system.

1 → Click E-mail.

Another Method

The menu equivalent is **F**ile/**Sen**d to/**M**ail Recipient.

Your screen should look similar to Figure 5.73

E-mail message box

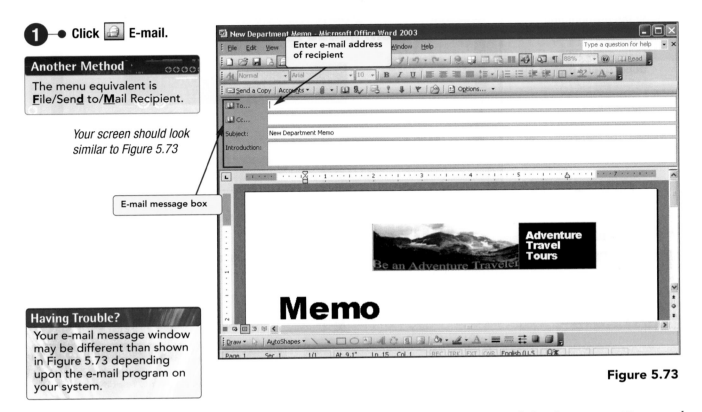

Enter e-mail address of recipient

Figure 5.73

Having Trouble?

Your e-mail message window may be different than shown in Figure 5.73 depending upon the e-mail program on your system.

Additional Information

To send an e-mail message to multiple recipients, separate the e-mail addresses with semicolons.

An e-mail message box is displayed at the top of the document. You use the message box to specify the recipient's e-mail address, the e-mail address of anyone you want to send a copy of this message to (cc:), the subject of the message, and the text of the message. You can also use the toolbar buttons to select recipient names from your e-mail address book, attach a file to the message, set the message priority (high, normal, or low priority), include a follow-up message flag, and set other e-mail options. The name of the document appears in the Subject box by default. You will enter the e-mail address and a brief message in the Introduction text box.

2 ● Enter the e-mail
    address of the person

Sends a copy of the document
as an e-mail message

ce Word 2003

Table   Window   Help

Type a question for help ▼ ×

lab exercises

Rock Climbing Classes ★ ★

3. You work in program development at Lifestyle Fitness Club. The company has recently added a rock climbing wall in several club locations. Response to the new feature has been very positive. You have been asked to consult the climbing instructors and gather data which will help determine if it is necessary to add additional classes. The completed memo is shown here.

a. Create a new document using the Professional Memo template.

b. Replace the Company Name placeholder with **Lifestyle Fitness Club**. Increase the cell size to display the name on a single line.

c. Replace the remaining placeholders with the following information:

To: **Susan O'Reilly**

From: **[Your Name]**

CC: **Kathy Wright**

Re: **Cardio Climbing Attendance Figures**

d. Change the date field format to d MMMM yyyy.

e. Replace the sample body text with the following:

Attendance at the Cardio Climbing Class has increased by 57% since the Rock Climbing Fair last month. Elaine believes that we may need to add three classes to the schedule to accommodate the growth in attendance. She has also suggested that we offer an Adult Climbing Class and a Family Climbing Class at 4:00 P.M., based on the age variations in these afternoon classes. I have included the numbers on attendance for these classes below to aid in your decision. Please contact Elaine at the Fort Meyers location to inform her of your decision regarding class development.

f. Create a table with five rows and four columns. Insert the following information:

Cardio Climbing Attendance by Age			
	6-15 years	15-25 years	26-50 years
Cardio Climbing 8:00 A.M.	9	6	50
Cardio Climbing 4:00 P.M.	42	63	21
Cardio Climbing 8:00 P.M.	7	26	58

g. Merge and center the cells in the title row. Increase the font size to 12 pt. and bold.

h. Add a row at the bottom of the table. Total the attendance for each group in the new row. Add an appropriate row label. Center the contents of cells B3:D6.

i. Add cell shading of your choice to the table. Remove the border line between cells A1 and A2. Add bold to the text in row 6.

j. Size the table appropriately and center the table in the memo. Save the document as Rock Climbing Memo and print it.

Adoption Statistics Memo ★ ★ ★

4. Annabelle works in the fundraising division at Animal Rescue Foundation. She has been very busy this month preparing for upcoming charity events and the annual silent auction. The director of the foundation has asked her to compile the adoption rates for the past three years for use in the auction brochure and send them to his office. The completed memo is shown here.

a. Create a new document using the Elegant Memo template.

b. Replace the text "Interoffice Memorandum" with **Animal Rescue Foundation**.

c. Replace the placeholders with the following information:

To:	**Sam Johnson**
From:	**[Your Name]**
Subject:	**Animal Adoption Statistics**
CC:	**Mary Munson, Fred Samuels, Sara Joseph**

d. Change the date field to the dddd, MMMM dd, yyyy format.

e. Replace the sample title text with **Animal Adoption Rates**.

f. Replace the sample body text with the following:

I have finished compiling the adoption statistics for use in our upcoming fundraising events. Below you will find the adoption rates for the past four years. Please note the period in 2003 with zero adoptions corresponds with the renovation of the kennel area.

g. Insert the following information in an appropriately sized table:

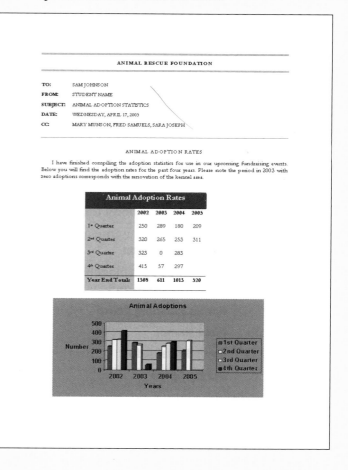

Animal Adoption Rates			
	2002	2003	2004
1st Quarter	250	289	180
2nd Quarter	320	265	253
3rd Quarter	323	0	283
4th Quarter	415	57	297

Concept Preview

The following concepts will be introduced in this lab:

1   **Forms**   Forms are documents that contain fill-in blanks or spaces reserved for entering information.

2   **Tracked Changes and Comments**   To make online reviewing of documents easier, you can add tracked changes and comments to a document.

3   **Mail Merge**   The Mail Merge feature combines a list of data (typically a file of names and addresses) with a document (commonly a form letter) to create a new document.

4   **Data Source**   The data source is a table of information that contains the data that varies in each copy of a merged document.

5   **Field Name**   Field names are used to label the different data fields in the recipient list in a mail merge.

Creating a Form

The first project you are working on is to create a form for clients to use to order a catalog.

Concept 1

Form

1   **Forms** are documents that contain fill-in blanks or spaces reserved for entering information. Forms are used to get information or feedback from users or to provide information. The several different types of forms you can create are described in the table below.

Type of Form	Description
Printed	The form is printed and filled in on paper.
E-mail	The form is distributed and collected using e-mail.
Web	The form is displayed on a Web page, completed and submitted online.

When creating a form, you need to first decide the purpose of the form and what information you need to collect to meet that purpose. Then, it is a good idea to sketch a layout of what you want the form to look like before creating it in Word.

The purpose of this form is to identify the catalog a client would like to receive and to provide the mailing information where the requested materials should be sent. After considering the information you need, you have sketched out a layout for the form shown below.

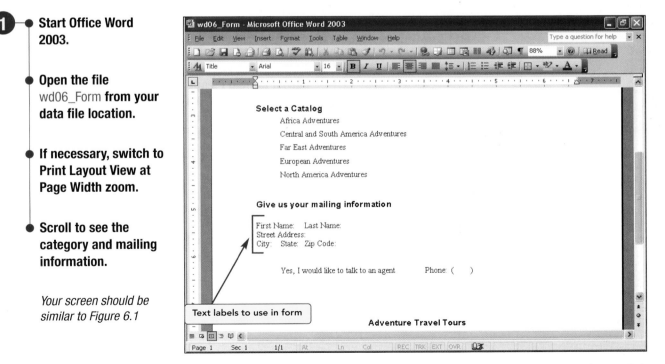

Select a Catalog
☐ Africa Adventures
☐ Central and South America Adventures
☐ Far East Adventures
☐ European Adventures
☐ North America Adventures
Give us your mailing information

First Name:	Last Name:	
Street Address:		
City:	State:	Zip Code:

Many different features can be used to create a form. Commonly, forms are based on a grid and use a table to help align the entry areas. Most also use graphical objects, called **controls**, that make the form easier to read. Controls include such items as check boxes and text boxes where information is entered. E-mail and Web forms commonly use interactive controls that display data choices and perform actions, such as submitting the completed form. Additionally, lines can be used to identify areas to fill in information.

You have already started working on the content for the form. It includes a heading and introductory text with information about how to complete the form.

1 ● Start Office Word 2003.

● Open the file wd06_Form **from your data file location.**

● If necessary, switch to Print Layout View at Page Width zoom.

● Scroll to see the category and mailing information.

Your screen should be similar to Figure 6.1

Figure 6.1

The document also includes text labels identifying the items you want the user to complete. You want to use a table to help align the mailing information in the form. Then you will add lines to show where the information should be entered.

Converting Text to a Table

Additional Information

You can also convert the contents of a table to regular text.

Many times, a document already contains text that is appropriate for display in a table. Rather than creating the table and entering the text in the cells, you can save time by converting existing text to a table format. You will use this feature to display the mailing information.

2
- **Select the three lines of mailing information.**

- **Choose Table/Convert/Text to Table.**

Your screen should be similar to Figure 6.2

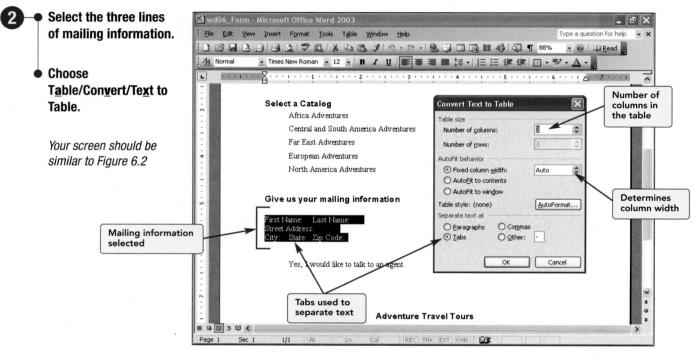

Figure 6.2

Additional Information

A paragraph mark indicates where a new row starts.

From the Convert Text to Table dialog box, you need to specify the number of columns and rows you want in the table, how the column widths are to be determined, and what means the program will use to separate text into columns. Common separators are a comma and a tab.

This table will have three columns and three rows. You will use the default selection of a fixed column width for the columns, which is automatically determined by the program. Finally, because the text in the document used tabs to separate the labels, the separator setting of Tabs will be used. Word attempts to determine these settings for you automatically from the selected text and displays the most likely selections.

3

- If necessary, change the number of columns to 3.

- If necessary, select Fixed Column **W**idth and **T**abs.

- Click [OK].

- Click outside the table to deselect it.

- Save the document as Catalog Request Form to your data file location.

Your screen should be similar to Figure 6.3

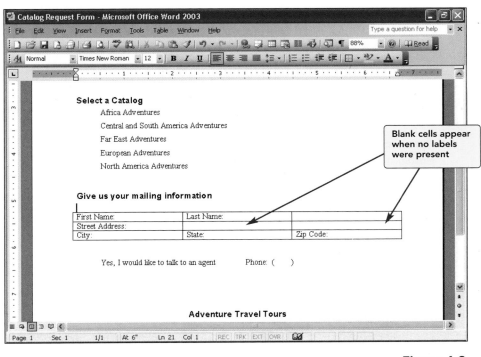

Figure 6.3

Each text label appears in a separate cell of the table. Blank cells appear when there was only one or two labels on the line that was converted. Next, you need to modify the table by merging cells and changing column widths.

4

- Click in the Last name cell.

- Display the Table and Borders toolbar if necessary.

- Merge the Last Name cell with the cell to the right.

- Merge the three cells in the Street Address row.

- Adjust the column widths as in Figure 6.4.

Your screen should be similar to Figure 6.4

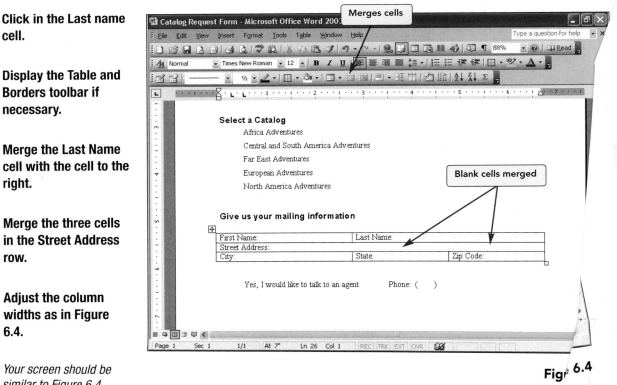

Fig 6.4

Next, you want to remove the interior table vertical border lines and increase the height of the row space by increasing the line spacing. You also want to change the alignment of text in the cell from the default of top left-aligned to bottom left-aligned.

5 • Select the table.

• Open the ▣ ▾ Outside Border drop-down menu and click ⊞ Inside Vertical Border to remove the interior vertical border lines.

• Increase the size of the row spacing to double by dragging the row border lines.

• If necessary, select the table again.

• From the ▤ Align Top Left drop-down list, select ▤ Align Bottom Left.

• Deselect the table and close the Tables and Borders toolbar.

Your screen should be similar to Figure 6.5

Figure 6.5

The table is now formatted how you want it to look.

Adding a Check Box Control

Next, you want to add a graphic box in front of each catalog name that the clients will check to identify which catalog they want to receive. You do this using the Check Box control. Controls are added using the Forms toolbar.

1
- Display the Forms toolbar.

- Move to the .25-inch tab stop in front of the Africa Adventures catalog item.

- Click ☑ Check Box Form Field.

- In the same manner, insert check boxes in front of the other four catalog items.

Your screen should be similar to Figure 6.6

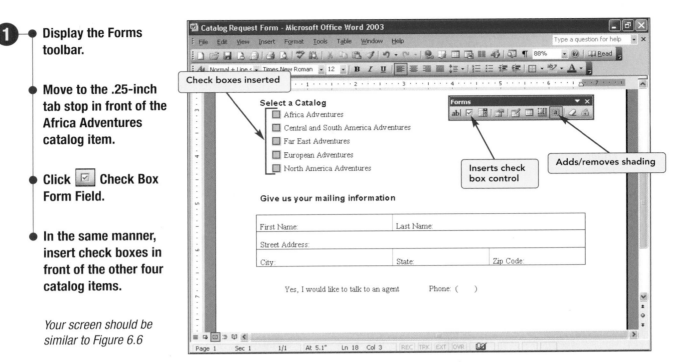

Figure 6.6

Because this is a paper form, you do not want shading to appear in the check boxes. You also want to display a check box in front of the "Yes, I would like to talk to an agent" text.

2
- Click Form Field Shading to remove shading from all controls.

- Move to the .25 inch tab stop in front of the "Yes, I would like to talk to an agent" label.

- Click ☑ Check Box Form Field.

- Close the Forms toolbar.

- Save the document.

Your screen should be similar to Figure 6.7

Figure 6.7

A check box without shading is created at this location.

Adding Lines to the Form

Finally, next to the phone label you want to display a line to show where the user should enter the information. You will create this line using the Line feature in the Drawing toolbar. Using this feature creates a line in the drawing canvas.

1 ● **Click in the blank space below the table.**

● **Display the Drawing toolbar.**

● **Click ◣ Line and drag in the drawing canvas to create a line approximately 2 inches long.**

Your screen should be similar to Figure 6.8

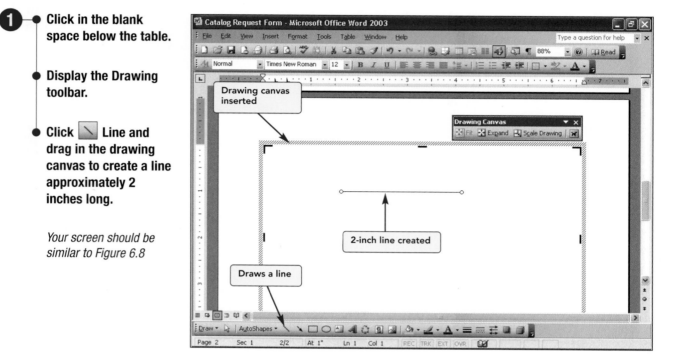

Figure 6.8

Now you want to move the line to the space to the right of the Phone label and delete the drawing canvas.

2 • Drag the line out of the drawing canvas.

• Select and delete the drawing canvas.

• Select the line and move it to the right of the phone label below the ( ).

Your screen should be similar to Figure 6.9

Figure 6.9

3 • Add your name and the current date in the footer.

• Preview the completed form and, if needed, adjust the document to fit on a single page.

• Save the file and print the form.

• Close the document.

• Close the Drawing toolbar.

Your printed form should be similar to that shown here.

Using Collaboration Features

Your next project is to review a document about the Africa Safari tour that a co-worker wrote for the new Africa Adventures catalog. Writing documents, such as travel brochures and newsletters, is often not a solo effort. One person is typically responsible for assembling the document, but several people may be involved in writing and/or reviewing the text. Office Word 2003 includes many features that make it easy to collaborate or work with others to complete a project. These features include the capability to circulate documents for review, to insert, view, and edit comments, and to track and accept or reject proposed changes.

Tracking Changes to a Document

You have a copy of the text file and want to enter your suggested changes and return it to the author. To show the author what changes you are suggesting, you will use the Track Changes feature and add comments.

Concept 2

Tracked Changes and Comments

2 To make online reviewing of documents easier, you can add tracked changes and comments to a document. **Tracked changes** identify any insertion, deletion, or formatting change that is made to the document. Notes or annotations called **comments** can also be added to a document without changing the document text. Tracked changes and comments are displayed using markup. **Markup** elements include colored and underlined text and balloons. **Balloons** show text that has been deleted and the text of comments. They appear in the right margin so that they are easily visible and to preserve the layout of the original document.

Typically a document is sent out for review by several people. When it is returned to the author, a document that has been edited using tracked changes can then be quickly reviewed to evaluate the suggested changes. As the author reviews tracked changes and comments, each change can be accepted or rejected as appropriate. Comments can be deleted when they are no longer needed.

You will open the document file you want to review and turn on the Tracked Changes feature before making any changes.

1 ● Open the wd06_Camping Safari file.

● If necessary, switch to Print Layout view at Page Width zoom.

● Hide the spelling errors.

● Save the file as Camping Safari Edited.

● Choose **T**ools/**T**rack Changes.

Another Method

The keyboard shortcut is Ctrl + ⇧Shift + E. You can also double-click TRK in the status bar to turn this feature on and off.

Your screen should be similar to Figure 6.10

Additional Information

You can change the color and other formatting used in the markup.

Having Trouble?

If the Reviewing toolbar is not displayed, open it from the toolbar shortcut menu.

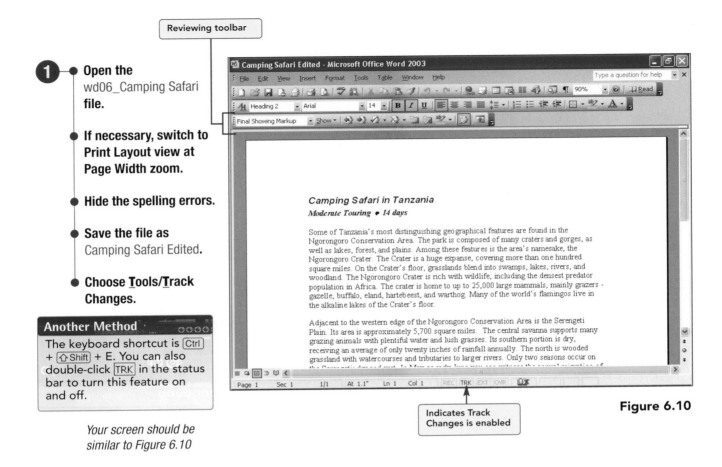

Indicates Track Changes is enabled

Figure 6.10

When Track Changes is enabled, "TRK" appears in the status bar and the Reviewing toolbar shown below is displayed. Now, when changes are made, the document will display markup of the tracked changes.

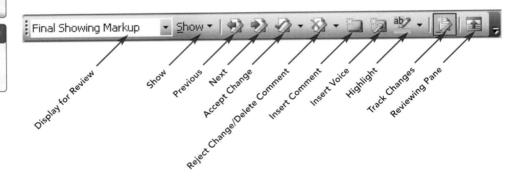

First, you want to delete some text in the first paragraph and replace it with new text.

2 Move to the end of the third sentence, after the word "Crater" and before the period.

- Select the text to the right through the end of the word "covering."

- Press [Delete].

- Type **, which covers.**

- Scroll the document horizontally to display the right edge of the page.

Your screen should be similar to Figure 6.11

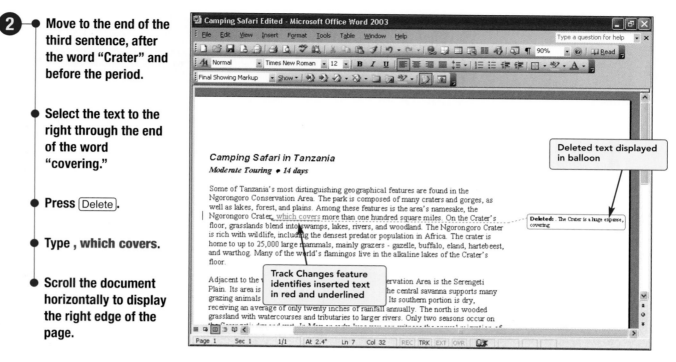

Figure 6.11

Having Trouble?

If revision marks are not displayed, choose **V**iew/Ma**r**kup to turn on this feature.

Additional Information

Balloons appear only in Print Layout and Web Layout view.

The inserted text is identified with the markup of red text color and an underline. The text you deleted is displayed in a balloon in the right margin. Dotted lines connect the balloon to the location where the text was deleted.

The next change you want to make is to change the word "Crater" to all lowercase characters when it does *not* follow the name Ngorongoro.

3 ● Use Find and Replace to locate all occurrences of "Crater" and replace them with "crater" when they are not following Ngorongoro.

● When you are finished, close the Find and Replace dialog box.

Having Trouble?
Use the Match case Search option while using Find and Replace.

● Point to any markup for the word "crater."

Your screen should be similar to Figure 6.12

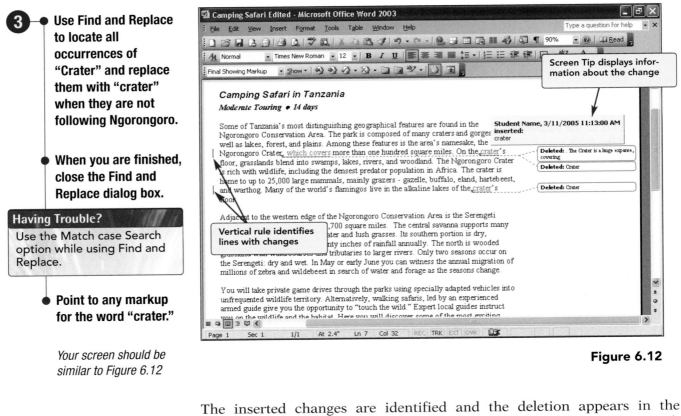

Figure 6.12

The inserted changes are identified and the deletion appears in the balloon. Pointing to a markup element displays a ScreenTip with information about who made the change and when the change was made. The lines of the document that have been changed are identified with a vertical rule along the left margin. The different markup elements help preserve the layout of the document while changes are being tracked.

In the second paragraph you have several changes to make.

4 ● At the end of the first sentence of the second paragraph, delete the period and "Its area is" and replace it with covering.

● At the beginning of the third sentence, change "Its" to In contrast, the.

Your screen should be similar to Figure 6.13

Figure 6.13

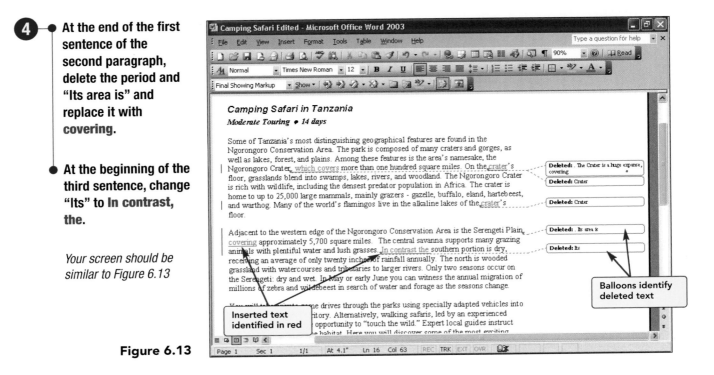

Adding Comments

As you read the final paragraph, you decide it does not contain enough information about the activities and camping experiences that will be encountered on the safari. Rather than making these changes, you decide to add a comment about this to the author.

1 ● **Move to the beginning of the third paragraph.**

● **Click** [ ] **Insert Comment on the Reviewing toolbar.**

Another Method ・ ○○○○
The menu equivalent is Insert/Comment.

Your screen should be similar to Figure 6.14

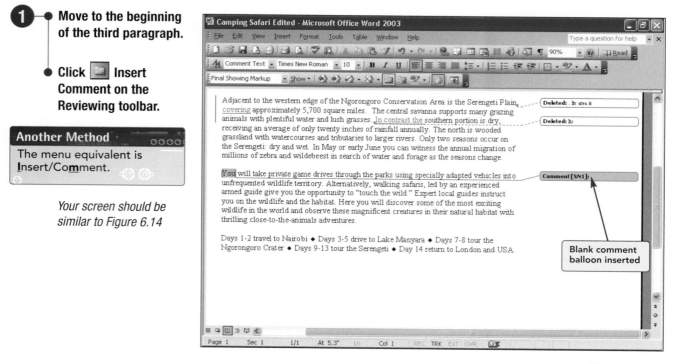

Figure 6.14

Additional Information
In Normal view, a reviewing pane opens where you enter the text for the comment, much like entering the text for a footnote. You can also click [ ] to display the reviewing pane in any view. To close the reviewing pane, click [ ] again.

A blank comment balloon is displayed in the margin and a line connects it to the location where you inserted the comment. The comment balloon displays the initials of the person who added the comment followed by the comment number. Comments are numbered sequentially in a document much like footnotes. Next you need to add the text of the comment.

2 • Type **Add more information to this paragraph about the activities and camping experiences on this tour.**

• Click [icon] Track Changes to turn off this feature.

Your screen should be similar to Figure 6.15

Camping Safari Edited - Microsoft Office Word 2003

File   Edit   View   Insert   Format   Tools   Table   Window   Help   Type a question for help

Adjacent to the western edge of the Ngorongoro Conservation Area is the Serengeti Plain, covering approximately 5,700 square miles. The central savanna supports many grazing animals with plentiful water and lush grasses. In contrast the southern portion is dry, receiving an average of only twenty inches of rainfall annually. The north is wooded grassland with watercourses and tributaries to larger rivers. Only two seasons occur on the Serengeti: dry and wet. In May or early June you can witness the annual migration of millions of zebra and wildebeest in search of water and forage as the seasons change.

You will take private game drives through the parks using specially adapted vehicles into unfrequented wildlife territory. Alternatively, walking safaris, led by an experienced armed guide give you the opportunity to "touch the wild." Expert local guides instruct you on the wildlife and the habitat. Here you will discover some of the most exciting wildlife in the world and observe these magnificent creatures in their natural habitat with thrilling close-to-the-animals adventures.

Days 1-2 travel to Nairobi ◆ Days 3-5 drive to Lake Manyara ◆ Days 7-8 tour the Ngorongoro Crater ◆ Days 9-13 tour the Serengeti ◆ Day 14 return to London and USA.

Deleted: Its area is

Comment displayed in comment balloon

Comment [SN1]: Add more information to this paragraph about the activities and camping experiences on this tour.

Page 1   Sec 1   1/1   At 5.6"   Ln   Col 11   REC   TRK   EXT   OVR

Status indicator dimmed when Track Changes turned off

Figure 6.15

The comment text appears in the balloon. Now the status indicator TRK is dimmed, and any further changes you make will not be tracked.

Viewing Changes

As a final check, before returning the marked up document to the author, you want to view the document without the markup showing. There are four different views, described below, that are used to specify the type of changes you want to see in a document that contains tracked changes.

Option	Effect
Final Showing Markup	Displays the final document with the insertions underlined and the deletions indicated in the revision balloons.
Final	Displays how the document would appear if you accepted all the changes.
Original Showing Markup	Displays the original document with the deletions underlined and the insertions indicated in the revision balloons.
Original	Displays the original unchanged document so you can see how the document would look if you rejected all the changes.

You want to read the document as it will appear with the changes, but without the markup.

1 • **From the**
Final Showing Markup
**Display for Review
drop-down list, select
Final.**

• **Scroll the document
to see the three
paragraphs.**

*Your screen should be
similar to Figure 6.16*

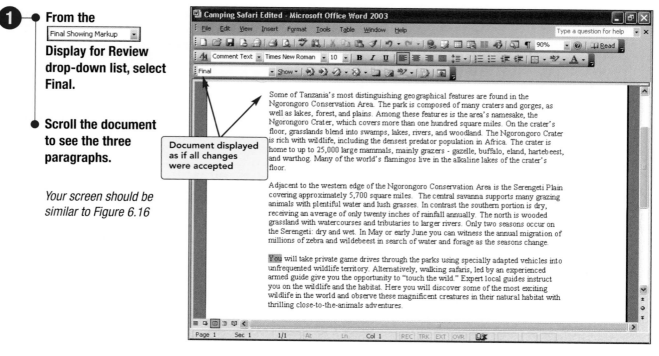

Document displayed
as if all changes
were accepted

Figure 6.16

The document appears as it would look if all changes were made except
for those suggested in comments. Next you want to see the original
document before the changes were made.

2 • **From the**
Final Showing Markup
**Display for Review
drop-down list, select
Original.**

*Your screen should be
similar to Figure 6.17*

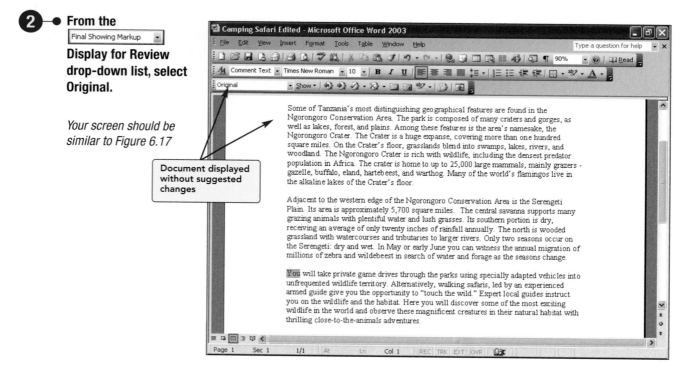

Document displayed
without suggested
changes

Figure 6.17

The original document appears without the suggested changes. You can quickly switch between the document views to check the changes. You will display the final document with markups again and make one final addition to the file before returning it to the author.

Adding Text Animation

You are quite pleased with the content about the Africa Safari tour that your co-worker provided and want to include a brief note to this effect in the document. A clever way to make the note stand out is to animate it.

1 ● **Change the view back to Final Showing Markup.**

● **Move to the blank line above the first paragraph of the document.**

● **Type Nice job!.**

● **Select the text and apply a font color of your choice.**

● **Choose Format/Font/Text Effects.**

Your screen should be similar to Figure 6.18

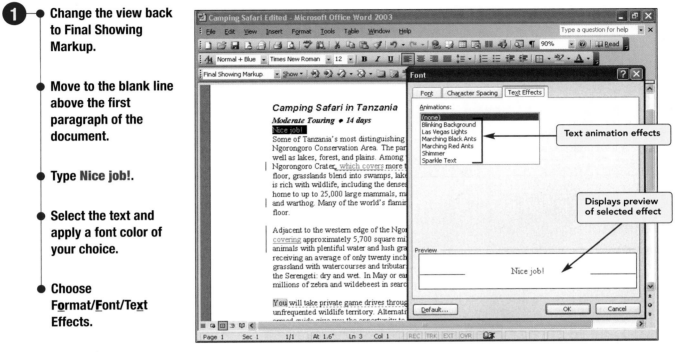

Figure 6.18

The available effects are listed in the Animations list box, and a sample of the animation effect associated with the selected text appears in the Preview area. Since no effect has been applied yet, the text is not animated.

2 • Select each effect to preview how it will appear.

• Select **Las Vegas Lights**.

• Click [OK].

• Deselect the text.

• Save the document.

Your screen should be similar to Figure 6.19

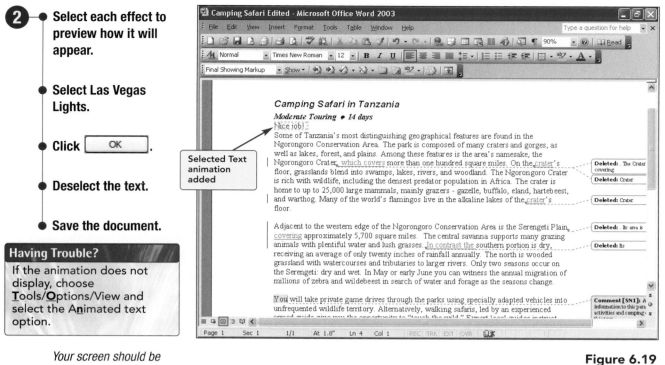

Selected Text animation added

Figure 6.19

The text will blink when viewing the document, but the animation effect will not print. Because the Track Changes feature was off, this change is incorporated immediately into the document, just like any normal editing change. The changes you made while the Track Changes feature was on are not permanently added to the document until the author decides to accept or reject the change.

Next, you will return the document with your suggested changes to the author.

E-mailing a Document as an Attachment

You will return the document via e-mail with the document as an attachment. An **attachment** is a file that is sent with the e-mail message but is not part of the e-mail text. You open the attachment with the application in which it was created.

Note: Skip this section if you do not have an E-mail program installed on your system and an Internet connection.

1 ● Choose **F**ile/Sen**d** To/**M**ail Recipient (as Attachment).

Your screen should be similar to Figure 6.20

Having Trouble?
Your e-mail message window may look slightly different depending on the E-mail program on your system.

Figure 6.20

An e-mail window is displayed in which you can address your e-mail message. Notice that the Subject and the Attach fields display the file name of the attached document. The extension indicates the application in which the file will open, which is helpful to know.

2 ● In the To field, type your e-mail address.

● In the message area, type **I reviewed the Camping Safari document and made my suggested changes using the Track Changes feature.**

Your screen should be similar to Figure 6.21

Figure 6.21

Now you are ready to send the message. If you have access to the Internet, you will send the message; otherwise, you will save it to be sent at a later time.

3 ● If you have Internet access, click ▢ Send .

● If you do not have Internet access, choose **File/Save As** and save the message as **Camping Safari Reviewed.**

● Close the e-mail window.

● Close the Reviewing toolbar.

● Print the reviewed document showing markup.

> **Having Trouble?**
> The Print What option in the Print dialog box will automatically display "Document Showing Markup" whenever you print a document with markup showing.

● Close the Word document.

The program automatically sets the zoom level and page orientation needed to best display the tracked changes in the printed document.

Comparing and Merging Documents

While checking your e-mail for new messages, you see that two co-workers have returned a document you sent to them to review with their comments and tracked changes. You have saved the two attachments on your system and now you want to review the suggested changes.

When you receive comments and changes from multiple reviewers for the same document, the easiest way to review them is to combine or merge the documents together. This way you can review the changes from a single document.

You will first open the original document you sent to the reviewers. Then you will merge the reviewers' documents with the original. You can display the results of the merge in the currently open document, in the next document you open, or in a new document. You will merge the reviewed documents into the original document.

1
- Open the file wd06_Everest Original.

- If necessary, switch to Print Layout view and Page Width zoom.

- Choose **T**ools/**C**ompare and Merge **D**ocuments.

- Select the file wd06_Everest ChangesDan.

- Open the [Merge ▼] drop-down menu and choose Merge into **c**urrent document.

- Scroll the document to see the changes.

- Point to the first markup to see the ScreenTip.

Your screen should be similar to Figure 6.22

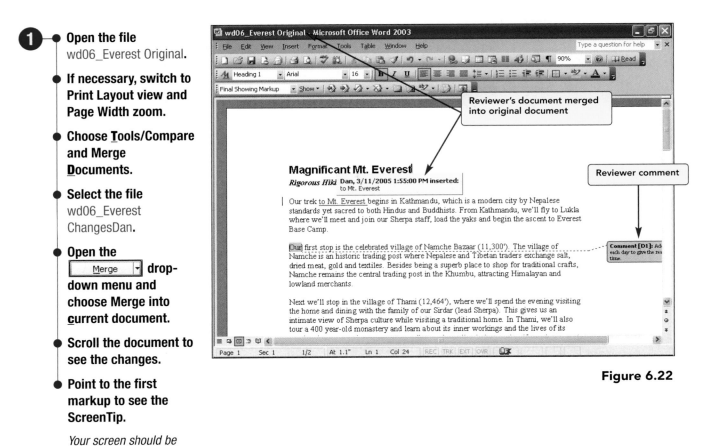

Figure 6.22

This reviewer, Dan, inserted only one comment and made two editing changes. Now you will merge the document containing changes made by the second reviewer with this document.

2
- Choose **T**ools/**C**ompare and Merge **D**ocuments.

- Select the file wd06_Everest ChangesCarol.

- Open the [Merge ▼] drop-down menu and choose Merge into **c**urrent document.

- Point to the first markup change to see the ScreenTip.

Your screen should be similar to Figure 6.23

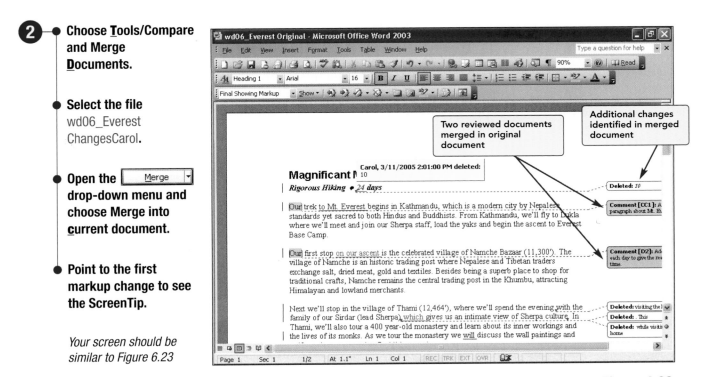

Figure 6.23

The markup from both reviewed documents is displayed in the original document. Word automatically assigns unique colors to the comments and tracked changes made by each reviewer.

Accepting and Rejecting Changes

Now you are ready to review the changes and comments and decide whether to accept or reject them. You will review each item in sequence to evaluate the suggestion. To make it easier to read the text in the balloons, you will use the Reviewing pane.

1 ● If necessary, display the Reviewing toolbar.

● Click 🔲 Reviewing Pane.

● If necessary, move to the beginning of the document.

● Click ⏩ Next.

Your screen should be similar to Figure 6.24

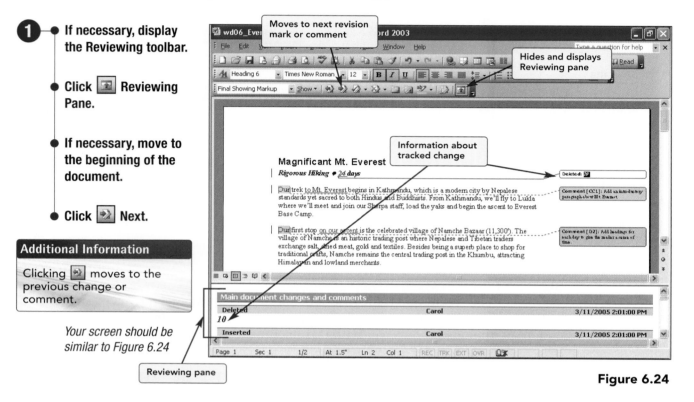

Figure 6.24

The first tracked change made by Carol to delete the number 10 is highlighted. The Reviewing pane also displays the information about this change. Since this tour is 24 days in length, you want to accept the change.

2 ● **Click** ▨ ▾ **Accept Change.**

Your screen should be similar to Figure 6.25

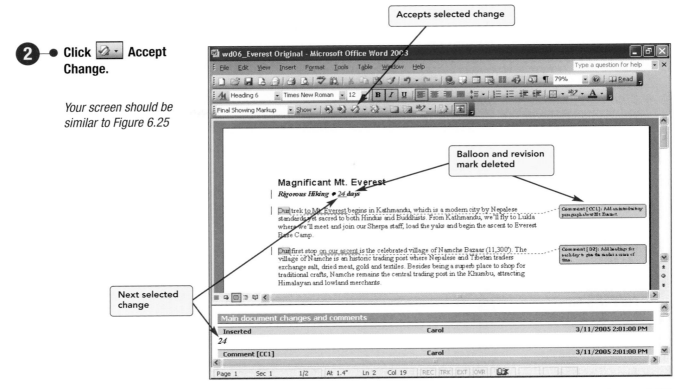

Accepts selected change

Balloon and revision mark deleted

Next selected change

Figure 6.25

The number 10 is deleted along with the revision mark and the balloon. The next suggested change, to insert the number 24, is selected. Again, this is correct and you want to accept the change.

3 ● **Click** ▨ ▾ **Accept Change.**

● **Click** ⯈ **Next.**

Your screen should be similar to Figure 6.26

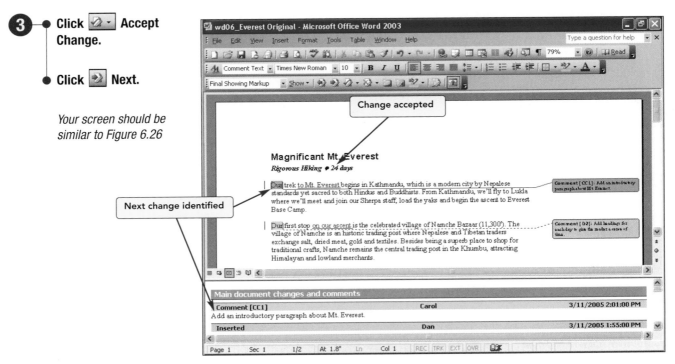

Change accepted

Next change identified

Figure 6.26

The next change is a comment. You decide you do not want to consider the comments at this time, and will hide them. This way you will focus mainly on the insertions and deletions. You will address the comments after you review the editing changes.

4 • Click Show ▾ and choose **C**omments to clear the checkmark.

• Click ➡ Next.

• Click 🖉 ▾ Accept Change to accept the insertion of the words "to Mt. Everest."

• Click ➡ Next.

Your screen should be similar to Figure 6.27

Next identified change

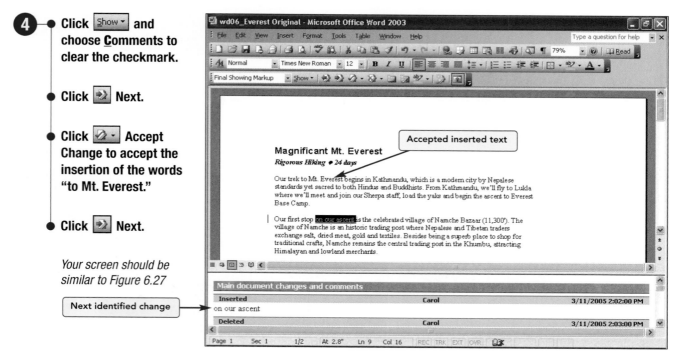

Figure 6.27

With the comments hidden, you can move directly to editing changes and respond to them accordingly. The next change is to insert "on our ascent." You feel this change is unnecessary and you will reject it.

5 • Click 🖉 ▾ Reject Change.

Having Trouble?
You can use 🖉 ▾ to undo the last acceptance or rejection of a tracked change.

• Scroll the document to see the markup in the remainder of the document.

• Display the third paragraph.

Your screen should be similar to Figure 6.28

Figure 6.28

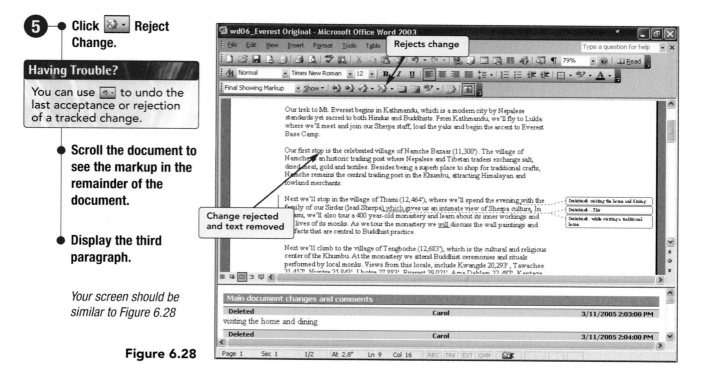

Lab 6: Creating Forms and Form Letters and Collaborating on Documents

www.mhhe.com/oleary

The inserted text was removed. As you look at the other editing changes in the document, you decide they are all acceptable. Rather than moving to each one independently and accepting it, you can quickly accept all changes.

6 ● **From the [icon] ▾ Accept Change drop-down list, select Accept All Changes in Document.**

Your screen should be similar to Figure 6.29

All remaining changes accepted

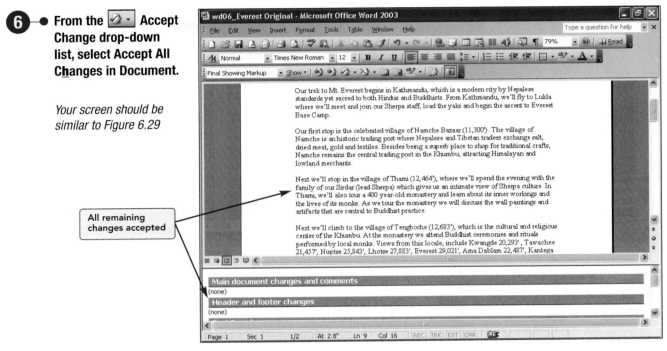

Figure 6.29

Now, you want to review the comments.

Reviewing Comments

You will show the comments in the document again and then move to the first comment to consider the suggestion.

1 ● Click **Show ▾** and choose **C**omments to display the checkmark.

● Click **↔** **Previous** twice to move to the first comment.

Your screen should be similar to Figure 6.30

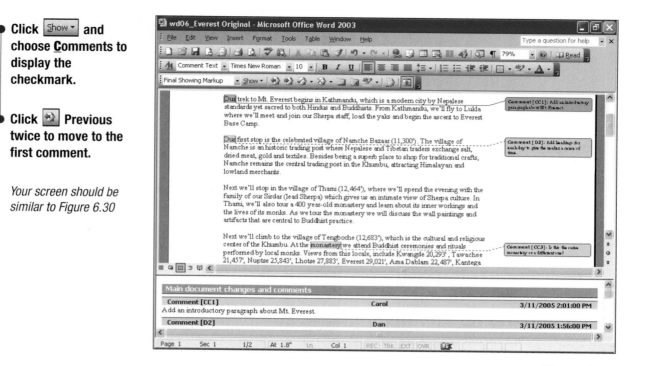

Figure 6.30

In the first comment, the reviewer wants you to add an introductory paragraph about Mt. Everest. This sounds like a good suggestion. In fact, you already have a paragraph you had written and saved in a separate file that you can add to the document that will take care of this.

2 ● Click **⊗ ▾** **Reject Change/Delete Comment.**

Your screen should be similar to Figure 6.31

Another Method

You can also choose Delete Comment from the comment balloon's shortcut menu.

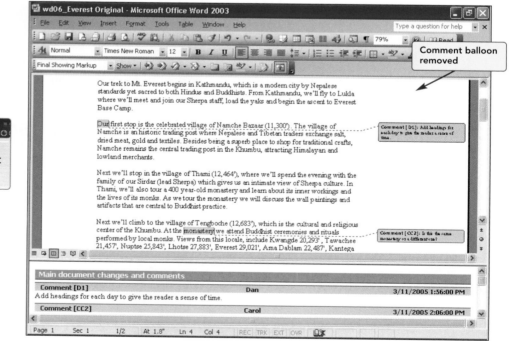

Figure 6.31

The comment is deleted and you are ready to add the paragraph. Rather than opening the file and copying the paragraph into the document, you can insert the contents of a file directly into an open document.

3 • Move to the beginning of the first paragraph.

• Choose **Insert/Insert File**.

• Select wd06_Everest Paragraph **from your data file location**.

• Click .

Your screen should be similar to Figure 6.32

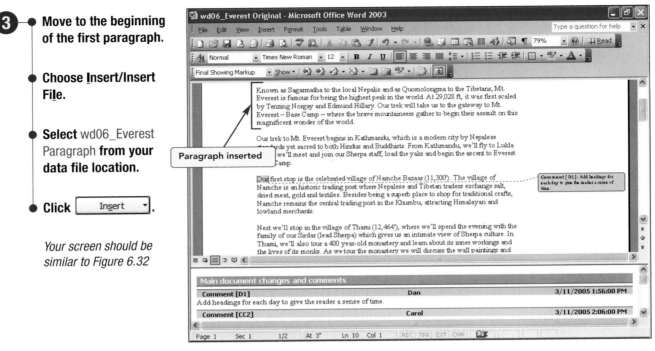

Figure 6.32

You feel the remaining comments require some discussion with the reviewers and will leave them in the document for now.

4 • Click 📄 **Reviewing Pane to close the Reviewing pane.**

• **Close the Reviewing toolbar.**

• **Add your name and the current date in a header.**

• **Save the document as** Everest Revised.

• **Preview then print the document with markup showing.**

• **Close the document.**

Note: If you are running short on time, this is a good place to end this session.

Collaborating Online

In addition to collaboration through the exchange of documents and accepting and rejecting tracked changes, there are two other ways that you can collaborate with many reviewers at once. The first way is to hold an online meeting using the Microsoft Windows NetMeeting feature. Each person you invite to the online meeting must also be running NetMeeting to receive your invitation.

In an online meeting, you are in control of the collaboration. Each person in the meeting can add comments to the document in real time, if you give them access. When you turn on collaboration, each person in the online meeting can take turns editing the document. The person whose turn it is to edit the document is the only one whose mouse will operate, and their initials will appear next to the mouse pointer.

The second way to collaborate is by using the Web Discussions feature, which needs to be set up by a system administrator. It enables you and other people to insert comments into the same document at the same time. This makes your job as document author much easier. You can see all the comments made by the reviewers, and they can too. Thus, if there is a discrepancy with the comment, the reviewers can discuss it among themselves.

Using Mail Merge

Your last project is to personalize the letter you wrote about the new tours and presentations by including each client's name and address information in the inside address and his or her first name in the salutation. To do this you will use the Mail Merge feature to create a personalized form letter and mailing labels to be sent to all clients.

Concept 3
Mail Merge

1 The **Mail Merge** feature combines a list of data (typically a file of names and addresses) with a document (commonly a form letter) to create a new document. The names and addresses are entered (merged) into the form letter in the blank spaces provided. The result is a personalized form letter.

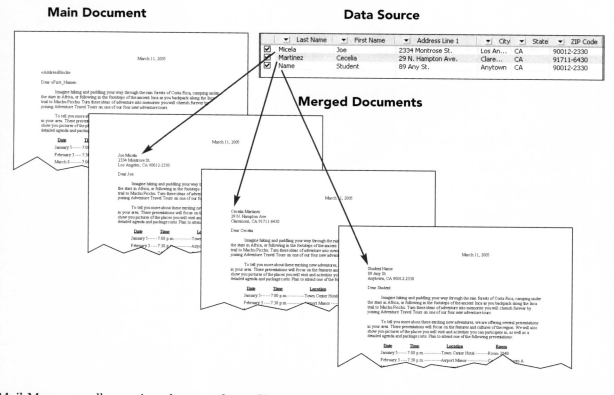

Mail Merge usually requires the use of two files: a **main document** and a data source. The main document contains the basic form letter. It directs the merge process through the use of merge fields. A **merge field** is a field code that controls what information is used from the data source and where it is entered in the main document. The **data source** contains the information needed to complete the letter in the main document. It is also called an **address list** because it commonly contains name and address data.

To complete the process of performing a mail merge, you follow these four steps:

1. Open or create a main document.
2. Open or create a data source with individual recipient information.
3. Add or customize merge fields in the main document.
4. Merge data from the data source into the main document to create a new, merged document.

You will open the tour letter as the main document and create the data source of clients' names and addresses. Then you will add the merge fields to the main document. When you perform the merge, Word takes the data field information from the data source and combines or merges it into the main document.

Creating the Main Document

You are going to use an existing letter as the main document. This letter is similar to the tour letter you saved in Lab 2.

1 • **Open the file wd06_Tour Letter.**

• **If necessary, switch to Print Layout view and set the zoom to Page Width.**

• **Change the name in the closing to your name.**

• **Move to the top of the document.**

• **Choose Tools/Letters and Mailings/Mail Merge.**

Your screen should be similar to Figure 6.33

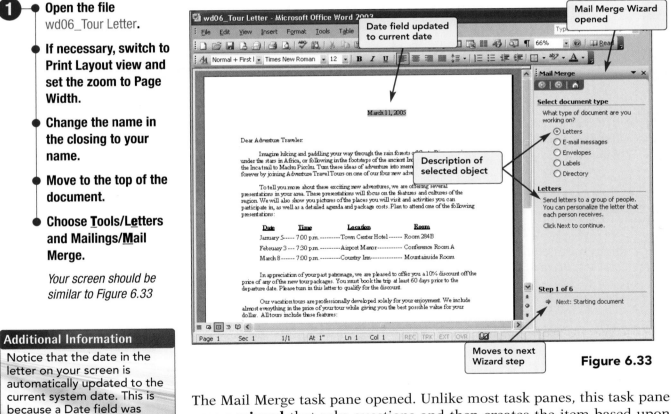

Figure 6.33

Additional Information

Notice that the date in the letter on your screen is automatically updated to the current system date. This is because a Date field was entered in the document.

Another Method

You can also use the buttons on the Mail Merge toolbar instead of the Mail Merge task pane to create a merge document.

The Mail Merge task pane opened. Unlike most task panes, this task pane uses a **wizard** that asks questions and then creates the item based upon your responses. There are many different wizards available in Word 2003 that are designed to help you quickly create many types of documents such as a memo, a form or a Web page. The Mail Merge task pane will guide you through the four steps in the mail merge process.

The first step is to specify the type of document you want to create. An explanation of the selected document type is displayed below the list of options.

2 • If necessary, select Letters.

• Click Next: Starting document.

Your screen should be similar to Figure 6.34

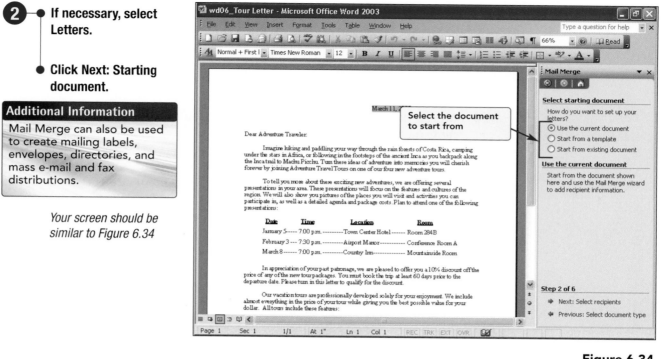

Figure 6.34

In the next step you identify the starting document. Since you already opened the file containing the letter you want to use, you will select the "Use the current document" option.

3 • If necessary, select Use the current document.

• Click Next: Select recipients.

Your screen should be similar to Figure 6.35

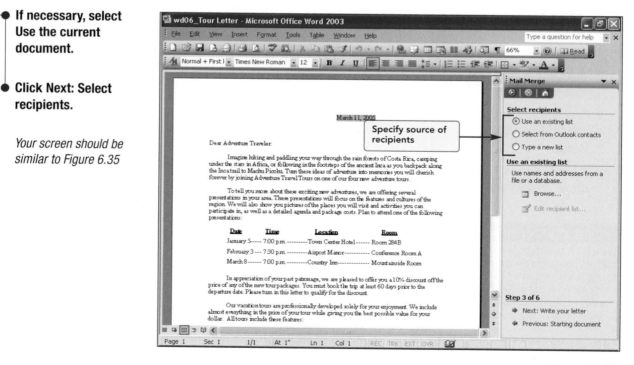

Figure 6.35

Creating the Data Source

Next you select the recipients to use as the data source for the mail merged document. You can use an existing list, select from your Outlook contacts, or type a new address list.

You are going to type a new Office Address List using Word.

1 ● **Select Type a new list.**

● **Click Create.**

Your screen should be similar to Figure 6.36

Common field names

Figure 6.36

The New Address List dialog box is used to specify the field names for the data that will be entered in the recipient list.

Concept 5

Field names

5 **Field names** are used to label the different data fields in the recipient list. A field name can contain only letters, numbers, or the underline character. It can be a maximum of 40 characters and cannot contain spaces. The first character of a field name must be a letter. Field names should describe the contents of the data field.

Commonly used form-letter field names are displayed in the New Address List list box. You can remove from the list any field names that you do not need in your letter, or you can add field names to the list or rename the field names. In this case, you will remove several field names from the list.

2 ● Click [Customize...].

Your screen should be similar to Figure 6.37

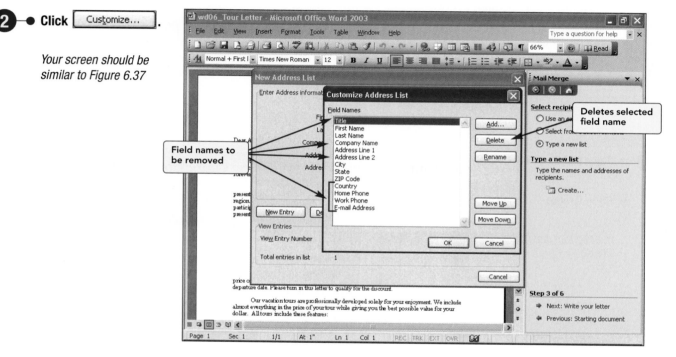

Figure 6.37

Additional Information

The [Move Up] and [Move Down] buttons let you rearrange the order of the fields.

Because you only need basic address information, you will remove any extra field names. Since the title field name is already selected, you will delete it first.

3 • Click [Delete] to remove the Title field from the list.

• Click [Yes] to confirm the deletion.

• Select and remove the following field names: Company Name, Address Line 2, Country, Home Phone, Work Phone, and E-mail Address.

• Click [OK].

Your screen should be similar to Figure 6.38

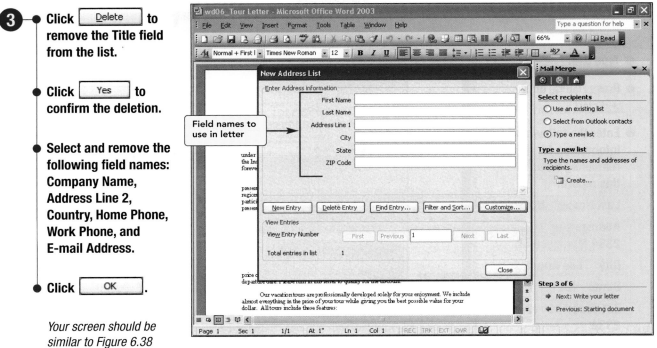

Field names to use in letter

Figure 6.38

The New Address List dialog box now displays only the six field names you want to use in the letter, and text boxes for entering the information for each data record. The information must be entered exactly as you want it to appear in the letter. If you do not have the information you need to complete a field, you can leave it blank. You will enter the information for the first field of the first data record, the client's first name.

4 Click in the First Name field text box.

7 Click [OK].

Your screen should be similar to Figure 6.42

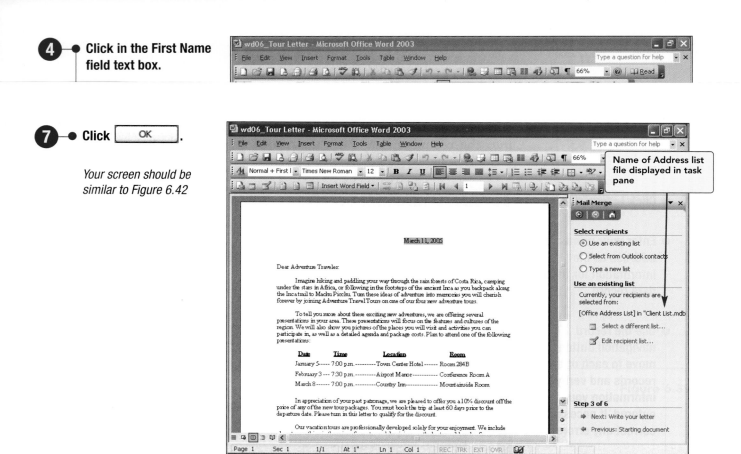

Figure 6.42

Now the name of the address list file you created appears in the Use an existing list section of in the task pane. You will use this address list and advance to the next step. In addition, the Mail Merge toolbar, shown below, is displayed.

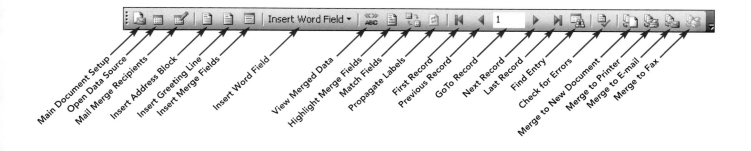

8 ● If necessary, select
       Use an existing list.

   ● Click Next: Write your
     letter.

*Your screen should be
similar to Figure 6.43*

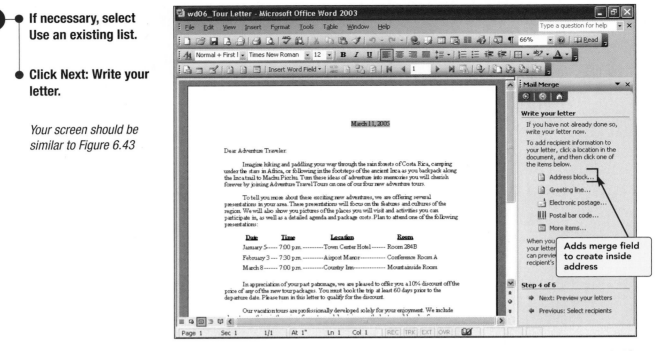

Figure 6.43

Entering Merge Fields in the Main Document

The next step is to create your letter, if you have not done so already, and to include the recipient information in it. How will Word know where to enter the client's name and other source data in the main document? Word uses merge fields to do this. Merge fields direct the program to accept information from the data source at the specified location in the main document. To prepare the letter to accept the fields of information from the data source, you need to add merge fields to the letter.

The letter needs to be modified to allow entry of the name and address information for each client from the data source. The inside address will hold the following three lines of information, which are the components of the address block:

> First Name Last Name
> Address Line 1
> City, State Zip Code

The first line of the inside address, which will hold the client's full name, will be entered as line 5 of the tour letter. A merge field needs to be entered in the main document for each field of data you want copied from the data source. The location of the merge field indicates where to enter the field data. First you need to position the insertion point on the line where the client's name and address will appear.

1 • Move to the blank line above the salutation.

• Click Address block.

Your screen should be similar to Figure 6.44

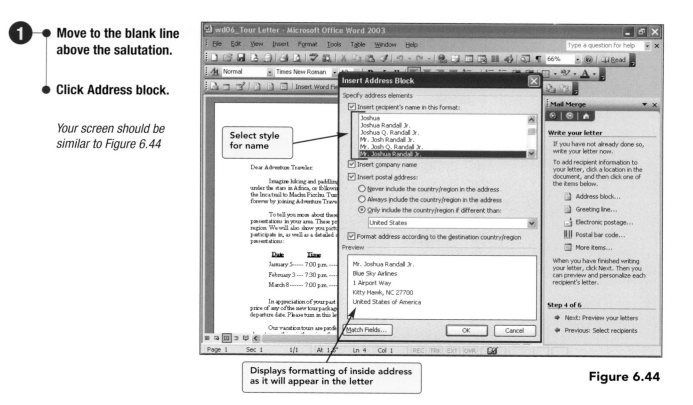

Select style for name

Displays formatting of inside address as it will appear in the letter

Figure 6.44

The Insert Address Block dialog box has many options for customizing the appearance of the fields. The Preview area displays how the Address Block will appear in the letter.

2 • Choose the example "Joshua Randall Jr." as the format for the recipient's name.

• Click Insert Company name to deselect it.

• Click   OK   .

Having Trouble?

You can also click 📄 Insert Address Block on the Mail Merge toolbar or 📄 Insert Merge Fields and insert the merge fields one at a time.

Your screen should be similar to Figure 6.45

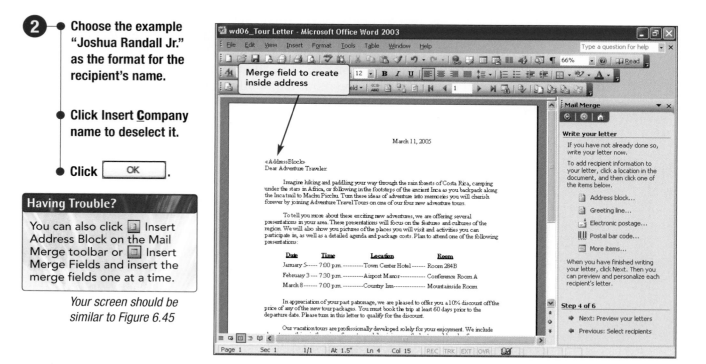

Merge field to create inside address

Figure 6.45

The merge field <<AddressBlock>> is displayed at the insertion point in the main document. It is a field code that instructs Word to insert the information from the data fields (from the data source) at this location in the main document when the merge is performed.

3 • Enter a blank line between the Address Block merge field and the salutation.

• Select "Adventure Traveler" in the salutation.

• Click 🖹 Insert Merge Fields (on the Mail Merge toolbar).

• Select the First Name merge field.

• Click [Insert].

• Click [Close].

Another Method ○○○○

You can also select the entire salutation and click 🖹 in the Mail Merge task pane to access several options for formatting the salutation.

Additional Information

The same merge field can be used more than once in the main document.

Your screen should be similar to Figure 6.46

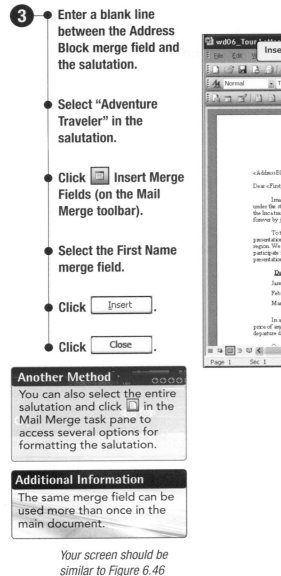

Figure 6.46

Previewing the Merged Letter

The next step is to see how the form letter appears with the merged data.

1 ● **Click Next: Preview your letters.**

Another Method

You can also click 🔲 View Merged Data on the Mail Merge toolbar.

Your screen should be similar to Figure 6.47

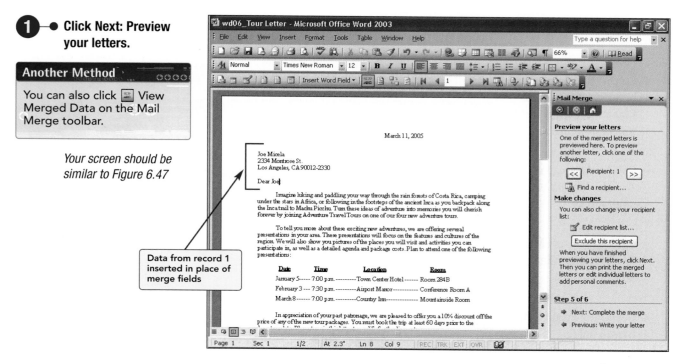

Data from record 1 inserted in place of merge fields

Figure 6.47

The data from the first record of the address list is displayed in place of the merge fields.

2 ● **Click** `>>` **to see the address information for the next recipient in the letter.**

● **Change the zoom to Two Pages.**

Your screen should be similar to Figure 6.48

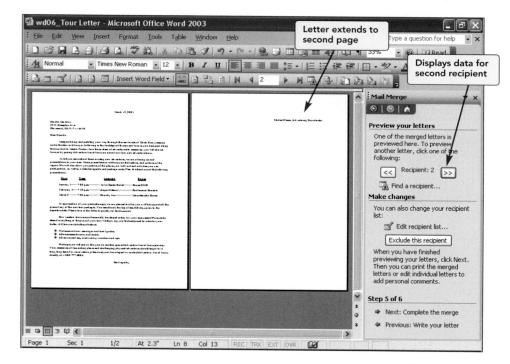

Letter extends to second page

Displays data for second recipient

Figure 6.48

With the addition of the address information, the form letter no longer fits on one page. You can easily fix this using the Shrink to Fit feature to make the letter fit on one page.

3 ● Click 🔍 **Print Preview.**

● Click 📑 **Shrink to Fit.**

Your screen should be similar to Figure 6.49

Shrink to Fit

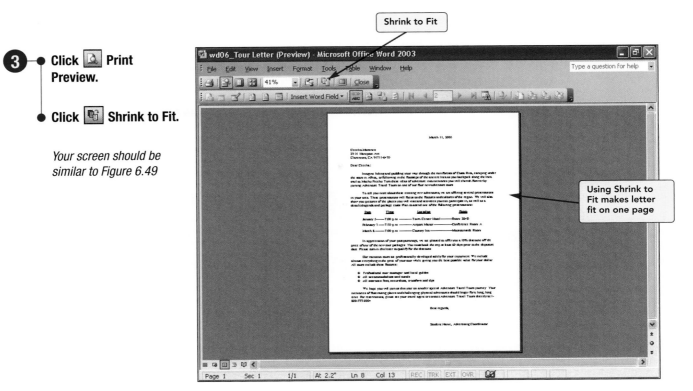

Using Shrink to Fit makes letter fit on one page

Figure 6.49

The font size of the letter has been reduced just enough to make the letter fit on a single page.

Font size reduced to 11.5 points by Shrink to Fit feature

4 ● **Close the Print Preview window.**

● **Return the zoom to Page Width.**

● **Save the letter as Tour Letter Main Document to your data file location.**

Your screen should be similar to Figure 6.50

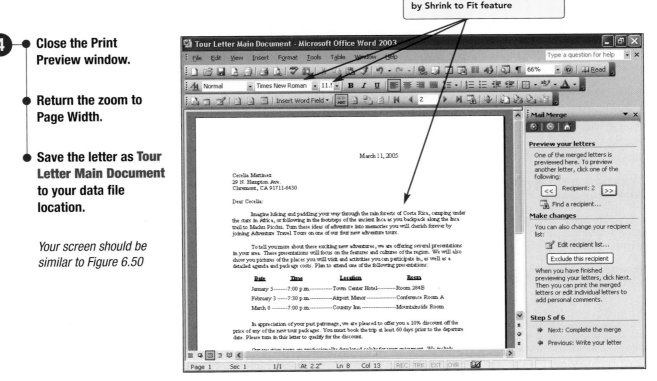

Figure 6.50

The Tour Letter Main Document file contains the merge field codes that are needed to direct the mail merge process. Each merge field code includes links to the appropriate fields in the data source file that are needed to create the individualized form letters.

Printing the Merged Letter

Now that you have created the main document and data source file, you are ready to complete the merge and print the new personalized tour letter.

1 ● **Click Next: Complete the merge.**

Another Method

You can also click 📋 Merge to New Document on the Mail Merge toolbar.

Your screen should be similar to Figure 6.51

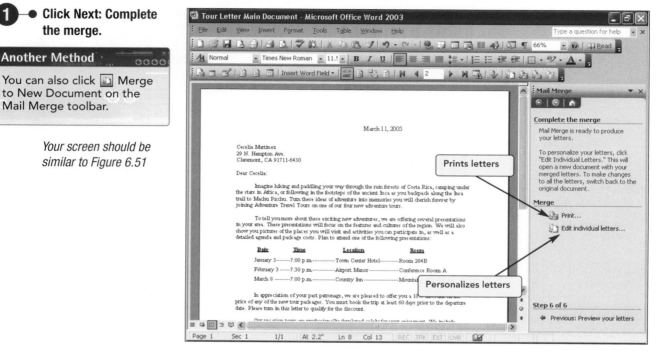

Prints letters

Personalizes letters

Figure 6.51

Another Method

The toolbar shortcut to edit merge letters is 📋 Merge to New Document on the Mail Merge toolbar.

Another Method

The toolbar shortcut to print merged documents is 📋 Merge to Printer in the Mail Merge toolbar.

Additional Information

To narrow the recipient list or set criteria, click 📋 Mail Merge Recipients to open the data source and then make your changes in the Mail Merge Recipients dialog box.

From the Mail Merge task pane, you can print the merged letters immediately or you can further edit the letters before you print them. If you want to edit the letters, Word opens a new document that contains all the individual letters. Then you can modify the letters, save the file and print the document just as you would any regular Word document. You can also direct the merge to output the form letters to e-mail or a fax if your system is set up to include these features.

Finally, if you do not want every record in your data source to receive a copy of the form letter, you can specify a range of records to merge. You can also narrow down the recipients to receive letters by deselecting specific data records in the address list or by setting specific criteria for data records to meet. In this case, you only want to print the letter that contains your name and address, which is record 3.

2 ● Click Print in the task pane.

● Click in the From field and type **3**.

● Click in the To field and type **3**.

● Click OK .

● Make the necessary selections from the Print dialog box for your system.

● Click OK .

Your printed output should be similar to that shown here.

3 ● Close the Mail Merge task pane.

● Close the Mail Merge toolbar.

● Close the document.

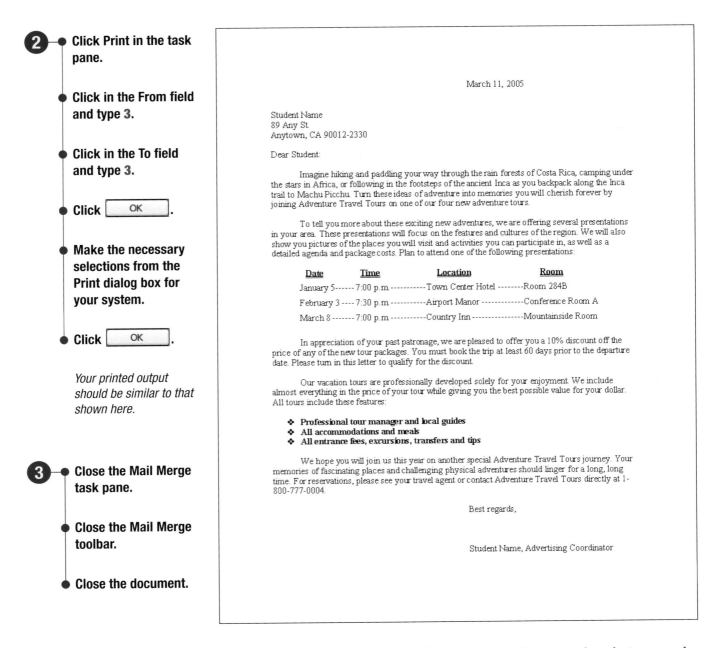

March 11, 2005

Student Name
89 Any St.
Anytown, CA 90012-2330

Dear Student:

Imagine hiking and paddling your way through the rain forests of Costa Rica, camping under the stars in Africa, or following in the footsteps of the ancient Inca as you backpack along the Inca trail to Machu Picchu. Turn these ideas of adventure into memories you will cherish forever by joining Adventure Travel Tours on one of our four new adventure tours.

To tell you more about these exciting new adventures, we are offering several presentations in your area. These presentations will focus on the features and cultures of the region. We will also show you pictures of the places you will visit and activities you can participate in, as well as a detailed agenda and package costs. Plan to attend one of the following presentations:

Date	Time	Location	Room
January 5	7:00 p.m	Town Center Hotel	Room 284B
February 3	7:30 p.m	Airport Manor	Conference Room A
March 8	7:00 p.m	Country Inn	Mountainside Room

In appreciation of your past patronage, we are pleased to offer you a 10% discount off the price of any of the new tour packages. You must book the trip at least 60 days prior to the departure date. Please turn in this letter to qualify for the discount.

Our vacation tours are professionally developed solely for your enjoyment. We include almost everything in the price of your tour while giving you the best possible value for your dollar. All tours include these features:

❖ **Professional tour manager and local guides**
❖ **All accommodations and meals**
❖ **All entrance fees, excursions, transfers and tips**

We hope you will join us this year on another special Adventure Travel Tours journey. Your memories of fascinating places and challenging physical adventures should linger for a long, long time. For reservations, please see your travel agent or contact Adventure Travel Tours directly at 1-800-777-0004.

Best regards,

Student Name, Advertising Coordinator

Now each time you need to send tour letters, all you need to do is open the Tour Letter Main Document file, use the Mail Merge command, edit the client data source file and print the letter.

Printing Mailing Labels

Now that the form letter is ready to be sent to clients, you want to create mailing labels for the envelopes. To create mailing labels for your form letter, you will use the Mailing Label Wizard.

1 ● Choose <u>F</u>ile/<u>N</u>ew.

● From the Templates section of the New Document task pane, click On my computer.

● Open the Letters & Faxes tab.

● Select .

● Click [OK].

● Select Cr<u>e</u>ate labels for a mailing list.

● Click [OK].

Your screen should be similar to Figure 6.52

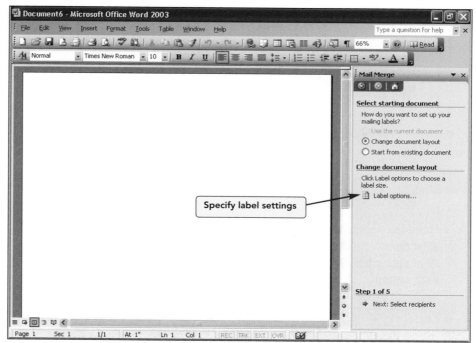

Specify label settings

Figure 6.52

A blank document window opens and the Mail Merge task pane displays. The Wizard first needs to know how you want to set up the mailing labels. The default will use the new blank document as the starting document. You can also choose to use another existing document.

2 ● Click Label options.

Your screen should be similar to Figure 6.53

Printer setting

Standard mailing labels

Figure 6.53

The next step is to select a ready-to-use mail merge template. The Label Options dialog box displays the type of printer and the manufacturer of mailing labels. Avery Standard is the default. The Product Number list shows all the types of labels for the selected manufacturer.

3 ● **Select 5260-Address.**

● **Click** OK .

Your screen should be similar to Figure 6.54

Table will be used to hold mailing label information

Figure 6.54

The document displays a three-column table that will be used to hold the mailing label information. You will use the Client List, which is the same data source you used for the merged letter as the source for the mailing label information.

4 ● **Click Next: Select recipients.**

● **Click Browse.**

● **Select** Client List **from your data file location.**

● **Click** Open .

● **From the Mail Merge Recipients dialog box, click** OK .

● **Click Next: Arrange your labels.**

Your screen should be similar to Figure 6.55

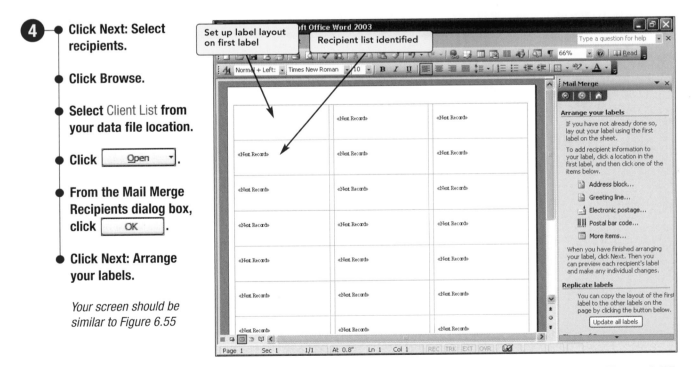

Figure 6.55

Next, you set up the first label on the sheet and replicate that setup to the rest of the labels.

5 ● **Click Address block.**

● **Select a format for the recipient's name.**

● **Deselect Insert company name.**

● **Click** OK .

● **Click** Update all labels .

Your screen should be similar to Figure 6.56

Figure 6.56

Next you will preview the labels before you perform the merge.

6 ● **Click Next: Preview your labels.**

Having Trouble?

You may need to scroll the task pane to see this option.

Your screen should be similar to Figure 6.57

Figure 6.57

Lab 6: Creating Forms and Form Letters and Collaborating on Documents

www.mhhe.com/oleary

The labels look good, so you can complete the merge and, if you wanted, print the labels. Instead, you will save the merged label file. Now when you send the tour letters, you can create mailing labels using the same data source as the letter.

7 ● Click **Next: Complete the merge.**

● **Save the document as** ATT Mailing Labels.

● **Close the Mail Merge task pane and close the document.**

Preparing and Printing Envelopes

Sometimes you may want to quickly address a single envelope. To see how this feature works, you will address an envelope for one of the letters in the Tour Letter Main Document file.

1 ● **Open the** Tour Letter Main Document **file.**

● **Click** Yes **to insert the data.**

● **If necessary, change the zoom to Page Width.**

● **Copy the inside address of the letter.**

● **Choose Tools/Letters and Mailings/ Envelopes and Labels.**

● **If necessary, open the Envelopes tab.**

● **If necessary, select the entire entry in the Delivery Address text box.**

● **Press** Ctrl **+ V to paste the copied address into the Delivery Address text box.**

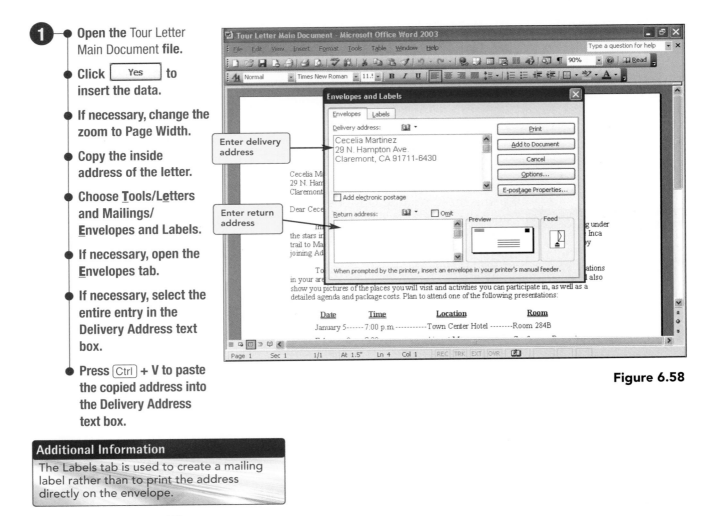

Figure 6.58

Additional Information

The Labels tab is used to create a mailing label rather than to print the address directly on the envelope.

Your screen should be similar to Figure 6.58

Another Method

You can also type an address directly in the Delivery Address text box.

To complete the information for the envelope, you want to add the return address. Then you will check the options for printing and formatting the envelope.

2 • Enter your name and your school's address in the Return Address text box.

• Click [Options...].

• If necessary, open the **E**nvelope Options tab.

Your screen should be similar to Figure 6.59

Figure 6.59

Using the Envelope Options dialog box, you can change the envelope size and the font and placement of the delivery and return addresses. The Preview area shows how the envelope will appear when printed using the current settings.

The default envelope size of 10 is for standard 8½-by-11-inch letter paper. This is the appropriate size for the letter. Next you will check the print options.

Additional Information

You can select other envelope sizes from the Envelope Size drop-down list.

4 • Open the **P**rinting Options tab.

Your screen should be similar to Figure 6.60

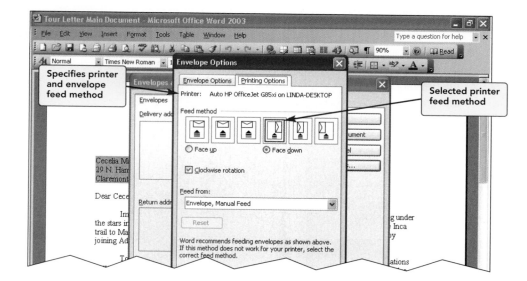

Figure 6.60

The options in this tab are used to specify how the envelope is fed into the printer. Word automatically selects the best option for the selected printer. You do not need to change any of the envelope options. If you were printing an actual envelope, you would need to insert the correct size envelope in the printer at this time. However, you will simply print it on a sheet of paper.

5 ● **Close the Envelope Options dialog box.**

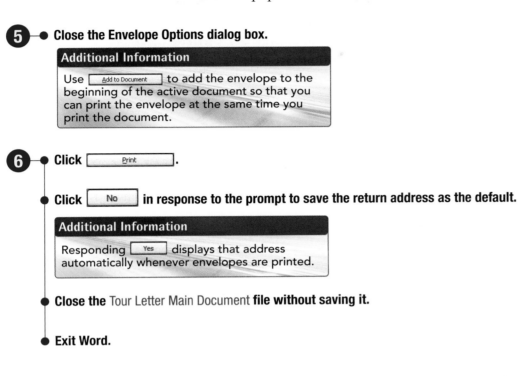

> **Additional Information**
>
> Use [Add to Document] to add the envelope to the beginning of the active document so that you can print the envelope at the same time you print the document.

6 ● **Click** [Print].

● **Click** [No] **in response to the prompt to save the return address as the default.**

> **Additional Information**
>
> Responding [Yes] displays that address automatically whenever envelopes are printed.

● **Close the** Tour Letter Main Document **file without saving it.**

● **Exit Word.**

Focus on Careers

EXPLORE YOUR CAREER OPTIONS

Forensic Science Technician

Do you like murder mysteries? Are you fascinated by court dramas? Forensic science technicians are involved in the investigation of crimes and are often called to testify in court to explain their findings to the jury. Most forensic science technicians specialize in one area of the field, such as DNA analysis or firearms. They must prepare reports that clarify their findings and explain the techniques used in the laboratory. Most positions require relevant experience and at least an associate degree in applied science; however, a bachelor's degree in forensic technology may be preferred. The typical salary range for forensic science technologists is between $19,000 and $35,000.

concept summary

LAB **6**

Creating Forms and Form Letters and Collaborating on Documents

Forms (WD6.4)

Forms are documents that contain fill-in blanks or spaces reserved for entering information.

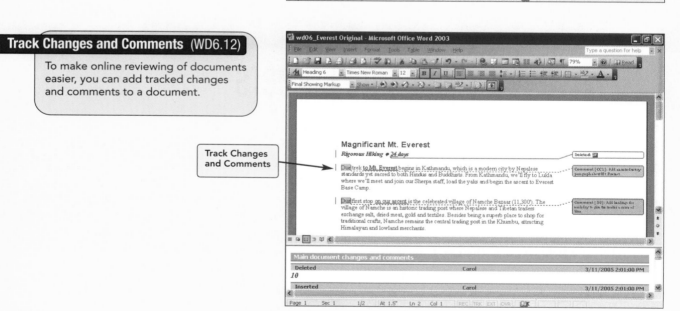

Forms →

Track Changes and Comments (WD6.12)

To make online reviewing of documents easier, you can add tracked changes and comments to a document.

Track Changes and Comments →

Lab 4: Creating Forms and Form Letters and Collaborating on Documents

www.mhhe.com/oleary

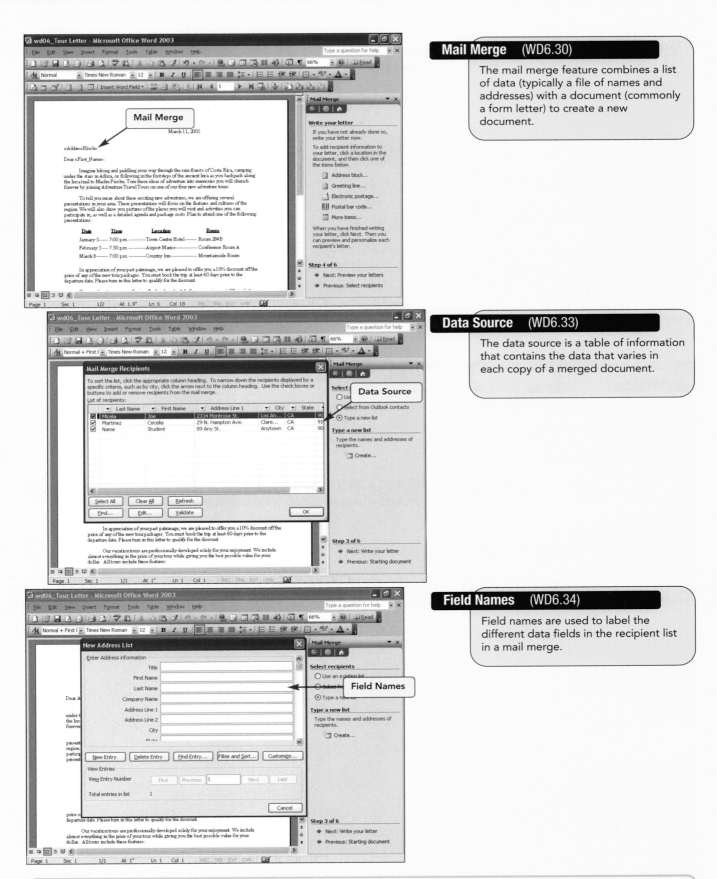

Mail Merge (WD6.30)

The mail merge feature combines a list of data (typically a file of names and addresses) with a document (commonly a form letter) to create a new document.

Data Source (WD6.33)

The data source is a table of information that contains the data that varies in each copy of a merged document.

Field Names (WD6.34)

Field names are used to label the different data fields in the recipient list in a mail merge.

key terms

address list WD6.30	data source WD6.30	merge field WD6.30
attachment WD6.20	field name WD6.34	Tracked Changes WD6.12
balloon WD6.12	form WD6.4	wizard WD6.31
comment WD6.12	header row WD6.33	
control WD6.5	Mail Merge WD6.30	
data field WD6.33	main document WD6.30	
data record WD6.33	markup WD6.12	

microsoft office specialist skills

The Microsoft Office Specialist certification program is designed to measure your proficiency in performing basic tasks using the Office 2003 applications. Getting certified demonstrates that you have the skills and provides a valuable industry credential for employment. After completing this lab, you have learned the following Microsoft Office Word Specialist skills:

Skill	Description	Page
Organizing Content	Insert and modify tables	WD6.6
Collaborating	Circulate documents for review	WD6.20
	Compare and Merge Documents	WD6.22
	Insert, view, and edit comments	WD6.12
	Track, accept, and reject proposed changes	WD6.24
Formatting and Managing Documents	Print documents, envelopes, and labels	WD6.49

command summary

Command	Shortcut Key	Button	Action
File/Sen**d** to/**Ma**il Recipient (as attachment)			Sends document as an attachment via e-mail
View/M**a**rkup			Displays markups made to a document
Insert/Co**m**ment			Inserts a comment
Insert/Fi**l**e			Inserts contents of an entire file
F**o**rmat/**F**ont/Te**x**t Effects			Applies effects such as animation to characters
Tools/**T**rack Changes	Ctrl + ⇧ Shift + E		Marks changes made to a document
Tools/Compare and Merge **D**ocuments			Combines documents and identifies differences
Tools/Le**t**ters and Mailings/ **M**ail Merge			Starts Mail Merge Wizard
Tools/Le**t**ters and Mailings/ **E**nvelopes and Labels/**E**nvelopes			Prints delivery and return addresses on envelopes
T**a**ble/Con**v**ert/Te**x**t to Table			Changes existing text in a document to text displayed in a table

lab exercises

matching

Match the item on the right with the correct description on the left.

1. Element that contains comments in reviewed documents.   _____ **a.** wizard
2. Elements used to display tracked changes.   _____ **b.** forms
3. Document that directs merge process.   _____ **c.** field name
4. Combines a list of data with a document.   _____ **d.** comment
5. Documents with blanks for entering information.   _____ **e.** data source
6. Table of information that contains data fields.   _____ **f.** balloon
7. Feature that monitors changes to a document.   _____ **g.** Mail Merge
8. A note added to a document without changing the
   document text.   _____ **h.** Track Changes
9. Feature that leads you step-by-step through a process.   _____ **i.** Original
10. Used to label different data fields in the data source.   _____ **j.** main document

_____ **k.** Markup

multiple choice

Circle the correct response to the questions below.

1. A(n) _____ asks questions and then uses your answers to automatically lay out and format a document.
   a. template
   b. placeholder
   c. wizard
   d. merge

2. The _____ document contains the text that will become the basis of a form letter.
   a. letter
   b. data source
   c. address file
   d. main

3. _____ names are used to label each data field in the data source.
   a. Row
   b. Record
   c. Field
   d. File

4. The _____ feature combines a list of data with a document to create a new document.
   a. Mail Format
   b. Track Changes
   c. wizard
   d. Mail Merge

5. A(n) _____ is used in the main document for each field of data that is inserted from the data source.
   a. merge field
   b. data record
   c. row
   d. data field

6. A(n) _____ is a note inserted in a document that does not change the text.
   a. comment
   b. balloon
   c. tracked change
   d. attachment

7. The data source is also commonly called the _____.
   a. main document
   b. address file
   c. balloon
   d. data field

8. The _____ can be a maximum of 40 characters and cannot contain spaces.
   a. data field
   b. field marker
   c. field name
   d. address file

9. The first row of the data source table is called the _____.
   a. field name row
   b. category name row
   c. data record row
   d. header row

10. Graphical objects called _____ make a form easier to read.
    a. address files
    b. data fields
    c. field names
    d. controls

true/false

Circle the correct answer to the following questions.

1.	An attachment is not part of an e-mail text.	True	False
2.	Each person in an online meeting can add comments in real-time.	True	False
3.	A data source is also known as the main document.	True	False
4.	A Wizard commonly contains data fields and addresses.	True	False
5.	Field names can be letters, numbers, and the underline character.	True	False
6.	Controls may be check boxes or text boxes.	True	False
7.	Markup includes balloons, underlines, and animation.	True	False
8.	Comment balloons are displayed within the text.	True	False
9.	Text animation can be printed.	True	False
10.	Even if Tracked Changes was not on, Word always detects changes in a merge document.	True	False

step-by-step

Lifestyle Fitness Form ★

1. You work at Lifestyle Fitness Club headquarters in the marketing and public relations department. Recently introduced yoga classes have been very popular, and you are researching additional alternative health programs for the clubs. To measure interest you have created a series of informational courses and would like to begin registering members for the free classes. You will create a form to gather enrollment information. Your completed form is shown here:

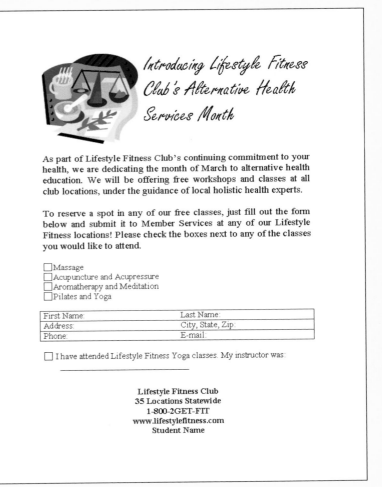

   a. Open the file wd06_Alternatives Form.

   b. Change the font of the form title to one of your choice. Increase the font size appropriately. Add a clip art graphic of your choice to the top of the document as shown in the example, or use wd06_Alternatives.

   c. Increase the font size of the two paragraphs to 16 pt. Justify the paragraphs.

   d. Increase the font size of the remaining text to 14 pt. Bold and center the company name and address lines.

   e. Convert the name and address lines of the text to a table with two columns. Remove the interior vertical border line.

   f. Add check box controls without shading to the list of classes.

   g. Insert a new line below the table with the following text: **I have attended Lifestyle Fitness Yoga classes. My instructor was:**

   h. Add a check box field at the beginning of the new sentence.

   i. Add a line approximately 2 inches long below the new sentence.

   j. Add your name below the Web address. Save the document as Alternatives Form2. Send the document as an attachment to your instructor. Close the file.

Downtown Internet Café Form ★

2. Jennifer Ellison works at the Downtown Internet Café as an event coordinator. She is planning a number of events to help celebrate National Tea Month. In order to gauge customer interest, she has created a form. Jennifer has completed a rough draft and sent a copy to Evan and Melissa, the owners, for review. They have several suggestions for the form. Your completed form is shown here.

   a. Open the file wd06_Tea Month.

   b. Read the comments from Evan and Melissa. Change the color of the WordArt object as suggested, and delete the comment.

   c. Melissa has suggested you change the bulleted list to check boxes. Delete the bullets and then insert check boxes without shading for each class. Delete the comment.

   d. Evan asked that your form contain a table for the customer's information. Add them using information and convert the text to a table. Remove the vertical interior border lines. Your completed table should look like the table shown in the example.

   e. Respond to Evan's final comment, and include the café contact information at the bottom of the flyer.

   Downtown Internet Café

   1-800-4-COFFEE

   www.downtowninternetcafe.com

   Your Name

   f. Remove the hyperlink for the Web address.

   g. Save the document as Tea Month2. Send the document as an attachment to your instructor. Close the file.

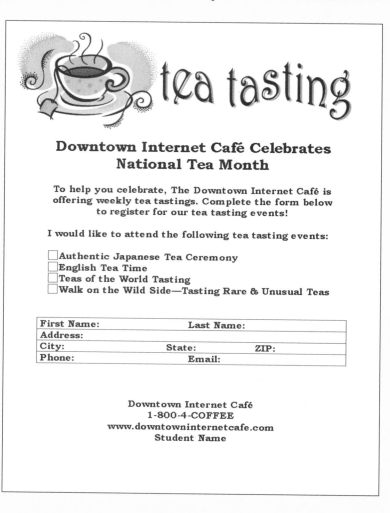

Animal Angels Merge Document ★ ★

3. Animal Angels is sending a letter to all the local veterinarians in the Cedarwood area to enlist their help in finding and caring for homeless pets. You have been asked to compose the new letter and create a form the recipient can return for more information on donation programs. You have begun working on the letter, but need to complete the form and mail merge. Your completed letter is shown here.

a. Open the file wd06_Animal Angels Form.

b. Insert your name in the closing of the letter.

c. Add a line below your name approximately 6 inches long.

d. Convert the text below the line to a table. Remove the interior vertical border lines. Your table should be similar to the example.

e. Enter the following text below the table:

Yes, please send me the Animal Angels Newsletter.

Yes, please send me more information about making a donation.

f. Add unshaded check boxes before each of the new sentences.

g. Open the Mail Merge task pane. Choose Letters as the document type and the current document as the starting document.

h. Create a new recipient list and enter the following information in the appropriate fields of the "Enter address information" form:

Dr. Helen Navarro

1895 S. DePalma Road, Suite 129

Cedarwood, CO 80631

Dr. Blake Wilkins

6272 E. Kennedy Loop

Cedarwood, CO 80631

Dr. Deborah Perry

8233 W. Armstrong Road, #2

Cedarwood, CO 80631

i. Save the data file list as ARF Donation List.

Animal Rescue Foundation

122 Pine Tree Lane
Cedarwood, CO 80631
February 7, 2005

Dr. Helen Navarro
1895 S. DePalma Road, Suite 129
Cedarwood, CO 80631

Dear Helen:

Animal Angels is the volunteer organization of the Animal Rescue Foundation. We strive to make a difference in the quality of life of homeless pets through fundraising and foster parenting. The Foundation achieves success on a daily basis through the immediate care of these animals, but there is so much that still needs to be done.

Animal Angels has identified several things you can do to help meet the needs of this homeless population:

1. Increase exposure to local humane organizations resulting in higher placement rates.
2. Provide a low cost spay/neuter program to the general public.
3. Subsidize extraordinary medical expenses for animals referred by local humane groups.
4. Participate in the regional lost and found service.
5. Help educate the public on owner responsibility through presentations, displays, and literature.

Take this opportunity to make a difference!

For more information, or copies of the Animal Angels Newsletter to distribute to your clients, complete and return the form below:

Sincerely,

Student Name

First Name:Helen	Last Name:Navarro	
Address:1895 S. DePalma Road, Suite 129		
City:Cedarwood	State:CO	Zip:80631
Phone:	E-mail:	

☐ Yes, please send me the Animal Angels Newsletter.
☐ Yes, please send me more information about making a donation.

h. You will create a new list of recipients. Create a list with the following fields:

First Name
Last Name
Address Line 1
City
State
ZIP Code
Home Phone
E-Mail Address

i. Enter the following names in the list:

[Your Name]
2337 W. Skylark Lane
Santa Fe, NM 87505
(505) 555-9834
[your e-mail address]

Sandra Mosiman
78007 La Puente Avenue
Santa Fe, NM 87505
(505) 555-8744
mosiman@mail.mosiman.net

Manuel Rojero
68805 N. Saddleback Place
Santa Fe, NM 87505
(505) 555-8321
rojero@mail.org

Save the data list as Anthology Cinema List.

j. Insert the merge fields into the table you created. (Hint: Use the "More items..." option in the recipient information list.)

k. Preview the document and shrink it to fit on one page. Perform the merge. Save the file as Anthology Cinema Letters. Print the letter displaying your name in the table.

l. Print mailing labels using the Anthology Cinema List.

Frequent Flyer Letter ★

1. Your job with a new low-cost airline company is to manage the company's frequent flyer program. Use the features you learned in this lab to create a form letter that will be sent to new customers of your airline's frequent flyer program. Use the program information provided in the file wd06_Frequent Flyer to create the letter. Enter your name as the signature name on the letter. Create at least three addresses in the data source file. Include a sentence with a check box control, and a table customers can fill out to receive more information on the program. When you are finished, save the document as Frequent Flyer Letter. Print the letters.

Video Club Membership ★ ★

2. The Video Tower sends membership cards to all its new members. You have been asked to create a form letter that can be used to inform customers of membership benefits that will accompany their permanent membership cards. Use the file wd06_Video Tower to create a merge document with at least three addresses. Enter your name as the signature name on the letter. Include a sentence with a check box control that customers can use to request additional cards, and convert the fields at the bottom of the letter to a table. When you are finished merging the documents, save the file as Video Tower Letter. Print the letters. Send the file to your instructor as an attachment.

Historical Society Letter ★ ★

3. Janet Bowers works for the local historical society. She leads tours of historical homes in her area and coordinates fundraising for restoration. She has composed a letter to send to society members regarding membership in the society. Janet's co-chair has reviewed the document and returned it to her. Use the file wd06_Historical Society to create the merge document Janet will send to members. Respond to the comments, making the suggested changes. Use at least three addresses in your recipient list. Save the document as Historical Society Letter. Send your completed document to your instructor as an attachment.

Safari Park Membership Letter ★ ★ ★

4. Nigel Peterson works for the Safari Park, a preserve for elephants. He has created a letter to attract new donations for the park and the preservation of habitat. Nigel sent a draft of the letter to his media relations director for review and will now complete the letter and create the merge document. Open the file wd06_Safari Park, review the comments, and make the suggested changes. Create a merge document with at least three addresses. Save the document as Safari Park Letter. Send the file to your instructor as an attachment.

Rewards Program Letter ★ ★ ★

5. You work for National Hotels Incorporated. You have been asked to create a merge letter that will inform customers about the company's reward program. Create a draft of a letter informing customers about the rewards program. Add comments to the document that inquire about the types of free gifts offered, and whether you should be specific about the gifts in the letter or not. After completing your draft, send a copy to a classmate for review and comment. Review the comments and keep any relevant suggestions. Your completed document should have a table, check boxes, and lines. Create a merge document with at least three addresses. Print the letters. Save the document as Hotel Rewards Letter. Send the file to your instructor as an attachment.

Working Together 2: Copying, Linking, and Embedding Between Applications

Case Study

Adventure Travel Tours

You recently prepared a memo to the regional manager that contained a table showing the sales figures for the four major tours for the past three years. You realize that this information will be updated each year with the previous year's sales figures. Rather than create the table each year for the sales information, you decide it would be easier to create an Excel worksheet of this data and then copy the Excel information into the Word memo when requested. Because you have done a lot of work creating the table in Word already, to save time you will copy the information from the Word table into an Excel workbook.

A second project you are working on is to provide a monthly status report to the regional manager showing the bookings for the four new tours.

You maintain this information in an Excel worksheet and want to include the worksheet of the tour status in a memo each month. You will link the worksheet data to the memo.

The last thing you need to do is to create a memo to the regional manager that shows the sales from the four new tours. Because the manager also wants a copy of the file, you will embed the worksheet data in the memo.

You will learn how to share information between applications as you create the worksheet and the memo. Your completed documents will look like those shown below.

Note: This lab assumes that you already know how to use Excel and that you have completed Labs 2 and 3 of Excel.

Linking an Excel worksheet to a Word document allows the Word document to be quickly updated when data in the worksheet changes.

An embedded object can be updated by opening the server application inside the destination file.

Copying Between Applications

All Microsoft Office applications have a common user interface such as similar commands and menu structures. In addition to these obvious features, they have been designed to work together, making it easy to share and exchange information between applications. For example, the same commands and procedures to copy information within a Word document are used to copy information to other Office System applications such as Excel. The information is pasted in a format the application can edit, if possible. Information can also be copied as a linked object or an embedded object. You will use each of these three methods to copy information between Word and Excel.

First you will use Copy and Paste to copy sales data to Excel. The table of sales data for the four major tours is in a Word 2003 file. You will open the file and copy the table to the Clipboard.

1 • **Start Office Word 2003 and open the document** wdwt2_Annual Tour Sales.

• **If necessary, change the zoom to Page Width.**

• **Select the six rows of the table that include the years and tour names through the last row of tour data (excluding the totals).**

• **Click** 🗐 **Copy to copy the selection to the system Clipboard.**

Your screen should be similar to Figure 1

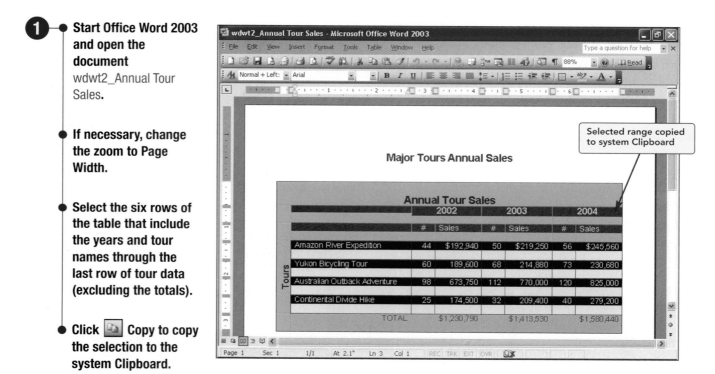

Figure 1

Now you are ready to paste the information into a new Excel workbook file.

2 • Start Office Excel 2003.

• Close the Getting Started task pane.

• Click on cell B4 of the worksheet and, if necessary, maximize the worksheet window.

Your screen should be similar to Figure 2

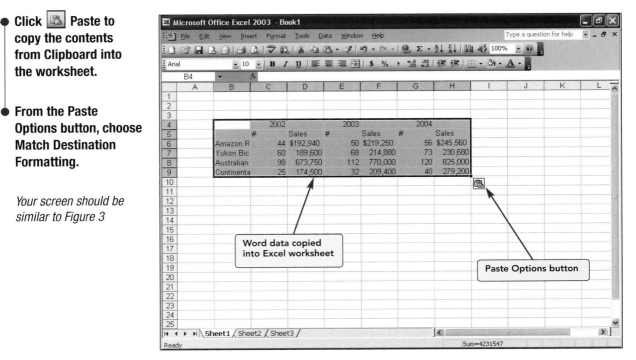

Two open applications

Figure 2

There are now two open applications, Word and Excel, and both application buttons are displayed in the taskbar. You are now ready to paste the table into the worksheet. While using Word, you have learned how to use cut, copy, and paste to move or copy information within and between documents. You can also perform these operations between files in the same application and between files in different Office applications.

3 • Click 🗐 Paste to copy the contents from Clipboard into the worksheet.

• From the Paste Options button, choose Match Destination Formatting.

Your screen should be similar to Figure 3

Word data copied into Excel worksheet

Paste Options button

Figure 3

The content from each cell of the copied table has been inserted into individual cells of the Excel worksheet. The data can now be edited and formatted using Excel commands. You will make a few quick changes to improve the appearance of the worksheet.

4 • Choose **Format/ AutoFormat.**

• **Select the Classic 2 style.**

• **Click** OK .

Your screen should be similar to Figure 4

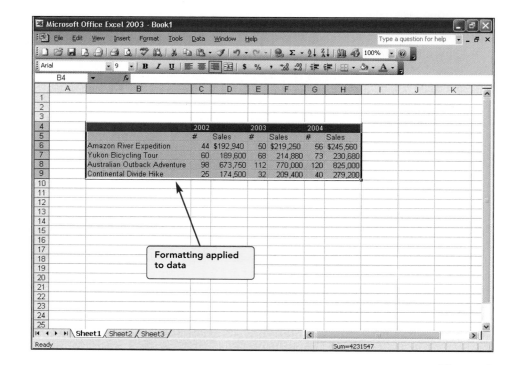

Figure 4

Much like a Word table, the Excel worksheet is formatted using a predesigned formatting style. Next, you want to calculate the total values.

5 • **Drag to select cells C10 through H10.**

• **Click** Σ **AutoSum.**

Your screen should be similar to Figure 5

Figure 5

The total values were quickly calculated. It is much easier to use Excel to perform calculations than Word. Finally, you will copy the title from the Word document to above the worksheet.

6 • Switch to the Word document.

Having Trouble?

Click on the taskbar button to switch to the Word window.

• Select the title text.

• Click 📋 Copy.

• Switch to Excel and move to cell D2.

• Click 📋 Paste.

• Click on cell A1, type **your name** and press ⏎Enter.

• Click 💾 Save and save the Excel file as Major Tours Sales **to your data file location.**

• Print the worksheet.

Your screen should be similar to Figure 6

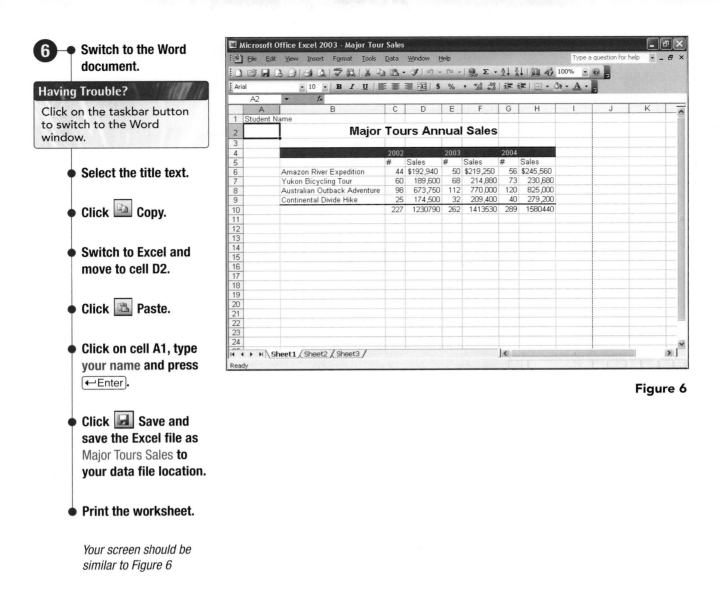

Figure 6

Copying the information from the Word table into an Excel worksheet was much quicker than entering all the data over again.

Linking Between Applications

Your second project is to create a memo to the manager each month to keep her apprised of the reservation status for the four new tours. This information is maintained in an Excel worksheet. You have already started the memo, and need to add the Excel worksheet data to the memo.

1 • **Switch to Word and close the** wdwt2_Annual Tour Sales **file.**

• **Open the file** wdwt2_New Tour Status.

• **In the memo header, replace "Student Name" with your name.**

• **Change the zoom to Page Width.**

• **Save the file as** New Tour Status.

Your screen should be similar to Figure 7

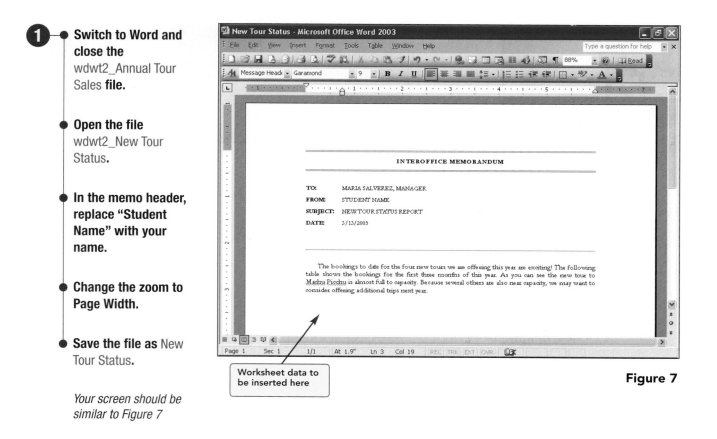

Worksheet data to be inserted here

Figure 7

You will insert the worksheet data below the paragraph. To insert the information from the Excel workbook file into the Word memo, you need to open the workbook file and copy the worksheet range. You will then tile the two open application windows to make it easier to see and work with both files.

2

- **Switch to Excel and close the** Major Tour Sales **file.**

- **Open the workbook file** wdwt2_New Tour Bookings.

- **Save the file as** New Tour Bookings Linked **to your data file location.**

- **Change the zoom to 75%.**

- **Tile the two open windows vertically.**

Having Trouble?

Select Tile Windows Vertically from the Taskbar shortcut menu.

- **Click in the Excel window to make it active.**

- **Select the worksheet range A3 through F10.**

- **Click** **Copy.**

Your screen should be similar to Figure 8

Another Method

You can also insert an object as an embedded object, which stores the entire source file in the document in which it is inserted. Opening the embedded object opens the program in which it was created.

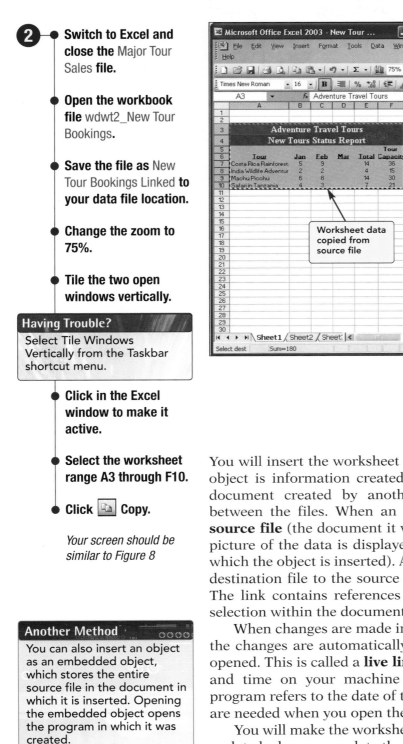

Figure 8

You will insert the worksheet into the memo as a **linked object**. A linked object is information created in one application that is inserted into a document created by another application while maintaining a link between the files. When an object is linked, the data is stored in the **source file** (the document it was created in). A graphic representation or picture of the data is displayed in the **destination file** (the document in which the object is inserted). A connection between the information in the destination file to the source file is established by the creation of a link. The link contains references to the location of the source file and the selection within the document that is linked to the destination file.

When changes are made in the source file that affect the linked object, the changes are automatically reflected in the destination file when it is opened. This is called a **live link**. When you create linked objects, the date and time on your machine should be accurate. This is because the program refers to the date of the source file to determine whether updates are needed when you open the destination file.

You will make the worksheet a linked object, so it will be automatically updated when you update the data in the worksheet.

3

- Click on the Word document window to make it active.

- Move to the blank space below the paragraph.

- Choose **E**dit/Paste **S**pecial.

- Select Paste **L**ink.

Your screen should be similar to Figure 9

Figure 9

The Paste Special dialog box displays the type of object contained in the Clipboard and its location in the Source area. From the As list box you select the type of format in which you want the object inserted into the destination file. There are many different object types from which you can select. It is important to select the appropriate object format so that the link works correctly when inserted in the destination.

The Result area describes the effect of your selections. In this case, you want to insert the object as an Excel Worksheet object, and a link will be created to the worksheet in the source file. Selecting the Display as Icon option changes the display of the object from a picture to an icon. Then to open or edit the object, you would double-click the icon. You need to change the type of format only.

4 • Select Microsoft Office Excel Worksheet Object.

• Click [OK].

• Click Center.

Your screen should be similar to Figure 10

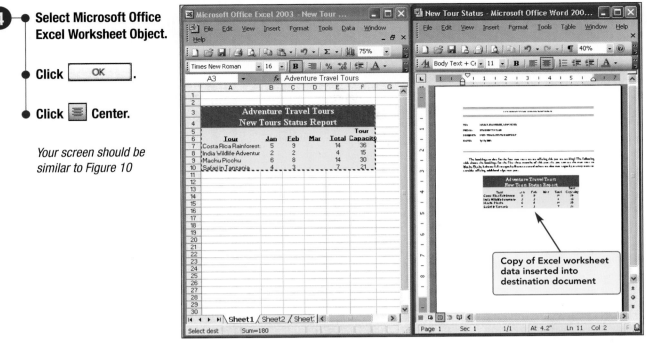

Figure 10

Another Method

The menu equivalent is **E**dit/Linked Worksheet **O**bject/**O**pen Link.

Updating a Linked Object

While preparing the memo, you received the tour bookings for March and will enter this information into the worksheet. To make these changes, you need to switch back to Excel. Double-clicking on a linked object quickly switches to the open source file. If the source file is not open, it opens the file for you. If the application is not open, it both opens the application and the source file. Because the Excel application and worksheet file are already open, you will just switch to the Excel window.

1 • **Click in the Excel window.**

• **Enter the values for March in the cells specified.**

D7	6
D8	4
D9	13
D10	8

• **Press ⏎Enter.**

• **If necessary, click on the linked object in the Word document and press F9 to update the link.**

Another Method ○○○○

The menu equivalent is **E**dit/Up**d**ate Link or Up**d**ate Link from the object's shortcut menu.

Your screen should be similar to Figure 11

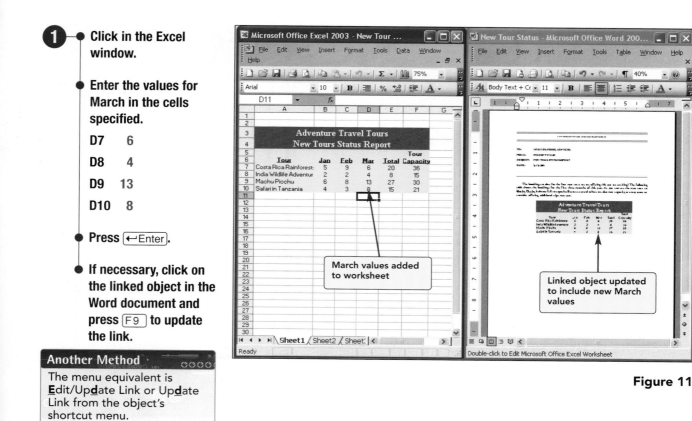

March values added to worksheet

Linked object updated to include new March values

Figure 11

The worksheet in the memo reflects the changes in data. This is because any changes you make to the worksheet in Excel will be automatically reflected in the linked worksheet in the Word document.

Editing Links

Whenever a document is opened that contains links, the application looks for the source file and automatically updates the linked objects. If there are many links, updating can take a lot of time. Additionally, if you move the source file to another location or perform other operations that may interfere with the link, your link will not work. To help with situations like these, you can edit the settings associated with links. You will look at the links to the worksheet data created in the Word document.

1 • If necessary, switch to the Word document.

• Choose **E**dit/Lin**k**s.

Your screen should be similar to Figure 12

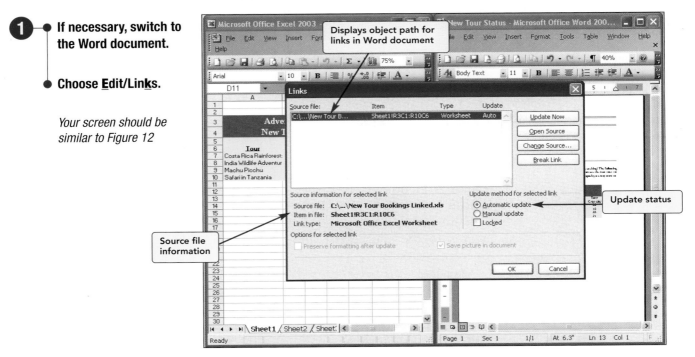

Figure 12

The Links dialog box displays the object path for all links in the document in the list box. The field code specifies the path and name of the source file, the range of linked cells or object name, the type of file, and the update status. Below the list box, the details for the selected link are displayed.

The other options in this dialog box are described in the table below.

Option	Effect
Automatic	Updates the linked object whenever the destination document is opened or the source file changes. This is the default.
Manual	The destination document is not automatically updated and you must use the Update Now command button to update the link.
Locked	Prevents a linked object from being updated.
Open Source	Opens the source document for the selected link.
Change Source	Used to modify the path to the source document.
Break Link	Breaks the connection between the source document and the active document.

As you can see, the link in the Word document is to the New Tour Bookings Linked workbook file and the link is set to update automatically. You do not need to make any changes to these settings. Now that the memo is complete, you will untile the windows and save the documents.

2 ● Click [OK].

● Undo the tiled windows.

● Print the memo.

● Close and save the Word document.

● Switch to Excel and close and save the Excel worksheet file.

Linking documents is a very handy feature, particularly in documents whose information is updated frequently. If you include a linked object in a document that you are giving to another person, make sure the user has access to the source file and application. Otherwise the links will not operate correctly.

Embedding an Object in Another Application

The last thing you need to do is to create a memo to the regional manager that shows the sales from the four new tours. Because the manager also wants a copy of the file, you will embed the worksheet data in the memo. An object that is embedded is stored in the destination file and becomes part of that document. The entire file, not just the selection that is displayed in the destination file, becomes part of the document. This means that you can modify it without affecting the source document where the original object resides.

1 ● Open the Word document wdwt2_New Tour Sales.

● In the memo header, replace "Student Name" with your name.

● Save the document as New Tour Sales.

● Switch to Excel and open the workbook file wdwt2_New Tour Income.

Your screen should be similar to Figure 13

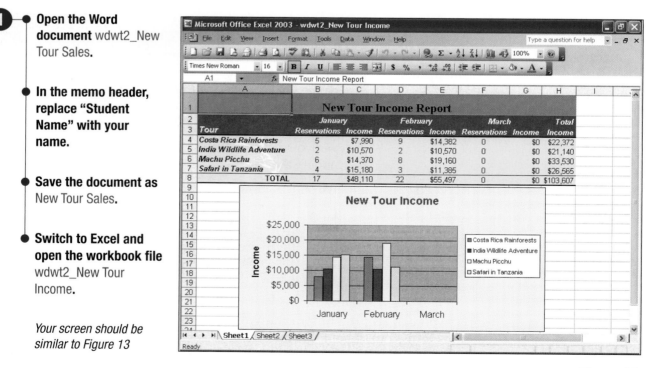

Figure 13

You will embed the worksheet in the Word document.

Working Together 2: Copying, Linking, and Embedding Between Applications

 www.mhhe.com/oleary

2 • Copy the range A1 through H24.

• Switch to the Word document window.

• Move to the second blank line below the first paragraph of the memo.

• Choose <u>E</u>dit/Paste <u>S</u>pecial.

Additional Information

To embed an entire file, use <u>I</u>nsert/<u>O</u>bject/Create from <u>F</u>ile.

Your screen should be similar to Figure 14

Figure 14

The Paste option inserts or embeds the Clipboard contents in the format you specify from the As list box. To embed the contents of the Clipboard into a document so it can be edited using the server application, select the option that displays the server name, in this case Excel.

3 • Select Microsoft Office Excel Worksheet Object.

• Click [OK].

Your screen should be similar to Figure 15

Figure 15

The selected portion of the worksheet is displayed in the memo at the location of the insertion point.

Updating an Embedded Object

You want to add the March reservations to the worksheet. Because the worksheet is embedded, you can do this from within the Word document. The server application is used to edit data in an embedded object. To open the server application and edit the worksheet, you double-click the embedded object.

1 • Double-click the worksheet object in Word.

Your screen should be similar to Figure 16

Having Trouble?

If the worksheet does not fully display the numbers, click outside the worksheet to close the server application. Select the worksheet object, increase the width of the object, and then double-click on the object to open the server application again.

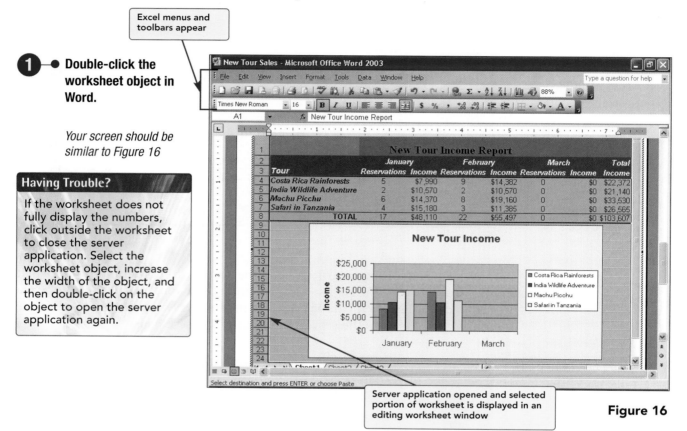

Excel menus and toolbars appear

Server application opened and selected portion of worksheet is displayed in an editing worksheet window

Figure 16

Additional Information

The user must have the server application on his or her system to be able to open and edit the embedded object.

The server application, in this case Excel, is opened. The Excel menus and toolbars replace the menus and toolbars in the Word application window. The selected portion of the embedded object is displayed in an editing worksheet window. Now you can use the server commands to edit the object.

2 ● **Enter the values for March in the cells specified.**

F4   6

F5   4

F6   13

F7   8

● **Press** ←Enter.

● **Close the server application by clicking anywhere outside the object.**

● **Scroll the window to display the entire worksheet object.**

● **If necessary, resize the worksheet object to fit within the page width.**

● **Preview, print, and save the document.**

Your screen should be similar to Figure 17

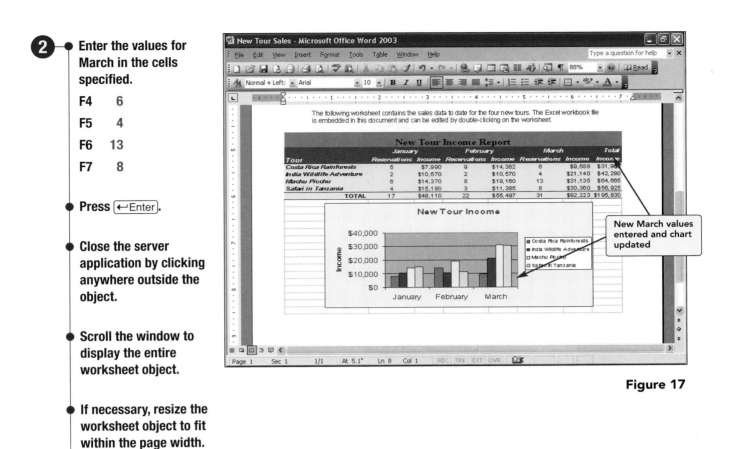

Figure 17

The embedded object in the memo is updated to reflect the changes you made. Notice the chart also updated to reflect the addition of the March data.

3 ● **Switch to the Excel window.**

Your screen should be similar to Figure 18

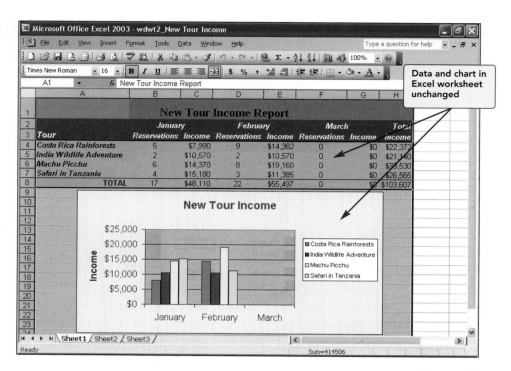

Figure 18

The data in the Excel worksheet is unchanged. This is because it is not linked to the Word document and is a separate file.

4 ● **Enter the March reservation data as you did in the memo.**

● **Save the workbook as** New Tour Income **and exit Excel.**

● **Exit Word.**

Copying, Linking, and Embedding Between Applications

key terms

destination file   WDWT2.7
linked object   WDWT2.7
live link   WDWT2.7
source file   WDWT2.7

command summary

Command	Shortcut Key	Action
Edit/Paste **S**pecial/Paste l**i**nk		Pastes contents of Clipboard as a linked object
Edit/Lin**k**s		Edits settings associated with linked object
Edit/Up**d**ate Link	F9	Updates the linked object to reflect changes made to source
Edit/Linked Worksheet **O**bject		Opens the source application and file of the linked object
Insert/**O**bject/Create from **F**ile		Embeds an entire file

step-by-step

Sales Analysis Memo ★

1. Tamira Jones manages the Animal Rescue Foundation's new retail store. The Foundation director has requested a summary of the sales and expenses for the board of directors. She has completed the memo and worksheet and will now complete the assignment. The completed memo is shown here.

   a. Start Word and open the document wdwt2_Animal Angels Sales.

   b. In the memo header, replace the From placeholder with your name.

   c. Start Excel and open the workbook file wdwt2_AA Sales. Copy the worksheet data below the paragraph in the Word memo. Center the Sales data in the memo.

   d. Save the Word document as AA Sales Memo. Preview and print the document.

   e. Exit Excel.

Animal Rescue Foundation

Memo

To: Sam Johnson

From: Student Name

CC: Sally Lamy

Date: July 18, 2005

Re: Retail Sales Figures

Biannual Sales Review

Below is a spreadsheet showing the sales and expenses for the first six months of operations at the retail store. Sales show a steady increase over the six months and have been greater then anticipated. Expenses have been trimmed and profits have increased accordingly.

	JAN	FEB	MAR	APR	MAY	JUN	TOTAL
Sales	$7,419.98	$7,477.64	$7,548.97	$8,445.82	$9,007.62	$9,059.33	$48,959.36
Expenses	$7,188.71	$5,330.05	$5,484.41	$4,445.82	$4,507.62	$4,050.49	$31,007.10
Profit	$231.27	$2,147.59	$2,064.56	$4,000.00	$4,500.00	$5,008.84	$17,952.26

Payroll Department Memo ★ ★

2. Karen works for a large hotel chain in the payroll department. She has recently created a new time sheet to be used to track hours worked and wants to send a memo informing department managers of the new procedure. She also wants to include a copy of the time sheet from Excel in the memo. The completed memo is shown below.

a. Start Word and open the document wdwt2_Time Sheet Memo.

b. In the memo header, replace the From placeholder with your name.

c. Start Excel and open the workbook file wdwt2_Time Sheet. Copy the range containing the time sheet to below the first paragraph in the Word memo as a linked object. Center the time sheet in the memo.

d. You still need to complete the sample by entering the hours worked on Saturday. In the Excel Worksheet, enter **4** as the Saturday hours worked.

e. Save the Excel workbook as Time Sheet. Exit Excel.

f. Update the linked worksheet object.

g. Save the Word document as Time Sheet Linked. Preview and print the document.

Memorandum

To: All Department Managers
From: Student Name
Date: April 19, 2005
Re: New Time Sheets

Starting with the next payroll period, a new time sheet form will be used. Below is an example of a completed new time sheet.

Time Sheet				
Employee Name:				
Week of:				
Day	Total Hours	Regular Hours	Overtime Hours	Adjusted Total Hours
Monday	10	8	2	10
Tuesday	8	8	0	8
Wednesday	9	8	1	9
Thursday	9	8	1	9
Friday	8	8	0	8
Saturday	4		4	4
			Weekly Total:	48

Please make sure the time sheets for all your employees are turned in no later than 9:00 am the Monday after each pay period.

Thank you for your cooperation.

CONFIDENTIAL

1

lab exercises

Opera Donors Memo ★ ★ ★

3. The City Opera Foundation has decided to hold a spring fundraising event. They would like to extend invitations to the top donors and have asked you to provide the appropriate donor records to the board. You have compiled the records in a worksheet and started the memo. Your completed memo is shown here.

   a. Start Word and open the document wdwt2_Opera Donors.

   b. In the memo header, replace the From placeholder with your name.

   c. Start Excel and open the workbook wdwt2_COF Donors.

   d. Copy the range containing the donations and paste it as an embedded object below the text in the memo. Center the worksheet in the memo.

   e. You received a memo that contains anticipated donation information that has not yet been entered in the Excel worksheet. Include the following text at the end of the memo: **Please note that the 2005 donation listed for Palmquist Equipment has not been finalized, but Mary assures me that this donation has been promised and "is in the works".**

   f. Open the embedded Excel worksheet and enter **12400** as the Palmquist Equipment 2005 donation.

   g. Switch to the Excel application window and enter **12400** in cell E7. Save the Excel workbook as COF Donors2. Exit Excel.

   h. Save the Word document as Opera Donors2. Preview and print the document.

City Opera Foundation

Memo

To: City Opera Foundation Board

From: [Click **here** and type name]

Date: March 29, 2005

Re: Top Donors

I have finished reviewing the foundation donation records. The table below shows the organizations that have contributed more than $50,000 over the past four years.

	2002	2003	2004	2005	Total Donations
T.W.B Foundation	$25,000	$25,000	$20,000	$28,000	$ 98,000
Red Finch Antiques	$10,500	$15,500	$14,800	$13,800	$ 54,600
Café Trocadero	$13,700	$14,900	$12,800	$13,000	$ 54,400
Fulton Farms	$16,800	$17,500	$19,000	$15,000	$ 68,300
Palmquist Equipment	$15,300	$14,800	$17,500	$12,400	$ 60,000
Total	$81,300	$87,700	$84,100	$82,200	$ 335,300

Please note that the 2005 donation for Palmquist Equipment has not been finalized, but Mary assures me that this donation has been promised and "is in the works".

Command Summary

Command	Shortcut Key	Button	Voice	Action
File/**N**ew	Ctrl + N	🗋	New file	Opens new document
File/**O**pen	Ctrl + O	📂	Open	Opens existing document file
File/**C**lose	Ctrl + F4	✕	Close Document	Closes document
File/**S**ave	Ctrl + S	💾	Save	Saves document using same file name
File/Save **A**s				Saves document using a new file name, type, and/or location
File/Save as Web Pa**g**e				Saves file as a Web page document
File/Ve**r**sions				Saves, opens, and deletes document versions
File/We**b** Page Preview				Previews Web page in browser window
File/Page Set**u**p				Changes layout of page including margins, paper size, and paper source
File/Page Set**u**p/Layout/ **V**ertical Alignment				Aligns text vertically on a page
File/Print Pre**v**iew		🔍	Preview	Displays document as it will appear when printed
File/**P**rint	Ctrl + P	🖨	Print	Prints document using selected print settings
File/Sen**d** To/**M**ail Recipient (as attachment)		✉		Sends document as an e-mail attachment
File/Sen**d** To/**M**ail Recipient		✉		Sends a copy of the current document in an e-mail message
File/Proper**t**ies				Displays file statistics, summary, and property settings
File/E**x**it	Alt + F4	✕		Exits Word program
Edit/**U**ndo	Ctrl + Z	↺ ▾	Undo	Restores last editing change
Edit/**R**edo	Ctrl + Y	↻ ▾	Redo	Restores last Undo or repeats last command or action

Command	Shortcut Key	Button	Voice	Action
Insert/Picture/AutoShapes		AutoShapes ▾		Inserts selected AutoShape
Insert/Diagram		[icon]		Inserts a diagram
Insert/Text Box		[icon]		Inserts a text box
Insert/File				Inserts contents of an entire file
Insert/Object/Microsoft Graph Chart				Creates a chart in document
Insert/Object/Create from File				Embeds an entire file
Insert/Hyperlink	Ctrl + K	[icon]		Inserts hyperlink in Web page
Format/Font/Font/Font		Times New Roman ▾		Changes typeface
Format/Font/Font/Font Style/Italic	Ctrl + I	*I*		Makes selected text italic
Format/Font/Font/Font Style/Bold	Ctrl + B	**B**	On bold	Makes selected text bold
Format/Font/Font/Size		12 ▾		Changes font size
Format/Font/Font/Color		A ▾		Changes text to selected color
Format/Font/Font/Underline style/Single	Ctrl + U	U		Underlines selected text with a single line
Format/Font/Font/Hidden				Hides selected text
Format/Font/Character Spacing				Changes spacing between characters
Format/Font/Text Effects				Applies effects such as animation to characters
Format/Paragraph/Indents and Spacing/Alignment/Center	Ctrl + E	[icon]	Centered	Centers text between left and right margins
Format/Paragraph/Indents and Spacing/Alignment/Justified	Ctrl + J	[icon]		Aligns text equally between left and right margins
Format/Paragraph/Indents and Spacing/Alignment/Left	Ctrl + L	[icon]	Left justify	Aligns text to left margin
Format/Paragraph/Indents and Spacing/Alignment/Right	Ctrl + R	[icon]	Right justify	Aligns text to right margin
Format/Paragraph/Indents and Spacing/Special/First Line				Indents first line of paragraph from left margin
Format/Paragraph/Indents and Spacing/Line Spacing	Ctrl + #			Changes amount of white space between lines
Format/Bullets and Numbering		[icon] [icon]		Creates a bulleted or numbered list
Format/Borders and Shading				Adds borders and shadings to selection
		[icon]		Adds outside border

Command	Shortcut Key	Button	Voice	Action
		⊡		Adds top border
		⊡		Adds bottom border
Fo**r**mat/**C**olumns		▤		Specifies number, spacing, and size of columns
Fo**r**mat/**T**abs				Specifies types and position of tab stops
Fo**r**mat/**D**rop Cap/**D**ropped				Changes character format to a dropped capital letter
Fo**r**mat/Change Cas**e**				Changes case of selected text
Fo**r**mat/Th**e**me				Applies a predesigned theme to Web page
Fo**r**mat/Pi**c**ture				Changes format settings associated with selected picture
Fo**r**mat/Pi**c**ture/Layout/ Wrapping Style		▣		Specifies how text will wrap around picture
Fo**r**mat/Re**v**eal Formatting	⇧Shift + F1			Opens Reveal Formatting task pane
Fo**r**mat/W**o**rdArt/Size				Sizes, rotates, and scales WordArt object
Fo**r**mat/W**o**rdArt/Colors and Lines		▣		Applies fill and line color to WordArt object
Fo**r**mat/Text B**o**x/Layout		▣		Changes wrapping style and alignment of text box
Fo**r**mat/Te**x**t Direction/**O**rientation				Changes direction of text in a table
Fo**r**mat/**O**bject				Applies formatting to selected object
Tools/**S**pelling and Grammar	F7	▣		Starts Spelling and Grammar tool
Tools/**R**esearch	Alt + Click			Opens the Research task pane
Tools/**L**anguage/Thesaurus	⇧Shift + F7			Starts Thesaurus tool
Tools/**L**anguage/**H**yphenation				Specifies hyphenation settings
Tools/**W**ord Count				Reviews document statistics
Tools/**T**rack Changes	Ctrl + ⇧Shift + E	▣		Marks changes to document
Tools/**C**ompare and Merge **D**ocuments				Combines documents and identifies differences
Tools/L**e**tters and Mailings/ **M**ail Merge				Starts Mail Merge Wizard
Tools/L**e**tters and Mailings/ **E**nvelopes and Labels/**E**nvelopes		▣		Prints delivery and return addresses on envelopes

Command	Shortcut Key	Button	Voice	Action
Tools/**A**utoCorrect Options/**E**xceptions			Options button	Option to exclude words from automatic correction
Tools/**A**utoCorrect Options/ **Sh**ow AutoCorrect Options buttons			Options button	Displays or hides AutoCorrect option buttons
Tools/**C**ustomize/**O**ptions/**S**how Standard and Formatting toolbar				Displays Standard and Formatting toolbars on two rows
Tools/**O**ptions/Edit/ O**v**ertype Mode	Insert	OVR		Switches between Insert and Overtype modes
Tools/**O**ptions/ Spelling & Grammar				Changes settings associated with the Spelling and Grammar checking feature
Tools/**O**ptions/View/**A**ll	Ctrl + ⇧Shift + * ¶		Show formatting marks	Displays or hides formatting marks
Table/Dra**w** Table		▨ or ▨		Creates a table using Draw Table feature
Table		▦		Inserts table at insertion point
Table/**I**nsert/Rows **A**bove				Inserts a new row in table above selected row
Table/**I**nsert Columns				Inserts new columns in a table
Table/Sele**c**t/**T**able				Selects entire table
Table/**M**erge Cells		▣		Merges cells in a table
Table/Table Auto**F**ormat				Applies pre-designed formats to table
Table/**A**utofit/Distribute Rows Eve**n**ly		⊞		Evenly sizes selected rows
Table/Con**v**ert/Te**x**t to Table				Converts selected text to table format
Table/Sort				Rearranges items in a selection into sorted order
Table/F**o**rmula				Inserts a formula into a table
Table/Show **G**ridlines				Displays gridlines in a table
Table/Table P**r**operties/**T**able/**C**enter				Centers selected table
Table/Table Properties/T**a**ble/**O**ption/ Automatically resize to fit contents				Automatically resizes columns in table to fit text or graphic
Table/Table P**r**operties/Col**u**mn				Adjusts width of selected columns
Table/Table P**r**operties/C**e**ll				Adjusts cell size and alignment

Command	Shortcut Key	Button	Voice	Action
Window/**S**plit				Divides a document into two horizontal sections
Help/Microsoft Word **H**elp		⑦		Opens Help window
O**r**der/Bring to Fron**t**				Brings object to front of stack
Group				Creates a group from selected objects
Ungroup				Ungroups a grouped object
Regr**o**up				Regroups an ungrouped object
In**s**ert Shape/**S**ubordinate				Inserts a shape below the selected superior shape
Layout/**R**ight Hanging				Hangs subordinate shapes to right of superior shape
Layout/**E**xpand Organization Chart				Expands drawing canvas around organization chart
Checkbox				Allows selection of more than one item
Drop-Down box				Displays available choices in a list
Textbox				A box where you can enter one line of text
Text Areas				A box where you can enter more than one line of text
Reset				Clears entries in form
Submit				Submits data in form to specified location
Chart Commands				
F**o**rmat/**S**elected Walls	Ctrl + 1			Formats chart walls
F**o**rmat/**S**elected Data Series	Ctrl + 1			Formats selected data series
F**o**rmat/**S**elected Axis	Ctrl + 1			Formats selected axis
F**o**rmat/**S**elected legend	Ctrl + 1			Formats selected legend
Chart/Chart **t**ype				Changes the chart type

Glossary of Key Terms

active window   The window you can work in identified by a highlighted title bar, the insertion point, and scroll bars.

address list   The data source file used in a merge; it typically contains name and address data to be combined with the main document.

alignment   How text is positioned on a line between the margins or indents. There are four types of paragraph alignment: left, centered, right, and justified.

antonym   A word with the opposite meaning.

attachment   A file that is sent along with an e-mail message, but is not part of the e-mail text.

attribute   A feature of an object, such as line color or fill color.

author   The process of creating a Web page.

AutoComplete   A feature that recognizes commonly used words or phrases and can automatically complete them for you if chosen.

AutoCorrect   A feature that makes basic assumptions about the text you are typing and automatically corrects the entry.

AutoFormat   A feature that makes certain formatting changes automatically to your document.

AutoShape   A ready-made shape that is supplied with Word.

AutoText   A feature that provides commonly used words or phrases that you can select and quickly insert into a document.

balloon   A box that displays markup elements such as comments and tracked changes in the margin of the document.

browser   A program that connects you to remote computers and displays the Web pages you request.

bullet   A dot or other symbol that is placed before text.

bulleted list   Displays items that logically fall out from a paragraph into a list, with items preceded by bullets.

caption   A title or explanation for a table, picture, or graph.

case sensitive   The capability to distinguish between uppercase and lowercase characters.

cell   The intersection of a column and row where data is entered in a table.

character formatting   Formatting features, such as bold and color, that affect the selected characters only.

chart   A visual representation of numeric data. Also called a graph.

Click and Type   A feature available in Print Layout and Web Layout views, that is used to quickly insert text, graphics, and other items in a blank area of a document, avoiding the need to enter blank lines.

collect and paste   The capability of the program to store multiple copied items in the Office Clipboard and then paste one or more of the items.

comment   A note that can be added to a document without changing the document text.

controls   A graphic object designed to automate the process of completing a form.

cross-reference   A reference in one part of a document to related information in another part.

cursor   The blinking vertical bar that shows you where the next character you type will appear. Also called the insertion point.

custom dictionary   A dictionary of terms you have entered that are not in the main dictionary of the Spelling Checker.

data field   Each category of information in the data source.

data record   A record that contains a complete set of related information for one person (or other entity).

data series   Each group of related data that is plotted in the chart. Each data series has a unique color or pattern assigned to it so that you can identify the different series.

datasheet   A table containing the data used to create a chart.

data source   The file that supplies the data in a mail merge.

default   The initial Word document settings that can be changed to customize documents.

destination   The location to which text is moved or copied.

destination file   A document in which a linked object is inserted.

diagram   A graphic object that can be used to illustrate concepts and enhance documents.

docked toolbar   A toolbar fixed to an edge of the window and displays a vertical bar called the move handle, on the left edge of the toolbar.

Document Map   Displays the headings in the document in a separate pane.

document window   The area of the application window that displays the contents of the open document.

drag and drop   A mouse procedure that moves or copies a selection to a new location.

drawing layer   The layer above or below the text layer where floating objects are inserted.

drawing object   A simple object consisting of shapes such as lines and boxes.

drop cap   A large, uppercase character with the top part of the letter even with the line and the rest of the letter extending into the paragraph below it.

edit   The process of changing and correcting existing text in a document.

embedded object   An object, such as a picture graphic, that becomes part of the Word document and that can be opened and edited using the program in which it was created.

em dash   A single long dash line.

endnote   A reference note displayed at the end of the document.

end-of-file marker   The horizontal line that marks the end of a file.

field   A placeholder that instructs Word to insert information in a document.

field code   The code containing the instructions about the type of information to insert in a field.

field name   A name used to label each data field in the data source of a mail merge.

field result   The results displayed in a field according to the instructions in the field code.

file property   A setting associated with a file.

floating object   A graphic object that is inserted into the drawing layer and which can be positioned anywhere on the page.

floating toolbar   A toolbar that appears in a separate window and can be moved anywhere on the desktop.

font   A set of characters with a specific design. Also called a typeface.

font size   The height and width of a character, commonly measured in points.

footer   The line or several lines of text at the bottom of every page just below the bottom margin line.

footnote   A reference note displayed at the bottom of the page on which the reference occurs.

form   A document that contains fill-in blanks or spaces reserved for entering information.

format   To enhance the appearance of the document to make it more readable or attractive.

Format Painter   The feature that applies formats associated with the current selection to new selections.

formatting marks   Symbols that are automatically inserted into a document as you enter and edit text and that control the appearance of the document.

Formatting toolbar   The toolbar that contains buttons representing the most frequently used text-editing and text-layout features.

formula   Table entry that does arithmetic calculations.

function   A prewritten formula that performs a calculation automatically in a table.

global template   The Normal document template whose settings are available to all documents.

grammar checker   The feature that advises you of incorrect grammar as you create and edit a document, and proposes possible corrections.

graphic   A non-text element in a document.

group Two or more objects that are combined so that you can work with them as you would a single object.

hard page break A manually inserted page break that instructs Word to begin a new page regardless of the amount of text on the previous page.

header The line or several lines of text at the top of each page just above the top margin line.

header row The first row in the data source containing the data field names.

heading style A style that is designed to identify different levels of headings in a document.

HTML (HyperText Markup Language) The programming language used to create Web pages.

hyperlink A connection to locations in the current document, other documents, or Web pages. Clicking a hyperlink jumps to the specified location.

hyphenation Inserts a hyphen (-) in long words that fall at the end of a line to split the word between lines.

hyphenation zone An unmarked space along the right margin that controls the amount of white space in addition to the margin that is allowed at the end of a line.

indent To set in a paragraph from the margins. There are four types of indents: left, right, first line, and hanging.

inline object An object that is inserted directly in the text at the position of the insertion point, becoming part of the paragraph.

Insert mode Method of text entry in which new characters are inserted into existing text, which moves to the right to make space for the new characters; the text on the line is reformatted as necessary.

insertion point The blinking vertical bar that shows you where the next character you type will appear on the line. Also called the cursor.

kerning To adjust the spacing between particular pairs of letters, depending on the font design.

landscape Orientation in which text is printed across the length of page

leader characters Solid, dotted, or dashed lines that fill the blank space between tab stops.

legend A box containing a brief description that identifies the patterns or colors assigned to the data series in a chart.

line spacing The vertical space between lines of text.

linked object Information created in a source file from one application and inserted into a destination file of another application while maintaining a link between files.

live link A linked object that automatically reflects in the destination document any changes made in the source document when the destination document is opened.

Mail Merge A feature that combines a text document with a data document or file containing names and addresses to produce a merged document or form letter.

main dictionary The dictionary of terms that comes with Word 2003.

main document A document that contains the basic form letter.

markup Elements that include colored and underlined text and balloons.

menu bar Located below the title bar, this bar displays the application's program menu.

merge field A field code that controls what information is used from the data source and where it is entered in the main document.

newsletter-style columns The arrangement of text in a document so that it flows from the bottom of one column to the top of the next column.

Normal template The document template that is opened when you start Word.

note pane Lower portion of the window that displays footnotes.

note reference mark A superscript number or character appearing in the document at the end of the material being referenced.

note separator The horizontal line separating footnote text from main document text.

note text The text in a footnote.

numbered list Displays items that convey a sequence of events in a particular order, with items preceded by numbers or letters.

object An item that can be sized, moved, and manipulated.

Office clipboard A temporary Windows storage area in memory.

operator Specifies the type of calculation to perform. The most common operators are + (add), – (subtract), * (multiply), and / (divide).

optional hyphen A hyphen that is inserted automatically when a word is broken between two lines because the full word did not fit.

outline numbered list   Displays items in multiple outline levels that show a hierarchical structure of the items in the list.

Overtype mode   Method of text entry in which new text types over the existing characters.

page break   Marks the point at which one page ends and another begins.

page margin   The blank space around the edge of the page.

paragraph formatting   Formatting features, such as alignment, indentation, and line spacing, that affect an entire paragraph.

picture   An illustration such as a scanned photograph.

placeholder   Text in a template that marks the space and provides instructions for the text that should be entered at that location.

portrait   Orientation of the page, in which text is printed across the width of the page.

Reading Layout view   Displays a document like pages in a book.

ruler   The ruler located below the Formatting toolbar that shows the line length in inches.

sans serif font   A font, such as Arial or Helvetica, that does not have a flair at the base of each letter.

scroll bar   Used with a mouse to bring additional lines of information into view in a window.

section   A division into which a document can be divided that can be formatted separately from the rest of the document.

section break   Marks the point at which one section ends and another begins.

select   To highlight text.

selection cursor   A colored highlight bar that appears over the selected command.

selection rectangle   The rectangular outline around an object that indicates it is selected.

serif font   A font, such as Times New Roman, that has a flair at the base of each letter.

shortcut menu   By right clicking on an item, this menu displays only the options pertaining to that item.

sidebar   An article set off from other articles or information, which highlights an article next to it.

sizing handles   Black squares around a selected object that can be used to size the object.

Smart Tag   A feature that recognizes data such as names, addresses, telephone numbers, dates, times, and places as a particular type.

The recognized item can then be quickly added to a Microsoft Outlook feature.

soft page break   A page break automatically inserted by Word to start a new page when the previous page has been filled with text or graphics.

soft space   A space between words automatically entered by Word to justify text on a line.

sort   To arrange alphabetically or numerically in ascending or descending order.

source   The location from which text is moved or copied.

source file   The document that stores the data for the linked object.

source program   The program in which an object was created.

spelling checker   The feature that advises you of misspelled words as you create and edit a document, and proposes possible corrections.

split window   A division of the document window into two horizontal sections making it easier to view different parts of a document.

stacking order   The order objects are positioned in the drawing layer.

Standard toolbar   The toolbar that contains buttons for the most frequently used commands.

status bar   A bar displayed at the bottom of the document window that advises you of the status of different program conditions and features as you use the program.

story   Text that is contained in a single text box or linked text boxes.

style   A named combination of character and paragraph formats that can be applied to a paragraph.

synonym   A word with a similar meaning.

system Clipboard   Where a selection that has been cut or copied is stored.

tab stop   A marked location on the horizontal ruler that indicates how far to indent text when the [Tab] key is pressed.

table   Displays information in horizontal rows and vertical columns.

table reference   The letter and number (for example, A1) that identify a cell in a table.

tag   Embedded codes that supply information about a Web pages structure, appearance, and contents.

Task Pane   Displayed on the right side of the document window, it provides quick access to features as you are using the application.

template A document file that includes predefined settings that can be used as a pattern to create many common types of documents.

text box A container for text and other graphics.

text wrapping Controls how text appears around a graphic.

theme Predesigned Web page effects.

thesaurus Word feature that provides synonyms and antonyms for words.

thumbnail A miniature representation of a picture.

titles In a chart, descriptive text used to explain the contents of the chart.

toolbar A bar of buttons below the menu bar that are shortcuts for many commonly used commands.

Tracked Changes A feature that marks every change to a document, such as insertions, deletions, and formatting changes.

TrueType A font that is automatically installed when you install Windows.

typeface A set of characters with a specific design. Also called a font.

URL The address that indicates the location of a document on the World Wide Web. URL stands for Uniform Resource Locator.

version A "snapshot" of a document at a specific time, that is saved with the file.

Web page A document that can be used on the World Wide Web and viewed in a browser.

wizard A guided approach that takes you step-by-step through the process to create many types of documents.

WordArt A supplementary application included with the Word program that is used to enhance a document by changing the shape of text, adding 3-D effects, and changing the alignment of text on a line.

word wrap A feature that automatically determines where to end a line and wrap text to the next line based on the margin settings.

X Axis The bottom boundary of the chart.

Y Axis The left boundary of the chart.

Data File List

Supplied/Used	Created/Saved As
Lab 1	
wd01_Flyer1	Flyer
wd01_Lions	Flyer1
Step-by-Step	
1.	Web Site Memo
2.	Volunteers Needed
3. wd01_Coffee	Grand Opening
4. wd01_Note Taking Skills	Note Taking Skills
5. wd01_Conserve Water	Water Conservation
wd01_Water Hose	
On Your Own	
1.	Hawaii Cruise Flyer
2.	Lab Rules
3.	CPR Classes
4.	Computer Cleaning
5.	Career Report
Lab 2	
wd02_Tour Letter	Tour Letter2
wd02_Flyer2	Flyer 2 Versions
Step-by-Step	
1. wd02_Conservation Tips	Water Conservation2
Water Conservation (Lab 1)	
2. Note Taking Skills (Lab 1)	
wd02_Note Taking Tips	Note Taking Skills2
3. wd02_Yoga Flyer	Yoga Flyer
4. Volunteers Needed (Lab 1)	Orientation Schedule
	Volunteers Needed2
5. wd02_Coffee Flyer	Coffee Flyer2
On Your Own	
1.	Reference Letter
2.	Phone Rates
3.	For Sale Flyer
4. wd02_New Orleans	New Orleans2
5.	Election Results
Lab 3	
wd03_Tour Research	Tour Research
wd03_Giraffe	Research Outline
wd03_Parrots	

Supplied/Used	Created/Saved As
Step-by-Step	
1.	Donation Sites
2.	Coffee Outline
3. wd03_Kayaking Flyer	Kayaking Flyer
wd03_Kayacker	
4. wd03_Yoga Practice	Yoga Guide
wd03_History	
wd03_Yoga Pose	
5. wd03_Triple Crown	ATT Triple Crown
wd03_PCT	
wd03_Lightweight	
wd03_Backpack	
wd03_Tracey	
On Your Own	
1. wd03_Digital Camera	Digital Cameras
2. Coffee Outline (Lab 3)	Coffee Report
3.	Job Search
4.	Research
5.	Computer Viruses
Working Together 1	
wdwt_Presentations	New Tour Presentations
wdwt_Locations	Locations
Step-by-Step	
1. Locations (from WT lab)	
wdwt_LosAngeles	LosAngeles
2. Volunteers Needed (Lab 2)	Volunteers Needed
3. Grand Opening (Lab 1)	Locations
	Cafe Flyer
wdwt_Coffee Cup	
wdwt_Café Locations	
On Your Own	
1.	Web Design

Lab 4

Supplied/Used	Created/Saved As
wd04_Headline	Newsletter Headline
wd04_Tanzania Facts	Tanzania Facts
wd04_Newsletter Articles	
wd04_Be An Adventure Traveler	March Newsletter
wd04_Costa Rica Adventure	
wd04_Giraffe	
Step-by-Step	
1. wd04_Fitness Club Headline	Yoga Newsletter
wd04_Lifestyle Yoga	
wd04_Bikram	
wd04_Bow Pose	
2. wd04_Water Headline	Water Newsletter
wd04_Water Tips	
wd04_Water	

Supplied/Used	Created/Saved As
3. wd04_Coffee wd04_City wd04_Coffee Beans wd04_Coffee Plant	Internet Café Newsletter
4. wd04_Air Travel wd04_Airline wd04_Pet Carrier wd04_Cargo	ARF Newsletter
5. wd04_Hike Triple Crown wd04_Trail wd04_Lightweight wd04_Forest wd04_Low Impact	ATT Hiking Newsletter

On Your Own

1.	Activity Newsletter
2. wd04_Water Exercise	Water Exercise Newsletter
3.	PTA Newsletter
4.	Garden Newsletter
5.	My Newsletter

Lab 5

wd05_Logo Elements	Logo Grouped Sales Analysis Memo ATT Memo (template) New Department Memo

Step-by-Step

1.	Yoga Memo
2.	Bubble Tea Memo
3.	Rock Climbing Memo
4.	Animal Adoption Memo
5. wd05_Opera	Opera Memo

On Your Own

1.	Movie Data
2.	Language Memo
3.	Pet Ownership Memo
4.	World Internet Use
5.	Cars Memo

Lab 6

wd06_Form wd06_Camping Safari wd06_Everest Original wd06_Everest ChangesDan wd06_Everest ChangesCarol wd06_Everest Paragraph wd06_Tour Letter	Catalog Request Form Camping Safari Edited Camping Safari Reviewed (e-mail) Everest Revised Tour Letter Main Document Client List (.mdb file) ATT Mailing Labels

Step-by-Step

1. wd06_Alernatives Form wd06_Alternatives	Alternatives Form2

Supplied/Used	Created/Saved As
2. wd06_Tea Month	Tea Month2
3. wd06_Animal Angels Form	ARF Donation Letters
	ARF Donation List
4. wd06_Betty's Birds	Betty's Birds2
wd06_Bird Coupon-Noel	Bird Coupon Final
wd06_Bird Coupon-Mary	
5. wd06_Anthology Cinema Reviewed	Anthology Cinema Complete
	Anthology Cinema List
	Anthology Cinema Letters

On Your Own

1. wd06_Frequent Flyer	Frequent Flyer Letter
2. wd06_Video Tower	Video Tower Letter
3. wd06_Historical Society	Historical Society Letter
4. wd06_Safari Park	Safari Park Letter
5.	Hotel Rewards Letter

Working Together 2

wdwt2_ Annual Tour Sales	Major Tour Sales.xls
wdwt2_New Tour Status	New Tour Status
wdwt2_New Tour Bookings.xls	New Tour Bookings Linked
wdwt2_ New Tour Sales	New Tour Sales
wdwt2_ New Tour Income.xls	New Tour Income

Step-by-Step

1. wdwt2_Animal Angels Sales	AA Sales Memo
wdwt2_AA Sales.xls	
2. wdwt2_Time Sheet Memo	Time Sheet Linked
wdwt2_Time Sheet.xls	Time Sheet
3. wdwt2_Opera Donors	Opera Donors2
wdwt2_COF Donors.xls	COF Donors2

Reference 2

Microsoft Office Specialist Skills

Office Word 2003 Specialist Certification

Standardized Coding Number	Skill Sets and Skill Standards	Lab	Page	Lab Exercises Step-By-Step	Lab Exercises On Your Own
WW03S-1	**Creating Content**				
WW03S-1-1	Insert and edit text, symbols and special characters	1	1.11	1,2,3,4,5	1,2,3,5
		2	2.12	1,2,3,4,5	1,4,5
		4	4.18,4.26,4.50	1,2,3,4,5,	1,2,3,4,5
WW03S-1-2	Insert frequently used and pre-defined text	1	1.21	1	3
		2	2.53	1,2,3,4,5	1,2,5
		3	3.68		
WW03S-1-3	Navigate to specific content	2	2.22	1,2,3,4,5	
		4	4.22	1,2,3,4,5	1,2,3,4,5
WW03S-1-4	Insert, position and size graphics	1	1.60	3,4,5	1,2,4
		2	2.55	2,3,4,5	2,3,4,5
		4	4.36	1,2,3,4,5	1,2,3,4,5
WW03S-1-5	Create and modify diagrams and charts	5	5.36,5.54	4,5	3,4,5
WW03S-1-6	Locate, select and insert supporting information	4	4.15	5	1,2,3,4,5
WW03S-2	**Organizing Content**				
WW03S-2-1	Insert and modify tables	3	3.55	1,3,5	1,3,4,5
		5	5.15	1,2,3,4,5	1,2,3,4,5
		6	6.6	1,2,3,4,5	
WW03S-2-2	Create bulleted lists, numbered lists and outlines	2	2.50	1,2,3	3,4,5
		3	3.4	2	2
		4	4.48	5	3,4,5
		5	5.44	5	3,4,5
WW03S-2-3	Insert and modify hyperlinks	2	2.58	1,4,5	1,2,3,4
		WT1	WT1.9	1,2,3	1
WW03S-3	**Formatting Content**				
WW03S-3-1	Format text	1	1.50	1,2,3,4,5	1,2,3,4,5
		2	2.45	1,2,3,4,5	3,4,5
		3	3.7	3,4,5	4,5
		4	4.11,4.23	1,2,3,4,5	1,2,3,4,5
		5	5.17	1,2,3,4,5,	1,2,3,4,5
WW03S-3-2	Format paragraphs	1	1.59	1,2,3,4,5	1,2,3,4,5
		2	2.33	3,4,5	2,3,4,5
		4	4.34	1,2,3,4,5	1,2,3,4,5
WW03S-3-3	Apply and format columns	4	4.27	1,2,3,4,5,	1,2,3,4,5
WW03S-3-4	Insert and modify content in headers and footers	3	3.65	1,2,3,4,5	1,2,3,5
		4	4.55	3,4,5	1,2,3,4,5
WW03S-3-5	Modify document layout and page setup	2	2.29	2,4,5	
		3	3.34	3,4,5	1,2,3,4,5
		4	4.28,4.30	1,2,3,4,5	1,2,3,4,5

Standardized Coding Number	Skill Sets and Skill Standards	Lab	Page	Lab Exercises	
				Step-By-Step	On Your Own
WW03S-4	**Collaborating**				
WW03S-4-1	Circulate documents for review	5	5.63	3,4,5	
		6	6.20	3,4,5	3,4,5
WW03S-4-2	Compare and merge documents	6	6.22	2	5
WW03S-4-3	Insert, view and edit comments	6	6.12	1,2,3,4,5	1,2,3,4,5
WW03S-4-4	Track, accept and reject proposed changes	6	6.24	1,2,3,4,5	1,2,3,4,5
WW03S-5	**Formatting and Managing Documents**				
WW03S-5-1	Create new documents using templates	5	5.4,5.50	1,2,3,4,5	1,2,3,4,5
WW03S-5-2	Review and modify document properties	1	1.69	1,2,3,4,5	1,2,3,4,5
		4	4.46	1,2,3,4,5	1,2,3,4,5
WW03S-5-3	Organize documents using file folders	3	3.14	3,4,5	2,3,4
WW03S-5-4	Save documents in appropriate formats for different uses	5	5.9,5.52	1,2,3,4,5	1,2,3,4,5
		WT1	WT1.3	1,2,3	1
WW03S-5-5	Print documents, envelopes and labels	1	1.67	1,2,3,4,5	1,2,3,4,5
		2	2.64	1,2,3,4,5	1,2,3,4,5
		3	3,76	1,2,3,4,5	1,2,3,4,5
		4	4.55	1,2,3,4,5	1,2,3,4,5
		6	6.49	1,2,3,4,5	1,2,3,4,5
WW03S-5-6	Preview documents and Web pages	1	1,67	1,2,3,4,5	1,2,3,4,5
		2	2.61	1,2,3,4,5	1,2,3,4,5
		3	3.76	1,2,3,4,5	1,2,3,4,5
		WT1	WT1.1	1,2,3	1
		4	4.55	1,2,3,4,5	1,2,3,4,5
WW03S-5-7	Change and organize document views and windows	1	1.8	1,2,3,4,5	
		2	2.18	1,2,4,5	
		3	3.16, 3.70	4, 5	
		4	4.42	1,2,3,4,5	1,2,3,4,5

Index

ABOVE, WD5.23
Active window, WD2.18
Address list, WD6.30
Alignment, WD1.57–WD1.59
All caps, WD1.55
Animation, WD6.19–WD6.20
Animations list box, WD6.19
Antonyms, WD2.10
APA style, WD3.18
Applying styles, WD3.21–WD3.23
Area chart, WD5.37
Attachment, WD6.20–WD6.22
Attribute, WD5.12
AutoComplete, WD1.22
AutoComplete ScreenTip, WD1.22
AutoCorrect, WD1.25–WD1.27
AutoCorrect Options button, WD1.26
AutoCorrect Options menu, WD1.27
AutoFormat, WD2.59, WD3.61–WD3.62
AutoFormat dialog box, WD3.62
AutoFormat styles, WD5.62
AutoRecover, WD1.30
AutoShape, WD2.55–WD2.61
    adding text, WD2.58–WD2.60
    filling, with color, WD2.57
    inserting, WD2.56–WD2.57
    moving an autoshape, WD2.60–WD2.61
AutoSum, WD5.25
AutoText, WD1.22
AutoText entries, WD2.53–WD2.55
AVERAGE, WD5.22
Avery Standard, WD6.47

Backspace key, WD1.12
Balloon, WD6.12
Banner, WD4.4
Bar chart, WD5.37
Bitmap files, WD1.60
Black text, WD1.56
Blank line, WD1.13
Block of text, WD1.43
.bmp, WD1.60
Body Text style, WD5.16
Bold, WD1.55
Border and shading, WD4.34–WD4.36
Border lines, WD5.34–WD5.36
Borders and Shading dialog box, WD4.13
Both Hanging, WD5.60
Break dialog box, WD3.34
Browse Objects scroll buttons, WD4.22, WD4.25
Bullet, customizing, WD4.48–WD4.50
Bulleted list, WD2.50, WD2.53
Bullets and Numbering dialog box, WD2.51, WD5.46

Calculations, WD5.22–WD5.26
Caption, WD3.48–WD3.50
Caption options, WD3.49
Case sensitive, WD2.24
Cell, WD3.55
Cell margin, WD5.33
Cell shading, WD5.28–WD5.29

Centered, WD1.58
Centering vertically, WD3.35–WD3.36, WD5.33–WD5.34
Change Case command, WD1.48
Change Case dialog box, WD1.49
Changing case, WD1.48–WD1.50
Character effects, WD1.55–WD1.56
Character formatting, WD1.50, WD2.44–WD2.50
    color highlighting, WD2.45
    Format Painter, WD2.48
    Styles and Formatting task pane, WD2.48–WD2.50
    underlining text, WD2.46–WD2.47
Character size, WD1.8
Character spacing, WD4.11–WD4.13
Character style, WD3.7, WD3.21
Chart, WD5.37–WD5.44
    background color, WD5.41–WD5.42
    data series, WD5.39–WD5.40
    datasheet, WD5.38
    defined, WD5.37
    modifying, WD5.40–WD5.44
    ports, WD5.37
    posting data from table, WD5.38
    removing 3D-effect, WD5.42–WD5.43
    sizing, WD5.40
    specifying chart data, WD5.38–WD5.40
    types, WD5.37
Check box, WD6.8–WD6.9
Checking grammar, WD1.18–WD1.21
Checking the document, WD3.69–WD3.75
    formatting inconsistencies, WD3.72–WD3.75
    Reading Layout view, WD3.69–WD3.71
    redisplaying spelling/grammar errors, WD3.71–WD3.72
Clear Formatting, WD3.25
Click and Type, WD3.18–WD3.20
Click and Type pointer, WD3.19
Clip art, WD1.60–WD1.62
Clip Art task pane, WD1.61
Clip Organizer, WD1.60
Clipboard, WD2.12
Clipboard task pane, WD4.19
Closing a file, WD1.33–WD1.34
Collaboration features, WD6.12–WD6.30
    accepting/rejecting changes, WD6.24–WD6.27
    comments, WD6.16–WD6.17, WD6.27–WD6.29
    comparing and merging documents, WD6.22–WD6.24
    e-mail attachment, WD6.20–WD6.22
    online collaboration, WD6.29–WD6.30
    reviewing comments, WD6.27–WD6.29
    text animation, WD6.19–WD6.20
    tracking changes to document, WD6.12–WD6.15
    viewing changes, WD6.17–WD6.19
Collect and paste, WD4.19
Collecting and pasting, WD4.18–WD4.23
Color, WD1.55
Color highlighting, WD2.45
Colors dialog box, WD5.28
Column
    inserting, WD5.20–WD5.21
    newsletter-style, WD4.27–WD4.31
    sizing, WD4.30–WD4.31
    three-column layout, WD4.30
    two-column layout, WD4.28–WD4.30

Keyboard shortcuts, WD1.16, WD4.50. *See also* Command summary
Key terms (glossary), WDG.1–WDG.5

Label Options dialog box, WD6.46
Labels, WD6.45–WD6.49
Landscape, WD5.30
Leader characters, WD2.41
Left Hanging, WD5.60
Legend, WD5.37, WD5.40
Line chart, WD5.37
Line feature, WD6.10
Line spacing, WD2.42–WD2.44
List style, WD3.7
Lists, WD2.50–WD2.53

Mail merge, WD6.30–WD6.44
    create data source, WD6.33–WD6.39
    create main document, WD6.31–WD6.32
    enter merge fields into main document, WD6.39–WD6.41
    preview merged letter, WD6.41–WD6.44
    steps in process, WD6.31
Mail Merge Recipients dialog box, WD6.37
Mail Merge task pane, WD6.31, WD6.46
Mail Merge toolbar, WD6.38
Mailing Label Wizard, WD6.45
Mailing labels, WD6.45–WD6.49
Main dictionary, WD1.23
Main document, WD6.30–WD6.31, WD6.32
Margin setting, WD2.30–WD2.33
Markup, WD6.12
Match Case, WD2.23, WD2.24
MAX, WD5.22
Memo templates, WD5.5–WD5.9
Memo Wizard, WD5.5
Merge field, WD6.30
Merging cells, WD5.26–WD5.27
Merging documents, WD6.22–WD6.24. *See also* Mail merge
Microsoft Graph, WD5.37
Microsoft Office Online Templates Web page, WD5.4
MIN, WD5.22
Mirror margins, WD2.30, WD2.32
MLA style, WD3.18, WD3.36, WD3.62
Modify Style dialog box, WD4.24
Modifying styles, WD4.23–WD4.26
Mouse pointer
    arrow, as, WD1.6
    crayon, WD5.17
    drag and drop, WD2.16
    hide white space, WD3.16
    I-beam, as, WD1.6, WD1.7
    sizing row/column, WD5.31
    upright pitcher, WD4.43
Moving and copying selections, WD2.12–WD2.19
    copy and paste, WD2.13–WD2.15
    copying between documents, WD2.17–WD2.19
    cut and paste, WD2.15–WD2.16
    drag and drop, WD2.16–WD2.17
    moving an autoshape, WD2.60–WD2.61
Moving through text, WD1.15–WD1.18

Nameplate, WD4.4
Navigating a document, WD1.36–WD1.39
Navigating by headings, WD3.29–WD3.32
    Document Map, WD3.30–WD3.32
    table of contents hyperlink, WD3.29–WD3.30
NetMeeting, WD6.29
New Address List dialog box, WD6.33, WD6.35
New Address List list box, WD6.34
New documents, WD1.7–WD1.11
New folder, WD3.14–WD3.15
New Folder dialog box, WD3.15

New Style dialog box, WD3.24
Newsletter
    adjusting the layout, WD4.54
    collecting and pasting, WD4.18–WD4.23
    customizing bullets, WD4.48–WD4.50
    drop cap, WD4.52–WD4.53
    headline, WD4.4–WD4.15
    horizontal rules, WD4.13–WD4.15
    hyphenation, WD4.31–WD4.33
    justification, WD4.33–WD4.34
    modifying styles, WD4.23–WD4.26
    newsletter-style columns, WD4.27–WD4.31
    Office Clipboard, WD4.18–WD4.23
    printing, WD4.55–WD4.56
    refining layout/position of graphics, WD4.53–WD4.54
    removing hidden text, WD4.47–WD4.48
    researching on the Web, WD4.15–WD4.17
    sidebar, WD4.34–WD4.45
    special characters/symbols, WD4.50–WD4.52
    text box, WD4.36–WD4.45
    word count, WD4.46
    WordArt, WD4.5–WD4.13. *See also* WordArt
Newsletter headline, WD4.4–WD4.15
Newsletter-style columns, WD4.27–WD4.31
Next Column button, WD5.32
Normal.dot, WD5.4
Normal template, WD5.4
Normal view, WD1.8
Note reference mark, WD3.37
Note separator, WD3.37
Note text, WD3.37
Num Lock, WD1.16
Numbered list, WD2.50–WD2.52, WD5.44–WD5.50
Numbered mark, WD3.38
Numeric keypad, WD1.16

Object, WD1.60
Office Address List, WD6.33
Office Clipboard, WD2.12, WD4.18–WD4.23
Office Clipboard gallery, WD4.20, WD4.21
Online collaboration, WD6.29–WD6.30
Online meeting, WD6.29
Open dialog box, WD1.34
Opening a file, WD1.34–WD1.36
Operators, WD5.22
Optional hyphen, WD4.31
Options dialog box, WD3.17
Organization chart, WD5.55, WD5.57–WD5.59
Original, WD6.17
Original Showing Markup, WD6.17
Outline, WD1.55, WD3.4–WD3.14
    changing outline levels, WD3.7–WD3.9
    collapsing/expanding, WD3.11–WD3.14
    moving/inserting topics, WD3.9–WD3.11
    Outline view, WD3.5–WD3.7
Outline levels, WD3.7–WD3.9
Outline numbered list, WD2.50, WD5.44–WD5.50
Outline symbol, WD3.5, WD3.6, WD3.8
Outline toolbar, WD3.5, WD3.8
Outline view, WD1.8, WD3.4–WD3.5
Overtype mode, WD1.41–WD1.42

Page break, WD2.20–WD2.21
Page layout, WD2.29–WD2.33
Page margin, WD2.30–WD2.33
Page Number Format dialog box, WD3.67
Page orientation, WD5.29–WD5.31
Page Setup command, WD2.31
Page Setup dialog box, WD2.32
Pane, WD1.6
Paragraph, WD1.50
Paragraph alignment, WD1.57–WD1.59